2,239
Tested Secrets for
Direct
Marketing
Success

DENNY HATCH ▪ DON JACKSON

NTC Business Books

NTC/Contemporary Publishing Group

Library of Congress Cataloging-in-Publication Data

Hatch, Denny.
    2,239 tested secrets for direct marketing success : the pros tell you their
time-proven secrets / Denny Hatch and Don Jackson.
        p.   cm.
    Includes bibliographical references and index.
    ISBN 0-8442-3007-3 (cloth)
    ISBN 0-8442-0349-1 (paper)
    1. Direct marketing.   2. Success in business.   I. Jackson, Donald R.,
1938–   .   II. Title.   III. Title: Two thousand two hundred thirty-nine tested
secrets for direct marketing success.
    HF5415.126.H38   1997
    658.8'4—dc21   97-37280
                                                                          CIP

Cover and interior design by Jeanette Wojtyla
Interior production by Hespenheide Design

Published by NTC Business Books
A division of NTC/Contemporary Publishing Group, Inc.
4255 West Touhy Avenue, Lincolnwood (Chicago), Illinois 60712-1975 U.S.A.
Copyright © 1998 by Denny Hatch and Don Jackson
Printed in the United States of America
International Standard Book Number: 0-8442-3007-3 (cloth)
                                                  0-8442-0349-1 (paper)
     01 02 03 04 HP 21 20 19 18 17 16 15 14 13 12 11 10 9 8 7 6 5

What the Leaders Are Saying About
2,239 Tested Secrets for Direct Marketing Success

A 10-pound heart of Godiva chocolates couldn't possibly be more delicious and satisfying than the juicy nuggets that fill this anthology of direct marketing wit and wisdom. Read it slowly. It's a book to be studied, to be savored, and—of course—to be unashamedly stolen from.
> **Emily Soell, Vice Chairman/Chief Creative Officer Worldwide**
> **DraftDirect Worldwide**

What a brilliant idea this book is . . . for learning and reference by professionals and novices alike. It's a great read, well-organized.
> **Martin Baier**

Denny Hatch and Don Jackson have done our industry a great service. . . . Anyone who reads this book and puts its lessons to work will profit mightily from it.
> **Arthur Middleton Hughes, Executive Vice President**
> **ACS, Inc.**

They left out one "secret": Buy this book.
> **Murray Raphel**
> **Raphel Marketing**

Hatch and Jackson rule with their new 2,239 *Tested Secrets for Direct Marketing Success.* There's nothing else like it!
> **Jim Rosenfield, Chairman**
> **Rosenfield & Associates**

Denny and Don have done it! . . . Their unique collection of the direct marketing industry's best secrets—covering alternate media to creative and databases . . . to design, fulfillment and Internet marketing . . . to testimonials and telemarketing, and so much more—will prove to be an invaluable yardstick for seasoned direct marketers and neophytes alike.
> **John Harrison, President**
> **DiMark, a Harte-Hanks Company**

Jackson and Hatch have . . . organized a readable anthology of the rules for making direct response and advertising work in any business.
> **Henry R. "Pete" Hoke, Publisher Emeritus**
> *Direct Marketing Magazine*

This one's for all of us . . . whether you just entered the business or have gray in your hair, this book is a must. . . . The "rules" that Hatch and Jackson provide are the result of the experiences of some of the most important innovators in direct marketing. The result is not only a useful tool which I will use frequently, but a compendium of truly BIG ideas!
> **Jerry Reitman, Executive Director**
> **Chicago Direct Marketing Educational Foundation**

I was delighted to find this volume is more than just a gold mine of ideas. It's more like a good novel. Open to any page, and it's hard to put down.
> **Jim Kobs, Chairman**
> **Kobs Gregory Passavant**

Contents

Acknowledgments	vi
Welcome!	vii
Seven Secrets for Dealing with Rules	1
General Secrets of Marketing	3
General Management	12
Alternative Media	17
Analysis of Results	24
Arithmetic	30
Back-End Marketing	44
Brochures	51
Business Segments	55
Catalogs	62
Copy	72
Creative—General	102
Database Marketing	110
Design	123
Direct Mail	133
Direct Mail Production	138
Direct vs. General Advertising	142
Direct-Response TV	149
Envelopes	162
Fulfillment	167
Fundraising	171

Guarantees   187

Headlines   190

Internet Marketing   194

Lead Generation   200

Letters   205

Lift Pieces   213

Lists   215

Media   250

Offers   259

Order Forms   279

Premiums   283

Reply Envelopes and Cards   286

Space Ads   288

Strategy   304

Sweepstakes   313

Telemarketing   319

Testimonials   328

Testing   330

Bibliography   341

Index   349

Direct marketing: an aspect of total marketing

Direct marketing is an interactive system of marketing that uses one or more advertising media to effect a measurable response and/or transaction at any location, with this activity stored in a database.

Martin Baier, Henry R. Hoke, Jr., and Bob Stone

Acknowledgments

Many, many thanks are due Axel Anderson not only for his input, but for helping create the magnificent bibliography of books on advertising, marketing, and direct marketing at the back of this volume. Quite simply, Axel has forgotten more about direct marketing than I will ever know.

Others in my life who shared their knowledge and wisdom with me: Walter Weintz, Franklin Watts, Helen Hoke Watts, Dave Goodnough, Elsworth Howell, Bob Clarke, Lew Smith, Bob Scott, Bill Houghton, Lester Doniger, Harold Schwartz, Jim Prendergast, Paul Goldberg, Frank Vos, Bob Doscher, artists Ted Kikoler and Heide Follin, M. Hughes Miller, publicist and former Zeigfield Follies dancer Evelyn Lawson, Malcolm Decker, Bob Hacker, Lee Epstein, Bob Teufel, Annette Brodsky, and Dick Benson. Also, sincere thanks go to the wonderfully gifted staff at *Target Marketing* and *Who's Mailing What!* whose energy and hard work freed me up to work on this book: Alicia Orr, Hallie Mummert, Lisa Yorgey, and Debbie Gershon.

Denny Hatch

Thanks go to the people who shared their help and wisdom and supported my journey along the road of direct marketing practices: Dick Nevins, Ed Stern, Martin Baier, "Pete" Hoke, Peter Bonnani, Stan Winston, David Reichberg, Kathleen O'Shaugnessy, Jim Rosenfield, Jim Prendergast, George Abouzeid, Carl Bloom, Art Demoss, Sy Okner, Bernie Weiner, Neil Zelenetz, Jerry Reitman, Jim Kobs, of course Bob Stone, Irwin Lower, Dale Steiger, and more than 100 clients over the last 32 years.

Don Jackson

And from both of us: Putting together a book of 2,239 secrets was a considerable undertaking that could not have been accomplished without the help and encouragement of a legion of people. First and foremost, a million thanks go to our life partners, Peggy Hatch and Betts Jackson—both consummate professionals in the field of direct marketing whose input, advice, and encouragement were invaluable. Jennifer Herring, who logged in and organized the material and maintained contact with the contributors, was our anchor. We appreciate NTC/Contemporary editor Rich Hagle for both his faith in and fine touch on the finished product.

Above all, we want to thank the 167 great direct marketers and other contributors who provided everything from one-liners to highly technical articles on every facel of this complex and endlessly facsinating profession.

Thank you all!

Welcome!

From the moment the cat wakes you at first light, testing its claws on the dust ruffle of the bed, to the epic lunacy of Leno and Letterman late at night, we are bombarded with tens of thousands of sights, sounds, smells, touches, and tastes each and every day of our lives. Jerry Reitman calls it sensory overload.

The general advertiser's challenge: get a message that will be retained through the clutter of words and images.

The direct marketer's challenge: get through the clutter with an offer so interruptive that it keeps on interrupting until action is taken.

Direct marketing is the business of intimate, highly personal advertising to individuals where they live and work—or catching them on the fly with an irresistible offer in a magazine or a down-'n'-dirty ad in a supermarket take-one rack or on an airline ticket jacket.

It is the business of acquiring customers and donors and getting to know them—keeping track of their transactions with you and then continuing to delight them by serving their needs, creating new wants and, above all, persuading them to act.

As Joan Throckmorton, the great practitioner, teacher, and author, points out:

> As direct marketers we're not here primarily to make a sale; we're here to get a customer. Sales are important, of course. (Where would marketers be without them?) But the name of this game is repeat sales rather than one-shots. And to have that, you need a customer.
>
> Some marketers today use a form of advertising that I call "response advertising." It consists of customers who answer their promotions via coupon redemption or electronic means like telephones and computers. But generally these marketers do not record customer names and establish a database; therefore, this is sampling—or coupon redemption or sales promotion. It is not direct marketing.

Direct marketing is also a business of common sense, arithmetic, and the precise and constant measurement of your successes and failures.

Every discipline, from brain surgery to auto manufacture to marketing—is based on the work of those who have gone before. You learn their thought processes, study their tests, capitalize on their successes, and remember their failures, so you don't repeat them.

In short, every art, science, and industry has a set of canons, caveats, codes, constants, considerations, codicils, constraints, criteria, and customs that have been developed and refined over the years. This is especially true of direct marketing, which has been around for over 400 years.

Four hundred years?

According to Cecil Hoge, Sr., in his wonderful book *Sears and Montgomery Ward: The First Hundred Years Are the Toughest:*

> Mail order itself did not originate in 1872 when Montgomery Ward first started in the mail order business. In the 1500s, the first book catalogs were printed in Venice. By the 1600s there were garden catalogs, and by the 1700s they included stunning woodcuts of each species. By then, elegant catalogs for Wedgwood China and of the Sheffield plant and other pioneer English factories were printed in different languages. Orders came in from countries around the world. In America, before the Revolution, Benjamin Franklin published a book catalog asking for mail orders.

Direct marketing today has become huge. In 1996, using the process of direct marketing, U.S. companies and individuals generated revenues of more than a trillion bucks. If U.S. direct marketing were a country, it would be the fourth largest in the world, its GDP trailing only those of the United States, Japan, and Germany.

The exponential explosion of direct marketing has resulted in the traditional apprentice system being blown sky high. Bright new people are pouring into direct marketing, but many of them—especially those joining large corporations—end up pigeonholed, specializing in one specific discipline and then going from job to job as specialists in that area.

Probably the most important single secret in this entire book was submitted by freelancer Marty Gross:

> Whoever knows only one direct marketing skill, whether it's art direction, copywriting, or list management, does not even know that properly.

The result of this pigeonholing: faulty assumptions and, ultimately, vast sums of money needlessly wasted.

For this reason we conceived of this book.

Over the last 400 years a formidable body of knowledge has developed, not only about the techniques of reaching people where they live and work but also in human psychology, which is crucial to the business of persuading people to respond—to act.

To codify at least some of the 400 years of experience, we sent requests to hundreds of direct marketers, asking them to share their knowledge and wisdom. The result, some 2,239 secrets, maxims, and formulae, are here to guide you in your work and give you the opportunity to take advantage of the best direct marketing arena in the world. The United States has 280 million relatively affluent people, all of whom speak the same language and all of whom are literate. To reach these consumers in their homes and workplaces, marketers can use some 24,000 lists and other delivery services. Break down those lists into smaller demographic and psychographic units, and you're probably looking at a quarter of a million separate lists.

As a result of this wealth of lists—unmatched anywhere in the world—American direct marketers can test and refine those tests down to a gnat's eyebrow. Once the numbers are confirmed, the campaign can be rolled out nationally—and often internationally, because people are people the world over and what works here can work wherever people can read, there is money to spend, and mail is delivered.

And make no mistake about it, if you know what you're doing, you can still start from the kitchen table.

It was Sir Isaac Newton who wrote, in a letter to Robert Hooke: If I have seen further, it is by standing on the shoulders of giants. We hope you will benefit from the sage advice of those who have gone before you and in turn pass on these secrets to your newer associates as they enter the business.

While we have included the words of more than 160 past and present direct marketing practitioners—many of them giants in the fields of advertising, marketing, and direct marketing—this is but a beginning. An extraordinary wealth of information is also available to you from myriad other sources. For that reason, you will find on page 340 what may be the most comprehensive bibliography of literature in the field of direct marketing—books and periodicals as well as seminars, courses, and major conferences. Also included: a directory of local and regional direct marketing clubs that will enable you to network with your colleagues.

To longtime practitioners, it is our hope that this review of the basics and the complexities of direct marketing will help you rethink your strategy and tactics.

For relative newcomers, it is our hope that this book will serve you well but that it will be just the beginning of your exploration—and success—in direct marketing.

And from all, we welcome comments, criticisms, and, above all, your ideas for the second volume!

Warmly,
Denny Hatch and Don Jackson

Seven Secrets for Dealing with Rules

John J. Fleider's Dictum
Learn the current rules so you'll know when you are violating them.

> In direct marketing, as in any other field, if you don't know the rules, you will fail. It's true that rules are made to be broken, but to be successful you have to know them first. Only then can you break them, expand on them, or go on to create new rules of your own.
>
> All real breakthroughs have been made by people who went outside the so-called rules of their time. In retrospect, these breakthroughs seem logical—because they have now become the new rules.
>
> Following a rule or predetermined answer causes us to stop asking the key questions that might lead to a new discovery. The way to discovery, I believe, is to stop when you've arrived at the logical answer or the rule, then reassess the question and push on for a new answer. Creativity, it is said, is looking at the same thing as everyone else but seeing it in a different way.

Anver Suleiman's Rule of Rules
Start by absolutely following all the rules (except when they conflict—seemingly), then select the rule authored by the person with the most success in the market you are serving. Don't violate the rules without using controls and tests!

Ed McLean's Codicil
Rules are good things to test!

> If a rule says never to send a letter that is longer than a page, don't accept the rule as gospel. Test different lengths to see which works best for *your* offer.

Bob Hacker's Three Rules for Breaking the Rules
Play by the rules until you have solid controls; you have a higher chance of success and less risk.

Break the rules only after you have solid controls, because in breaking rules risk—and sometimes cost—is much higher.

There are two ways to find a breakthrough: Play the rules better than anybody else. Break the rules better than anybody else!

Bill Jayme's Coda
The only real rule I know for success in life, business, and even direct marketing is that there are no rules, including this one.

> If it all worked on rules, there never would have been Shakespeare. I have spoken.

General Secrets of Marketing

Anver Suleiman's Ethic
Rank-order everything you can. Viewing things in rank order provides stark comparisons from which you can make judgments, create models, place bets.

Don Jackson's Immutable First Commandment
Ask yourself what business you are in.

> You are emphatically not in the direct marketing "business" or "industry." Direct marketing is a process—a way of doing business. Everybody from catalogers and publishers to banks and insurance purveyors uses the direct marketing concept.

Don Jackson's Immutable Second Commandment
You are in the business of acquiring customers (or donors) and then continually delighting them.

> The next time some wonk gets up at a conference and starts using the current industry buzzwords—*retention marketing, back-end marketing,* and *customer satisfaction,* let fly with a noisy raspberry cheer. This is old hat. Anybody with half a brain and half a computer can satisfy a customer. But only when you *continually delight* your customers will they keep coming back for more.

Example A

A friend of mine bought a Lexus—a $45,000 piece of machinery. He could afford a Mercedes, a Jaguar, a Cadillac, but he went with the Lexus. His lifetime value to that automobile manufacturer could be in the high six figures.

My friend took delivery of his elegant new Lexus from the dealer and started to drive it home, luxuriating in the smell of the leather interior and the glorious handling qualities. On a whim, he turned on the radio. His favorite classical music station came on loud and clear in splendid quadraphonic sound. He pushed the second button; it was his favorite news-weather-traffic station. The third button was the talk radio station he listened to to keep awake on long trips. In fact, every button was set to his specific tastes.

Was the Lexus psychic? No. The mechanic at the Lexus dealership had noted the radio settings on the old trade-in and duplicated them on the new Lexus. My friend was, in a word, delighted.

Was setting the radio the mechanic's idea? Or was it the policy of the dealership? Or did it come from Lexus-on-high? Apparently it was the technician's idea. Delight a customer and you have a customer for life (which, for an automobile mechanic—and all of us working stiffs—translates into corporate growth and a steady income).

Remember, what this technician did for my friend cost Lexus nothing. Zip. Nada. Not one cent. Yet it solidified the relationship. Over the coming years, Lexus will have to screw up big time to negate that divine moment.

Example B

For Christmas of 1995, Betts and I ordered $1,500 worth of goodies for the kitchen from Williams-Sonoma. Because of lousy weather and a Federal Express slowdown, not all of the merchandise arrived in time to be under the tree on Christmas morning. For us it was less than a merry Christmas.

On the Monday after Christmas, I called Williams-Sonoma and complained. The telephone sales representative was not only sympathetic but took immediate action. First, he forgave all the shipping charges, thus knocking off about $150 from our bill. Second, he overnighted to us all the merchandise we had not received—with no charge for shipping—so we would be sure to have it for the remainder of the holidays. Third, he included merchandise return labels, so when the first shipments arrived we could simply slap these labels on the cartons and ship them back—at Williams-Sonoma's expense. Fourth, he sent a free gift—a marvelous top-of-the-line glass turkey baster that retails for $25.

Betts and I were delighted.

P.S. The merchandise did indeed arrive the next day.

Elsworth Howell's Edict
Always try to convert a disadvantage into an advantage.

Williams-Sonoma has competitors—the Chef's Catalog, Hanover's Colonial Garden Kitchens, as well as major department stores that not only offer much of the same merchandise but also blitz the mailbox with traffic builders. Had the incident described in Example B on page 4 not occurred, Betts and Don Jackson might be seduced into trying another catalog because of price or merchandise. Following the Christmas debacle and incredible make-good, Williams-Sonoma is now the Jacksons' purveyor of kitchenware. Period.

To lose the Jacksons, the company would have to perpetrate a major-league screw-up. It won't.

Malcolm Decker's Corollary
Times of adversity and screw-ups may be the only times when you can really show your customers how much you love them.

Comment by Don Jackson: When the relationship is as smooth as silk, the customer may feel unloved. For example, if everything from Williams-Sonoma had arrived in time to be put under the Christmas tree, we may well have taken the company for granted. Would we not, then, entertain offers from Chef's Catalog and Colonial Garden Kitchens? Only when Williams-Sonoma blew it did we realize how much we were loved.

P.S. Do not orchestrate deliberate customer screw-ups so you can show them how much you care. Remember Murphy's Law.

Anver Suleiman's Lodestar
Nothing is more powerful than goodwill except ill will.

If you have a dissatisfied customer, make good—fast—and then give a bonus.

Joseph C. Kligge, Jr.'s, Admission
The market is always smarter than I am. I rely on it rather than my own intuition for guidance.

Wendell Forbes's Ethic
The purpose of being in business is not to make money; the purpose of being in business is to be of unique, important, and meaningful help and value to the customer.

Then it will follow, "as night the day," that you cannot help making money. Cause marketing? What's that? I thought all marketing routinely held the welfare of the customer as the top priority.

John J. Fleider's Canons

Basic human motivations are a constant; only the how in satisfying them changes.
Maslow's "Hierarchy of Human Needs" remains a constant. So, while the means of satisfying human needs changes and adapts, the needs stay the same. They are just recognized in different ways.

When emotion and reason come into conflict, emotion always wins! While people like to believe they react rationally to offers and other stimuli, the truth is they react emotionally and then look for the rationale to assuage their intellects. The smart marketer will acknowledge this in presenting any product or offer.

Don't rely on other people's numbers.

Looking for the secret-response rates, conversion rates, etc., is a waste of time except as a guide. Can you duplicate everything the other party did? Do you have the same list? Are all conditions the same? The economy? Consumer attitudes?

Look outside your industry for best-in-class examples and benchmark them.

What firm has the best billing system? The best track record in customer retention? The best new customer acquisition processing? If you measure yourself solely against your competition, you'll be only as good as or a little better than they are. But your customers are experiencing those best-in-class processes from someone, and they are measuring your delivery against that someone, whether it's your direct competitor or not.

It's much more rewarding to keep a customer than to get a new one. What are your processes for keeping customers with you? Many firms don't give that end as much attention as they do the front end, but that is where the money is to be made. Cross-selling, repeat purchases, renewals, and word of mouth all reflect customer loyalty. If your customers will switch for a few dollars or an offer on the Internet, beware. You don't have a customer base at all. Like a garden, it takes constant care and nurturing.

Bill Williams's Eight Steps to Generating and Evaluating Ideas

Take the customer's point of view.

This will force you to examine everything as the customer sees it, from the order blank to correspondence to online order entry/customer service. Make all your customer interactions as simple and error-free as possible. Ask yourself: are you communicating as clearly, consistently, and professionally as your customers expect you to?

Meet or exceed the competition's service.

People don't shop with you because of sentimental attachment. If your products have competition (and whose don't?), service will determine loyalty. Try to raise the competitive bar over time. Remember, a competitor that is playing catch-up loses credibility with the customer and will probably operate less efficiently than you.

As an industry, we are a lot closer to totally satisfying our customers than we were 10 years ago. As professionals and as competitors, we must challenge ourselves to achieve total customer satisfaction in the decades to come. If this becomes our industry standard, we'll all be well prepared to face any changes and challenges the future brings.

Know thyself.

Only by understanding what's unique about your company can you leverage your strengths and address your weaknesses in customer relationships.

Consistently meet your commitments.

Virtually every company consistently honors its product guarantee. But how many companies miss delivery deadlines, fail to update the customer on the changing status of an order, or give great service only when a customer requests an extra effort? Too many. Don't allow inconsistency to exist in your business!

Service must be efficient to be successful.

Not a company exists that can maintain both profits and market share while operating less efficiently than its competitors. The easiest way to lose profits, market share, or both is failing to focus on efficiency in the pursuit of being an effective market-share competitor.

Anticipate everything.

Please your customers by knowing what they'll appreciate before *they* know it. Win over new customers by accurately anticipating your competitors' service capabilities and strategies and then beating them to the punch. There's not a market leader in the business that can keep its position by being complacent.

Commit long-term.

If you have a well-thought-out idea of where customer expectations and competitors' capabilities will be in five or 10 years, begin to lay the groundwork now to gain an advantage. For example, those direct marketers who thought customers would be increasingly time-constrained now state second and next day as their delivery standard. These companies gain market share at the expense of their competitors. Building operational capabilities is a long-term commitment that will win over customers and yield huge competitive advantages.

If you can't measure it, you can't manage it.

This is an adage that is true in spades when it comes to service. Everyone measures gross margin, SG&A expense, and capital expenditures. But how many companies measure on-time delivery, the timely acknowledgment of orders, notification of delays and cancellations, or a customer's repeated attempts to resolve a product or service issue? Operating focus groups to evaluate order forms, having "mystery shoppers" report on telemarketing transactions, and tracking actual versus scheduled production units are the absolute minimum in measurement of service required to achieve continuous improvement.

Don Jackson's Immutable Law
People will buy from you for four reasons only: (1) price and/or (2) service and/or (3) quality and/or (4) exclusivity.

> If you have the lowest price available, they will buy. If you offer excellent quality, they will buy. If you offer great service—quick delivery, easy returns policy, guarantee of satisfaction, marvelous merchandise, pleasant and helpful sales representatives—they will buy. If your product or service is unique and available from no other source, they will buy from you.

Jackson's Corollary
If you cannot offer at least two of the four reasons for buying in the previous secret, you do not have a business.

Frank Knight's Observation
Marketers create better wants.

> Herbert Stein remembers in the *Wall Street Journal* (10/25/94), "I had forgotten what my professor Frank Knight used to say, that what people wanted was not the satisfaction of their wants, but better wants."

Franklin Watts's Dictum
People love to be sold.

> *Comment by Denny Hatch:* It is fashionable in the Information Age to say that people don't like to be sold. "Tell; don't sell" is one of the current phrases used by techies who have never sold anything in their lives and would be scared to death to ask for an order for fear of rejection.

Jerry Reitman's Certainty
Bait the hook to suit the fish, *not* the fisherman.

> The only way to improve results, regardless of medium (and we've counted over 350 different kinds of media) is to *increase personal relevance.*
> The concept: We are living in an increasingly cluttered world, with a consumer who is suffering from sensory overload. And that is likely to increase with even more ways to reach the consumer, from CD-ROM to interactive TV to God-knows-what. The more relevant we make a communication to the individual consumer we are trying to persuade, the more likely we are to capture attention—and an order.
> Too often, with all the sophistication offered by new database technologies for selection and segmentation, we forget about tailoring what we say in

print, mail, and, increasingly, broadcast so that we are speaking to the differences in people, not their similarities.

To adapt the old line "Test and then test again," I would say, "Be relevant and then more relevant to the consumer."

Don Peppers and Martha Rogers, Ph.D.
The central proposition, the defining goal, for any business in a 1:1 world, is share of customer.

Trying to increase your market share means selling as much of your product as you can to as many customers as you can. Driving for share of customer, on the other hand, means ensuring that each individual customer who buys your product buys more product, buys only your brand of product, and is happy using your product instead of some other type of product as the solution to his problem.

Consider this: If you have a 10 percent market share, then for every dollar spent on products like yours, you get about a dime. Maybe every single consumer in your market spends equally in your product category, and maybe every single one buys your brand about 10 percent of the time. Then you would be getting about 10 percent of the business from each of them. But more likely, your business is coming from only 80 percent of consumers, who are buying your brand 12 percent of the time on average. Or maybe 20 percent of them are buying your brand about 50 percent of the time.

The key share-of-customer requirement is to know your customers 1:1. You must know which consumers will never purchase your product at all so you can stop spending money and effort trying to get them to do something they never will. And you must know who your loyal customers are so you can take steps to make sure that yours is the only brand they choose even more often.

Tom Peters's Prescription
The customer creates his or her own carnival (I call it "customerizing").

The carnival is a set of opportunities, a canvas on which the customer paints his or her own customized experience. If there are 5,000 customers tonight, they are painting 5,000 substantially different pictures.

John Francis Tighe's Guide
A no may not be a no at all but a future yes.

There are a lot of reasons why a given recipient doesn't respond at a given time—not because of your mailing but because of his or her circumstances at the moment.

Don't take my word for it. Read Dick Benson's book *Secrets of Successful Direct Mail*. One of his rules of thumb is that follow-up mailings two weeks after the first mailing pull 50 percent of the original response.

Raymond Rubicam's Rubric
The object of advertising is to sell goods. It has no other justification worth mentioning.

Claude Hopkins's Tenet
The only purpose of advertising is to make sales.

Advertising is profitable or unprofitable according to its actual sales. It is not for general effect. It is not to keep your name before the people. It is not primarily to aid your other salespeople.

Treat advertising as a salesperson. Force it to justify itself. Figure its costs and results. Accept no excuses (which good salespeople do not make). Then you will not go far wrong.

The difference is only in degree. Advertising is multiplied salesmanship. It may appeal to thousands while the salesperson talks to one. It involves a corresponding cost. Some people spend $10 per word on an average advertisement. Therefore, every ad should be a supersalesperson.

A salesperson's mistake may cost little. An advertising mistake may cost a thousand times as much. Therefore, be more cautious, more exacting. A mediocre salesperson may affect a small part of your trade. Mediocre advertising affects all of your trade.

Gary Kauffman's Beacon
Nothing is more profitable than the right offer powerfully stated to the right person at the right time.

Simply put, people accept offers more frequently than they buy products or services. It is the "What's in it for me?" syndrome.

Elbert Hubbard's Homily
Big business makes its money out of by-products.

It's not what you sell; it's what *else* you sell that's important. That's the whole point to the system and processes of direct marketing.

Don Jackson's Fundamental
The better known you are (the greater the brand equity), the less you have to fight the credibility of the offer.

Frank Watts's Cobweb Clearer
Sell what you've got.

> Marketers can get so excited about creating new products that they give short shrift to their existing business.

Angel Martin, "The Rockford Files"
You can't make one thin dime giving people what they need. You've got to give 'em what they want.

General Management

 Two constants pervade the direct marketing concept. The first is the people who do all the tasks and execute all the functions within the company environment. The second is the customers—the people who make the purchases, the multiple purchases, that fuel the system and all of its processes.

Dick Benson's Rule of Thumb
Marketing is only as good as the supporting infrastructure.

George Mosher's 12 Management Maxims
Do the simple things quickly and the complex things carefully.

Small and incremental changes add up to big dollar savings.

Continually ask yourself: "Is this function or process necessary?"

Reach solutions and prevent problems; do not react to crises.

Walk around; know what's going on.

Do not blame people; focus on establishing an environment where employees are excited about their jobs.

Employees must take full responsibility for their jobs—be open to all possible ways to solve a problem.

Expect people to do their jobs; train them, but do not do it for them.

Remember that employees' time is valuable; use it correctly.

Hire carefully and try very hard not to lay off; prune people who are not producing.

Try hard to hire highly skilled people and pay above average wages for above average work.

Agonize over only one thing: hiring.

> The wisdom is apparent as we shift to the purpose-process-people business model from the form-follows-function models of the past. Note that seven of the 12 maxims focus on people!

John J. Fleider's Fundamentals

> **A company can become world class when it gets discretionary effort from its people.**
> People will work to the level needed to keep their jobs. It's only by involving them to where they will give the organization their discretionary effort—they are totally aligned with the company's purpose and objectives and they think about and act on what is best for meeting them—that a company or an organization can move into a class by itself. The team that worked on Windows 95 decided for themselves to go one day to an Egghead Software store and buy one of every piece of software offered—and then to test them against their own product and thinking.
>
> Most companies do not have the leadership style or culture in place to achieve this type of breakthrough contribution from their employees at every level.

> **Never discard an idea—even if it didn't work the first time.**
> Young people come to the marketplace fired up with "new ideas" based on their life perspective. Their creativity can be stifled quickly by the old-timer's statement "We tried that and it didn't work." Times change. Technology intervenes. The consumer's level of sophistication advances. For example, means of payment, such as credit card payments over the Internet, change the equation for the consumer. Trust your original instincts that said this was an idea worth trying and see if the conditions have now changed enough to make it work—or worth testing again.

Drayton Bird's Precepts
Great work comes from people who exceed the bounds of what they are expected to do.

Fear of failure does as much as hope of success.

Wendell Forbes's Certainties

Where we stand determines our horizon.

Each of us views events from our own particular perspective. We can stand on high ground and have a cosmic view or stand in the dense underbrush of a valley and see little.

If the people who do the work would increase their productivity by 5 percent and top management would reduce its ego by 90 percent, we could experience prosperity such as the country has never seen.

If you want to be right 90 percent of the time, say no to all new ideas.

Franklin Watts's Cobweb Clearers

When in doubt, do the obvious.

Always see a salesperson once.

In business and in love, when you ask a direct question, be prepared for a direct answer.

Always answer your own phone.

Denny Hatch's Corollary

Do not allow fictitious people to sign your letters and represent your company.

A number of direct marketing companies are represented by noms de plume: Publisher's Clearing House (Robert H. Treller); *Reader's Digest* (Carolyn Davis); Cox Direct/Donnelly Marketing (Carol Wright); Frank Cawood (Frank K. Wood).

The advantages of a fake name: Anybody can take the call. Corporate turnover is irrelevant.

The disadvantage: Many top guns do not want to be known by name because they could receive angry calls at three in the morning from disgruntled customers. In fact, angry calls from disgruntled customers at three in the morning provide valuable information about your business—information others in the organization would like covered up.

Don Jackson's Hypothesis of Modern Management Technique

The people on the front lines who are dealing with customers or clients—whether it be retail, wholesale, a service business, or mail order—must know the business, know the customer, and, above all, be empowered to act.

> Customers want to deal with decision makers. The minute a representative—in person or on the phone—says "I'll have to ask my boss" or "I'll have to get permission," you've lost credibility.

Frank Gerson's Law
The problem in business today is that companies are quick to embrace the "next great management concept," such as TQM (total quality management), reengineering, downsizing, or whatever. In reality, all they ever have to do is listen to the customer and do whatever it takes to delight that customer. Everything else will fall into place.

Jim Rutz's Ethic
God will not let you starve because you refused to promote a product that is unethical, harmful, or at odds with the greater good of society.

Don Jackson's Adage
Treat every dollar you spend on every program you manage as if it were your own money!

> If you wouldn't spend your own money on an idea, a concept, a program, a promotion, a campaign, why would you spend your company's money on it?

J. Peterman's 10 Management Principles

> Catalogs and business should be simple. Simple is wonderful, elegant, and sophisticated. That goes for deals, too.

> If everyone waits for me to make a decision, decisions aren't going to be made.

> There's more to running a company than training managers: it's creating a culture.

> I want people to develop themselves to a point where they can get a job somewhere else but they want to stay because they like the culture here.

> Managing, in its simplest form, is common sense.
> Trouble is, most people in the world don't have common sense.

> Nobody's ever been fired for making a mistake.
> In fact if you haven't made a mistake I cast a jaundiced eye, because you're probably not doing anything.

To create a great organization, you need great people.

The guy who succeeds is the guy who says "I'm going to succeed."

Successful businesses are driven forward with different kinds of minds. Accountants can't make any revenue. They can account for revenue and do a lot of good things. But the creative mind creates revenue.

If something fails and it destroys you, you should have been a nine-to-fiver. To be an entrepreneur you cannot be afraid of failure.

Alternative Media

Linda Callahan's
Eight Alternative Media—a Glossary

(Remember, prices represent ballpark averages and generally do not include the production and delivery of the insert pieces.)

Package inserts.
These are freestanding promotional pieces delivered to a mail-order customer via the fulfillment package (e.g., the insert is delivered in a box containing a shirt you ordered from a catalog). Naturally the product shipment types vary dramatically: catalog generated vs. space generated, continuity or club oriented, business to business vs. consumer. Correspondingly, the responses to the outside insert will also vary. The going rate for package inserts is nonetheless an average of $50/M. The number of outside inserts varies from four to eight. Generally only noncompetitive pieces are included together.

If one goes heavily into a club or continuity-oriented program, the rate of duplication needs to be monitored. The response rates also vary significantly, depending on a number of other variables: whether the insert is generating a lead or producing an order, the average ticket price of the items being sold, the size of the insert, etc. A large-ticket item may be profitable with two responses per thousand, whereas lead-generating devices having a strong affinity between the insert and the products being delivered would require and will produce responses from 2 to 5 percent.

The current universe approaches half a billion names and includes distributors like Arizona Mail Order, Hanover House, and Fingerhut. There are also scores of smaller distributors such as Albert Constantine (woodworking), Atlas Pen & Pencil, and Performance Diver.

Ride-alongs.
In this instance a company mails a catalog, circular, or announcement to its customer base and allows outside advertising to go along. An advertiser can

count on this method of distribution since the company doing the mailing has a vested interest in getting out its own promotional pieces. Companies like Columbia House and BMG dominate this category and offer regular mailings in blocks of two to six million to their club members. Advertisers' response from this category is strong—comparable to that from package inserts. Average prices range from $40/M to $60/M. Four to six outside inserts are included in each mailing. Response curves are similar to direct mail.

Co-op mailings.

This category, by definition, presents a group of noncompetitive advertising mailings to a common market. Carol Wright is typical, including both mail-order and direct-response offers along with package goods participants (coupons on brand items). Co-ops represent large numbers (up to 40 million) in a single drop and can usually provide good demographic selections. Although responses are not as high as those generally received from packages, co-ops are priced more competitively, at an average of $15/M.

Other types of co-ops include mail-order and direct-response offers but instead of the package goods coupons, include local coupons (e.g., a dry cleaner, ice cream shop, bank, or gas station). These programs are usually sold on a local level by neighborhood franchises. Good examples include Super-Coups (mostly New England), Val Pak, and Money Mailer. Most of them are available in a number 10 envelope format, but some mail in a six- by nine-inch envelope. Circulation exceeds 50 million per quarter.

Statement stuffers.

These mailings include invoices and statements generated by cable TV companies, utilities, credit cards, magazines, clubs, continuity programs, retailers, businesses, and so on. They are usually distributed in small envelopes so your insert needs to be no larger than $3\frac{1}{2}$ by $6\frac{1}{2}$ inches to fit. Outside inserts are generally limited to three since statements get mailed first class (which means the highest possible percentage of deliverability) and additional outside advertising would bump them into the next higher postal rate. Response tends to be strong. The average price is running at $45/M.

Sampling.

Sampling offers a variety of goody bags distributed free to specific markets, such as college students, new mothers, and other special-interest groups. Inserts accompany product samples and coupons. Packages are usually given out free in high-traffic situations. Pricing ranges from $25/M to $40/M. Shelf life can be difficult to pinpoint.

Card deck mailing.

This vehicle usually consists of 20 or more $3\frac{1}{2}$- by $5\frac{1}{2}$-inch cards delivered polybagged together. Some are business reply cards; others give a phone or fax number for the order. Rate card prices average $25/M to $30/M and include printing from film. Most business-to-business and some consumer card decks have come onto the market in recent months. Currently, 750 decks are available in approximate circulation of 100,000 to 250,000 each. Most decks will accept preprinted inserts at a higher cost per thousand. Many are also mailing in a larger format—5$\frac{1}{2}$ by 8$\frac{1}{2}$ inches—that is more preprint friendly.

Catalog bind-ins/blow-ins.

This distribution has been used in big numbers for years by the horticultural set (e.g., a magazine subscription offer or a lead generator for a lawn tool product bound into a catalog). Many catalogs are now beginning to offer blow-in space, traditional advertising space, and business reply card (printed three up to make a page) space in their catalogs to further serve the direct-response advertiser. Blow-ins can run as little as half the price of package inserts to the same customers.

Other alternatives.

Inserts have been included in newspapers and supermarket take-one racks, have ridden along with pennysavers, order acknowledgments, and freestanding inserts (FSIs in runs of Sunday supplements), and the list goes on.

Leon Henry's 10 Guidelines for Getting Started with Package Inserts/Co-ops

Use a broker.

Don't do it yourself. It's tough and unnecessary. A reliable broker will tell you what's good for your product and what you should avoid.

Test.

But test smart. Some mailers test for test's sake, which unfortunately means when they are through they don't know what and why they tested. It is axiomatic in the insert market—because of its varied nature—that you test. But testing smart means testing with a proven insert wherever possible. Test statistically reliable numbers relative to your offer. Test with no more than two copy approaches. Test as many programs initially as your budget allows. Remember that the batter who comes to the plate once is a hero only if he gets a hit—and even the great Ted Williams hit the ball only 40 percent of the time over his lifetime. Test smart by coming to bat as often as possible. A strikeout won't look so bad among the homers.

Test new programs.

Along with standbys such as Hanover House, Newfield, Carol Wright, and Fingerhut, you want to test others, such as Viking Office Products, Global Computer Suppliers, and Buyer's Choice. You've never heard of these? Of course, you're not using a broker who has a research staff to ferret out the new programs. But don't just test the new ones because they have not yet stood "the test of time" and usage. Make some room for the tried and true, but leave test cells for those that are new today and tomorrow.

Use one insert.
Look at all the smart mailers, and you will see that they have been going out with one insert format for years. Why? Because you want to test the medium and not the message. If you are confident in your message, each test of the medium (the various package insert programs you go into) will be clear in its results.

Ask lots of questions.
Don't be afraid to ask your broker every silly question that you can think of about the source of the program presented. Just as you would ask other media salespeople, you should inquire about the source of the customers, the media used to obtain the customers, the number of years in business, other inserters that have used and continued with the program, the time that it takes for your inserts to be distributed, and so on. The more you ask, the better informed you will be. The better informed, the more likely you will be successful.

Be sure to key by program.
You'd be surprised by how many sophisticated mailers forget to insert an identifying key on each program's order device. They also forget to key in such a way that when the distribution takes too long they can't research how and when their inserts were distributed. For example, if the distribution will take three months, it makes sense to key your inserts in such a way that you can tell when the first month is completed and so forth. The small extra expense with the printer can save you headaches and cut your aspirin bill.

Use the right sources.
Just as you should be using a knowledgeable broker, you should have the right printer, direct mail consultant, and, where necessary, the correct mailing house working for you. Ask for competitive bids from everyone that you use. The printer who is an expert with your catalog may not be right for the insert market. Your artist should know that inserts must be machine insertable.

Ask for proof of receipt and of delivery.
The old days are gone, so you can be reasonably assured that the inserts you send to be distributed will be used. Why? Because too many companies are making too much money from the service to "fuss" around. But you can never be too sure. Your broker should obtain an insert sample upon receipt and upon completion and have it in his or her file. Your printer should have receipt of delivery. Your inserts should be boxed professionally and marked clearly. The insides of some of the warehouses dwarf the imagination, and your insert can get lost.

Pay the right price.
Because of the variety of insert programs, you want to pick the best for your offer and then decide on the right ones based on the top price you are will-

ing to pay. After you've received the test results, there's plenty of time to negotiate for price reduction. As with other media, prices change with volume and frequency. After all, the worst your broker can report is "the rate card or nothing." It pays to ask.

Expect less; get more.

The package insert field is still being developed. For all of the success stories, this medium is just like the other forms of direct response. It is a numbers game. If you watch the cost of printing and the cost of distribution, your response should be sufficient to provide you with a satisfactory cost per inquiry or cost per order. If you're expecting miracles, this is not the medium for you. But for steady production of orders at reasonable and competitive costs, this medium is hard to beat. And for ease of entry, low visibility, and low cost, what could be better? Where is the cost of a television commercial or the heavy postage and four-color envelopes? Not here. Inserts are inexpensive, and for most products they are extensive. Many magazines, catalog houses, clubs, and photofinishers are having tens of millions of inserts distributed yearly.

Iris Shokoff's Four Tips for Buying Co-ops and FSIS

Buy remnant space.

You can find some really good deals at the last minute; you just need to be in the know. If you forge close working relationships with knowledgeable list brokers and managers, you'll know which programs have leftover space that can be negotiated for. Be sure to have an insert ready and waiting, since these deals can come up close to the mail date.

In competitive product categories, expect to pay higher rates to clear circulation.

Most insert program managers are pushed to offer category-exclusive deals to participants. For example, a children's book club might not want another children's education offer in the pack. To keep from being edged out by the competition, you may need to pay more to ensure exclusive circulation of your insert.

In noncompetitive product categories, negotiate a lower cost per thousand.

Why should you pay more than you have to? Insert program managers like to offer a wide variety of products in their packages. If you have the advantage of being the only participant offering a certain type of product, use your uniqueness to negotiate a cheaper price.

Use experienced direct-response media buyers.

Buying media wisely is a very time-consuming business. Prices, percentage points, and response rates are constantly changing, and media buyers dedicate

100 percent of their time to being one step ahead of the game. In media buying how you play the game greatly affects whether you win or lose.

Dick Benson's Beacon
Think of alternative media, co-ops, and FSIS as short-copy media.

Bob Doscher's Formula
Think of alternative media, co-ops, and FSIS as offer-driven media.

Elliott Segal's Six Tips on Fax Marketing

Target your audience.
Selling fax paper or fax-related supplies via the fax machine has a natural synergy. If you were trying to market insurance policies, it would be doomed to failure.

Limit your fax to one 8½- by 11-inch page.
You are not likely to offend if your flyer is short and to the point, offering an immediate benefit.

Fax after business hours only.
The threshold of tolerance is greater after normal business hours than it is during fax-intensive prime time. Mr. Fax sends out flyers from 9:00 P.M. to 6:00 A.M. only. This avoids tying up the prospect's fax machine during normal business hours. It also reduces phone line expenses.

Remove names on request.
This basic courtesy must be honored. When people ask to be removed from your fax list, remove them immediately. Mention on your flyer that you will do this. The last thing you want to do is send unwanted information to someone who has asked that it be stopped.

Promote an 800 number.
This will enable your prospect to contact you toll-free to order or to be removed from the prospect list.

Remember, the issue is not whether the faxed document is unsolicited but whether the message has any value.
When the receiver sees value in the message, there can be no negative feeling toward the incoming fax.

Denny Hatch's Five Additional Tips on Fax Marketing

Avoid the cover sheet.
The recipients pay for the fax paper. Why needlessly stick them for your excesses?

Remember, small type often breaks up in fax transmissions.
How many times have you received a fax on standard company letterhead where some "artsy" designer decided the phone and fax number should be in six-point serif type that is absolutely unreadable when it comes off the machine? Fax technology demands bold type that is large enough for mistakes.

Treat your fax message like an ad.
Spend as much time on writing and designing a fax promotion as you would a full-page advertisement; your message deserves no less.

Before you fax your flyer, fax it to yourself to see how it looks coming off the fax machine.

Remember, it is a violation of federal law to send an unsolicited fax to a company or an individual with whom you have had no prior relationship. Be aware: this is a murky area—and getting more so.

Analysis of Results

One of the most significant differences between the direct marketing concept and other forms of advertising is the notion of measurement. Perhaps the first rule of the concept is measure *everything*—advertising results, administrative results, operations results, and customer service results.

Drayton Bird's Adage
Discovering why things flop teaches us more than success does.

Gary Hennerberg's Checklist of 17 Items to Monitor and Analyze with Each Direct Marketing Effort

Inquiries and conversions by media source.
What It Is. The number of people who "raised their hand" and responded to your offer and the number of those "raising their hand who also reached into their pocketbook." Both of these numbers must be segmented by the individual medium used (list, publication, etc.) to evaluate the effectiveness of the effort and media used.

How You Use This Data. It permits a comparison of the number and percent response among lists, publications, etc. (Note: List response percentages should be compared with other lists, for example, and should not be compared to space ad or DRTV percentages.) It also permits comparison of response and conversion rates among sources to evaluate the best performing media used.

Response by media by month.
What It Is. The number of people who "raised their hand" and responded to your offer on a monthly basis as well as the number of inquiries that converted each month.

How You Use This Data. Analysis of response by month allows you to (1) arrive at the best season or months for offering your product, (2) plan future marketing promotions for those months, and (3) reveals months that may have high inquiry response but low conversion so you can factor this information into future promotions.

Remember this caveat: the nature of your offer will impact results. A super freebie will raise the number of inquiries, but to be successful it must raise the number of conversions as well.

Cost per acquired lead and converted sale.

What It Is. The cost for each lead generated. Simply, the total cost (production, medium, and other related costs) divided by the number of leads. This report should also include the cost for each lead converted to a sale.

How You Use This Data. Comparing costs for each effort informs future marketing plans about the cost-effectiveness of the medium. Cost per conversion is more important to know than cost per inquiry because one medium may have a low number of leads (with a high cost per lead) but a very high conversion rate, which brings down the overall marketing cost per sale. Remember that a medium that appears more expensive than others—it has the highest cost per thousand, e.g.—may end up costing you less if it produces more cost-effective inquiries and conversions than other media.

Media and production cost by source.

What It Is. The total of all costs associated with the marketing program. You have two ways to go: (1) amortize creative agency fees, production time, and all other expenses related to the preparation of the campaign over the life of the campaign by per-thousand circulation or (2) treat creative and production time as a onetime expense. The latter is probably a tidier accounting system, because if the ad or direct mail effort is a raging control that runs for years, trying to amortize the original creative costs accurately over the life of the campaign becomes a nightmare.

How You Use This Data. Using cost per thousand makes all comparisons equal. It also reveals the true total cost of your efforts and allows you to compare the results of efforts by dividing the number of inquiries or conversions by the cost of the program to measure the program's effectiveness.

Sales force disposition of qualified inquiries.

What It Is. Tracking how many inquiries were sent to the sales force as well as whether leads were followed up by a sales representative call or by telesales.

How You Use This Data. This information pinpoints good follow-up and reveals problem areas. It gives you an early warning about customers who have had no follow-up and triggers actions aimed at those who have, such as thanking newly sold customers or including them in a survey of customer satisfaction. It also allows measurement of back-end marketing efforts. Note: Flow charts created before a campaign will ensure that no lead is overlooked or lost.

Inquiries receiving fulfillment packages and sales histories.
What It Is. Inquiries not forwarded to the sales force but sent other fulfillment information.

How You Use This Data. This, too, reveals what's happening with the inquiry. Was the prospect simply sent information with no additional follow-up? Graded for lead level of importance? Importantly, it provides an early warning for leads who have had no additional follow-up and allows you to track the time that has elapsed between receipt of an inquiry and conversion into a customer. It also enables measurement of the medium source of the inquiry by the customer. It's possible some media types will produce more "tire kickers" than others. Because follow-up timing is critical, elapsed time from the inquiry receipt until material is sent can be managed.

Inquiries converted to sales.
What It Is. The number of inquiries, by source, that have converted to sales.

How You Use This Data. Permits a comparison of inquiries converted to sales by source to determine cost per inquiry and cost per converted sale. Remember, it's most important to search for the lowest cost per inquiry or lowest cost per sale, not necessarily where the most leads or conversions originated.

Customer types.
What It Is. The consumer or business type of the core customer base. If this information does not exist on the customer file, demographic and lifestyle data and standard industrial codes (sics) can be appended, along with sales volume, number of employees, number of locations, and more.

How You Use This Data. It permits better targeting of lists and other media so you can maximize your marketing investment. It's possible to append outside data to your list, and by profiling your best customers you can discover where to prospect for more of them.

Key titles.
What It Is. In the business environment, knowing who inquires, who influences the purchase, who has the authority to purchase.

How You Use This Data. Usually several people inside a prospective customer company have some influence in a purchase. Having titles or functional responsibilities/job descriptions permits you to target much better. If you know who is inquiring, you can formulate creative strategy to appeal to the right target audience.

Sales value of a customer from first sale.
What It Is. The dollar value of the customer from the first sale.

How You Use This Data. This information provides the basis for future sales projections. Are subsequent purchases always about the same size? Growing? Declining? It also reveals the benchmark for future media selection based on the value of customers. Some media may simply have prospects who have higher sales values. If you must base your allowable marketing costs on the first purchase, accumulating historical data will provide more accurate information. As you assemble historical data over time, you can see trends emerging about the value of new customers' first purchases. Are new customers trending toward bigger sales? Smaller?

Sales value/number of purchases from new customer in first year.

What It Is. The number of times a new customer has purchased over a consecutive 12-month period from the date of his or her first purchase, the dollar value of each purchase, and the cumulative sales after the first 12 months as a new customer.

How You Use This Data. It's essential to know the retention or persistence of customer purchases. New customers who purchase often and purchase in high volume should be treated specially early on to solidify the relationship through targeted direct marketing. If a significant number of customers purchase once from you and don't purchase again, you have the opportunity to learn why.

Projected sales value/number of purchases by average customer after one year.

What It Is. Unlike the sales and purchases from a new customer, this number is an average value of all customers after one year of purchase history. This will include every customer with one year or more of history.

How You Use This Data. You will be able to select the best-performing media for future marketing efforts, since every customer should have a source code appended to it from now into perpetuity. It will also help you determine the longtime value of a customer and better evaluate how much money you can invest in marketing costs to acquire a new customer.

Quintile analysis of sales.

What It Is. The breakdown of sales in order from the largest customer sale in dollars to the smallest customer sale. Customers are segmented into quintiles (five groups) with an equal number of customers in each group. If there are 100 customers and the sales are arranged from the highest to the lowest, the top 20 customers will represent the first quintile with the largest volume of sales dollars. Usually, sales from the largest 20 percent of customers represent 60 percent or more of sales volume.

How You Use This Data. You can target your best customers or ensure they receive special treatment from your marketing efforts or sales force. You have the option of turning over your lowest 20 percent of customers to lower-cost marketing contact cycles. Knowing the profile of your best customers will permit you to use media where more of those customer types can be found.

Customer profile analysis.

What It Is. The history of the customer, along with detailed data about his or her sales value (what the customer buys from you), demographics or psychographics, business type, geography, and more.

How You Use This Data. This information permits more selective media choices and can be used to develop marketing strategy, including creative, offers, and media choices.

Allowable marketing cost.

What It Is. The amount of money remaining after cost of goods sold (COGS), fulfilling the product, overhead, and profit objectives are subtracted from sales that can be used for marketing programs. (See related articles from the March 1993 and April 1995 issues of *Target Marketing.*) Allowable marketing costs can be based on:

- Cost to generate an inquiry
- Cost to generate an inquiry with an assumed conversion rate
- Cost to generate a sale
- Cost to generate a sale with long-term value

How You Use This Data. This information permits you to use marketing dollars where you have a history of response and conversion. If no response history exists, you learn what you must generate before going into the campaign. Most important, it helps you establish objectives.

Profit and return on investment.

What It Is. The final scorecard. Reveals how much every dollar spent on marketing costs returned in profit.

How You Use This Data. It enables you to justify to yourself and management if the marketing program made sense. Many times precise numbers regarding COGS, overhead, etc., are not available, so use your best estimate of percentages with input from coworkers who can provide a qualified estimate.

Key learning, indicated actions, recommendations.

What It Is. The direction and conclusions you will come to after completing the analysis.

Hints About How to Draw Your Own Conclusions: As ideas strike you while analyzing the data, jot down your thoughts so you can use them as you wrap up an analysis. As you analyze and review data, additional ideas should come to mind about data you should examine. A word of caution: Be careful not to let the data paralyze you into inaction, the analysis/paralysis syndrome.

How You Use This Data. This becomes the road map you will follow. The best predictor of the future is what has happened in the past.

Arithmetic

 Nothing seems to put people off more than mathematics. The word *arithmetic* seems far less threatening. The manipulation of numbers is basic and fundamental to the execution of the direct marketing concept. After all, one of the distinguishing characteristics of direct marketing is measurement—measurement of everything that can be measured.

Mastering four basic mathematical functions—addition, subtraction, multiplication, and division—allows most direct marketing practitioners to handle almost all necessary calculations. The rest of us now know the reason the Almighty caused Lotus 1-2-3 and Excel to be born.

Anver Suleiman's Standard
Think in ROM (return on marketing dollar), not RR (response rate).

This will help you think more clearly and make all comparisons, regardless of package/product costs, comparable. A step beyond this would be to think margin vs. revenue so you truly are focused on the bottom line.

Old Marketing Adage
It costs five times as much to acquire a new customer or donor as it does to keep an existing one happy and continually buying from you.

Comment by Denny Hatch: The greatest mistake a direct marketer can make is to concentrate heavily on acquiring new customers or donors and give short shrift to the back end. A typical scenario is frequently found in magazine publishing:

The circulation director hires a series of high-priced writers and designers to create new acquisition packages. Yet the billing series—those key communications that persuade the new subscriber to pay the bill—are often left to junior writers. "I've got the customer," the logic goes. "Why should I pay exorbitant prices to a copywriter for a billing series?"

The high-priced writer who generated the order in the first place found the right voice for that publication to use with those subscribers. Anytime the magazine talks to that group of subscribers, it should be in the original voice.

Rebecca Klem Mills's Gospel
Customer long-term value includes the profit that can be generated from future upgrades and cross-sells as well as the profit that can be expected from the original purchase. Including the future value of customers in the initial profitability calculation allows the marketers to increase their file penetration and contact more customers.

Overhead should include all office expenses unless management has decided to price the business on a marginal basis to be more competitive.

Shareholder value is the excess of all future profit over that required to meet the company's cost of capital.

Return on equity is a yearly measure calculated as the profit divided by the total investment in the business, including required risk capital.

Denny Hatch's Addition
The most elementary piece of direct marketing arithmetic: Know your allowable cost per order.

How much can you afford to spend to get an order? If you spend more on marketing and fulfillment than what you bring in, you will lose money—*unless* you know your new customer or donor will be profitable in year two or three, in which case you can lose money on the acquisition and make it back—and then some—on the lifetime value.

Let's say you're running a space ad for $1,200 to sell a $40 product. You have paid for the creative; your ad is standing and ready to run. Your markup is five to one; in other words, your cost of goods sold is $8. You will accept cash with order (check or money order) or a credit card. No bill-me option. Let's say you will charge $5 for shipping, and it costs you $5 to ship, so this is a wash.

Revenue per order		$40.00
Cost of goods sold	$ 8.00	
Reserve for returns (15%)	6.00	
General and Administrative (15%)	6.00	
(Includes credit card processing)		
Profit (15%)	6.00	
Total Costs	$26.00	26.00
Allowable Cost Per Order		$14.00

If you are spending $1,200 in a publication to run an ad, then $1,200 ÷ $14 = 85.7.

You need 86 orders to break even.

If you offer a bill-me option, you have to factor in a percentage for bad debt—bandits who take your product and don't pay. This will cause your cost to go up and your allowable cost per order to go down, which means you will need more orders to break even.

If you have just one product in your line, you have a problem. Assuming the ad breaks even, you have spent $14 to acquire each of 86 customers. Presumably they know you, they like you, and they will buy from you again. But if you don't have something else to sell them, the only way you can make money off these people is to rent your list to others. And since consumer lists go out of date at the rate of 2 percent a month (people move, die, change their names) and business lists go out of date at the rate of 1 percent a week (that's 50 percent a year!), your list will get dirty quickly, and rentals will cease.

Therefore, we can see that arithmetic reinforces a fundamental point made in earlier chapters: to stay in business using the direct marketing concept, you need to have continuing sales to your existing customers.

Robert C. Hacker's Truths

Direct Marketing Truth 1: Direct marketing is the only marketing system that allows you to use hard numbers to plan, engineer, and measure marketing programs.

Direct Marketing Truth 2: Most people still don't use the numbers to plan, engineer, and measure programs.

People think running the numbers is too hard, probably due to all the hype about factor analysis, step regressions, neural networks, and other expensive, complicated computer-generated statistical modeling—it's just too scary and expensive.

Another reason is that nobody shows people how easy it is to become a numbers maven. A simple calculator and a cocktail napkin can often lead to startling discoveries—sometimes uncovering new opportunities, often saving us from disaster.

Hacker's Six Indispensable Formulas

Raw cost per response.
If you have a package that costs $.489 per unit and a response rate of 2.78 percent, what's the cost per response? The formula is: cost per response = cost per package ÷ response rate. In this example $.489 ÷ .0278 = $17.59 cost per response.

Loaded cost per response.

Using the preceding example, let's assume that fulfillment cost is $3.75 and telemarketing averages $4.50 per call. To figure your loaded cost, use this formula: loaded cost per response = (cost per package ÷ response rate) + fulfillment + telemarketing. The loaded cost in this example would be ($17.59) + $3.75 + $4.50, or $25.84.

Cost per sale.

In a one-step sale, the loaded cost per sale in this example would be $25.84. But if this were a two-step sale, $25.84 would be the loaded cost per lead. With a closing rate of 22 percent, the cost per sale would be $25.84 ÷ .22 or $117.45 since cost per sale = cost per lead ÷ closing rate.

Response rate required to hit breakeven.

There are times when you need to know what response rate you'll need to hit breakeven. Let's assume that a package cost $.654 and the raw cost per response was $25. The response rate required to hit this target is calculated with the following formula: response rate = cost per package ÷ cost per response. In this case, $.654 ÷ $25.00 = 2.62%.

Allowable cost per package (in the mail).

Let's assume the consensus is that a specific offer will generate a response rate of 1.5 percent to 2.0 percent and that the cost per response is $48. Using the worst case (1.5 percent), the most you can afford to spend on the package (in the mail) is $48 × .015 = $.720 each, based on the formula package cost = cost per response × response rate.

Figuring package cost at any quantity.

In the engineering process, questions like this often come up: "What happens to production costs if I increase the drop quantity from 50,000 to 100,000?"

Typically this means going back for another bid, but it doesn't have to. Here's how you can estimate the cost at a quantity of 100,000. Let's assume you have bids at two quantities:

- 25,000 costs $356/M
- 50,000 costs $256/M

1. Calculate the cost of the second 25,000.

    - 25 × $356 =$ 8,900
    - 50 × $256 = $12,800
    - So, the second 25,000 costs you $3,900 ($12,800 − $8,900).

2. The cost per thousand (CPM) for the second 25,000 is $3,900 ÷ 25 = $156/M.
3. The setup cost for the job is ($8,900 − (25 × $156)) = $5,000.
4. The cost for any new quantity is setup cost + (CPM × (quantity ÷ 1,000)).

So, the cost of 100,000: $5,000 + (156 × 100) = $20,600 or $206/M.

This methodology will calculate within a few percentage points unless the vendor changes presses or is willing to live with lower margins for higher volume. In both cases, your estimate will be on the high side and safe for planning purposes.

Gary Hennerberg's Procedure

Measurability is a hallmark of targeted marketing programs.
It should come as no surprise that many people find direct marketing math overwhelming. Scores of those who use direct marketing methods haven't learned how to determine financial objectives and measure program performance. Yet no matter what your role in your organization, you need a basic understanding of how to arrive at the numbers. Knowing the numbers lets you think through your marketing program from a highly quantifiable standpoint. With that information at your fingertips, you'll know if your marketing assumptions are sound.

Once you know the numbers, you may find you need to rethink your program. You may need to reduce costs by decreasing the cost of your promotional activity. Will the extra color on your letter pay for itself? Can adjusting the trim size of your brochure save a few crucial dollars? Will an unusual-sized envelope pull the extra orders you need?

Of course, testing will answer these questions, but the math will help you analyze every situation. It'll also be to your advantage to make sure your production staff is your ally so that you'll always know when and how you can knock a few dollars off your costs.

Perhaps you need to improve your offer. How many extra paid orders do you need to justify an expensive premium? Is there an item with high perceived value that doesn't cost as much? Should the premium go to everyone who responds or only those who pay? Maybe you'll need to increase your price or decrease your returns and cancellations or alter one of dozens of other tactics that will change the dynamics of the numbers.

Marketing math needn't be a mystery. Perhaps the biggest challenge is collecting data and using it right.

Knowing how much an average customer is worth from the first purchase is a good starting point.
The key word here is *average*. If you sell one product at one price to every customer, the customer's worth is a no-brainer. But companies prosper because of a variety of products and offers. An average customer may vary depending on the offer (discounted vs. full price). Average customers could buy from several product lines, which increases their value. In the catalog arena, "average customer" will mean average order size.

Another critical number is the retention percentage rate and average order from future purchases—not necessarily the response rate from your next contact.

Since the next purchase may not occur during the next contact, it is important to evaluate over an established period (a year, for example) the number of times you contacted each first-time buyer, the number of first-time buyers who purchased from you again, how frequently, in what dollar amount, and within what period.

You should also know how much time elapses between the first and second purchase and each purchase thereafter.

Knowing this may lead you to conclude that if you can make the second purchase occur faster with a special offer, the overall value of the customer could improve.

If you've already realized you should be making these calculations, but your computer system is not up to tracking and analyzing such data, take a flight of customers (for example, 1,000) and track their sales activity manually.

Better: Go back one year, and randomly select 1,000 customers, and retrace their buying habits. It may not take as long as you think, and you will at least have information you can extrapolate for future planning. (Note: Those 1,000 customers need to be first-time buyers, not 1,000 who are still customers today.)

One strength that large companies have is their ability to offer several product lines; that strength, however, can be a curse when trying to measure the long-term value of a customer.

To determine long-term value, calculate sales from related products, including those from different divisions. In some organizations this is a hornet's nest. Managers from one product group don't usually fork over part of a marketing budget or sales to another group. While evaluating long-term value doesn't necessarily mean forking over sales to another product group, that perception can exist.

Know your required response levels by medium and medium source and evaluate response based on first purchase or longtime value.

Although it takes time and research, the best way to determine these factors is to back in to the numbers. Here are four key steps:

1. Research long-term sales value as just discussed. Account for returns or cancellations in this equation so that you know net sales.
2. Calculate every imaginable fixed and variable cost associated with selling your product, including cost of goods sold, inbound 800 number costs, business reply mail postage, fulfillment, premiums, bad debt, returns processing, commissions, and overhead. Now subtract these costs from your sales value. This is your contribution to profit and marketing cost.
3. Establish your profit objective. If, for example, it is 20 percent of net sales, subtract that number from your contribution.

4. The number remaining is your allowable marketing cost (or cost to acquire a customer). Divide your allowable marketing cost into your media cost per thousand to learn how many orders per thousand (which you can translate into a response percentage) you'll need to meet your objectives.

Don't like the allowable marketing cost and response percentage you see? Refine the numbers.

Are you padding your costs too much? Is your profit percentage realistic? Only after these numbers are tight (understanding that some numbers may be your best assumption) will you know how your marketing efforts must perform. All the numbers can be put on a spreadsheet that you can manipulate on a PC.

Usually your models using a spreadsheet program are best if customized for your operation.

Once you've set up your program, you can make new assumptions and see the profiles or required results by simply changing one number. Since the computer automatically recalculates your numbers, it's math made easy. You'll evaluate your creative, offers, and other elements in a new light when you know exactly what those elements have to produce in response and sales.

Lifetime Value (LTV)

 Customer lifetime value (or long-term value) is the present value of the net contribution to overhead and profit expected from the customer over a period of time certain. There is no more important measurement for organizations following the direct marketing. Unfortunately the concept is not universally applied, though the underlying logic is indisputable. What follows are techniques for calculating this complex quantity and applying it in your own business. First, some foundation ideas:

Bob Stone's Doctrine

All customers are not created equal.
Comment: The foundation of "loyalty" programs, this absolute rule is supported by decades of test results. It addresses the importance of customer file segmentation, which leads to . . .

Eighty percent of repeat business comes from 20 percent of your customers.
Comment: In short, you need to direct your customer communications at the most fertile portion of your database. Stone combines database segmentation

techniques with this verity to produce his notion of *customized communications*—a foundation concept of both loyalty and database marketing. And it is essential to understanding the notion of customer lifetime value.

Don Jackson's Bylaw

Customer contact strategy is the essence of the direct marketing concept. The growth of a business following the direct marketing concept is dependent on consistent communication with customers—Stone's idea of customized communications.

There are six applications of the customer lifetime value concept.
- Assigning an acquisition allowance for customer acquisition
- Developing product pricing
- Setting selection criteria for customer marketing
- Allocating distribution channels, media, promotions, and offers for initial customer acquisition
- Investing in reactivation of former customers
- Assigning an asset value to your customer base

Alan Weber's Lifetime Value Methodology

Not only do you need to know whether your current customers are profitable, but you also need to acquire new customers affordably.

New customers are the lifeblood of any company. Most marketers agree, while it costs money to gain customers and profits come from existing ones, without new customers a business will soon have none at all.

The question is: how much can you prudently spend to gain a customer?

To answer this question we need to take a step-by-step approach. We will use some basic marketing math, combined with information that should be in any good database. In addition, we need to look at the company's capital position. That is, how much money does the company have access to for prospecting, and what is the rate of return the company must earn on the money it uses?

Prospecting—and acquiring new customers or donors—can be viewed as a simple matter of making a financial investment.

Money is invested at the beginning, and time passes before the investment is recovered. Once the investment is recovered, additional income is profit. For example, the cost of producing and mailing a catalog is borne before the first sale from that catalog is made. It may be some time before new customers acquired through that catalog spend enough to more than cover the initial cost of acquiring them.

In the following example, let's assume we are spending $0.60 per catalog (total in-the-mail cost, with list rental and postage) and getting a 1.10 percent average response from rental files.

- Cost to reach a prospect: $0.60
- Average response: 1.10%
- Cost to reach a prospect ÷ average response = advertising
- Cost to acquire a customer: $0.60 ÷ 1.10% (.011) = $54.55

Next, we need to determine how much profit margin is earned on the average initial sale. By subtracting this amount from the cost to acquire a customer, we will know how much we initially invest in a new customer. Let's assume an average initial order of $70 and an average margin of 40 percent, after fulfillment costs.

- Average initial order: $70
- Average margin: 40%
- Advertising cost to acquire a customer: $54.55
- Average initial order × average margin = profit margin on initial sale
- Thus: $70.00 × 40% = $28.00
- Advertising cost to acquire a customer − profit margin on initial sale = initial investment (per customer)
- Thus: $54.55 − $28.00 = $26.55

Now we need to determine our likely future profits.

At this point we have determined the initial investment to acquire a new customer. In the preceding example, the amount is $26.55. We must subtract for the cost of recontacting the customer and for the required rate of investment return, which we will call the time value of money discount factor (TVMDF).

We use the TVMDF to recognize the fact that a dollar one, two, or three years from now will not be worth as much as a dollar today. The TVMDF is based on a rate of interest we require on our investment, including what we demand as a result of risk. Using this factor will give us customer lifetime value in terms of net present dollars (what future profits are worth to us today).

The first step is to determine how much it costs to acquire a new customer.

In this example, we will base lifetime value on three years of purchases. (The optimal number of years varies from industry to industry and should be appropriate to your situation.) To determine at what rate new customers will buy, we need to look at past data. We also need to know how many mailings per year are sent to customers and at what cost.

Let's assume we are mailing four catalogs per year to existing customers at $0.50 each. (The cost is higher for prospect catalogs because list rental expense must be added.) Then we look at what the response of customers has been during each of the past three years. Note, this is based not on the most recent purchase (recency) but on the amount of time since their first purchases.

We will assume a group of customers who made their first purchases in the past year responds at a rate of 16 percent to each of the four offers. A customer who made his or her first purchase two years ago responds at 13 percent, and the three-year customer group responds at 11 percent. The numbers drop off, as customers tend to drop off over time, and fewer are recent buyers.

- 4 mailings per year
- $0.50 cost per mailing
- 16% response per mailing year one
- 13% response per mailing year two
- 11% response per mailing year three
- Number of Mailings × Response per Mailing = Annual Response Rate

Thus:

- Year One: 4 × 16% = 64%
- Year Two: 4 × 13% = 52%
- Year Three: 4 × 11% = 44%
- Number of mailings × cost per mailing = annual marketing cost: 4 × $0.50 = $2.00

By determining the cost per year of reaching an existing customer (annual marketing cost) and the responses we expect from existing customers (annual response rate), we can simplify the math. We can look at each year as if it were a single $2 catalog mailing, with a 64 percent response rate for one-year customers, a 52 percent response rate for two-year customers, and a 44 percent response rate for three-year customers.

Now we need to consider our TVMDF. We will assume this is 20 percent per year (which is the same as paying interest at 20 percent per year to our investors). In other words, if we can achieve a 20 percent or greater return, we can attract additional investment. Below 20 percent per year, investors will place their money elsewhere.

The TVMDF for year one is 1.2, which is the principal (one) plus 20 percent. For year two it is 1.44 (1 + 20 percent for 2 years, or 1.2 squared) and for year three 1.73 (1 + 20 percent for 3 years). This is the opposite of calculating what an investment would be worth with interest because we divide by one plus the interest rather than multiply. We do this because we are calculating what a future dollar amount is worth today, not what a dollar amount today will be worth in the future. We also need to determine the margin of repeat sales, which differs from the margin on initial sales but is calculated the same way.

- 20% TVMDF
- $75 average repeat order
- $30 margin on repeat sales (average repeat order $75 × 40% average margin)

- $2 per year marketing cost
- 64% response year one
- 52% response year two
- 44% response year three

- (Margin on repeat sales × response) − marketing cost = profit per year
- ($30.00 × 64%) − $2.00 = $17.20 (year one)
- ($30.00 × 52%) − $2.00 = $13.60 (year two)
- ($30.00 × 44%) − $2.00 = $11.20 (year three)
- Sum (profit per year − TVMDF) = present value of future profit
- ($17.20 − 1.2) + ($13.60 − 1.44) + ($11.20 − 1.73) = $37.63

Finally, we subtract the initial investment to acquire a customer from the present value of future profit to determine if we exceeded our investment goals.

In this example:

- Initial investment to acquire a customer = $26.55
- Present value of future profit = $37.63
- Present value of future profit − initial investment to acquire a customer = Lifetime Return on Investment
- $37.63 − $26.55 = $11.08

In this case, we acquired customers at an almost 50 percent loss on the initial sale, but by the end of the year we have recovered our investment—with interest—and are making a profit.

If the sample catalog company could attract investors who would demand less than a 20 percent return, it would be able to expand its prospecting into more marginal lists and still make a profit. This would be particularly wise if by expanding it could lower fixed expenses as a percentage of sales.

On the other hand, if investors view the company as an increasing risk, they may demand more than a 20 percent return on investment. In this case the company would be forced to prospect more selectively and increase its initial response rates.

Lifetime value calculations show the importance of mining your customer base.

If the company undermails its own list, it will not achieve the future profits necessary to gain new customers. If the sample company were to mail to customers only three times per year, it would not make a profit. On the other hand, if it could get similar response rates from five mailings per year, it would make more profit and new customers would have a greater lifetime value.

Try these formulas with your own customers. By using this approach, you will be able to determine if you are prospecting too much or too little. You will also see how improvements in marketing to your existing customers allow you to attract new customers who would otherwise be unprofitable.

Robert C. Hacker's Road to High-Ticket Sales

If you have your heart set on a certain package, you need to start with your average sale and work backward.

Typically, clients with high-ticket products think they have to sell with high-priced packages. You hear this all the time with high-end real estate developments, particularly when the developer can't separate his or her ego from the project.

Often the opposite is true.

To hit cost-per-sales targets, you must use inexpensive packages, particularly if there are multiple steps in the sales process. In many cases, if the lead generation package is too expensive, you can never recover.

Let me show you how to use a spreadsheet to determine the investment you can make to sell a $1 million piece of property. This example is based on real numbers for a real client we've been working with for the past three years.

The company uses a five-step sales model, similar to the one shown here. Leads are qualified and converted to prospects, who are then converted to hot prospects, who are then persuaded to visit and attend a sales presentation.

Most prospects live 200 to 400 miles away, and ongoing communication is by mail and telephone until they make their first visit.

First you must determine the major economic targets and performance assumptions of the business. Typically the sales manager is a better source for this information than the marketing manager, so we usually start there. During the interview we have the sales and/or marketing managers commit to program performance assumptions. If they give us a range, we'll model the high, low and midpoints of the range. To avoid migraines, I'll show you the midrange assumptions only.

In this case, the most expensive sale price was a waterfront property for $1 million. The average sale was expected to be about $360,000. The other key performance assumptions discovered during the interviewing process are noted in the boxes in the chart.

Based on the numbers the developer provided (we provided only the response rate assumptions), the maximum amount we could spend on the package was $.95. After list and postage expenses, we had about $.55 per package left for production.

We showed the client the best package we could have produced for $.55. The client hated it.

After all, this company had already invested $170 million and knew we had to put more into the package. The developer showed us an example of a package he loved. It cost about $2 per unit in the mail. Using the $2 cost, we ran the same model backward, playing "what if?" games with packages at various costs.

- If the package cost $2, could we increase response rates and conversion ratios enough to hit the cost-per-sale target? Did the sales man-

ager think he could increase closing rates by putting more money in the mailbox? The answer was no.
- What about $1.50? Could we gain enough efficiency to offset the high package cost? Again, the answer was no.

The final decision: The developer made a rational choice to increase costs to protect brand image. We mailed the $1.50 package, and the client accepted a slightly higher cost per sale.

You might say to yourself, "This is a lot of work." Is it worth it? You bet. The system protected the developer from going with his heart and spending $2, a cost too high to pencil. The creative development process was rational, not the typical "my opinion vs. your opinion" harangue we've all been trapped in from time to time. The client could make rational trade-offs and see the direct effect of his dreams on the bottom line.

DIRECT MARKETING'S EFFECT ON LEAD GENERATION

Step Five: Closing the Sale	$.95 Package	$1.50 Package
Average Sale	$360,000.00	$360,000.00
Target Marketing Cost %	1.75%	2.22%
Target Marketing Cost $	$6,300.00	$7,992.00
Closing Rate Target	7%	7%
Cost per Presentation	$441.00	$559.44
Hospitality Expense	$50.00	$50.00
Cost "to the door"	$391.00	$509.44

Step Four: Hot Prospects	$.95 Package	$1.50 Package
Presentation Rate	33.0%	33.0%
Ghost Cost per Prospect	$129.03	$168.12
Mail Contact	$5.00	$5.00
Telemarketing Support	$10.00	$10.00
Net Cost per Prospect	$114.03	$153.12

Step Three: Prospects		
Conversion to "Hot" Rate	75.0%	75.0%
Gross Cost per Prospect	$85.52	$114.84
Mail Contact	$5.00	$5.00
Telemarketing Support	$10.00	$10.00
Net Cost per Prospect	$70.52	$99.84

Step Two: Raw Lead Trapping & Qualification

Conversion to Prospect Rate	75.0%	75.0%
Gross Cost per Prospect	$52.89	$74.88
Fulfillment	$5.00	$5.00
Telemarketing Support	$10.00	$10.00
Net Cost per Prospect	$37.89	$59.88

Step One: Lead Generation

Response Rate	2.5%	2.5%
Target Cost per Package	$0.95	$1.50

Work the numbers: To determine what cost per sale you can justify—and therefore determine how much you can spend on direct mail creative and production—you need to start with the average sale and work backward. If you're set on a particular package price ($1.50), you'll need to calculate from there.

Bill Butler's Codicil to All Lifetime Value Pronouncements

Actuaries beware; lifetime value calculations sometimes assume biblical life spans just to finance questionable "relationships."

Don Jackson's Tenet

Lifetime value calculations must include a risk hedge.

To combat Bill Butler's warning, since predictive lifetime value models frequently use long-term assumptions to calculate profitability, it is wise to insert some numerical risk hedge device. Many users double the discount rate to accomplish this. Others calculate LTV, then use only a percentage of the calculated LTV—50, 60, or perhaps 70 percent—for its applications.

Back-End Marketing

 Back-end marketing accomplishes two critical tasks within the direct marketing approach. First, back-end marketing increases customer lifetime value, delivering a host of benefits to both company and marketer. Second, back-end marketing increases customer persistence, and, by inference, customer loyalty. It is a critical part of the system.

Maxwell Sackheim's Gospel
The most important order you ever get from a customer is the second order.

Why? Because a two-time buyer is at least twice as likely to buy again as a onetime buyer.

Comment: Throughout this book and in countless articles and seminars and meetings and speeches you will hear this mantra chanted over and over again by the faithful. Believe in this. It is true!

Dick Benson's Precept
A special discount to customers as compared to outsiders will increase response by more than the discount.

Hatch's Laws of Initial Response

Ignore the first response.
When you have dropped a mailing, the first replies you get are from the nuts and cranks who hate junk mail and want to send you a message, often filling your business reply envelopes (BREs) with religious tracts and occasionally sticking it to you by wrapping a building brick in paper and taping your BRE to it as a reply mechanism. Ignore them.

If you get a few crank callers who are offended by your mailing, be nice, be gracious, and then ignore them.

Often CEOs—and especially lawyers—get upset when a few people take offense at a mailing. Always look at the total number of objections, crank letters, and nut case calls you get as a percentage of total response before you take action.

Malcolm Decker's Theory

You cannot buy customer loyalty; it must be earned. *Customer loyalty* is a misnomer; loyalty is a consistent attitude and pattern of behavior *by marketers* toward their customers, instills consumer confidence, and encourages greater consumption.

> The Stamp Collectors Society of America continuity series with 55 personal transmittal (resell) letters sent over a period of 55 months demonstrated our commitment to the customer and produced a *51 percent completion rate.*

> ***Comment by Don Jackson:*** The notion that it is impossible to generate customer loyalty is false. Note the success of frequent flyer programs, hotel programs, AT&T True Rewards, and hundreds of other programs. But perhaps the most important example is at the retail level. In every town and village and city in the United States, effective retailers generate customer loyalty by simply providing superior products and service to their customers. The key, it seems, is delivering consistent value. Marketers *do* play an extraordinarily important role in customer retention, especially following Stone's concept of customized communications. The more relevant the communication, the more likely it is that customer will remain loyal.

John Yeck's Caveat

Have your fulfillment pieces ready before you mail the offer.

> You cannot close what you cannot fulfill—especially true for lead generation programs.

Judith Schalit's Five Ways to Bolster Customer Service

Don't assume that people are happy if they don't complain.

Encourage customers to talk to you—offer an 800 number.

Turn each problem into a sales opportunity.

Properly handle disgruntled customers, who can be your best customers.

Remember, companies go out of business due to poor customer service.

Collecting money is an essential part of business. And it is as much a part of back-end marketing as the fun of upselling customers.

Hank Rossi's Prescription: The Four Key Components of an Effective Credit-Granting and Collection Program
Credit screening.

The collection series.

Efficient and effective billing systems.

Check recovery planning.

Rossi's Essential Elements of a Good Credit-Screening Program

The initial do-not-promote file.
This file is comprised of the names of customers you do not wish to do business with for a variety of reasons and wish to exclude from future promotions. Its purpose is to prevent people who have previous unsatisfactory history from ordering again.

The offer.
More and more companies are using the order form to ask credit questions to identify prospects who match their credit rejection profile. This includes time-honored devices such as requiring a signature on the order form and/or the customer's telephone number. Asking such questions as "Do you have a credit card?" or "Have you purchased anything by mail before?" also provides valuable credit data.

These devices are generally used in combination with the phrase "subject to credit approval" or "subject to credit acceptance." This phrase can deflect response if overemphasized, so it is usually presented in very small type. Even if it depresses response slightly, your responders will be more profitable.

The objective is to deflect as much of the potential bad debt as possible without discouraging good customers.

The order-screening system.
While the do-not-promote file will suppress promotions to known unprofitable prospects, many orders are generated by insert cards, space, or TV, which by its very nature is unscreened. An order-screening/rejection system should be tied in to the data entry/capture system that is a duplicate of the do-not-promote file. This file should be maintained on-line as part of your data capture systems.

Prospect or customer segmentation.
This should be based on information contained in your company database. It may be based on order source or previous payment habits of that order source in general or known customer habits.

How you talk to a customer determines whether you get paid.
Even more important, it determines whether the customer will come back to make another purchase. A targeted series of letters with personalized copy and graphics goes a long way toward accomplishing the profit goals of your company.

Rossi's Eight Ingredients for a Collection Series That Will Maximize Revenue and Minimize Collection Expense

Meaningful segmentation initially by prospect and customer and later by customer payment history.
Too many companies still lose customers by offending them with tough collection copy when they have purchased and paid multiple times.

Different approaches to prospects versus customers.
Prospect collection series should utilize a frequent billing pulse (time between efforts), be relatively tough, and generally be short. Customer collection series usually have a slower billing pulse and contain letters that are relatively mild and much longer.

Collection copy targeted to the audience addressed.
With the billing packages available today, we can remind customers that their subscription was ordered from an ad in *Better Homes & Gardens* and contains a special planter premium that will be shipped immediately upon receipt of their payment.

Graphics that attract attention and remind the customer of what was ordered.
Laser printing has done for collection departments what it did for marketing efforts several years earlier. Effective use of variable fonts and point sizes enables us to write attention-getting letters. Pictures of products offered or premiums to be shipped on payment serve as effective reminders of what this bill is for.

Early third-party letters that will improve collection pay-up by providing a legal letterhead change and also entice customers who are ignoring your letters to talk to the third party.

Phone calls to "with pay" accounts or customers who have previously renewed and for some reason are not paying the current bill.

Very often the phone call serves to eliminate confusion on the customer's part and results in the desired payment. In other cases it identifies the reason for nonpayment; if the issue cannot be resolved, prompt cancellation saves on billing expense.

Late third-party efforts to cream accounts and squeeze out as much of the receivable as possible before assigning that receivable to a collection agency on a commission basis.

Assignment to a collection agency that can maximize your collections while minimizing problems resulting from overzealous collectors.
To find an agency, get a referral. Then carefully and continually monitor results.

Rossi's Components for an Effective Billing System

The ability to segment prospects and customers into as many billing groups as needed to maximize the return on collection expenses.
Many people forget that where credit granting is involved, collection expense (the cost of generating bills, postage, and payment application costs) is the largest line item expense after fulfillment.

Too many systems do not have this ability, and some that do require too much programming to maintain.

New systems coming on-line today have this flexibility, which gives the credit manager the same testing ability that the marketers have.

A fulfillment operation with enough capacity to do a file maintenance update, generate a billing tape, laser-print the bills, burst, fold, insert, meter, and mail the bills within 24 to 48 hours of generation and obtain the best postal discounts.

Collection software that produces images and graphics that get the customers' attention.

The ability to vary the billing pulse to create a sense of urgency with the billing messages.

A good "pay-up by effort" reporting system.
This tool allows the credit manager to determine the exact number of bills that should be mailed to each billing group. The report will also show the results of third-party efforts, collection phone effectiveness, and the efficiency of any collection agency you might be using.

A comprehensive check collection program will result in a recovery rate somewhere in the neighborhood of 75 percent.

With that kind of recovery rate, why would any marketer want to antagonize its customers by sending harsh collection letters or imposing service charges?

Rossi's Steps to a Good Check Recovery Plan

The bank is instructed to automatically redeposit all checks that bounce due to insufficient funds.

When checks come back from the bank as uncollectible, a sales-oriented letter asking for a replacement check is sent out automatically.

Thirty days after the first letter, a follow-up reminder is sent.

Thirty to 45 days after the in-house letter, a collection agency is retained to create a sense of urgency. The initial agency communication should be conciliatory but to the point and professional. Subsequent efforts should be increasingly firm and urgent. The practice of debiting customers' accounts and then resuming normal billing only confuses and results in more bills being mailed to collect less.

Even your good customers will sometimes make calculation errors when paying bills, resulting in bounced checks. Or a customer who's moving might close out one checking account without allowing sufficient time for checks to clear.

When this happens, banks typically impose a penalty in the form of a bounced check charge. Some direct marketers do the same thing. Unfortunately, they may have lost sight of the customer service side of our business. You could lose good customers—who made a mistake—by treating them like deadbeats.

Any credit-granting and collection effort is not 100 percent foolproof; there will always be bad debt you cannot collect.

George Mosher's Maxims

With customer service, look at both saving the customer and the collectability of problem accounts.

Always state: "I am sorry you had that problem."

In business-to-business situations always escalate who you are speaking to on collection calls one level each call.

You lose customers when they have to go through a hassle.

Customer service needs to be broken down between in-call and out-call handling. In-call people need to be available when the calls come in. Out-calls need to work down in piles.

When you have a similar problem across 10 or more orders, write a printed letter. Do not make telephone calls. Send a printed letter to everyone with that problem.

Keep statistics to one or two digits and make them simple to understand.

Accurate and timely accounting is a major key to successful operation of the business; up-to-date numbers are critical.

Increased profit is directly proportional to back-end marketing activity. The greater the customized customer contact, the lower your attrition rate. The lower your attrition rate, the higher your profitability.

Don Jackson's Absolute
Your own customers are your best prospects for future sales.

Brochures

 If the letter in a direct mail package is your salesperson, the brochure is the "prove it" part of your sales pitch. Brochures contain the detail, the features, and the specifics to support your offer and your sales pitch.

Drew Allen Miller's 19 Surefire Techniques to Spark Up Brochures
Brochure Covers

Use a single visual on the cover; research shows that one large photo works better than several small ones.

Show things happening; use action photos and be sure your models are appropriate, because too perfect a subject can elicit disbelief.

Place the headline below the photo/illustration; this can get you 10 percent more readership.

"Focal subheads" can be placed at the top.
If your brochure is going to be racked, put your name, activity, and/or location at the top.

Brochure Headlines

Keep headlines short; according to studies, those headlines with fewer than 10 words get more readership.

Focus your headline on your target group.
If they are golfers, show golfers in the cover photo. And use the word *golf* in your headline. Example: "Be a better golfer."

Try giving your headline news appeal.

More than 21 percent of readers recall headlines containing news. Write it like this: "9 out of 10 golfers immediately improve their swing with Acme clubs."

Brochure Text Copy

Keep text lines a comfortable length.
Body copy lines should never be shorter in picas than the point size (12-point type should not run less than 12 picas in width). Body copy lines should never be longer than double the point size (12-point type should not run longer than 24 picas).

Keep lead paragraphs short—no more than 12 words—to avoid intimidating the reader.

Consider using quotes; in headlines, subheads, text, or call-outs, quotes can generate up to 28 percent more recall.

Avoid typographic overkill; setting too much type in all caps, bold, or italics can slow the reader.

Visual Elements

Use graphic dingbats to ad interest—bullets, check boxes, hyphens, and asterisks.

Consider call-outs and sidecars.
Call-outs, with their attention-getting arrows, are a great way to stop the reader's eye. The same is true with those in-set panel boxes called *sidecars*.

Keep maps and charts simple.

Use bar charts rather than pie charts.
Although artists find a pie chart more exciting to produce, readers actually understand bar charts better. This is because a bar chart requires only a line-length judgment. Pie charts may look creative, but they require the reader to judge quotients at an angle.

Brochure Captions

Use captions wherever possible.
Next to the cover, captions are the most-read items in a brochure. But many designers think they clutter an otherwise clean layout. Crisp captions work hard to inform and involve the reader, yet only one out of five brochures uses them.

Caption width should match the photo width.

Place captions under photos.
Designers sometimes like to position them in more creative ways, but readers expect to find captions below photos. A prospect will give your brochure only so much time, so don't slow him down my making him search for the appropriate caption.

Set captions in a different style . . . different typeface . . . smaller type size . . . italics.

Pat Friesen's 14 Brochure Hot Spots
• Front and back cover • Headlines • Subheads • Bulleted copy • Photo captions • "Violators"—corner slashes, bursts, etc. • Sidecar stories • Graphs and charts • Icons used with phone numbers and fax numbers • Reversed-out type (used very sparingly) • Product photos with people in them • Top right- and left-hand corners • Bottom right-hand corner • Photo call-outs that point to specific product benefits

Malcolm Decker's Tips

The folder or brochure is show-and-tell time.
This piece should illustrate what the letter describes, proving that everything the very enthusiastic salesman said in the letter is true. Because it is impersonal—it is the company, not an individual, talking to the prospect—the voice should differ in tone and color from the letter. Its job is to add visual dimension and amplify certain points touched on lightly in the letter, thereby gaining further credibility for the offer.

The circular is frequently—but not necessarily—four-color. The pace is much different from that of the driving letter or the greased order card. The reader should be given as much time with the piece as needed or wanted. Although it must be designed carefully to unfold in the way you want to bring your prospect into the offer, the prospect should be able to read every panel or page or spread independent of the others. Think of it as a smorgasbord rather than a seven-course sit-down dinner.

Every panel and spread and broadside of this major illustrated piece has its own particular function.
You can't expect the deadfold (the part not visible until the piece is opened) to do the same job as the cover. Vitally important as the designer is, the organization of the piece—and the decisions about what panel or spread does what job—are still primarily the responsibility of the writer.

I read books and articles and any kind of authoritative materials about my subject I can find until I feel comfortable—or, as Frost said, "easy in my harness." Then I take some 8½- by 11-inch bond (web presses all print multiples of this dimension) and make up as many dummies as I need until I finally "see" all the things I want to say in the right space and in the right relationships. I make notes of all the pictures, and then I start my letter. When I'm through, I go back and write the brochure. I haven't thought about colors or white space or decorative borders or any of the innumerable things that make a brochure sing, but I do have a sturdy piece of architecture in the form of a thumbnail layout to give the designer—with copy that almost fits. The rest of it comes out of working together with the designer all the way down to the signed press sheet.

Business Segments

Business to Business

Denny Hatch's Observation

According to the U.S. Postal Service, business lists go out of date at the rate of 1 percent a week—or roughly 50 percent a year.

> Easily proven. Next time you're at a conference, ask those whose business card is different this year from this time last year—different address, different mail stop, different phone number, different department, different title, different company—to raise their hands. Half the hands in the room will go up. Do you really want to personalize mailings to lists that you are not absolutely certain are up to date?

Clubs and Continuities

Bill Gohring's Three Practices

Clubs (record, CD, or book) function well only when the initial promotion clearly represents the character of the club and the content of all subsequent offers.

The successful club manager will seriously consider the initial selections made by respondents and make sure that future offerings cater to their indicated taste in listening or reading.

Alternates and inserts will offer adequate opportunity to explore their broader interests, but for main selections, stick to the primary interests of your customer.

Financial Services

Rebecca Klem Mills's Fundamental

Acquisition allowance is calculated as the amount of the premium left over after expenses, claims, taxes, and profit have been deducted.

> Allowable acquisition cost is much higher for business solicited through the mail than for business solicited over the telephone due to the higher persistence for mail-solicited business. While the marketing allowance is greater, the response for a typical telemarketed nonbonus AD offer is over 10 times higher. Even with lower persistence, telemarketing generates more revenue.

> *Comment:* Acquisition allowance (or marketing allowance) is the sum you can afford to spend to acquire a new customer. The protocol for calculating this sum is complex and looks at revenue and expenses over time—frequently 10 or 20 years. This "profit study" is the classic iteration for customer lifetime value.

Jay M. Jaffe's 30 Truths About Direct Marketing Insurance Offers

> The lapse rate for insurance products sold by direct response is related directly to the level of the premium.
> Everything else being equal, a policy with a $30 monthly premium is more likely to lapse than a policy with a $15 monthly premium.

> The longer the time required to process an insurance application, the more likely it is that the applicant will not pay for the policy.

> "Free" insurance offers have inherently higher lapse rates than policies marketed without the "free" period.

> An insurance company's current customers, regardless of how they were sold insurance, will be more responsive to insurance offers than any other group of prospects.
> Customers are many times more responsive than noncustomers.

> Premiums for insurance sold using direct-response marketing seem to be limited by an invisible threshold.
> The monthly premium for accident policies is usually $6 to $12, for example, and for senior life insurance products, it is $20 to $25.

> The greater the customization of an insurance offer, the greater the response rate.

> Since customization costs more, the increased response rate is somewhat offset by the extra marketing costs.

Marketing costs expressed in terms of paid policies are much more meaningful than response rates when reviewing program profitability.
The only thing that matters is whether the costs per paid policy are within allowable acquisition costs.

Policy lapse rates for direct response insurance business are related directly to the underlying billing mechanism as much as any other single factor.
For example, premiums billed using credit cards have persistence rates mirroring the persistence rates of the credit card.

Insurance applications that require more information from the applicant generate lower responses than applications requiring less.

There is no material difference between insurance offers for which the premiums end in 95 or 99 cents and premiums where the cents are lower amounts.

Insurance offers that provide more than one benefit or premium option are more effective than insurance offers which present only one.
Some customers want the coverage but can't afford the premium if only one option is presented.

Telemarketing of insurance results in greater responses per 1,000 prospects but not necessarily greater profits per insured because telemarketed policies have higher lapse rates.

Make part of each rollout campaign a test; there is always something to learn.

Expanding a program too fast often results in overlooking important program parameters.
Most direct-response programs are complex; you need time to work out all the bugs.

Use surrogate or inferred information if original data are unavailable.
Of course, test to be certain the cost of appending the information is worthwhile. For example, if it is useful to know if the insurance applicant has an alcohol problem, the records of a state motor vehicle bureau may reveal any DUI or DWI convictions.

Use data enhancements only if they are economical.

Utilize intellectual property law (copyrights and patents) to protect successful ideas—why not make imitators pay a price?

Market ownership is preferred over market rental.

Remember, it is the owner of the market who controls the market. Years ago Colonial Penn wrote all of AARP's new business, but it did not control AARP. Today several companies write AARP's business, and Colonial Penn is not one of them.

Repeated rollouts by a competitor normally means the program is working; companies don't usually waste money on unprofitable programs.

Insurance offers with plastic cards usually are economically justifiable.

Plastic cards cost money to add, but this is offset by higher response rates. Why? Who knows? And who cares?

When formulating strategic plans, create a list of your company's strengths and weaknesses; concentrate on programs that capitalize on your strengths and avoid programs that highlight your weaknesses.

The amount available to spend for a new sale is equal to the "allowable acquisition cost."

Some companies acquire new business only until the cost for each sale does not exceed the allowable acquisition cost, while other companies continue marketing as long as the average cost per sale does not exceed the allowable acquisition cost. Either approach can be appropriate under the proper circumstances.

Direct marketing can be used to enhance other distribution systems rather than considered a distinct distribution system.

Some of the least expensive forms of market research can be most effective.

For example, informal telephone surveys by company employees can be an effective technique for obtaining qualitative feedback.

Customer lifetime value must be considered when developing marketing models and allowable acquisition costs.

This is especially critical for insurance or other programs, which rely on a stream of income over several years to repay marketing costs. Typically insurance acquisition costs are at or close to the premiums collected in the first policy year. When the expenses are considered (claims, for example), it will take several years to recover acquisition costs.

Significant income can be obtained from the sale of additional products to policyholders during the time the policy is on the books, adding considerable value to the initial sale.

Creating customer lifetime value models is a complex mathematical process that requires considerable data accumulated over a long period. (See Arithmetic Chapter.)

You need to go slowly and understand what is really working and what assumptions are unreasonable to have a model that is realistic.

Financial services marketed using some form of sponsorship produce better responses, on average, than when such products are marketed without any sponsorship.

Direct-response purchasers are often impulse purchases; therefore, materials must appeal to a prospect's real and perceived needs.

Don Jackson's Rule
The insurance direct marketing concept applies to the four insurance distribution channels: agency, brokerage, direct selling, and mail order.

There are only four distribution channels for insurance products. There are more distribution systems. The fact is that only a licensed individual or company can market an insurance product in the United States.

Ed Drake's Checklist for Developing a Lead Generation Program
This material is adapted from the Safeco Lead Management System guidelines for independent insurance agents.

Staffing.
- Who is responsible for screening leads, coordinating, production, and other elements of the lead-handling process?
- What training is needed?
- Are all staff members familiar with the program and their individual responsibilities?

Mailing information.
- Mail date
- Description of the letter/offer
- Areas targeted
- Number of leads expected
- Timing of primary responses
- Date fulfillment expected to reach prospect

Support media.
- Media used and schedule
- Advertising tie-in
- Advertising message
- Handling phone
- Date most calls expected
- Person responsible for handling incoming calls
- Response to calls

- Information to be obtained from caller
- Handling of existing customers

Follow-up.
- Markets to be used
- Rating software and information needed
- Underwriting guidelines from each company
- Company advantages or values
- Major competition information (both advantages and disadvantages)
- Letters to be used with proposal and other correspondence
- Telephone scripts
- Overall follow-up plan for staffing, handling declinations, expiration-date system

Checklist of material needed.
- Copy of mailing
- Blank quote cards or quote information form
- Fulfillment order form
- Sales brochure
- Letters and scripts
- Critical phone numbers (e.g., marketing rep, marketing manager, home office)
- Production log
- Extra gifts for walk-ins

Publishing

Dick Benson's Thoughts

For magazines, a "soft" offer ("Try a complimentary copy at our risk") is better than a hard offer (cash or "bill me").

Offers of subscriptions using two terms (e.g., eight months and 16 months) will pull more money—but 10 percent fewer orders.

Continuities average 5½ to 6 shipments.

Benson's 10 Thoughts on Renewals

Disclaimer: My views on renewal are mine alone. I know of no one who agrees with them.

I don't believe copy and format of renewal efforts have any effect, assuming that the renewal series is adequate to start.

I believe the product or, if you will, the editor, is responsible for renewals.

I do believe timing counts.

The number of efforts is important.

First-class instead of third-class postage will often more than pay for itself in a renewal promotion.

I don't believe in paying reply postage for rentals, although I understand Time, Inc., has recently gone back to using prepaid business reply envelopes.

Offers—i.e., premium and price—are important.

Advance renewals are 50 percent incremental.
You wouldn't have received those orders in the normal course of the renewal series.

If you can turn your subscription offer into a membership offer, you can bill for dues rather than ask for a renewal.
In my experience membership renewal is regularly 10 points above subscription levels. This is the result of billing for dues rather than asking for a renewal of membership.

Subscriptions sold at half price for at least eight months will convert at renewal time just as strongly as subscriptions sold for a full year at full price.
Initial subscriptions sold for an eight-month term at half price convert at roughly the same percentage as first-time subscriptions sold at full price for one year. An initial sale of a seven-month or shorter subscription will definitely have a negative impact on the conversion percentage.

Denny Hatch's Mantra
Very short-term subscriptions may look good up front, but the back end can be dismal.

Take a monthly magazine as an example. Sell a six-month trial subscription with a bill-me option and it may take two months to collect. The subscriber will be receiving billing efforts and renewal efforts at the same time.

John Klingel's Edict
The renewal effort must reflect how the person came in—a sweepstakes renewal to sweeps-sold subs, a premium offered to those who came in on a premium, or a short-term renewal offer to short-term trial subscribers—and you can't dramatically raise the price on renewals.

Catalogs

Susan McIntyre's 32-Point Checklist for Starting a Catalog

Almost anything can be (and probably has been) sold in a mail-order catalog.

People who want to start catalogs fall into two categories: (1) entrepreneurs in search of financial independence and (2) established companies that want to add a mail-order catalog to their existing sales channels.

For the entrepreneurs: Yes, you can still start a catalog business from your kitchen table, but the rules are tougher today, with success demanding creativity, savvy, and sweat.

For the established businesses: Your path to adding a catalog is quite a bit easier, thanks to the many synergies you can take advantage of.

Products in catalogs should have the following characteristics: (1) They can be photographed attractively. (2) The main benefit can be understood instantly just by looking at the photo and reading a short, clear headline. How do you select hot-selling products? Some catalogers have an instinct for knowing exactly what the public wants—but for most, merchandising involves a lot of trial and error. You must learn your audience's likes.

All the focus groups in the world won't tell you what will happen when you finally mail the first catalog.

Even top catalogers with years of experience seldom beat the Rule of Thirds: For any given catalog, one-third of the merchandise will sell well, one-third will sell OK, and one-third will bomb.

Take advantage of these two personal merchandising edges: (1) You're an expert in something. (2) You can get better prices.

A 20 percent gross margin won't do it.

Your gross margin (price minus cost of goods) must cover all your marketing and operational costs, and 20 percent is not enough.

Importers/resellers often work with a 50 percent gross margin and a $75-plus average order size. Manufacturers work with a 70 percent gross margin and somewhat lower average order size. Either way can be profitable.

But if your average order size is low, even 50 percent may not be enough. For example, food catalogers often have an average order size of $40, and for them a 50 percent gross margin leaves only $20 to cover all operational, marketing, and overhead costs. That's simply not enough. By contrast, upscale gift and decor catalogers commonly have a much higher average order size ($120 is typical), and the same 50 percent gross margin yields $60 per order, which should cover all costs and leave some profit behind.

Don't go to a general agency for a catalog.

Catalog design is a specialized field, and you will be better off using designers and copywriters who have catalog experience.

Speak directly to your audience.

I have seen simple, inexpensive catalogs pull three to four times better than fancy, professionally produced catalogs, because the underfinanced entrepreneur's little catalog really speaks to the audience's needs and wants. That's because the key to great catalog creative is to genuinely understand your audience and then to tell them your product's benefits clearly and persuasively.

But large companies generally send their designs through layers of committees, and the result is often expensive photography, beautiful printing, and no personality or meaningful message for the audience.

Beginning catalogers generally must choose between accepting high per-catalog costs for printing and mailing in test quantities and risking large sums of money on large volume printing.

Ideally, the beginning cataloger would prefer to print and mail in small test quantities with many versions to test various design concepts, merchandise selections, and pricing levels. The winning combinations could then be rolled out in higher volumes.

But the economics of printing and mailing won't permit this. The price penalty for printing quantities below 100,000 becomes severe.

I believe you should opt for lower-volume printing to limit total financial exposure until your new catalog has proven itself. The alternative is simply too risky. Of course, this means you won't be profitable at first. But you won't go broke either while you learn about your audience and merchandise. After you've fine-tuned your operation, you can graduate to high-volume production and dramatically lower your printing/mailing costs.

The key to long-term profitability is to build a large house list of repeat customers.

New catalogers are always surprised to learn that rental lists and ads are so expensive that they usually soak up all the profit generated by the first sale to each customer. In other words, your first sale to a new customer will usually generate a loss. It's repeat sales where catalogers earn their profits.

The fast, expensive way to build a house list is to rent outside lists and take out ads.

You can tap huge customer universes, build a house list fast, and spend a lot of money doing it.

The slower, more economical way to build a house list is to use a variety of nonstandard techniques.

These techniques deliver "free" names that you generate via channels like public relations, using other lists you may already own, piggybacking your prospecting message with other vehicles that you're already sending out (packages, inserts, warranty cards, labels, general ads), using in-store guest books, and so on. Except for PR, these apply mostly to established firms, but PR can work particularly well for entrepreneurs. Several major catalogers have built their businesses primarily with PR.

You will not get an 8 percent response rate from any rented list.

If you mail a well-constructed catalog to a well-qualified response list (meaning a list of proven mail-order buyers who have bought something similar to your product by mail), you will get a 1 percent response if you are fortunate. If you mail to a compiled list (one containing people identified only by their demographic characteristics), you will get less.

A little arithmetic shows that with any reasonable set of costs you will lose money on the first sale to customers gathered via mailing lists.

You rent lists to build your house list, not to earn money on the first sale.

Can you do better than 1 percent on a cold mailing to a rented list? Probably not. Many beginning catalogers pump up their projections by applying 3 percent or 4 percent response rates to their rented lists, but this is unrealistic. It's better to use reasonable response rates and think of the loss on the first sale as your cost to add a new customer to your house list.

Catalogers commonly earn house lists responses of 3 percent to 10 percent—sometimes more from certain subgroups.

Since you own your house list, your costs are lower, too. Repeat sales to your house list customers will be your main source of profits.

Each cost you incur from the moment an order arrives until the moment it ships is order processing and fulfillment.

I've seen total costs as low as $7 per order and as high as $30 per order. And there's no correlation between cost and customer benefits; the $7-per-order operation was fast, responsive, and efficient, while the $30-per-order operation was slow, sloppy, and irritating to customers.

Nine Rules of Inventory

For a manufacturer, getting merchandise is easy because it's already in inventory.

For the rest of us, acquiring merchandise is a tedious process of shopping merchandise marts, trade shows, foreign travel negotiation—whatever is required.

How much inventory to buy depends on actual sales experience. Only after you have a track record with a product will you be able to predict sales (and hence appropriate inventory levels) quite well—but for catalogers just starting out, I urge caution.
It's true that buying smaller quantities increases your cost of goods and back orders. But that's better than getting stuck with a warehouse full of something you can't sell.

Expect returns.
Food returns are usually less than 1 percent. Hard goods/gifts frequently show a 3 percent to 6 percent return. And apparel is the worst—returns are as high as 25 percent to 40 percent. Some will be restackable; some won't.

Control your SKUs.
A stock-keeping unit (SKU) is one item of inventory, regardless of quantity. One small women's blue-and-white plaid skirt is one SKU. Fifteen small women's blue and white plaid skirts represent one SKU. Fifteen small, six medium, and three large women's blue-and-white plaid skirts equal three SKUs. A women's small skirt with matching belt sold together is one SKU—even if the belt and skirt come from different manufacturers.

More merchandise in your catalogs means more opportunities for each customer to find something to buy.

Doubling your SKUs won't double your response rates, sales, and profits; but they will all rise by a healthy percentage until your catalog becomes quite large.

Some experts say you need 150 products (plus sizes and colors) to be profitable, but I've seen highly targeted niche catalogs make profits from just 25 products and 75 SKUs.

Higher product density per page lets you offer more products without increasing your printing or mailing costs.

That's why so many catalogs are looking jam-packed these days.

Four Proven Ways to Keep Order Processing and Fulfillment Below $15 per Order, and Preferably Below $10

To keep your return rate (and hence your customer service costs) low, show each product in your catalog realistically, so customers won't be disappointed.

Pick and pack accurately.

Answer as many questions as possible in your catalog.
When customers call with questions, that means your catalog isn't doing its job.

Keep a question log and pack the answers in your next catalog.

Jack Schmid's 16 Musts for Catalog Success

You must have a long-range plan.
While the business plan is nothing more than a road map, it clearly shows the thought process that is in place. The plan is the catalog team's communication to:

- Management or those funding the venture
- The key people who manage the catalog
- The subordinates who execute the day-to-day operations of the catalog

Two distinct types of long-range planning are generally needed:
A new cataloger should conduct a feasibility study that looks at the market, competition, and overall economics of the venture.
All catalogers should create a strategic business plan, which looks at the five key management aspects of direct marketing:

1. The merchandising plan
2. The marketing plan
3. The fulfillment plan
4. The financial plan
5. The people plan

In addition, you must have solid short-range marketing plans.
Successful catalog companies put together intelligent campaign marketing plans for every season. These include clearly defined objectives, well-thought-out merchandising, a creative concept that stands out, decisive testing, and realistic financial forecasts.

It is not acceptable to plan a good campaign every once in a while. To grow and prosper, catalogs must build on solid, every-season campaign planning.

A catalog must not try to be all things to all people.

In my judgment the catalog business has grown and prospered in the last two decades because of one word—*niche*. A niche business starts with the product and goes on to the creative execution. Everything from the way you price product to your attitude toward customer service fills a void in the market.

You must have a "competitive edge."

Catalogs fail when management has not adequately studied the competition, particularly its merchandise. We are dealing with fickle customers in the nineties and beyond—customers who will easily be lured away by better prices or innovative new products. In many large market segments, there might be room for a number two. But it's not true of every product or market segment.

Every catalog needs to articulate how its product is different from the competition. *Differentiation* is a key word for every new cataloger.

You must not skimp on the kickoff for the creative campaign.

Regardless of the size of the company, there must be a formal and logical transfer of information from those who select the product and define the target audience to the designer and copywriter who will creatively execute the catalog. Bypass this kickoff meeting and you will surely have regrets down the road.

You must have a well-conceived offer.

A formal definition of an offer is what you are willing to give to your customers in return for their responding to your mailing. Problems arise when catalogers fail to think about what will stimulate the prospect or customer to action.

You must be clear about your target audience.

It's next to impossible to select merchandise, write copy, or select lists or magazines to advertise in if you do not know precisely who your target customer is.

Business-to-business catalogers need to go one step farther and define who places the orders, who the decision makers are, and who influences the purchase decisions.

You must have an alternate plan for reaching and attracting new customers.

Believe it or not, there is life after list rentals. Successful catalogers realize that renting lists of other mail-order buyers is but one of dozens of ways to find and attract new customers. Consider the following alternatives for building your customer list that don't require postage:

• Referrals • Package inserts • Co-op mailings • Television/radio • Card decks • Credit card inserts • Magazine advertising • Newspaper advertising • Trade shows • Doctors' or dentists' offices • Public relations

You must have an experienced creative/marketing team.

Cataloging is by nature the most complex creative process in direct marketing. The creative team is challenged to present multiple, often quite diverse, items in one vehicle. Lead times are longer than those for solo mail or self-mailers. Testing is far more difficult. Catalogs are design driven, while most other direct mail pieces are copy driven.

You must think through format carefully.

What do you do if you have only six or eight items? Is a catalog the best marketing vehicle? Does every multiproduct offering have to be in a bound $8^{1}/8$- by $10^{1}/4$-inch format?

These and about 100 other creative questions need to be answered before the creative team begins. Failure to think these options through will surely lead to disappointment in response rates and average order size.

You must have a plan for tracking results.

Ask many catalogers how their campaign did, and they have no more concrete answer than "not bad." Often the mailing got a lot of orders but there was almost no tracking of lists, offers, mail drops, or other important criteria of the mailing.

Business catalogs struggle with tracking results because so many orders come in via purchase order or through purchasing agents. Planning for and tracking results is one of the prime ways to keep improving from season to season.

You must have an adequate fulfillment plan.

Why does fulfillment always get short shrift? Why is that the last function planned?

Fulfillment is vitally important to a catalog's long-term health. Strong fulfillment helps build customer loyalty, aids in getting repeat business, contributes to a sound P&L, and decreases the number of complaints received. Fulfillment is one of those functions that isn't very glamorous but is a major contributor to profitable catalog growth.

You must have a clear understanding of database marketing.

The database has been called the secret weapon of marketers. For anyone wishing to build repeat sales—like all catalogers must—capturing purchase activity of your customers is a necessity. Simple segmentation by recency, frequency, and dollars spent can do wonders in driving up the sales per catalog.

You must analyze every aspect of every promotion.

The secret to building a growing successful business is making every mailing better than the last. I know of no other way to accomplish this plan than to postanalyze every aspect of performance and draw conclusions to make improvements in the efforts that follow. Catalogers must work in an analysis mind-set to study merchandising, media, testing, timing of mail drops, offers, and P&L of every campaign.

You must give yourself enough time.

Not a year goes by that we aren't approached by an enterprising person or company that wants to launch a new catalog in 45 to 60 days. But a new venture really demands complete attention and your best work. I like to think that the first catalog is like the model that others will follow. If you don't give the strategic plan, merchandise selection, circulation plans, and creative execution your very best shot, what's to follow? As a rule of thumb, I recommend time frames like these:

Function	Days
Strategic planning	60–90
Merchandise/product development and inventory planning	60–90
Fulfillment preparation	60–90
Circulation planning	60
Creative execution through printing—first catalog	120

That adds up to a minimum of 12 months' lead time before the first catalog is ready to mail.

You must know when to seek outside professional help.

The most common fault that I observe in new ventures is that the company doesn't know what it doesn't know. Typically the catalog assignment is handed off to product or marketing experts in another channel. But this doesn't make them catalog experts. Smart companies seek outside help in avoiding these nasty pitfalls, which often mean the difference between success and failure. It's a good practice to realistically assess your company's internal skills and, where necessary, to complement them with outside professionals.

Bob Stone's Four Tips

You will get far more new catalog customers if you put your proven winners in the front pages of your catalog.

Assuming items of similar appeal, you will always get a higher response rate from a 32-page catalog than from a 24-page catalog.

A new catalog sent to a catalog customer base will outpull cold lists by 400 to 800 percent.

Credit card privileges will increase the size of the average catalog order by 20 percent or more.

Murray Raphel's Pricing Strategy

Recent surveys on the pricing pattern in a catalog of a leading mail-order house showed two-thirds of all prices under $10 end in odd numbers.

For prices above $10 the most popular prices end with .95 ($15.95, $16.95).

When the item becomes a big ticket of $25 or more, a dollar or two below the even price is most popular ($28 or $29 rather than $30).

A dollar or two *below* an even price sells well.

A dollar or two *above* an even price sells badly.

Even prices suggest higher quality.
You don't increase sales of a $10,000 diamond necklace by offering it at $9,995.

Multiple-unit pricing increases sales.
For example, a national brand of tomato juice that sold for 33 cents increased sales 70 percent when the price changed to three for 99 cents.

Even prices work well in multiple sales (three for $1).

Prices ending with even numbers are rarely used (e.g., $2.44, $3.66, etc.).

Using zeros with round numbers makes the price seem higher. (Say $88, not $88.00.)

Jack Schmid on Catalog Design

Catalog design is a critical element because, first and foremost, more than for any other type of direct mail, the catalog is a visual medium.
Customers browse through catalog pages much as they'd window-shop on Main Street or at the mall. When something catches their eye, they'll stop, look, and—hopefully—make a purchase.

    Catalogs have the additional design challenge of combining all the elements of a successful direct mail package—a letter, brochure, lift note, order device, and reply envelope—into one user-friendly piece.

Good design places all these elements into the book in such a way that the reader's eye is driven through the pages.
Not that copy isn't important—it certainly is. But in a catalog, page layout and design form the basis for the copy as well as the art.

Design and layout drive the photography or illustrative artwork.

Design and layout drive copy.
The writer should be writing to exactly specified copy blocks or headline lengths.

Design and layout drive production of the catalog (typesetting or copy fitting via computer).

There are four types of catalog layout (with variations): (1) grid or symmetrical, (2) free-form or asymmetrical, (3) single product per page and, (4) grouping by product type.

You need to select typefaces—for headlines, footlines, captions, charts, and body copy—that complement one another.

The order form is the most difficult and complex element of catalog design.
Normally talented designers have been known to lay huge "bombs" when it comes to creating order forms.

An order form that is difficult to complete, has a hidden phone number or inaccurate keying of product copy and photography, can cost a catalog as much as 5 or 10 percent or even more of its potential orders.
That means lost sales and unrealized profits—losses that could have been prevented.

Not all catalogs need an order form.
Many business catalogs receive 99 percent of their orders by phone and fax and could argue that an order form is a waste of printing, paper, and letter shop dollars. The counterargument is that even one order missed because of the absence of an order form is one too many. I urge business-to-business catalogers in particular to turn their order forms into "telephone organizers" to assist their customers in placing orders.

Since order forms are tricky but fun to design, my suggestion is to start by collecting order forms that are simple, easy, and clear to fill out. Emulate those elements that work for your catalog. But remember to pass the new version of the order form by your order entry people before adopting any revision.

Remember, the order form is for the ultimate convenience of your customers, not internal people and systems.

Copy

 It has become accepted that copy needs to arrest attention, create interest and desire, and propel readers to action. So the cognoscenti will notice that fundamental formulas (like AIDA = attention, interest, desire, action) have been excluded from this chapter. Much of the accumulated wisdom here addresses the logical next steps in the process of writing copy.

MBA Magazine's Maxim

Customers want ¼-inch holes, not ¼-inch drills.

Maxwell Sackheim's Principle

When you believe in an offer, you're a much better writer than if you're only an advertising person.

Joan Throckmorton's Seven Absolute Truths

Whatever you say, however you say it, however you present it, first ask, "Does this make sense to the customer?"
You'll have plenty of opportunities to apply this law at several important stages in creative development. Neglect it and you won't be protected from out-and-out failures. Use it and you'll be safe.

Too many of us have gotten shortsighted on this point today. The industry needs more questioners, and you should be among them. If you aren't, you might end up trying desperately to sell something to customers when you can't make sense or be honest about it. You may be faced with some unsolvable creative problems (including writer's block).

Today our customer base is growing and evolving right along with direct marketing. Customers now buy jewelry, expensive collectibles, boots, cosmetics, fine clothing and furs—even cars—through direct marketing. They are better educated and more sophisticated than customers of 20 years ago.

They have more money to spend; they are more demanding and more skeptical.

You have to be pretty good to sell them, so protect yourself. Make sure before you begin that you won't be forced to shake their credibility or try something on them that you don't believe in yourself. Here are some examples.

Don't run the big sale into the ground (same goes for "Last Chance") or you'll end up like the boy who cried "Wolf!"

Don't shout "Hurry" when a magazine subscription still has six months to go. (There are other things you can say to motivate your subscriber.)

Don't tell a customer how important he or she is to you when your computer can't even tell the customer's gender ("Dear B. Fish," "Esteemed P. Rock").

Don't exclaim "This invitation is not for everyone" when "Official Invitation #1,318,149,975" is printed on the reply card.

Don't promise something on your outer envelope or in a headline that you can't immediately substantiate in the copy that follows. (Customers get angry, and so would you.)

Don't try to hype a weak offer with deceptive phrases and weasel words.

Don Hauptman's Five Basic Principles and Techniques for Writing Direct Mail Copy

Start with the prospect instead of the product.
Avoid superlatives and brag-and-boast language. Wherever possible, incorporate anecdotes, testimonials, success stories, and other believable elements of human interest.

Do research.
Interview customers, ask questions, and listen carefully. My favorite question is "What are your [the prospect's] greatest problems, needs, and concerns right now?" At least half the time spent on an assignment—before you attack the blank page or computer screen—should be pure research.

Use specifics to add power and credibility.
Use precise, documented figures and facts in advertising. Cite data or opinions from outside, impartial sources. A lot of copy is anemic and ineffective because it's superficial, vague, and unspecific. Concrete statements and detail add a ring of truth. But to find this kind of material, you've often got to dig for it.

Don't try to change behavior.
It's time-consuming, expensive, and often futile. It's usually wise to capitalize on existing motivations. In other words, preach to the converted. Unless you have an unlimited budget, avoid products and services that require the buyer to be educated or radically transformed.

Be a creative plagiarist.
You can learn by studying the work of others. Don't imitate, emulate, or recreate, but when you see an idea you admire, try to identify the principles behind it. Then apply those principles in a fresh, original way to your own work.

Jim Rutz's Duo

Spend half your writing time on concept, teaser, offer, headline, and first paragraph.
Up to 90 percent of your rejections will be caused by those elements, not the many pages that follow.

Remember that your readers are as smart as you are.
Your readers aren't stupid; they're just not paying attention! So make sure you get that first. Then talk to them like adults.

Denny Hatch's 28 Emotional Appeals That Stimulate Action
• Greed • Flattery/affirmation • Fear • Salvation • Power • Self-improvement • Revenge • Love • Anger • Physical hunger/thirst • Envy • Guilt • Better health/physical well-being • Pride/ego/stature • Eternal life • Irresistible bargain • Grief/sorrow • Unbounded pleasure • Cuddly/sweet • Pity • Exclusive membership • Inside information • Quick fix • Fame • Make a discovery • Patriotism • Danger • Official notice of something

In his analysis of more than 250 direct mail packages that were in the mail for three or more consecutive years (and were therefore moneymakers), direct mail maven Axel Andersson found that the majority of them appealed to greed and/or flattered the person.

Goodman Ace's 12 Most Powerful Words in the English Language
You • save • money • easy • guarantee • health • results • new • love • discovery • proven • safety

Dick Benson's Certainty
Free is a magic word.

Walter Weintz's Pronouncement

There are three kinds of copy: "you" copy, "me" copy, and "it" copy.

"You" copy is the most important. It is found in letters where the writer is talking intimately to you, the reader, and about you—your wants, your loves, your wishes, your salvation.

"It" is found in the circular or brochure, where it—the product or service being sold—is described and pictured.

"Me" copy turns up in two places. First of all, you'll find it on the order form, which is a reprise of the offer in the reader's own voice. ("Yes, please send *me* the product and charge *my* Visa. *I* understand that if at any time *I* should become dissatisfied. . . ." The other occurrence is in testimonials or lift letters. ("Frankly, *I'm* puzzled. . . ." or "*I* tried this product and am a true believer. Here's *my* story.")

The beauty of direct mail is that it enables the salesperson to use all parts of the English language, plus illustrations, graphs, charts, and any other bells and whistles to capture attention and engage a reader.

Lea Pierce's Precept

There is no more beautiful or powerful word in the English language than *you*. You cannot use the word *you* too often in direct response if you want a response you'll be proud of.

Bill Christensen's Edict

The subject of any successful direct marketing effort in any medium is not the product or service being sold. The subject is *you,* the prospect.

This is one of the hardest concepts for sellers to grasp. When they have a good product, they want to tell the world about *it*—what it does, how it works, its splendid look and feel. They want to talk about how it was made and about the company that makes it. But . . . what does it do for me?

Gil Gabriel's Corollary

The subject is you, the prospect, except when it's me, the writer, identifying with you, the prospect.

If you make a connection, you're more likely to make a sale.

Quite a few years ago I was consulting and writing copy for *Teacher,* a magazine for elementary school teachers. We had commissioned three of the grand masters to write packages for an extensive (and obviously expensive) test mailing.

And they were grand packages! Four-color brochures, tokens, and other involvement devices—all the bells and whistles.

At the very last minute we found we had a test panel set aside and nothing to mail. So the client asked me to turn out and turn in a completely new package over a weekend and deliver it Monday morning.

I did, but there wasn't time to notice that four of the first five paragraphs started with *I* or that there was scarcely a *you* to be found anywhere or that the benefits didn't start until paragraph 11.

Yet (you guessed it!) this simple, written-over-the-weekend letter outpulled the other three packages (and my own previous control) by a wide margin, because the writer (the editor) made a connection with the reader (the teacher).

This inexpensive package continued to beat everything we tested against it for several years. We subsequently tested it in a personalized format; with a four-color envelope; in a six- by nine-inch format with a folder; in an envelope with a paste-on reply address label. And the original package always came out the winner.

In the intervening years, I tried similar approaches for other professional groups with mixed success—some hits, some misses.

Richard Armstrong's Dissent
The most important word in direct mail copy (aside from *free* of course) is not *you* as many of the textbooks would have it but *I*.

What makes a letter seem personal is not seeing your own name printed dozens of times across the page or even being battered to death with a neverending attack of *you*s. It is, rather, the sense you get of being in the presence of the writer—that a real person sat down and wrote you a real letter. A heavily computerized letter, by contrast, seems less personal.

Direct mail recipients, after all, don't need to be reminded that they are real human beings with real names. To the contrary, they need to be assured that the letter they are reading comes from a human being, not a computer and not a committee.

Ironically, it is sometimes more difficult for professional copywriters to write this kind of copy than it is for our clients (although Frank Johnson, Tom Collins, and Ed McLean were and are masters of it). Often it is the entrepreneurs and activists themselves—people like Joe Sugarman [JS&A/Marketing Wizards], Gary Halbert, Father Bruce Ritter [former head of Covenant House], Howard Ruff [newsletter publisher] and many others—who have the gift for putting their persuasive personalities on the printed page.

Comment: The issue here is less the word *you* than it is the *you* attitude. Simply put, a first-person letter is the most difficult to write, the type that most often fails, and should never be attempted by an inexperienced writer. The reason:

Bob Hacker's Addendum to Christensen and Armstrong
The prospect doesn't give a damn about you, your company, or your product. All that matters is "What will it do for me?"

Executing Christensen's and Hacker's Edict and Addendum
Every direct marketing effort must offer benefits and promises, not features.

> One way to tackle a promotional challenge is to make a list of all the features of the product or service being offered and then rank them according to the importance to the specific audience you are reaching. Turn these features into benefits and lead off with your top-ranked benefit.

Andrew J. Byrne's Corollary
Sell *benefits*—but *features* can be proof that you offer them.

Bill Jayme's Beacon
Two basic tenets of selling are that (1) people buy from other people more happily than from faceless corporations and (2) in the marketplace as in theater, there is indeed a factor at work called "the willing suspension of disbelief."

> Who stands behind our pancakes? Aunt Jemima. Our angel food cake? Betty Crocker. Our coffee? Juan Valdez. Anyone over the age of three knows that it's all myth. But like Santa Claus, the tooth fairy and the Easter Bunny, the myths are comforting.

Maxwell Sackheim's Five Canons
Give the reader a chance to make a deal with you—not tomorrow or next week but right away.

Make it easier to say yes than to say no.

It must be a bargain in one form or another.

If you can tell your story in 10 words, fine. But if you need 1,000 words, nothing less is fair to the space you pay for.

The greatest challenge to copywriters is to find something to say that will be worth the reader's while.

Gene Schwartz's Lowdown
The four most important characteristics of a copywriter are (1) indefatigability, (2) clarity, (3) craziness, and (4) humility.

> When I talk about indefatigability, I mean that copywriting is research. You can always determine the ad that has had the best research; it has something I call "claim density." It's packed with facts, with information, with ideas. You can't get that without doing a lot of research.
>
> Clear writing is strong writing.
>
> By craziness, I mean the copywriter is the person who looks at things that other people don't see. As a result, the copywriter writes in a way that's strangely fascinating, offbeat, and somewhat crazy.
>
> Finally, copywriters have to put themselves last. The customer comes first. The product comes second. The writing comes last. But above all, copywriters have to have integrity. They must never write an ad just to please the client, to make money, or to meet a deadline—and never, never write an ad for a bad product.

An Addendum
In mail order, the copy is the offer. Prospects buy dreams, not performances; the performances just keep them from sending back the dreams.

Lea Pierce's Duet

> Avoid "Huh? What?" copy.
> Clear, brief, fast-moving copy with a powerful offer will get you offers. Turgid prose will get you the circular file—every time.

All products are interesting; it's your job to find out why.

Emily Soell's Advice
A direct mail package (or print ad or television commercial) that convinces readers they are known, understood, and valued has gone nine-tenths of the way toward selling its wares.

Barbara Harrison's Tip
Interact with the reader.

> Challenge the reader's assumptions. Ask questions. Reveal the reader's weaknesses while offering the solution. Involvement is the first step toward response.

For *Catnip: The Newsletter for Caring Cat Owners,* I asked, "Do you and your cat speak the same language? See how well you understand your feline friend."

For *Mind/Body Approach to Weight Loss,* the outer envelope asked on the back, "Are you a Vata, a Pitta or a Kapha? Free Body Type Quiz enclosed."

Jim Allyn's Precept
Make your long copy seem like short copy.

It's popular in direct marketing seminars to ask beginners if they think long copy or short is better. Most hands go up for "short," and the instructor then proves "long" is best.

My answer to the long-short question is "Both!"

Most direct marketing pros know about breaking up long copy with subheads. But take that approach one step further. Since people *scan* the subheads, it's better to actually *make the subheads act as a short copy block* rather than a series of unconnected labels. An example. The subheads read:

Introducing a breakthrough new kind of novel
  (Copy goes here)
It's SOUTHERN GOLD, and it's been called a "G-Rated Thriller"
  (Copy goes here)
That means there's no graphic violence
  (Copy goes here)
. . . And there are no obscenities, either
  (Copy goes here)
Plus, it's a fast-paced story you'll love to read
  (Copy goes here)
All that, without paying a hardcover price
  (Copy goes here)
. . . From Thomas Nelson, a publisher you can trust!
  (Copy goes here)
So readers who scan in a hurry get *short* copy.

And those rare few prospects who read every word of my painstakingly crafted copy (bless their hearts!) get *long* copy.

Bob Stone's Pronouncement
The longer you hold a prospect's interest, the more sales points you can get across and the more likely you are to win an order.

Drayton Bird's Rubric
Discussing the length of copy is about as useful as wondering how tall a good general should be; you might as well ask how much string it takes to wrap a parcel.

Dick Hodgson's 100 Motivations for People to Buy

Satisfy curiosity.

Get a surprise.

Be successful.

Be more comfortable.

Make work easier.

Gain prestige.

Be sociable.

Be creative.

Be efficient.

Safeguard self and family.

Protect family's future.

Be good parents.

Be well liked and loved.

Appear different from others.

Gain popularity.

Add to life's pleasures.

Express a personality.

Be in fashion.

Avoid embarrassment.

Fulfill fantasies.

Be up to date.

Own attractive things.

Collect valuable possessions.

Protect or conserve possessions.

Satisfy ego.

Be "first."

Accumulate money.

Preserve money already accumulated.

Save time.

Protect reputation.

Satisfy appetite.

Enjoy exotic tastes.

Live in a clean atmosphere.

Be strong and healthy.

Renew vigor and energy.

Get rid of aches and pains.

Find new and uncommon things.

Win others' affection.

Be more beautiful.

Attract the opposite sex.

Satisfy sexual desires.

Bring back "the good old days."

Be lucky.

Live longer.

Feel important.

Gain knowledge.

Improve appearance.

Gain praise from others.

Be recognized as an authority.

Enhance leisure.

Save money.

Have security in old age.

Overcome obstacles.

Do things well.

Get a better job.

Be your own boss.

Gain social acceptance.

"Keep up with the Joneses."

Appreciate beauty.

Be proud of possessions.

Resist domination by others.

Emulate the admirable.

Relieve boredom.

Gain self-respect.

Win acclaim.

Gain admiration.

Win advancement.

Seek adventure.

Satisfy ambition.

Be among leaders.

Gain confidence.

Escape drudgery.

Gain freedom from worry.

Get on the bandwagon.

Get something for nothing.

Gain self-assurance.

Escape shame.

Avoid effort.

Get more comfort.

Gain praise.

Be popular.

Have safety in buying something else.

Take advantage of opportunities.

Protect reputation.

Be an individual.

Avoid criticism.

Avoid trouble.

Emulate others.

One-up others.

Be in style.

Increase enjoyment.

Have or hold beautiful possessions.

Replace the obsolete.

Add fun or spice to life.

Work less.

Look better.

Conserve natural resources.

Protect the environment.

Avoid shortages.

Relax.

Jim Punkre's Eight Laws

People want to know "What's in it for *me?*" first and foremost.

Negativity repels; positivity attracts.

Research, research, research!

It's more important to know the market than the product.

Our job is to make the new feel familiar and the familiar feel suddenly new.

Clients would rather have mediocre copy on time than outstanding copy late.

Great design will frequently save bad copy—but bad design will always destroy the most brilliant text.

A copywriter is the bridge between things and dreams.

Roger Keeling's Three Elements

Obsessive-compulsive editing has ruined more letters than it's helped. Don't alter any copy for mere aesthetic reasons or because it "sounds better" to you with those changes. Change copy only when it is clearly ungrammatical, factually erroneous, hopelessly unclear, staggeringly boring, structurally muddled, plainly offensive, or when cutting is necessary to make the package fit in the printed format you've selected.

If a professional copywriter has generated a letter with what *you* see as awkward diction, dubious sentence structure, messy format, or overt violations of other copywriting rules, it's possible that he or she did it on purpose . . . and he or she may well be right that it will outperform your neatly scrubbed and polished rewrite.

Consultants and clients are able to improve the products given them by their copywriters only often enough to cause lingering trouble.

Woe to all when consultants or clients are convinced that *they* could write better than the writer if they just had the time. Consultants and clients *do* occasionally substantially improve the packages their copywriters give them. Unfortunately, they too often later use these copyediting successes to justify subsequent forays into obsessive editing that do *not* actually improve the copy. You hired a copywriter, and you paid him or her good money—*now let his or her voice come through.*

Unless the package is an indisputable disaster, test, test, test—even if you hate it.

Even when consultants or clients are right, when a copywriter is known to generally produce competitive or out-and-out winning packages, it's best to mail at least a few test panels of the writer's original submission with only the lightest editing. The reasons: see Malcolm Decker's Two Inviolable Basic Rules about testing (Rule #1: Test everything; Rule #2: See Rule #1). You just may be surprised by the result.

Ed McLean's Guideline
When using outside writers, make sure they create a full package, from extra inserts to business reply envelopes.

Even if you aren't going to use every piece in the initial effort, you can use these pieces to test against and to revive the original package when it starts to flag.

Don Kanter's Bylaw
The main problem with copywriters is that they think their job is to write.

Saying that is equivalent to a salesperson saying "My job is to talk."

The salesperson's job is not to talk. The copywriter's job is not to write. For both, the job is to sell. Selling is the end result; writing is the means the copywriter uses to reach that end. This is true of all advertising copywriting; it is especially true of direct-response copywriting, because more often than not you are the *only* salesperson with whom the prospect will ever come in contact. If you don't make the sale, there's nobody else to do it.

Pat Friesen's Process
Write to one person.

This is a simple technique for writing copy that establishes rapport and talks to your audience. When you visualize your readers, envision an individual, not a group— someone who fits the description of your targeted audience.

Try to think of a real person, someone you know. Write to that individual as though you were talking to him or her, selling your product.

Friesen's 13 Proven Tips for Writing Copy That Gets Response

A good writer can never ask too many questions.

Make lists of everything you know about your targeted audience, offer, product features and corresponding benefits, and the customers' potential objections to buying.

Prioritize offer elements and product benefits for your targeted audience.

Try the product or service you're writing about; use it; live with it; test every feature.

Check out the competition.

When in doubt about what to say and how to say it, talk to a customer who's already bought the product.

Never write to fill space; write to tell your story.

Read copy aloud; you'll catch more errors and get a better reading of the conversational tone of your copy.

For greatest readability, keep your words, sentences, and paragraphs short.
Words: 75 to 80 percent should be five characters or less. Sentences: maximum 1 to $1\frac{1}{2}$ lines long. Paragraphs: maximum six to seven lines.

Never fall in love with a word, headline, or sentence so much you won't change it—there's usually more than one way to get a message across. Your first approach may or may not be the best one.

Work as a team member with the art director/designer.

An art director can write headlines, too.

Normally, the best lead paragraph for your letter is buried somewhere in the middle of your first draft copy.

Bill Josephs's Seven Copy Codicils

If it isn't "broke," don't try to fix it.

Do not tinker with a successful piece of copy, script, mailing package, or offer. Test against it, but don't alter success.

Don't tinker with a loser.
Learn all you can from your last-place finishers, but do not try to "adjust" them. It is seldom worth the effort and expense in money and time to test up from a losing package.

Strive to give the prospects more than they expect, such as useful information.

Copy should always be perfectly clear.
Never give the prospect the opportunity to put a negative spin on your words.

Never pad copy; edit out redundant words and phrases.

Be concise, friendly, and active; never use a passive voice.

Always use guarantees.

Anne Hall's 18 Steps to Commonsense Copywriting

Know your market.

Know your product and its benefits.

Know your lists.

Know your offer.

Write to a real person (think of someone you know).

Respect your reader's intelligence.

Respect your reader's time.

Respect your reader's budget.

Assume your reader is naturally curious—most people are.

Be sure your message is believable.

Express genuine enthusiasm through your message, your product benefits, and your offer.

Give directions that are easy to follow.

Make new members, subscribers, and/or donors feel welcome.

Thank donors and members early and often.

Touch people on points of human contact that make them say "Yes, that is just like me."

Avoid flat claims.
Use vivid portrayals of dramatic situations, humanized facts, word pictures to inspire readers to want, as soon as possible, what the product will do for—and get for—them.

Try to make it entertaining to read.
More adults go to the movies than to schools of instruction.

Use the vocabulary level of the least erudite of your prospects; then everyone will follow you.
Said Ernest Hemingway, "I use the oldest words in the English language. People think I'm an ignorant bastard who doesn't know the ten-dollar words. I know the ten-dollar words. There are older and better words which if you arrange them in the proper combination, you make it stick."

Robert Louis Stevenson's Truism
It takes hard writing to make easy reading.

Jack Maxson's Duet

Copy is for the ear as well as the eye.
When writing copy, pause every paragraph or so and read aloud. Do you keep stumbling over certain words or phrases? If so, it needs rewriting. Does it flow smoothly and easily? If not, rewrite. After all, if you can't read your own stuff, who can?

The best copy is the copy the reader doesn't notice because the writer has so skillfully found the reader's wavelength.

Bob Matheo's Six Techniques

Surprise your readers.
Disarm them. Appear different in some strikingly significant way. Reason: no matter how great the benefits you offer, if they sound or look like everybody else's, your readers will yawn.

Don't tease your readers.
Reward them for sticking with you for those many pages you've written. Present useful information in your copy or at least amuse them with some well-crafted phrases.

From the outset, think graphics, integrated with copy and not merely as an afterthought to ornament it.

Use negatives where appropriate; fear of loss is almost always more motivating than desire for gain.

Avoid formulas.
They make for boring mailings and ads. But do use checklists to make sure you haven't omitted something important.

Put yourself in the prospect's shoes before you start to create and start where the reader is.
My mentor, the legendary Tom Collins, called it "The Method Acting School of Copywriting."

Donna Stein's Certainty
Use the power of drama for all it's worth, especially in fundraising letters.

Rather than quoting statistics about how many primates are poached each year, tell the story of one baby monkey clinging to its mother's side as shots ring out.

Jack Maxson's Additions
Put your product in the reader's hands.

When you've got the right customer profile, the right list, the right price, the right product, the right graphics, the right timing, there's still another mountain to be climbed—the right copy. Show the reader through your carefully chosen words what your product will do for him or her. Put your product in the reader's hands. You can't lose!

Maxson's Three-Day Rule

First-draft copy always begs rewriting.
Ben Franklin told us, "Fish and visitors stink in three days." So can copy. After that first flush of victory, when you've won your battle with words, it's forgivable to experience a high. But let it sit for a few days and read it

again, aloud. Those shiny words may not work nearly as well as you thought they did.

Comment: Ernest Hemingway used to finish the first draft of a novel and stick it in a drawer. He would then go fishing or hunting in Africa or corrida hopping in Spain. Six weeks to six months later he would take the novel out and reread it with absolutely fresh eyes and rewrite accordingly.

In advertising, most of us are under deadline and can't afford one week, let alone six. But Jack Maxson's three-day rule is one to follow.

Build a big vocabulary, but use it sparingly.

George Duncan's 10 Copy Dos and Don'ts

Do build your teaser/headline around a major benefit.

Do preview the offer up front and merchandise it throughout your letter.

Do use teasers to target your market.

Do use the product name in the corner card and letterhead rather than the company name (IBM, AT&T, and such excepted.)

Do quantify claims as much as possible. Percents of performance, number of dollars saved or earned, minutes and seconds of time, etc., lend credibility.

Don't introduce yourself or your company.
Begin immediately writing about the reader and his or her problem and how your product will help.

Don't expound on the state of the industry, world, etc.
It may come across as preaching, especially to the converted. (If the reader doesn't already know what you're talking about, he or she may be too removed from the process to be a good prospect.)

Don't use puns.
They rarely translate to the reader's context.

Don't ask questions in teasers and headlines that can be answered yes or no.
That gives control of the communication to your reader.

Don't use your product name as a headline by itself (clever as it may be), without appending benefit or offer copy to it.

Milt Pierce's 30 Questions to Ask Before Submitting Copy
Is the vocabulary in my copy simple and unambiguous?

Does any sexism appear in the copy? (Kill it.)

Have words and phrases been repeated that should not be repeated?

Do five different people understand what you are attempting to accomplish when they read the copy?

Have you made it easy to order?

Are there words that can be eliminated? (Be merciless in excising them.)

Is the sentence structure simple, straightforward, and direct?

Does the copy contain every single benefit on your list of benefits?

Does your letter read like a warm and personal communication from one human being to another?

Are all the benefits explained in human, emotional terms?

Have you provided compelling reasons to make your customer buy without delay?

Does your copy treat the reader with respect?

Does your copy *look* exciting, dynamic, alive? Are there underlines, indentations, handwritten notes, etc.?

Are you prepared to prove the truth of your claims if asked to do so by federal, state, or postal authorities?

Does your copy begin with your strongest selling point?

Have you done everything to assure that your envelope will be opened?

Does every picture have a caption?

Does the copy flow from one idea to the next in a clear and logical manner?

Are you offering a money-back guarantee? (You should.)

Is your copy funny or cute? (Avoid humor at all costs.)

Is your type large enough to be read (no smaller than seven points)?

Are artist, copywriter, and account executive all in agreement regarding tone and theme?

Would you be embarrassed to show this package to your children?

Honestly now, does your copy ever get boring?

Have you checked spelling, grammar, punctuation?

Have you used the word *you* in the opening and in headlines?

Does your mailing try to sell more than one thing? (Don't!)

Are you using a question-and-answer piece? Should you?

Do all the parts of your mailing appear to be created by the same individual?

Are your sentences or paragraphs too long?

Milt Pierce's 99 Magic Copy Phrases
Act now!

Frankly, I'm puzzled.

Dear friend and fellow [e.g., *Chicagoan*].

Just one idea from one issue could easily repay the cost of your subscription many times over.

For superfast priority service, enclose $1 additional.

If you don't agree that [the product] saves at least [$XX], or if you're not satisfied for any reason, simply return it for a full refund. No questions asked.

Could any offer be more fair?

Perhaps you've heard about _____ on TV [or on radio, or in leading newspapers and magazines].

We need your help and financial support to continue this important work.

Due to rising costs, we can guarantee our prices only through [date].

Don't you owe it to your family and to yourself to give _____ a try?

There's no risk, no obligation to buy anything—now or ever.

If you'll give me just XX seconds of your time, I'll show you how you can _____.

Open immediately! Important time-dated materials enclosed.

Much has been accomplished already. But much more needs to be done.

Won't you take a moment right now to look over the enclosed _____?

And remember, your contribution is fully tax deductible.

Why not share this opportunity with a friend?

My name is _____, and I'm the editor [or president, etc.] of _____.

I'd like to share this _____ with you.

You are cordially invited to _____.

We're making this offer to a select group of people only.

Once again, when the supply is exhausted, this item may never again be available (at this low price).

A special invitation to _____.

Congratulations!

In looking over our records I noticed that _____.

This offer could change your life!

There's never been an offer like this before. And because _____, there won't be another like it for a long, long time to come.

Did you know that . . . ?

Here's a small sample of what you'll find in _____.

Discover _____ on a free trial basis.

It's the most exciting new _____ in America today.

Now you can try _____ without risking a penny.

So what are you waiting for?

You can't lose!

Now if I were you right now, I'd want to know [or I'd be asking]. . . .

Isn't it time you _____?

Reserve your place now!

Guard against future price rises.

Now here's where you come in.

Simple? You bet it is!

What's the gimmick?

Send no money.

No salesperson will ever call.

And here's an extra bonus. If your order is received within XX days, we'll send you a _____ absolutely free!

It's yours to keep even if you decide to return the _____ [or just for examining _____].

Like you, I'm _____.

Explore the world of _____.

There's never been a better time to _____.

Now, more than ever before, you need _____.

You can write your own subscription terms at this money-saving price. Just write [or check the box for] the number of issues you want. We'll gladly bill you later.

You may already have won a _____. But you'll never know unless. . . .

So please say yes today.

Every issue is packed with dozens of dramatic photographs, plus diagrams, charts, and drawings.

As a subscriber, you'll enjoy. . . .

Here's a sample of what you'll be missing.

Mail the convenient coupon today. We'll rush you your _____. Then use it [or read it, wear it, watch it, listen to it] at your leisure. Take up to XX days to decide whether you want to make _____ a permanent part of your _____.

If for any reason you're not satisfied with _____, you may cancel your subscription at any time. We'll send you a prompt and full refund on the unused portion. And you may still keep your bonus.

Supply [or Registration or Membership] is strictly limited.

This low price is guaranteed only for the next XX days.

Don't take my word for it. Find out for yourself.

How can we afford to make an offer like this? Because we know _____.

Here are 39 good reasons why you should _____.

Don't bother to read this unless _____.

I was surprised when your name turned up on our list of "missing persons."

Indications are that you're the type of person who _____.

If you're like most of us, you want _____.

What better way to _____?

You'll save time and money.

If you're the kind of _____ I think you are. . . .

You cannot be turned down for this service.

No one has to tell you _____.

As soon as we receive your card, we'll rush you _____.

Let us send you _____ to examine at your leisure, without cost or obligation.

More about that later. First let me tell you a little more about _____.

In a moment I'll tell you how you can _____.

As a charter member [or subscriber] you are guaranteed the lowest available rates on all future _____.

That's the lowest price the law permits us to offer _____.

Just write "cancel" on the invoice and return it to us, and you owe nothing.

This could be the most important letter you've ever received [or book you've ever read, etc.].

People who earn $100,000 a year don't work nearly as hard as those who earn $10,000. They've simply learned _____.

I won't even cash your check for 31 days.

Why should I want to share this secret with you? Frankly, because with a little luck, I'll earn $_____ from this _____.

It doesn't require education, capital, luck, talent, or experience. You don't have to give up your present job.

No matter what your age. No matter what your income.

If I'm wrong, you've lost only a couple of minutes and a postage stamp. But if I'm right. . . .

Perhaps you're still a little skeptical. I don't blame you.

Would you invest one dollar to _____?

This offer may not be repeated in the future.

Not available in stores.

Why not mail the convenient order form right now, while you're thinking about it?

Judge for yourself.

Now is an excellent time to give _____ a try, because you can take advantage of this special offer.

Welcome to the select family of _____.

I think you'll like what you see.

Reservations are accepted on a first-come, first-served basis. So you are urged to _____.

It's written in clear, easy-to-understand language.

Any questions? Why not pick up the phone and call me personally? My number is _____.

Does it sound too good to be true? Believe me, _____.

"Rocket" Ray Jutkins: Max Ross's eight "Bucket Brigade" phrases that get you from where you are to the next step in getting your reader to take some action:
"But that's not all."

"And now you can. . . ."

"So that is why. . . ."

"Or, if you prefer. . . ."

"Now—here is all you do."

"Better yet. . . ."

More important than that. . . ."

And, in addition to that. . . ."

> ***Comment:*** Also try "There's more," "There's still more," and "There's still much, much more."

Herschell Gordon Lewis's Three Basic Conclusions for Successful Communication

Inject yourself inside the brain of your typical target.
Using this simple formula, I've written many a package as a woman, as a member of an ethnic or religious or political or philosophical group to which I don't belong or subscribe, as a plain ol' country boy. The process parallels Method Acting.

Don't show off for your peer group (I hate that term).
One reason so many writers of "conventional" advertising fail as direct marketers is their insistence on showing the reader (or viewer or listener) how clever they are or how huge a vocabulary they can command. To me, this is a horrendous mistake.

For direct mail copy to work, it must have verisimilitude.
Verisimilitude is the appearance of truth. Raw truth has weeds in it; verisimilitude is an unblemished garden.

Truth: "Although the survey shows that readers spend more time with *Fortune,* and *Forbes* attracts greater advertising response, this magazine has shown a greater percentage of circulation growth."

Verisimilitude: "The marketplace knows what's best! We outstrip both *Fortune* and *Forbes* in rate of circulation growth."

Verisimilitude is also a brake on claims. I call this . . .

Lewis's Ballooning Number Rule
The further a number rises beyond the typical reader's personal experiential background, the less emotion the number generates.

So referring to the national debt in trillions of dollars has less impact than "*You* owe . . ."; computer monitor manufacturers whose copy talks about 16 million colors may be truthful, but they're outside the verisimilitude loop.

One more point about verisimilitude: It thrives on specificity. Example: Instead of "We've been in business a long time," a verisimilitude-conscious writer would say "My father opened his first store at 30th and Main thirty-two years ago."

I have an insurance client whose business began in 1784. In almost every mailing I add to that date, "That's five years before George Washington became president," which, in my opinion, is considerably stronger than "That's well over 200 years ago."

Lewis's Quotation Marks Rule
Putting quotation marks around a word or phrase that may not be immediately recognized tells the reader we share the novelty of the idea, which helps the reader accept the unknown.

For example, a description of a fax machine included the statement "Uses thermal paper."

Many who read this description interpreted *thermal* in its traditional sense—something hot. Clarity would have been improved by quotation marks: "Uses 'thermal' paper." A more powerful wordsmith would have combined quotation marks with an explanation: "Special 'thermal' paper means you never have to change a ribbon."

What is the difference between *Expensive "Look-Alike" Wristwatch* and "Expensive Look-Alike Wristwatch"? Note: Placement of the quotation marks influences the reader's total reaction.

HGL's Parentheses Rule

Parentheses increase distance.
Use parentheses when you want to downplay. Don't use parentheses when you want immediate involvement.

Example: Compare the dynamics of these two build-up questions:

1. What are the eight signs you should start looking for another job? (See page 120.)
2. What are the eight signs you should start looking for another job? See page 120.

Use parentheses to imply exclusivity.
"Original issue price for our preferred members just $99.50" or "Original issue price (for our preferred members) just $99.50"?

Lewis's Capital Letters Rule
For an extra-octane boost, use capital letters. "Original issue price (for our Preferred Members) just $99.50." Capitals suggest greater stature.

Lewis's Exclamation Point Rules

Use exclamation points.
What's the difference between "Easy to assemble: No tools needed" and "Easy to assemble: No tools needed!"?

The exclamation point says to the reader: "We think this is worth exclaiming."

Using more than one exclamation point is hard evidence: the writer is unsure of his or her ability to convince the reader.

Additional Secrets from Herschell Gordon Lewis

Never use an asterisk in direct-response copy.

Know the difference between hard and soft transitions.
A dash (—) provides a hard transition. Ellipses (. . .) provide a soft transition. Example: "The writer's talent—or lack of talent—combines elements of brightness and thoughtfulness . . . joy and sadness . . . leading the reader by an emotional leash."

Little words can add or reduce power.
It is one of the weakest words to begin a selling argument. But *it* has value when used properly. For example, "It was" followed by a predicate nominative adds historicity to fact: "It was Robert Tyler who discovered how to achieve high gloss on recycled paper." How does "It was . . ." add historicity to fact? In this use, it says a revelation is coming.

Think through the use of numbers.
"Accurate within five seconds per month" or "Accurate within sixty seconds per year"?

"Five seconds per month" wins because it seems to be less time. "Accurate within 10 minutes over a 10-year span" would be a miracle of accuracy, but the reader thinks, "Uh-oh, I'll be 10 minutes late and miss my plane."

Which phrase will sell more for you? "Two percent a month" or "Twenty-four percent a year"? If you're writing about what someone pays, it's "2 percent a month"; if you're writing about what someone gets, it's 24 percent a year."

Don't start with "There is."
The writer always has a stronger way to begin a message than the passive phrase "There is" or "There are."

Use *now*.
What is the difference between "Next month . . ." and "A month from now . . ."? Between "It's 3 o'clock. We leave at 4 o'clock" and "It's 3 o'clock. We leave an hour from now"?

Tying an event to *now* makes it more imminent. Eliminating the tie to *now* seems to stretch the time.

Claiming proprietorship at the wrong time can exclude a potential buyer.
"Our Reservation System is specifically created for municipal special events." Changing the first word from *our* to *the* ("The Reservation System is specifically created for municipal special events") enables us to participate. We're not outsiders.

Sell results, not circumstances.
Instead of "BURIED? You're no longer buried under that avalanche of written memos," write "BURIED? You're finally out from under that avalanche of written memos."

The writer can choose his or her persona.
Aggressive opening: "I want to add a personal note." Permission-asking opening: "May I add a personal note?" Bubbling-over-with-enthusiasm opening: "I couldn't wait. I had to add my own personal note."

When possible and logical, use the definite article, not the indefinite article.

The [whatever] is stronger than *a* [whatever] because it suggests: whatever you're selling stands alone, above competitors.

Use *one* instead of *a* to establish superiority.
"The gem in each earring is a full carat" versus "The gem in each earring is one full carat."

Gradually change *a* to *the* or *your* to increase the suggestion of reader possession.
The difference between these sentences can be the difference between making a sale and not:
"You pay considerably less for your subscription."
"Others pay considerably more for their subscriptions."
We've all grown up with the *you* benefit. But comparisons are the new kings of power. People read "You pay less" or "Others pay more."

The more a number departs from the anticipated rounded-off figure, the more credible it is.
Which is more credible? "Take five minutes to read this" or "Take four minutes to read this"? "I made $50,000 last month" or "I made $46,000 last month"? "Your profit: $100,000" or "Your profit: $96,000"?
Why not "Take 3 minutes and 24 seconds to read this" or "I made $46,738 last month" or "Your profit: $96,115"?

As soon as is sooner than *when* . . . ergo, more motivational.
Which is the more motivational sentence?
"When your referral deposit comes in, we'll credit your account an additional $5" or "As soon as your referral deposit comes in, we'll credit your account an additional $5"?

Shift *we* to *you*.

Instead of "It'll take just 10 seconds for you to indicate on the card whether we should keep you on our mailing list," write "Take 10 seconds to indicate on the card whether you want us to keep you on our mailing list."

A negative statement can be a hedge.
Hedge: Our planet isn't flat.
Definitive: Our planet is round.

Control the degree of negativism.
In order, with the most positive first:

1. It may or may not be that. . . .
2. It's debatable whether. . . .
3. It's questionable whether. . . .

Adding "Will you?" to a statement changes a cold imperative to a warm request.
Instead of "Call me tomorrow with a progress report," try, for warmth (which you may not want), "Call me tomorrow with a progress report, will you?"

"Have no . . ." is more desperate than "don't have any. . . ."
"They have no food" is a more desperate circumstance than "They don't have any food."

Use words with automatic power.
Examples: *free, free gift, limited time, right now, surprise, hot, not sold in stores, first time offered, good only until [date], don't miss out, I'll look for your order,* and *try it at our risk.*

Use *try* rather than *examine.*
"Try it at our risk" will pull more response than "Examine it at our risk" because "Try" is less of a commitment and suggests the need for less expertise or time commitment.

Avoid words with implicit weakness.
Here are 12: *administration, approximately, define, earn, facilitate, features, formulate, indeed, needs* (as a noun), *product, respond, work.*

Use these words sparingly: *therefore, however, furthermore.*

Think* is more potent than *thought.
"If you think that . . ." is a more potent opening than "If you thought that . . ." because present tense implies an immediate change of current attitude; past tense suggests that whatever follows will be a revision of history.

***When* is superior to *if* for suggesting something will happen.**

If is superior to *when* for suggesting something will not happen.

Eager is positive; *anxious* is negative.

To add sarcasm or ridicule to a negative, replace *isn't* or *aren't* with *anything but*.
"Your message isn't subtle" becomes "Your message is anything but subtle."

The same as establishes a closer relationship than *Identical to*.

Get rid of *in* between adjective and noun.
"The best ~~in~~ furniture."
"The newest ~~in~~ colors."
"The latest ~~in~~ fashions."

A replacement is superior to a substitution.
Replacement suggests upgrade; substitution suggests downgrade.

Always be on the lookout for word replacements that will give you a fractional increase in impact; that's what professionalism is supposed to be.

Wendell Forbes's Approach
The words *strive* and *try* are more positive, constructive, and realistic than the words *will* and *must*.

> *Must* and *will* set up a confrontational and demoralizing environment. A feeling of failure results from not achieving what has been set forth. *Strive* and *try* ask people to do their best to win or accomplish and thus create an environment of growth and learning. Winning is not the only thing; trying and striving and learning are the only things, for they create and build rather than destroy and humiliate.

Axel Andersson's Constraint
Don't promise savings in percentages; savings should always be given in money.

> The only percentage most people understand is 50 percent, and in that case I prefer "half price" or, better, "buy one, get one free."

Creative—General

While almost every business concept requires the application of *creativity,* none is as demanding as direct marketing. Creativity, of course, is composed of many parts and in many ways defies simple definition. Our favorite way of describing creativity is the process by which *the common is seen uncommonly* . . . and acted on. There's not much sense in being creative if you don't act. And direct marketing demands action.

Claude Hopkins's Ethic
Competent advertising people must understand psychology.

> The more they know about it, the better. They must learn that certain effects lead to certain reactions and use that knowledge to increase results and avoid mistakes. In most respects human nature is the same today as in the time of Caesar. So the principles of psychology are fixed and enduring. You will never need to unlearn what you learn about them.

John Francis Tighe's Coda
When the next "hot" freelancer you hire disappoints you with a single instead of a home run, give him or her another shot instead of the bum's rush.

> If you disagree with this strategy, ask yourself: would your present direct marketing agency—or any other—have signed a contract contingent on hitting the ball out of the park on its first time at bat?

Jay Abraham's Axiom of the Preemptive Advantage
You can score a huge victory over your business competitors simply by being the first to tell customers something that comes to them as a major revelation—or at least has the ring of inside information.

If you sell clothing that is triple stitched and inspected 14 times for durability and quality workmanship, let your customers know that. If the stuff is dyed, and the dye is imported from Europe, and the dye is applied four times, tell them that also. It might all seem boring and unimportant to you, but your customers—once they hear or read inside stuff—will feel better about what they buy and better about you. In fact they'll probably repeat what you tell them at the next party they attend.

Way back in 1919, Claude Hopkins was hired by the Schlitz beer people. They were in trouble, running 10th or 15th in beer sales. When he went out to Schlitz in Wisconsin, Hopkins asked for an explanation of how they brewed their beer, and they took him through the place, step by step.

They showed him how they had dug deep artesian wells just to get superior water; they showed him the mother yeast cell; they showed him the glass-enclosed rooms where the beer was condensed and recondensed for purity. And then they showed him the "tasters" and the place where their bottles were cleaned and recleaned 12 times.

"My God," Hopkins said, "why don't you tell people in your advertising about all these steps you're taking to brew your beer?" And they said, "Well, all beer is made this way. It's not just our process." And Hopkins said, "Yes, but the first person to tell the public about this process will gain preemptive advantage." Hopkins then launched an ad campaign based on the story of how Schlitz made beer and moved that company up to first place in sales in about six months!

Martin Conroy's Observation
If you're trying to find out what makes people tick, you might take a look at the Seven Deadly Sins from the old Baltimore Catechism.

Remember them? Pride, covetousness, lust, anger, gluttony, envy, and sloth. Of course, the deadly sins are all bad and all extreme and all no-nos.

But there's an unsinful, nonextreme side to every one of them where you can see how good and honest people act and react. On the sunny side of sinful pride, for example, nice people still take normal, unsinful satisfaction in what they are and what they have. Short of deadly covetousness, people have an understandable desire to possess some of the good things in life. Instead of sinful lust, there's good old love that makes the world go round. Without raging in anger, good people can still feel a reasonable annoyance with bad people and bad things. Without getting into gross gluttony, normal men and women can have a normal appetite for good food and drink. Short of envy, there's a very human yen to do as well as the next guy. And as for sloth, who isn't happy to learn an easier way to do things? If you want to know what makes people act like people, the Seven Deadly Sins are worth a look.

David Ogilvy's Observations

Give the facts.

Very few advertisements contain enough factual information to sell the product. There is a ludicrous tradition among copywriters that consumers aren't interested in facts. Nothing could be further from the truth. Study the copy in the Sears Roebuck catalog; it sells a billion dollars' worth of merchandise every year. In my Rolls-Royce advertisements I gave nothing but facts. No adjectives, no "gracious living."

The consumer isn't a moron; she is your wife. You insult her intelligence if you assume that a mere slogan and a few vapid adjectives will persuade her to buy anything. She wants all the information we can give her.

You cannot bore people into buying.

The average family is now exposed to more than 1,500 advertisements a day. No wonder they have acquired a talent for skipping the advertisements in newspapers and magazines and going to the bathroom during television commercials.

The average woman reads only four of the advertisements that appear in the average magazine. She glances at more, but one glance is enough to tell her that the advertisement is too boring to read.

Competition for the consumer's attention is becoming more ferocious every year. She is being bombarded by a billion dollars' worth of advertising every month. Thirty thousand brand names are competing for a place in her memory. If you want your voice to be heard above this ear-splitting barrage, your voice must be unique.

Be well mannered; don't be a clown.

People don't buy from bad-mannered salespeople, and research has shown that they don't buy from bad-mannered advertisements. It's easier to sell people with a friendly handshake than by hitting them over the head with a hammer. You should try to charm the consumer into buying your product. This doesn't mean that your advertisements should be cute or comic. People don't buy from clowns.

We make advertisements that people want to read. You can't save souls in an empty church.

Old Advertising Agency Maxim from Benton and Bowles

If it doesn't sell, it's not creative.

Ed McCabe's Lament

Every time we get creative, we lose money.

John Yeck's Advice
Write your reply element first; then you know precisely where you're going.

Start your copy thinking with "Hey! Have I got a deal for YOU!!!" and the rest is easy.

If copy can be misunderstood, it *will* be misunderstood.

Study the prospect more than the product.

The ballgame's in the other person's head—the only place you can score.

Copywriting is applied psychology.

The medium isn't the message; the *message* is the message, and nothing ever happens unless the message is received correctly.

If someone who's seen it before can't read your copy aloud without stumbling, rewrite.

Tell your readers exactly what to do next; save them the trouble of having to figure it out for themselves.

The only way to get someone to do what you want them to do is to get them to want to do it.

Wendell Forbes's Recollection
"We must view with profound respect the infinite capacity of the human mind to resist the introduction of useful knowledge."—Thomas Raynesford Lounsburty

Andrew J. Byrne's 10 Rules
Don't just say it—*prove it*! Use testimonials and case histories.

Specifics sell. Generalities don't.

Advertising doesn't have to *look like* advertising. Editorial ads do a great job because they look like *news*.

Tell *why* it pays to act *now*!

Don't create advertising for "readers." Create it for people who felt a need for the *benefits* of your product *before* they saw your ad.

If you haven't mentioned what *problem* your product solves, why should a reader be interested in your solution?

Don't begin your advertising with warm-up sentences. Say something important *fast*—about how the reader can gain. Advertising that's "different" won't bring you one extra sale.

Tell the readers exactly what you want them to do—maybe two or three times, using different words.

People read only what interests them. That includes advertising.

Don't be cute. Your advertisement can entertain a million readers—and not sell one of them.

Lea Pierce's Principle
Half the creative battle is finding the perfect angle.

> Some people call it the *unique selling proposition*. Finding that angle is not a marketing problem; it's a communications challenge.

Richard Jordan's Twin Tenets

Get to the point.
It may once have been that you had plenty of time to develop a creative story line in a direct mail piece; not so today. You have to get to the point and let readers know where you're taking them—and you have to do it quickly.

Most readers—with the possible exception of devotees of "thought magazines"—simply won't stay with you through a leisurely development of a creative idea. They're the Type A people behind your car at the stoplight; they beep their horns the minute the light turns from red to green.

There's a point in every creative piece when it turns the corner from the creative starting point to the discussion of what it's ultimately selling. The message is: turn this corner fast.

This is particularly important when you're selling to nonreaders. (I do a lot of this in selling audiocassette programs for Nightingale-Conant). But it's probably true in more cases than not that you're talking to people who are mentally saying, "C'mon! C'mon! C'mon! Get to the point! What's this whole mailing about?"

Test the result-boosting power of "hot potatoes."
Hot potatoes are one of my favorite ways to boost response. A hot potato makes a prospect feel obligated to take *some* kind of action in response to a mailing, rather than to take no action at all.

For example, a yes/no mailing gives the prospect a hot potato; a simple RSVP mailing is a more muted form of the same thing. (Requesting a yes *or* no response was an important element in my long-running membership-card control for *Natural History* magazine.)

The original lift note—created, I believe, by Paul Michael—was a hot potato. It started: "Frankly, I'm puzzled." It asked prospects if they were not accepting the accompanying offer to send in a note saying why.

I know of a local charity that mails out a little contribution booklet, requesting its return with or without a donation. Again, this is a hot potato to potential donors who feel cheap returning the booklet *without* a gift.

A live stamp, enclosed with a late-in-the-series renewal effort, creates an impetus for the subscriber to renew. No one likes to throw out a live stamp. And it's nigh on impossible to peel a live stamp off an envelope and use it elsewhere.

The "petition enclosed for your signature" by political and cause fundraisers is a hot potato; you feel you have to sign and return it, and while you're at it, why not send in a check?

Try the hot potato. It works.

Pat Farley's Aphorisms

While technology may change, people are still people and are motivated by the same things.

Avoid too much involvement such as puzzles or riddles.
They can occupy the reader to the detriment of the offer; instead, appeal to the emotions and self-interest.

Dealing with Client Changes

If anyone has to read twice to understand or ask what something means, change it!
Odds are that a substantial percentage of your audience will have the same problem.

If it won't result in the loss of an order, don't fight it.

When the request for change in copy is subjective, the writer should prevail; the writer's subjective judgment is what the client is paying all that money for.
Your job is to sell. When you work to please your client or boss, you aren't doing your job.

Legal changes are never cast in stone.

Remember two things: (1) Many lawyers think they're great writers (they aren't), and (2) *all* lawyers love to negotiate. Try to talk directly to the lawyer who's making the changes and find out what the real problem is, then negotiate alternative ways of dealing with the matter.

Jack Maxson's Two Tenets

Your job is to sell, not entertain.

Writing comedy is fun, but don't let it get in the way of your message. How many times have you chuckled at a clever piece of copy but realized afterward that you couldn't remember the name of the product or the sponsor?

Probably well over half of our buying choices are based on emotion.

We make buying decisions on the basis of reason—fire extinguishers, vacuum cleaners, smoke alarms, toothbrushes, and the like. But a very large percentage of our choices (probably well over half) are based on our emotions. We can buy quality cars for $13,000 or less, but a sizable number of us pop for models at $25,000 and more. Why? Emotion over reason. Almost everything we use or own makes some kind of statement about us—homes, hair coloring, painting, clothing, recreation, and more.

Bill Christensen's Two Guidelines

Most packages simply don't ask for the order aggressively enough, often enough, or in enough different ways.

A package that makes a single request for the order in the last paragraph of the letter is like a salesperson with a cold, weak handshake. If the seller isn't confident, neither am I.

I ask for the order, sometimes repeatedly, on every panel of every piece of paper. I ask first in the first paragraph of the letter, then I ask again by the third paragraph, I continue from there, over and over again. I can't emphasize this enough as a help to folks who want to learn direct mail selling.

Create substance where there once was none.

Instead of asking prospects to send for more free information from Mid-American Life (no substance, too vague), I'll have them "send for Information Packet No. 17" (the word *packet* automatically denotes tangible substance, and adding *No. 17* implies the existence of an established consumer information bureau).

In fact, I'll carry this through the offer copy and even the business reply envelope, with the offer reading something like this:

Information Packet No. 17 is available to you—for free—from Mid-American Life Information Service Group. The group is operated as a complementary service to people like you—to make sure you have all the knowledge you need to plan a brighter, more dynamic future.

I'll then carry that to the BRE, with the first address line reading "Information Service Group."

Don Jackson's Maxim
Creative thinking is the lodestone of the direct marketing concept.

Without creative thinking, no problem is solved, no offer is created, no process is developed, no information is manipulated, no knowledge is gained. In short, nothing happens!

Database Marketing

 There is some confusion about the definition of *database*. Some use it to describe a list, some use it to describe a type of marketing, and some information systems specialists use the term to describe the technical aspect of data accumulation. In fact a database is a comprehensive collection of interrelated and nonduplicated data, usually stored in a computer, serving multiple applications, allowing timely and accurate retrieval or manipulation. By extension, therefore, a database marketing system is a system of integrated information files, as just defined, about a company's customers, prospects, suspects, products, sales, and more, that is conveniently accessible for model building, updating, analyzing , and conducting marketing activities.

Peter Drucker's Qualifier
The computer is a moron.

Gary Halbert's Gospel
Nothing in business (or life) is more expensive than bad information.

> Obviously bad data leads to bad information. And having bad information in a marketing decision support system is like hitting the "delete" key.

Denny Hatch's Corollary
The only thing worse than no information is bad information.

> At least with no information, you know exactly where you stand. Bad information will destroy a program.

Denny Hatch's Observation
Database marketing is a state of mind.

The term *database marketing* is truly unfortunate. It reduces living, breathing, thinking, feeling human beings to blips in a computer.

A database is a collection of names and addresses plus personal information about those folks—either based on their purchases or donations with you or on appended outside information. You don't need a computer to be a database marketer.

Example: You like blue suits and yellow ties. Your regular salesman at the men's store gets a new shipment of blue suits and calls you to say they will be on the floor Wednesday; but if you will come in Monday or Tuesday, you can (1) have first pick and (2) receive a free yellow tie with each new blue suit you buy.

No computer was involved. His database was inside his head—or maybe on index cards.

Basically, database marketing is finding new customers and treating them with all the respect and love you give a family member. In effect, your database is your extended family. A better term, then, might be *extended family marketing*.

George Duncan's 11 Ways to Use Your Database for Consumer Marketing

Send timely reminders of needed services.
These could include doctor/dentist appointments, oil change/tune-ups, and the like. "The letterheads/memo pads you ordered last June 17th will be depleted soon. Order now with the attached form."

Send a card or letter on the anniversary of a purchase.

Send customers' kids birthday cards if you can get them on the database.

Do periodic surveys.

Invite customers/prospects to a product demonstration or an educational seminar.
These events should be offered free to customers; charge a slight fee for prospects.

Using careful segmentation, send notification of price, product, and policy changes as well as new product announcements.
Send previews to customers.

Provide contests and sweepstakes opportunities.
These efforts support mail order sales and in-store traffic-building programs.

Use frequent buyer programs.

But *you* keep the paperwork. Don't trust the customer to do it.

Newsletter.
Sending a newsletter is especially effective as part of a frequent buyer program.

Do an annual report.

Always include in ads—and press releases—an offer for something other than "more information."
Items you offer through space or mail should be of intrinsic value, tangible, and carefully targeted to the status of the recipient: suspect, prospect, customer, client, or advocate. Always include such items in shipments along with discount certificates, etc., designed to spur repeat business.

George Duncan's 13 Ways to Use Your Database for Business-to-Business Marketing

Produce a special report or white paper on technology or industry dynamics related to your product. Give it a *title* and offer it by name.

Compile case studies of successful implementation of your product.
Get permission early and have these on file. Example: "7 ways XYZ Widgets have saved companies like yours more than $13 million!" (Note the specificity of "7 ways" and "$13 million".)

Present profiles of successful client companies.
"Meet the pros who are making a difference in astrophysics today!" (Can be any level—CEOs, engineers, etc.)

Gather test results of product performance—trade publication reviews and articles of such performance.

Conduct an annual industry survey on some vital issue—executive salaries, corporate marketing practices, product or corporate performance benchmarks—publish the results, and mail them to customers.

Send press releases on new product announcements to customer prospect segments.
Include information on how to obtain product brochures.

Keep reprints of articles on your company or products.

Offer reprints of your ad campaign with a note.
Example: "In case you missed our ads when they ran in XYZ and ABC, we're sure you'll want to see them."

Run contests (for customers only).
Integrate these with sales incentive contests for sales reps.

Send invitations to informational (product or industry) seminars.

Offer product videos.
These can be integrated into all of the preceding mailings and offers when targeted properly.

Publish a newsletter.

Send annual reports.

Arthur Hughes's 14 Tenets for Database Marketers

Database marketing will be successful only if the customer benefits from it.
If the customer is able to say, "I'm glad that I'm in that database because . . .", then you will profit from the relationship. Otherwise you will be ignored.

The principal use of lifetime value analysis is to test the effectiveness of marketing strategies.
Before you implement any proposed new strategy, determine customer lifetime value before the strategy and after its successful implementation. If lifetime value goes up, adopt the strategy. Otherwise scrap it. This method won't tell you that your strategy will work, but it can help weed out many strategies that cannot work.

RFM (recency—frequency—monetary) analysis, which is based on customer behavior, is more powerful than any model based on demography.
This is the most powerful method for predicting future behavior. You don't need an expensive model; only a spreadsheet.

Database marketing is incremental.
You are selling the product anyway. Database marketing will help retain customers or increase sales. Evaluate the costs and benefits of database marketing on the incremental costs and incremental profits.

Outsourcing the construction of your marketing database will always save both money and time.
Why? A provider with experience in building many databases can get you up and running faster and at lower cost than any in-house operation that lacks experience in this specialized field. Once it's up and running, you can bring it in-house.

All new-customer databases should be up and running within six months.
You will make money from a database only when it is functional. What if
your database is so large it will take more than six months? Begin with the
top 20 percent of your customers. Expand to the other 80 percent when you
have learned what works and what doesn't. You will save money and time.

Know the two kinds of customers: (1) transaction buyers who first consider only price and have no loyalty; (2) relationship buyers who are looking for a reliable supplier who will give them super service.
Relationship buyers are the ones you want. You can train your customers to
be one or the other. Once you have acquired a customer, stop talking about
price and start talking up your service. You can train customers to be relationship buyers.

Make your customers work hard to achieve Gold Card status; then
reward them with super service.
Focus your attention on those customers just below the qualification level.
Encourage them to spend a little more to achieve gold. When they do, you
will have them for a lifetime. This is the main payoff from a gold program.

Keep in your database only the data you can profitably use for marketing during the next two years.
Too many people keep data that is "nice to have" but cannot be used to
increase profits. Such data costs money and reduces profits.

Keep track of the source of all new customers and determine the retention rate by source.
Often a source that provides a lot of new customers per dollar spent fails to
provide long-term customers. In most operations you are seeking long-term
customers, not one-shot sales. There are often differences in the persistence
of customers by media used for acquisition.

Customer loyalty is retention.
Loyalty can be measured. It is customers who are still buying from you in
year two and year three.

There are five ways that database marketing activities can increase lifetime value.
When considering any new strategy, figure out the effect of your strategy on
these five factors: increasing retention, increasing referrals, increasing spending rate, decreasing direct costs, and decreasing marketing costs.

There are two types of database marketing people—constructors and
creators—and you need both to be successful.
A constructor likes to play with computers: merging/purging, building databases, providing access. A creator knows how to make money with a database

and is good at strategy. If you lack either type in your database team, you will fail.

A fundamental mistake in database marketing is to focus on price instead of service.

Database marketing is a very inefficient way to distribute coupons or discounts. Mass marketing is in place for that. Once you have acquired a customer, concentrate on personal, helpful service and forget price. Your goal is to keep customers for a lifetime.

Bruce Ratner's Suggestion
Visual displays identify the best variable for your model.

When building a simple regression model in which only one independent variable X is used to predict the event or outcome Y, the scatter plot provides the necessary information for selecting the best predictor.

Bill Weil's Caveat
To maximize success in database marketing the standard for data integrity is 99 percent.

Data integrity is the reliability of data elements, both internal and external in the database. This echoes the notion of GIGO—garbage in, garbage out, a concept that has been part of the data processing environment for decades. Data integrity is the process of ensuring that all data is clean, elementized, standardized, matched, and documented and that policies, standards, and procedures for maintaining each of these over time are in place.

How much can bad data cost you? Quite a lot, according to Weil:

- Assume 90 percent accurate file.
- Of the 10 percent with inaccuracies, suppose 5 percent are usable and could have been repaired (i.e., 0.5 percent of the overall file would be affected).
- Assume annual value of cross-sell or retention $100 to $1,000 per customer.
- Assume 1,000,000 customers times 0.5 percent equals 5,000.
- 5000 times $100 to $1,000 equals $500,000 to $5,000,000 lost annually.

Don Jackson's Standards

Integration of relevant, clean data is the key to successful database marketing.

It's simple, really. Relevance needs to be the focus of database architecture. There is simply so much data available that you face choices when selecting data and data sets to house in your database.

Listen to the murmur of your market.
Create feedback loops in your database environment so that you can record what your customers and prospects are saying about your products, your service, your company, and your competition. There is no more valuable source of information.

David Shepard's 40 *Nevers* for Database Marketers

Never use focus groups to generate new ideas.
Focus groups are useful for evaluating concepts, not necessarily generating them.

Never start a database project without a plan to cost-justify it to somebody, sometime.
Trust me; you'll be asked.

Never assume that your loyalty program will make a difference.
If the product or service you offer is important to your customer, and if the reward program is significant, then a reward program will work; if your product or service is not important to the customer's lifestyle, then a loyalty program that offers more of the product or service or offers the product at a discount probably won't make an incremental difference.

Never enhance your entire database just to profile it.
If you want a customer profile, a small random sample will do.

Never assume that multiproduct promotions will work better than single-product promotions, even if each product is targeted against the same mailing.
No one's sure why, but more often than not this has proven to be true; maybe it has to do with providing too many choices. Maybe it's something else.

Never decide on a database platform without testing it at rollout volumes.
It's next to impossible for a marketing person to evaluate the claims of competing vendors. A live test of your data against your requirements is the only answer.

Never believe a modeling result that doesn't conform with your experience or intuition.
Models quantify expectations. If a result seems wrong, it's probably a data processing error, not a revelation.

Never assume a testable contact strategy doesn't need to be tested.
A new contact strategy is just like new creative—it may seem obviously superior to the current control, but you won't know for sure until you've tested it.

Never assume the data you are working with is correct.
Even though our quantitative-analysis tools have improved, the systems that deliver data can still turn out misleading or misinterpreted data.

Never trust anyone who tells you that their solution is proprietary unless they are paying you.

Never be product-driven.
Focus on the segment's needs, and the right product will get to the right person, hopefully at the right time.

Comment: If you follow a customer-driven process, this is so basic it is elementary. Remember our business is to create customers, not to make sales.

Never give a person with responsibility for marketing current products responsibility for developing new products.
It's too easy to work on current products, and new ones may not receive the attention they require.

Never use the results of small tests to roll out large quantities.
Unless, that is, you want to lose your job.

Never try to compare open-ended responses with a request for proposal.
The solution: lay out a set of very specific activities (file sizes, number of updates, number of mailings, etc.) and ask each vendor to tell you how much it will cost (in total dollars, not rates) to execute the plan.

Never sign off on a major application-development project whose costs will be estimated after the start of the project.
Guess what's likely to happen.

Never, in the presence of real data processing professionals, discuss anything technical, like relational or flat files.
You'll sound silly.

Comment: The problem is in definition. In our world people try to define themselves by redefining terms. Consider the conundrum posed by the definition of *direct marketing.*

Never, in the presence of a real statistician, say "multicollinearity." Just say "collinearity" and don't ask why.
No, I don't know why either.

Never assume that a marketing person will remain in charge of a database project.
In most cases top management will hold data processing responsible for data processing activities, and they'll need to be in control. This is slowly changing.

Comment: Marketers need to be in charge of information and the development of information decision support systems.

Never assume that all your marketing questions will be answered once you have built a marketing database.
Some questions can be answered directly (how many people bought product X in the last six months and live in New York), but most questions will require analysis that goes beyond simple queries (like how often you should mail to your best customers).

Never assume you are the only one in the room who doesn't understand the difference between a data warehouse and a marketing database; between data analysis and data mining; between relationship marketing, database marketing, and one-to-one marketing, etc.
The amount of database jargon is increasing exponentially (that's jargon, too) and few people mean the same thing when they say the same thing.

Never assume that a user-friendly, easy-access tool is either user-friendly or easy.
You probably already know that.

Never believe that increasing processing power will automatically improve database performance.
The problem is not processing; the types of calculations direct marketers make are trivial. The problem is getting data from storage (disks) into memory, where the processing takes place; thus more or faster processors are not the answer to queries that take hours to run.

Never believe that new releases of database software or operating systems have been completely debugged.
Just don't believe it; it's not true.

Never assume any one person knows all there is to know about technology.
It's impossible to know everything about mainframes, client-server systems, PCs, operating systems, and applications software. Be careful that the answers to your questions aren't just the answers that come to the mind of the person you've asked.

Never store more data than you plan to use on the assumption that you will figure out how to use it later.

You won't, and the more data you have to manage, the more complicated the management problem.

Never get excited about the fact that the cost of data storage is constantly going down.
It is going down and will continue to go down, but that's not the problem. Managing data and decision making are the problems.

Never assume that you can run an outbound telemarketing program without access to disposition data.
If you've ever seen the effect of repeat phone solicitations on response, you won't make this assumption.

Never assume an individualized marketing strategy is more cost-effective than a one-size-fits-all control strategy.
Customized marketing will always cost more than mass marketing or a control-driven traditional direct marketing strategy; the gain in response, retention, and/or purchase behavior from customization needs to be cost-justified. It works, but not all the time.

Modeling
Modeling is the attempt to describe relationships among variables. The secret to successful modeling is picking the "right" variable.

Never let an outside vendor develop and run all your models and never let a statistician control your modeling strategy.
Eventually, modeling needs to be internalized to become a true part of your operation, but vendors can help make that happen. The stuff about the statistician is just my having fun at the expense of our statisticians, but it's still true.

Never use a model without testing segments expected to perform below average.
Models need to be tested; if you promote only the top segments and response is below expectations, you won't know if the model stopped working or if the result was a seasonal aberration or a scoring error.

Never commission a segmentation study or a predicative model without an implementation plan.
Not every segmentation scheme nor every model can be implemented easily, and gearing up for implementation can take longer than the model-building process itself.

Never build an RFM model without the aid of a CHAID (CHI² Automatic Interaction Detector) program.

CHAID models can build RFM trees that are more accurate than trees built by trial and error.

Never assume a CHAID program, or even a regression model, will outperform an old-fashioned RFM analysis if the RFM has been refining the model for more than 20 years.
After 20 years the RFM modeler probably has it all figured out. But his or her activities can be duplicated fairly quickly using CHAID.

Never believe that a neural-net model will always beat a regression model.
Sometimes it will, sometimes it won't; and the times can't be predicted. Never believe that neural-net models don't require data preparation. The better the data preparation, the better the chance that the neural net will find a solution at least as good as, if not better than, a regression model.

Never assume that block-group or household-level models will be more cost-effective than zip code models.
The models will be stronger for sure, but not necessarily strong enough to justify the added costs measured in both dollars and extra lead time.

Never model the obvious.
You don't need a model to tell you that direct mail customers buy more than print customers.

Never model overlay data until you've modeled all your internal data.
Model them both together and you won't know if you could have done as well, or almost as well, without the purchased data.

Never use a variable in a model that doesn't improve your validation results, even if it's declared statistically significant.
The fewer the variables in a final solution, the more likely the model will hold up over time.

Never use dummy variables to code census variables or to classify purchase data when there's a large number of purchase options.
Just don't do it.

Never assume the results of a model (the spread tends to decrease from top decile to bottom decile) will hold up exactly on a rollout.
No one knows why for sure, but it happens a lot, so plan for it.

Comment: Shepard and his associates are some of the most knowledgeable practitioners in the business of database and modeling. *Nevers* turn into rules. Now let's take a look at the development of a database.

Most database marketing systems begin life as transaction files.

Your objective in developing a database is to field a powerful marketing tool.

Comment: The idea is to move from an operations support system to a marketing decision support system to a totally integrated marketing decision support system.

When you develop an integrated database marketing system (IDBMS), you must create a road map.

Comment: The very first step is to define and quantify marketing objectives, then to define specific database drive programs needed to meet objectives. Finally you build your database so it is capable of supporting programs in the real world.

Define, define, define.

Comment: First define the business functions the IDBMS will support by conducting an in-depth business needs analysis. Define the desirability of ad hoc queries. Determine the relevant records and how you will select them. Define the type of tracking and measurements you need and want. Then define the kind of contact control you want to exercise.

Make the decision you *have* to make.

Comment: You have to decide to build your system internally or to outsource it; next you have to decide what relevant files to include. Then you need to review data elements and then select the right data elements. Decide the view you want to take of statistics (cumulative statistics [if period data exists], period statistics [if cumulative data exists]). Decide on the relevant data enhancements. Decide on individual information consolidation methodology and household information consolidation methodology. Figure your update frequency and your access process. Finally, determine the speed of query satisfaction you need.

Review and think and review and think and review and think . . . and *test*.

Comment: Once you have a preliminary design, settle the hardware and software issues. Then subject your planning to a reality check, especially where costs are concerned. Revise if necessary. Remember, it is faster and cheaper to correct things before you go operational than after you go operational. But don't roll out before you test. Select a sample or a beta site and test your thinking. Do an A/B split to determine cost effectiveness.

When you test, consider these cost factors.

Comment: Are you achieving the functionality you planned? How fast is the performance of your analytic functions? About right? How about the enhancements: Are they right? Do you need more or less? What is your update strategy? All of these elements affect costs.

Finally, run a financial analysis.

Comment: Run various scenarios to determine ROI or ROE in differing circumstances. Develop an incremental cash flow analysis. And—most important—measure the impact of competition. If your competition is investing in database and database marketing, it is a sure thing you better, too.

All this leads to:

The First Rule of Database
The more you know, the more you grow!

> *Comment:* A self-evident truth. The more retrievable, relevant information you have about your customers, prospects, and suspects, the more effective your marketing is—and the more profit you accumulate.

Bob Hacker's Second Rule of Database
If you want to increase profits quickly, do not promote to the worst performing quintile (20 percent) of your list.

Hacker's Corollary
To be more conservative, don't promote to the worst decile.

Design

 The purpose of design in direct marketing is never purely aesthetic. In fact a "pretty" design may run counter to the purpose of all direct marketing packages, which is of course to sell. Design brings concepts to life. An effective design leads the reader or viewer through the ad, direct mail package, or TV commercial so the writer's words have maximum impact and thus lead to multiple sales.

Claude Hopkins's Notion

Use pictures only to attract those who may profit you; use them only when they form a better-selling argument than the same amount of space set in type.

John Lefton's Model

Every creative problem has at least one solution that is neat, simple, convenient, and totally wrong!

Don O'Brien's Formula

The old saying that "you've got only five seconds to capture a reader's attention" is true.

Putting a variety of attractive and interesting elements on a page increases the span from five seconds to 10 to 60—and to an order. So, no matter where the eye falls, the arrangement and variety sitting there spark interest—which the words amplify at once.

Ted Kikoler's 27 Design Tips to Lift Response

Don't fall into the desktop publishing trap.
If you have a Mac (or any other desktop publishing system), don't fall into the trap of making your letters prettier. If you are using a typesetting font

(such as Times Roman or, worse, Helvetica) instead of a real typewriter font (Courier or Prestige), you are giving your letters the kiss of death. I can't stress this point enough. A typewriter-written letter will almost always beat one that's typeset. It's true that more people in business are now using prettier type-faces than typewriter, but it's not the accepted norm. At least not yet. Wait about five to 10 years. Until then, give your letters a true typewriter look.

There's danger in shouting.

We all tend to back away from people who shout at us, so don't fall into the trap of believing you have to shout to be heard. Some of the best mail comes across like a one-on-one conversation instead of a shouting like a town crier. Large lettering and lots of color in your direct mail package are perceived as shouting. Try toning your graphics down to a whisper to bring the listener closer.

Don't forget human involvement.

Examine 10 direct mail packages, and nine of them will give you the feeling that they're coming from a machine instead of a live human being. There's a total lack of human involvement. Sure, there's a letter from a person, but the signature is printed. The reader's name is either a label or computer person-alized. It appears as if the only human that ever touched it was the mail car-rier. The envelope is full of printed things—not things touched by real people. Everything looks too neat—too perfect. If somehow you can give readers the feeling that the letter was written by a real human, the order form was filled out by someone in the office, the components were folded and inserted by hand, you stand a greater chance of getting them to pay attention to your mailing and thus lifting response.

Always have envelope tests in the mail.

You can bring a dying package back to life. It doesn't matter how good your control is, it will eventually suffer fatigue and die. As soon as recipients see the envelope a second or third time they will recognize it and tune out. Instead of going for brand-new copy and design, the first thing you should do is change the outer envelope. Keep the same teaser copy, but give it a new look. When that starts to wear out, take your entire package and give it a whole new look.

For example, Emily Soell's control for the launch of *Condé Nast Traveler* was mailed in the same envelope for more than five years. Whenever results began to flag, the envelope color was changed and responses popped right back up again. That envelope was mailed in red, yellow, green, blue, orange, and black poly.

You'd be surprised by how long a control can be kept alive with simple cosmetic changes. That's because we have a harder time remembering what we have read than what we have seen.

Don't overdo personalization.

People cannot resist looking at their name. But be careful. Unless you're running a sweepstakes, don't overdo it. The best two places for it are the letter and the order form, and even that can be costly. If you have to make a choice, personalize the order form. A simple trick that helps lift response is to repeat the person's name—or a part of the address—a second time somewhere on the order form. I guarantee this helps.

A simple overlooked response builder: perceived quantity.

If you can get an envelope in the mail with two-inch-high letters saying "YOU ARE OUR $1,000,000,000.00 WINNER!" you know there are millions of these in the mail. That makes yours worthless. On the other hand, if you get an envelope in the mail from your best friend, you know there's just one. That makes it valuable, so you read every word of it. Create the illusion of lower quantity of your mailing and your response will go up.

Jolt the reader.

Sameness puts people to sleep, whereas a jolt keeps them alert. Jolt them by having as many components as economically feasible in your envelope. It's better to break messages into two or three smaller pieces of paper rather than to save money by crowding it all onto one. Give each piece a separate theme such as a guarantee, a free bonus, an early bird bonus, testimonials, and so on.

It's important that every component in your envelope look different— different size, shape, color, typeface, fold, etc.

Yes, it can look like a three-ring circus, but it jolts the reader, and that increases your response.

Physically lead readers directly to your letter.

As your prospects open the envelope, they want to know what it's all about in as little time as possible. They make a beeline for the order form or brochure. But these two items spill the beans too fast. Instead, when you direct them to your sales letter first, you have a much better chance of getting the response you want. If you have a strong tease on the envelope—in both words and graphics—duplicate it at the top of your letter. Then make sure that your letter is folded with the message facing out and inserted so that it faces the back of the envelope. It should be the first thing they see when they open the envelope. If your envelope teaser copy did what it was supposed to do, your prospects will eagerly want to know more. When they open the envelope and see the same message, they will start there.

Don't be cute.

Being cute or clever or showing off can kill response. A homely, even ugly, appearance will many times beat a flashy look. It appears more sincere.

Regardless of how good your response is from a flashy mailing, it will have a short life in the mail. The longest controls look very plain. With small changes, you can keep them alive for many years.

Make graphics pay for themselves.

Copy is the undisputed king at the creative end of direct mail. The longer you can keep a person reading, the higher your response will be. Graphics tend to distract the reader from the words on the page with a "Hey, look at me" effect. We all know that a picture is worth a thousand words. But that doesn't work in direct mail. You get higher response when you use graphics that force people to read rather than distract them. Try toning down the color and visuals—especially around large blocks of text.

Remember the keyhole view.

A lot of people slice open an envelope and view it as looking through a keyhole. They peek inside without removing the contents. Take a look at your mailing this way and you may be surprised by what you'll discover. You may find things that give the sales pitch away too soon, or you may see that some of your powerful items—such as a stamp or burst that says "FREE"—are hidden from view because of the fold. Simply reposition these things to improve the keyhole view and draw more people in.

Purposely hide part of the headline.

It's important to direct and involve the readers; otherwise you lose them. A simple but powerful involvement and direction technique is to purposely hide part of the headline on a fold line, thus forcing the reader to unfold the piece of paper to see the whole message. Designers hate doing this because it looks off balance, but only by throwing your readers off balance do you get them to move.

Get the product into the reader's hands.

This does not mean giving away an actual sample but visually getting the product closer to the person. The closer the product seems, the more desirable it becomes. You can accomplish this by doing the following.

- Making photos and illustrations as large as possible.
- Cropping photos to show the essence. Cut away all the unnecessary material. Leave the part of the photo that still tells the whole story. The reader will automatically fill in the missing part of the product in his mind. This technique saves valuable space and can make unexciting photos appear more dynamic.
- Involving the reader in the picture. Have life-size hands (that could be the reader's) coming in from the sides of the page.
- Showing the product in actual use, if possible.

Make the reader's eyes go where you want them to go.

The mind will follow. Here are some things that work:

- The eye normally goes from dark areas to light areas, large objects to small, and bright areas to drab areas.
- The eye zeros in on things that are out of place (color, size, shape, and position).
- Have photos and illustrations face the copy or be in the direction you want the reader to go. Every photo has direction.
- The farther along in the sales pitch, the smaller the type size can be. The more interested readers get, the easier it is to keep them with you. So use your largest type at the beginning for the headlines and lead-in paragraphs.
- Captions and call-outs get high readership.
- If everything looks alike, readers can mistakenly believe they've already seen one of your messages. Make each side of a two-sided piece look different.

Handwritten messages get noticed.
They're an effective way of highlighting special thoughts or teasing a reader into a long letter. This little trick always works! But don't overuse it.

This little trick always works!

Make things move; don't leave anything static.
This can be dangerous, though. At the same time, too much movement on the page—or movement that takes the eye in the wrong direction—can hurt readability.

Break up large areas into smaller visual ones.
These smaller chunks are easier to digest as well as to notice. Massive blocks of copy look like a lot of work to the reader. Make it easy for your prospect.

Make different sections look different.
Readers get bored easily. If they see something with the same style throughout, it will look like a lot of reading to do—which means work.

Talk the reader's language.
Use colors, typefaces, layouts, and overall appearances the reader can relate to.

Talk the product's language.
Masculine products have to look masculine; female products have to look feminine, etc.

Use serif typefaces for body copy; they're easier to read.

Avoid reverse copy.

Light letters on a dark background are much harder to read. Exception: Reverse headings are fine. Use them for body copy only if they are being knocked out of a photo to attain a larger image area and more dramatic effect.

Warm colors get a warm response; cold colors get a cold response.
Use bright warm colors on order cards—red for example.

Keep things simple.
Make the eye move easily from information to information. Line up as many things as possible. This reduces eye strain and distraction.

Avoid a flat look.
Try to create several dimensions to prevent boredom. Varying the weight of typefaces helps—light, medium, bold, and extra bold. Use screen tints for panels to hold copy blocks together and add dimension.

Make the order cards stand out.
If they are part of a larger sheet and must be torn off, either screen the entire area with a tint and leave the card white or tint the card and leave the rest of the page white. Always add a heavy broken rule along the part where the tint and blank areas meet.

Denny Hatch's Precept
Never repeat the same copy or the same design in different places in the same package.

People who are looking for just one more reason to to say yes will lay the piece down whenever repetition elicits, "Oh, I've read this before." Then you've lost the sale.

Bob Hacker's Commandment
Ugly works.

Martin Davidson's Constraint
It doesn't have to be ugly to sell.

Bill Josephs's Advice
Never use four colors when two will suffice.

Learn what your production facilities can do *before* you design a package; find the most economical way to achieve the visual impression you want.

Murray Raphel's Observation
Purple means extra value in pricing.

> Supermarkets used this color to promote their special low prices for so many years that the color became identified with "extra value."

Ed Elliott's Fundamentals

It's copy that sells, not design.
But it's the design that sells the copy. It makes no difference how persuasive, how benefit oriented, or how well written the copy is if it isn't read. It's the designer's job to present the copy in a way that will overcome skepticism, busy schedules, and people's dislike of what they perceive to be "junk."

Have a healthy respect for your writer.
The good copywriters I know are great salespeople. It is part of their personality. But great writers often have one common shortcoming. Their expertise is conceptual and verbal but rarely visual. That's why teamwork with a good designer is so crucial.

Become the writer's assistant.
The designer's job is to create the right impression, get people to read the copy, draw visual emphasis to the appropriate text in the right way to bring the greatest response, and remove obstacles that might keep people from responding.

Ed Elliott's Four Conclusions from Testing
Serif text gets a better response than sans serif.

Narrow columns are more likely to be read than wide columns.

Positioning a coupon perforation so that you must tear through the photo of a person can depress response.

Glossy coated paper is not as readable as uncoated or matte stock.

Ed Elliott's 16 Devices That Can Turn a Skimmer into an Interested Reader

Table of contents.

Headlines and subheads.

Photography, especially of people and action.

Tables, charts, graphs.

Illustrations clarifying or reinforcing the text.

Captions under every visual.
People read captions as they skim.

A word or subhead that is bigger, bolder, blacker, or in a different color from other elements on the page.

Enlarged numbers, possibly followed by an enlarged or bold lead.

A word or line set off at an angle or in a box or a burst.

Text inside an arrow or a ruled box.

Anything that interrupts a page-by-page pattern of columns.

Text with a light screen behind it.

Pull quotes.

A paragraph set off in bold or with a double indent.

Handwritten indications.

Bulleted text, especially with bullets that are larger than or different from other bulleted text.

Ed Elliott's Three Ways to Get Maximum Readership

Use the right text type size.
Ten or 11 points is optimum for readability; maybe one point larger for older readers.

Use the correct column width.
A good target range is 35 to 55 characters. Ten or eleven point is generally most readable on a column width of about a third of a page. Larger than 11-point type should probably be about half a page wide. Columns wider than half a page are not read quickly.

Rag right alignment is often better than justified text. It creates a text shape that allows an area for the eye to rest. It can also appear more inviting, less imposing, and more personal.

Ed Elliott's Six Design Features to Avoid

Avoid text without sufficient contrast to its background.
Examples: a background screen that is too dark, paper color that is too dark, and text that is too light, printed in a color other than black.

Avoid text printed over, or reversed out of, a busy or distracting background.

Avoid text reversed out of a dark color.

Avoid flush right or centered paragraphs.

Avoid text that is too condensed.

Avoid character spacing that is too tight.

Denny Hatch's Two Prescriptions

If you use margin notes in a letter, make sure the handwriting matches the signature.

Make a black-and-white photocopy of your finished four-color design. If the copy is not immediately readable, go back to the drawing board.
Some designers put busy backgrounds behind the text or a red headline reversed out of a black background. A black-and-white photocopy will immediately reveal that these detract from readability.

Andy Byrne's Four Beacons

Use sans serif type for headlines, not for body copy.

Don't use reverse type in body copy. It badly hurts legibility.

Illustrations should tie in with the headline or product.
They are not there to decorate a brochure or an ad.

You'll never hear it in art school, but "busy" ads work better than orderly ones.

Lew Smith's Three-Word Dictum
Neatness rejects involvement.

An ad or a mailing that is neat and precise—the design school equivalent of Palmer penmanship—is uninvolving, uninviting, and not interruptive; the viewer will lose interest quickly, and you will lose the sale.

Example: You stay late at work to do a massive cleaning job in your office. Your desk is absolutely clear of everything—not a paper, not a telephone message, not a note pad, not even an appointment book. The next morning when you walk in with your coffee and your newspaper, you sit down at your empty desk and contemplate the day, think about where you're going to have lunch, maybe do a little strategic planning.

Conversely, your desk is a wreck—piled high with papers, telephone messages, reports, interoffice correspondence, and mail. With barely room to set down your coffee, something will catch your eye—an unanswered letter, an essential call-back, the agenda for an upcoming meeting. Immediately *you're involved*.

Direct marketers must keep the prospect involved and off-balance, forcing the eye to shift and move around the offer until finally, the package is so compelling that action will be taken—*now*.

Direct Mail

 Direct mail is the workhorse of direct marketing. Everybody does it, from mom-'n'-pop businesses at the kitchen table to American Express, Lands' End, and AT&T. It is the largest single advertising medium by far—bigger than TV, bigger than newspapers and magazines, bigger than freestanding inserts, bigger than alternative media. The telemarketing industry would have you believe otherwise, but you can take all the money that is claimed to be spent on telemarketing and cut it in half—half for outbound and half for inbound. The direct mail I'm talking about is outbound—over 70 billion pieces of standard (third-class bulk) mail per year plus probably another 10 billion first-class presort. At an average of $400/M, that's roughly $32 billion spent on outbound direct mail a year—the equivalent of the gross domestic product of Chile and Costa Rica combined.

Direct mail is the only practical way to communicate with your existing customers. Telemarketing is chancy at best (people either aren't home or find it irritating when they are). Fax is OK, but the recipient pays for the fax paper, which can also be annoying. All other communications are via mass media, and that's no way to talk personally to your existing customers.

Direct mail is also secret. Unlike space or broadcast—where once an ad runs it becomes public knowledge—you can drop a wee 10,000 test into Tucson and Phoenix, and chances are very good your competitor won't have a clue about what you're doing. For this reason it is the ideal test medium.

Dorothy Kerr's Axiom
The way to be successful in direct mail is to see what comes into your mailbox and your in box at the office, note those mailings that keep coming in over and over (which means they are successful), study them carefully, and then steal smart.

Axel Andersson's Edict
Creating direct mail without studying other people's successful direct mail is like trying to do brain surgery without studying brains.

Murray Raphel's Quartet
A letter accounts for 65 to 75 percent of the orders.

Brochures account for 15 to 25 percent of orders.

The order form accounts for five to 10 percent of orders.

The more choices you give a customer to buy from (phone, mail, fax),
the more sales you'll have.

Claude Hopkins's Postulate
Mail-order advertising must tell a complete story if the purpose is to make
an immediate sale.

> The theory that the more you tell, the more you sell has never failed to prove
> out in any test we know.

Bob Stone's Standard
A preprint of a forthcoming ad, accompanied by a letter and response
form, will outpull a postprint mailing package by 50 percent or more.

Maxwell Sroge's Trio (from *Mail Order Digest*, August 1986)

> Don't assume what sells well in a store will also sell well by mail.

> Don't assume that the same people who buy in your store will also buy
> by mail.

> Don't assume that it's easier to run a mail-order business than a retail
> business.
> Because you don't have visual contact with your customer, you've got to do
> a better job of anticipating problems.

Bill Jayme's Beacon
Of all practical advertising media, only direct mail offers a sufficiently large
canvas for telling a complex story.

George Duncan's Observation
Direct mail is theater in print!

Mike Manzari's Codicil
Direct mail should be used only to get a response, and image advertising should be left to the general agencies.

> That doesn't mean, however, that you should ignore prospects just because they aren't responding this time around. They could be your future customers. Let the direct mail piece carry your image along with your offer. Take the opportunity to say something positive and memorable about your company, your product, and/or your service.

Denny Hatch's Bylaw
Direct mail must interrupt and keep on interrupting until some action is taken.

> Here's the secret of successful advertising: interrupting what's going on in the front of a prospect's brain with headline and graphics that seize on a lurking fear or desire and exploit it. Nobody expects to receive a piece of direct mail. What's more, you have no control over the company it arrives in. If your letter is in the same batch of mail with a personal letter from the White House, you won't be read first—guaranteed.
>
> Your mailing must interrupt and keep on interrupting until some action is taken. If the package is laid down for any reason, chances are it will be covered with the sports pages and the whole thing chucked into the garbage (or recycling bin).

Anver Suleiman's Prototype
If you are marketing the same product to 10 different lists/categories, tailor the letter and/or brochure to who the prospects are, where they are, what they do—any identifiable characteristic—and watch your response rate soar!

Denny Hatch's Corollary
If you can have a common brochure and versionalize only your letter, order form, and lift pieces, life will be simpler.

> Usually brochures are the most complex and costly of all the elements—especially if you're using four-color process. In comparison, letters are cheap, as are order forms and lift pieces.
>
> Testing is the lifeblood of direct marketing. But to stop a web press and make a plate change on every 5,000 or 10,000 brochures is expensive and impractical. Try to confine your tests to the simple pieces and make the complex ones generic to all efforts.

Dick Benson's Four Rules

Tokens or stickers always improve results.
Adding elements to a mailing package, even though obviously adding cost, is more likely to pay out than cheapening the package.

Personalized letters work better to house lists (those who have bought or subscribed before) than to "cold" lists.

Brochures and letters should stand alone, and each of them should contain all the information.

Direct mail should be scrupulously honest.

Bob Stone's Dictum
Self-mailers are cheaper to produce, but they hardly ever outpull envelope-enclosed mailings.

Dick Hodgson's Hint
Self-mailers should be used for seminar offers and for offers being made to people in the workplace where mail handling is not a regular part of the job, such as barbershops or to factory foremen and the like.

Denny Hatch's Tenet
A mailing with a letter but without a brochure will almost always outpull a mailing with no letter.

Malcolm Decker's Principle
The direct mail package—especially a full-dress package—is a sales team.

First the envelope knocks on the door to see if anyone's home. Then the major letter—the salesperson—takes over. Once the envelope is opened, the letter is the most important member of the team. It sells soft, or it sells hard. It spins yarns, or it spouts facts. It's long (but never long-winded) or pithy. However it comes on, it's loaded with customer benefits . . . Customer Benefits . . . CUSTOMER BENEFITS.

Then the demonstrator—the folder or brochure—goes to work. Like the letter, it can stand on its own. But it's most effective when it demonstrates in graphics what the letter can only say in words. It should convince the reader in images that everything the letter said is true.

The publisher's letter (or lift letter) is yet another voice backing up the key salesperson, the long letter; its job is to convince the waverer and salvage the skeptics. The order device restates the offer in the pithiest, least ambiguous language possible. And the business reply envelope brings the order home.

Finally, it's important to remember that in direct mail the word is king. Copy is the architect of the sale. Design and art are strongly supportive interior designers that often set up the sale. Because lookers are shoppers while readers are buyers, if you can firmly engage your prospects—and keep them engaged—through reading, you're on your way to a sale.

Denny Hatch's Presumption
After opening the envelope, you have no way of knowing which piece the prospect will look at first.

Bob Hacker has pointed out that people process information in two ways: rationally and analytically as well as irrationally and emotionally. Right-brain people—who rely primarily on the emotional and irrational approach—will read the letter first. Left-brainers will go for the circular. This is why, in the words of Dick Benson, "A letter should look like a letter."

I always look at the order card first so I'll know exactly what the deal is.

When making the same offer to different audiences, have a common order form and brochure, but change the letter and outside envelope. It's easy to change a letter and an envelope. These two elements are specifically addressed to "YOU"—the prospect. The brochure—the demonstrator that shows and describes "it" (the product or service)—should be designed to be universal.

Direct Mail Production

Denny Hatch's Guide
All elements of a direct mail package must be machine insertable.

Otherwise your letter shop costs will go through the roof. The exception: The order form can be just a shade smaller than the reply envelope, because this is inserted by the customer by hand.

Think through how the different elements of your mailing are inserted into the envelope. What do you want the reader to see first? Most of us open an envelope at the flap, and the first thing we see is the top of the piece facing the flap.

If you are using a window envelope, presumably the addressing piece is the "turnaround document"—the order form. In a closed-face envelope (no window), the order form can be anywhere. However, you probably don't want someone to see the order form first, because that talks price—and you don't want to talk price until the prospect is salivating for your product or service.

The typical order of insertion from front to back is (1) order form with name facing front and showing through the window; (2) reply envelope (upside down so as to be machine insertable); (3) lift piece; (4) circular with main headline facing toward the flap; (5) main letter, folded into itself with the headline and salutation facing the outside (flap side) of the envelope. However, if you have a powerful lift note from a world-famous celebrity, you might want that to be the first piece the prospect sees.

Once you've decided on the order in which the elements are to be inserted, give the letter shop clear instructions *in writing* and send an actual sample showing exactly how the mailing should be inserted.

Coleman Williams Hoyt's Three Rules for Working with the U.S. Postal Service

If you want your mail delivered on time, tell the Postal Service your plans in advance.

You'd be surprised by how many mailers ignore this simple and effective courtesy offered by the USPS and then complain loudly to deaf ears about their delayed mail.

If you get into an argument with the Postal Service, go upstairs.
Sad but true, local postal people can be your friends but are often unable to make the simplest business decisions. Keep the locals as your friends (you may need them later), but do your arguing with the Washington bureaucrats upstairs, who are the only ones capable of making simple decisions without fear of being overturned by somebody even farther upstairs.

If there is postal work to do, you can do it cheaper.
The Postal Service gurus call it "work sharing." What it means in plain English is that anything you can legally do to your mail—address it, barricade it, sort it, drop ship it, etc.—can be done less expensively by you than by the Postal Service, so do it. I say legally, because there is one thing the private express statutes prevent you from doing, which is delivering it. So do everything else as long as it's practical for you.

USA DIRECT, INC.'s 11 Direct Mail Production and Quality Control Procedures
Clear your package with the post office.

Communicate all instructions in writing.

Assign codes to each printed component so no confusion among similar pieces exists at the letter shop.

Establish quality control standards and review them with all your suppliers.

Maintain a production flow chart for each project.

Attend all press checks and bring back a copy of each sign-off sheet to compare to production run.

Have quality control sheets pulled and sent daily.

Have quality control sheets pulled during each production step. This includes printing, card and label affixing, and all bindery operations.

Have finished samples sent to you for final approval before mailing.

Check bills from your suppliers carefully. Make sure the amounts tally with your receiving tickets and purchase orders and that the multiplication and addition are correct.

Finally, and most important of all, plan your job thoroughly and well in advance.

Paul Goldberg's Two Keys

Have someone knowledgeable from your staff at the letter shop while your job is running.

Know how 3602s work.
The 3602 is an official U.S. Postal Service form that is attached to your bill from the letter shop. If they total to the correct number—and the dates on them are correct—your quantities and mail dates have been verified by the post office.

Here's how the process works:

1. The front part of the form is filled out by the letter shop.
2. The two-part verification—(a) that the makeup of the mail conforms to regulations and (b) that the stated quantity is correct by weight—is done by the post office.

If there is a long-term good relationship between the USPS and the letter shop (and in most cases there is), the post office may employ a skip-interval verification, which means each and every mailing will not be checked. But in all cases—whether it's in-plant loading or post office delivery—the weight must be verified. A reasonable variation is allowed, but if the variation is too large the postal employee might ask to see the labeling records, etc.

Be aware that 3602s can be phonied. I remember a classic situation where circulation manager X had in her hands signed postal receipts for one million pieces from letter shop Y while the mail was still being inserted at letter shop Z. It turned out that letter shop Y had been backed up and had farmed out the job to letter shop Z without telling the circulation manager. Imagine her terror over the lack of returns during the first few weeks.

The biggest way a letter shop can screw you is through postage. I know a couple of letter shops that falsified post office receipts and wound up owing a quarter of a million dollars of the client's postage money.

David Thompson's Two Inviolable Dicta

Own your own permit!
Never mail through a letter shop's master permit account. If you do, all the money you send for your postage is out of your control. Recently I was asked by a friend in the banking industry, "How come a letter shop would have a million dollars in its account one day and two days later be in the bank asking for a 90-day loan?" Obviously, the mailing house was using clients' postage money to finance its own operation.

Make out all postage checks payable to your postmaster and deposit them in your own permit account.

You can also protect yourself by calling the post office at least twice a quarter and asking for a printout of the deposits and withdrawals from your permit account. Then you will always know the date that X amount was withdrawn. (There may be a slight variation in dates because of clerical variations at the post office.) But this printout keeps everybody honest.

A Denny Hatch Duo

Any company that intends to be profitable using direct mail must have continuing access to an expert on postal reclassification.

Postage is the single most expensive element in the direct mail package (with the possible exception of nonprofit mail). Mail must be prepared in strict accordance with USPS Reclassification Guidelines to reduce postage costs.

If your agency, writer, or designer (1) doesn't know the parameters for postal reclassification and/or (2) kicks and screams that reclassification hinders the creative process, find a replacement at once!

Direct vs. General Advertising

The distinctions between general advertising and direct advertising are blurring on a daily basis. In the past the general advertiser's objective was to support a brand and to enhance brand equity. However, take a look at the Internet addresses that are popping up all over television and in print media, the 800 numbers on brand packaging, and you have to wonder if general advertisers are finally getting it: It's not share of market that counts, it is share of customers . . . and measuring everything.

Bob Hacker's Theorem
The art of war is also the art of direct marketing: A good idea violently executed will beat a brilliant idea poorly executed—every time.

John Francis Tighe's Proof
Direct marketers have far more in common with commission salesmen than general advertisers; they must "close" on the spot.

Joan Throckmorton's Coda
As direct marketers we're not here primarily to make a sale; we're here to get a customer.

Sales are important, of course. (Where would marketers be without them?) But the name of this game is repeat sales rather than one-shots. And to have that, you need a customer.

Some marketers today use a form of advertising that I call "response" advertising. It consists of customers who answer their promotions via coupon redemption or electronic means like telephones and computers. But generally these marketers do not record customer names and establish a database; therefore, this is sampling—or coupon redemption or sales promotion. It is not direct marketing.

To capture yourself a customer (or prospect) you have to capture customer data in the computer so that you can build a relationship based on a growing knowledge of the customer and his or her habits.

We set up a positive dialogue with our customers via direct-response techniques.

Through this dialogue we constantly test and measure to determine what pleases or appeals to the customer. The customer is always right.

Smart direct marketers understand that they are dialogue marketers. Establishing a dialogue is, in fact, the name of the game, whether it is by mail or phone or computer.

What could be more sensible, once you have a number of customers by name and address, than to test and measure their likes and dislikes? If you want to keep your customers buying, ask them what they want.

The wisdom of direct marketers is gained from customers. Listen to the customers and they will tell you what to do, as long as you test carefully and scientifically. (Which means in two brief sentences: Test only one thing at a time. Test in quantities or numbers of customers that are statistically valid and can therefore be projected.)

Your customers will even tell you when they've had enough or when a product needs changing. And certainly, they will tell you when they are unhappy or disillusioned. In this sense, your customer is always right—and, of course, what's best for your customer is ultimately best for you.

Properly treated, the customer will continue to tell us reliably not only what to sell, but when to sell, how much to sell, and the best offer to use. All marketers know this—don't they? Certainly they should. But no one is equipped to demonstrate it better and more precisely than direct marketers because direct marketers were the first to develop and utilize customer records (the database) to establish a productive customer dialogue or an ongoing, repeat-purchase history.

In addition to this history, a well-run operation will record when an order was received, when it was shipped, how it was shipped, and when and how it was billed and paid for. This is known as fulfillment data (the complete operation of order processing), and it is part of customer service.

If order processing, or fulfillment, does its job, customer inquiries and complaints can be kept to a minimum and handled promptly and positively when they occur. (If it doesn't do its job, a good customer turns off, not just to one direct marketer, but often to direct marketing as a whole.)

Sadly, some very big marketers have come to direct marketing with a "quota-driven" approach, rather than "customer-driven" marketing: "We have to sell 100,000 of these widgets by spring. Find more customers. Roll out the advertising. Cut the prices!" instead of "Find out how the customer will react to the new widget. What can he or she tell us about price preferences that will increase sales volume?"

When we listen to the customer first, we can make money with considerable confidence.

Our computers can take customer information and tell us not only where we are, but also where we can logically expect to be over the years ahead.

You'll discover that every kind of direct marketing (magazine subscriptions, book clubs, continuity programs, catalogs, third-party mailings) not only has extensive testing programs all along the line, but also has established formulas based on consistent behavior of specific customer groups. Marketers develop entire computer models based on these formulas and use them to draw up their long-range marketing plans.

Nothing must destroy our credibility with the customer. The customer takes us very seriously. The customer listens to us. The customer remembers. (And she talks to her friends.)

Sounds a little corny, doesn't it? Well, so does "A penny saved, a penny earned," "The best things in life are free," "Too soon old; too late smart!" These are all old-fashioned adages—truisms. (Get it?) They live on.

Bob Hacker's Challenge
The medium isn't the message!

Direct mail is ink on paper in an envelope. A newspaper is just paper and ink. Database marketing is just a way of trapping and manipulating information. The Internet is just a new way of disseminating information. Technology is only a tool—it doesn't sell a thing! Direct marketing is the art and science of changing behavior—the medium doesn't matter! Technology does not replace selling! We're not technicians, we're not communicators—we're salespeople! The best salesperson will win in any medium.

Lew Smith's Edict
A successful direct marketing effort is generally predicated on the idea that it is an impulse sale.

If the person lays down a mailing with the idea of deciding later, chances are you've lost the sale; the mailing will be covered with the newspaper, and the whole thing will go out with the trash.

Exception: Catalogs that people can browse through as in a retail store, and offers into the business arena where several people may have to sign off on it.

Lew Smith's Codicil
If direct marketing is basically an impulse sale, it must be remembered that people have a short attention span.

In the workplace—where distractions are greater—that attention span is even shorter. Therefore your effort must interrupt and keep on interrupting until some definite action is taken.

Psychologists have found that we—all of us—walk around carrying on endless conversations with ourselves. These conversations are frequently interrupted by a baby crying, a kitchen timer going off, a dog barking, someone at the door, a fire engine going by, a piece of direct mail, a catalog, a TV infomercial, or a telemarketing call. If the marketing effort is dull—if it does not interrupt and keep on interrupting—the interruption is interrupted and we resume the conversation with ourselves. The marketer has lost money. Once the proposition is laid aside, chances are very high that no action will be taken.

Direct marketing is action advertising. If you do not make an offer, there is no reason for a response—no reason to march against Philip. This is not a business of awareness, of shooting out warm fuzzies in hopes they will be remembered somewhere down the line. Direct marketing is accountable advertising, measurable within tenths and hundredths of a percent. You can't measure anything if you don't get a response. You won't get a response if you don't make an offer.

Exception: A pre-alert, such as the letters from *Reader's Digest* telling you to watch your mail for the upcoming sweepstakes. These *Digest* pre-alerts have been known to raise response by as much as 30 percent. The pre-alert is also used on TV by Publishers Clearing House and American Family Publishers, urging consumers to watch their mail for the upcoming sweepstakes and showing the happy couple who won the last $10 million prize.

Bob Hacker's Tenets

Direct marketing doesn't have to make sense—it just has to make money.

Direct marketing isn't advertising in an envelope.

General advertising and direct marketing come from two different worlds. General advertising evolved from public relations and publicity. Its primary objective is to *change the way the market thinks.*

Direct marketing, on the other hand, developed out of personal selling. Its primary objective is to *change the way the individual acts.*

Direct marketing talks to individuals; advertising targets groups or markets. Direct marketing pushes for immediate action; advertising tries to change perceptions and attitudes over time.

Claude Hopkins's Hypothesis
The severest test of an advertising person is selling goods by mail.

That is a school from which he must graduate before he can hope for success. The cost and result are immediately apparent. False theories melt away like snowflakes in the sun. The advertising is profitable or it is not, clearly on the face of returns. Figures that do not lie tell one at once the merits of an ad.

Cecil Hoge Sr.'s Vision

Mail order is a feel-your-way . . . stop . . . start . . . test . . . project method, for the people with a "feel" for it, to get rich surprisingly fast.

> Mail order loses money for far more people than it ever makes money for, simply because they don't have a "feel" for any business but get tempted into mail order as an easy business—often by shrewd entrepreneurs or biased advisors who get rich luring the ignorant and unbusinesslike into activities they are unsuited for.
>
> Mail order is a rare opportunity for those with a feel for it, and it is not at all simple for anyone else. I call it mail order "*fingerspitzengefuehl.*" In German this means the tips of your fingers; it refers to a special sensitivity. For the man or woman with a feel for mail order, it's a gold mine—the secret of mail order success. That feel is the basic know-how of correct mail order principles. It's a sound sense of correct mail order strategy. It's quite vital in today's mail order.

George Duncan's 7 Differences

Advertising sells *products*; direct sells *offers*.

Advertising *creates* markets; direct *discovers* them.

Advertising *changes* behavior; direct *models* it.

Advertising is heavily *emotional*; direct is heavily *factual*.

Advertising copy tends to be *short*; direct copy tends to be *long*.

Advertising creates *sales*; direct creates *customers*.

Agreement with our proposition is not enough; to make our bones in direct, we have to get a response.

Emily Soell's Warning

In a direct marketing appeal, you cannot convince people to do something they never thought about doing.

> ***Comment by Axel Andersson:*** Save the Children did exhaustive research and found that people who never before thought about adopting a child would not consider the Save the Children program. I have had this experience in marketing home study courses. People who have never thought about studying on their own in their spare time at home would probably never be convinced to do so.

Four ftc Rules

The 30-Day Rule

When you advertise mail or telephone order merchandise, you must have a reasonable basis for stating or implying that you can ship within a certain time. If you make no shipment statement, you must have a reasonable basis for believing that you can ship within 30 days, which is why direct marketers sometimes call this the 30-Day Rule.

If, after taking the customer's order, you learn that you cannot ship within the time you stated or within 30 days, you must seek the customer's consent to the delayed shipment. If you cannot obtain the customer's consent to the delay, either because it is not a situation in which you are permitted to treat the customer's silence as consent and the customer has not expressly consented to the delay, or because the customer has expressly refused to consent, you must, without being asked, promptly refund all the money the customer paid you for the unshipped merchandise.

The Warranties and Guarantees Rule

The ftc's rule on Pre-Sale Availability of Written Warranty Terms requires that written warranties on consumer products costing more than $15 be available to consumers before they buy.

If you solicit orders for warranted consumer products through the mail or by telephone, your catalog or other advertisement must include either the warranty or a statement telling consumers how to get a copy. Under the ftc act, you must honor satisfaction and money-back guarantees.

Ftc cases have held that it is unfair or deceptive for a merchant to fail to honor an unqualified satisfaction or money-back guarantee promptly and fully, including the return of the purchase price as well as shipping, handling, or other fees. The ftc also has held that it violates the ftc act to advertise a satisfaction or money-back guarantee without disclosing, clearly and conspicuously, any material limitations or conditions, such as requiring the customer to supply proof of purchase, returning the unused portion of a product, or restricting the offer to a specific time period.

The Negative-Option Rule

In any promotional materials, the ftc's Negative-Option Rule requires you to clearly and conspicuously give the following information:

- how many selections the customer must buy
- how and when the customer can cancel the membership
- how to notify you if the customer does not want the selection
- when the customer must return the negative-option form to cancel shipment of a selection
- when a customer can get credit for the return of a selection
- how postage and handling costs are charged
- how often a customer can expect to receive announcements and forms

If your promotion provides this information and you conduct the negative-option plan as represented, consumers enrolled in the plan are obligated either to return the negative-option form within 10 days after receiving it or (if they don't return the form in time) pay for the merchandise after receiving it.

Merchandise-on-Approval Rule

Under the FTC act, you must obtain the customer's express agreement to order merchandise on approval.

Merchants sometimes confuse sales on approval with negative-option plans. Unlike negative-option sales, merchandise-on-approval sales permit the prospective customer to return merchandise, usually after a no-obligation or free-trial period, even though it is exactly as represented in the merchant's advertising.

These sales do not require the customer to pay for the order until the merchandise is received and approved.

Although you do not have to make the disclosure required by the Negative-Option Rule when offering merchandise on approval, you must obtain the customer's prior express agreement to receive the merchandise. Otherwise, the merchandise may be treated as unordered merchandise. The consumer has a legal right to keep unordered merchandise as a free gift.

Direct-Response TV

 Direct-response television has come a long way since the days of Ginsu Knives and Veg-a-Matics. Today, in addition to the talking head pitchman, we have slice-of-life formats and a growing number of infomercials. Television is a rich resource for development—especially for insurance marketers. And with a growing number of general advertisers including toll-free numbers and Web site information in their commercials, its use will continue to expand.

Steve Dworman's 11 Essential Elements Necessary to a Successful Direct-Response Television Campaign

It may seem obvious, but number one is your product selection.
Your product should solve an immediate problem. It should appeal to the greatest number of people possible. It should be easily demonstrable.

To sell on television, your product needs an average markup of five times your manufacturing cost.

Before you even begin to conceptualize your show, you must figure out your offer.
What are all the components of what you're selling? What's your upsell to persuade the customer to buy more? Can you effectively incorporate your upsell into the show? What can you do during the show to increase the perceived value of your product? What's the most effective direct marketing technique for what you're selling? Buy one, get one free? A huge discount for ordering now? Buy the product and get something extra for ordering now? Knowing all of this before you produce the show is essential for knowing how and what you want to present during the show.

Brainstorm your show!
What is the most dramatic, startling, convincing way to demonstrate your product? What can be done to add as much authenticity to your demonstrations?

If it's a beauty product, should it be shot on film or video? Do you want a well-known figure or a celebrity involved?

Your infomercial needs to accomplish two distinct and sometimes contradictory objectives: to sell and to entertain.
First it must sell your product; second, it has to be spellbinding and capture the attention of channel surfers.

Besides your offer, the scripting of your in-bound 800 number is of vital importance.
I have personally witnessed nothing more than changes in a few sentences result in 30 percent more revenue. Many times you'll see offers on television for a very low price (sets of instructional tapes, for example), yet through careful scripting 80 percent of the callers commit to purchasing the entire 12-tape series.

The fulfillment company is often the only direct link between you and your customer.
There are numerous stories about fulfillment companies claiming capabilities they can't really handle. Some of the things you need to check out are multipay processing, continuity programs, and seven-day-a-week customer service. One infomercial company trains its customer service reps to handle problem calls by converting the caller to additional sales rather than just taking back merchandise. It generated over $1 million in additional revenue within the first 90 days of the program.

It's often a good idea to check out the fulfillment company through your credit card processor.
The processor will be aware of charge-back problems or late delivery problems so you don't have to find out the hard way.

Your outbound telemarketing campaign can often make a difference between breaking even and making a considerable profit.
Many of the outbound services will work strictly on commission once your DRTV program is tested, so it costs you no out-of-pocket money. The two main types of programs used in direct-response television are calling your inquiries and converting them to sales and back-end selling your customers additional merchandise. On consumables, such as skin care lines or makeup, you can build up a $40-million-a-year business just in reorders by using direct mail and telemarketing.

If you're running a successful television campaign, capitalize on the exposure by advertising your product in alternate sources.
These include credit card inserts, print ads, catalogs, and even the television shopping networks. Any of these can generate significant additional revenue.

For every unit you sell on television, you can sell an average of six to eight units in retail.

Several direct-response television campaigns have run at breakeven just to generate retail sales. Several companies exist within the direct-response television industry specifically to take television products into retail. Many of them own space in such major retailers as Target, Wal-Mart, and other mass merchandisers. As Marvin Traub, past chairman of Bloomingdale's, remarked at a conference we held in New York: "Nothing moves product at retail like a successful infomercial."

Dan Kennedy's 11 Rules for Successful Direct-Response Television

Don't start with a flawed premise.

No amount of creativity, celebrity hosts, artsy production values, or money will overcome the burden of a flawed premise—whether it's the wrong product for your market (or vice versa) or the wrong offer.

Tilt the probabilities in your favor by sticking to proven categories such as weight loss or fast wealth and, even more important, to proven direct-response marketing foundations such as greed, beauty, youth, ego, and sex.

Infomercials are just one of many advertising media and marketing methods, and some products are better suited to other methods.

Make a strong offer.

Offers can be placed on a line, with soft at one end and hard at the other. A soft offer is "Buy this stuff, and you'll be a happier person with better self-esteem." A hard offer is "Buy this stuff and your friends will swear you had a face-lift."

Simply, the harder the better.

Evaluate the piled-up perceived value of your offer.

Nothing beats the "and you get this and this and this and—wait!—this too!" It's the Ginsu-knife style of building perceived value. You cannot get $10 for $10 in value; $20 for $10 isn't exciting enough; $200 for $10, maybe.

This is why in mail order, where audiocassette courses are sold based on content value to more discerning buyers, they tend to be packaged with six or 12 tapes in one shiny vinyl album. But on TV the masters put one tape in an album so that there are 12 individual albums spread out, and it looks like a wheelbarrow load of stuff.

Premiums and bonuses drive sales.

Too often the premium is an afterthought. I think it's at least as important as the core product.

Pay attention to sales basics.

Advertising should be "salesmanship" via media. For direct response that goes double. Yet many people decide to do an infomercial without the first iota of knowledge about the fundamentals of making a sale. At a bare minimum, required reading ought to include all of Bob Stone's books, Claude Hopkins's *Scientific Advertising*, and Victor Schwab's *How to Write a Good Advertisement*.

A lot more money has been made with ugly shows than glamorous ones.

Different production values and creative levels are needed for different types of products; beauty products generally require a higher level of production than do slicer-dicers.

Some people in this business, as in all categories of advertising, are more interested in winning peer approval, industry recognition, and creativity for creativity's sake than in bottom-line results. Making the sale must be the priority.

Use a seven- or eight-to-one markup.

Have the ability to spend 75 percent as cost of sales.

Create a budget that allows for testing and revisions, more testing and more revisions.

Bob Stone's Two Realities

A direct-response, direct-sale TV commercial of 120 seconds will out-pull a 60-second direct-response commercial better than two to one.

A TV support commercial will increase response from a newspaper insert up to 50 percent.

Andrew Cohen's Five Steps from Storyboard to Order

Start with a creative storyboard.

The look and idea of the commercial are explained in a storyboard: a series of pictures and words communicating the product, offer, and call to action. The cost of creative: $5,000 to $25,000 or more.

Make the infomercial.

The storyboard is sent to film companies, film editors, casting agents, music production companies, and others who submit an estimate for the cost of their services. Once these costs are approved, the commercial is shot, edited, and then duplicated to be sent to various TV stations.

More than 70 percent of DRTV commercials are shot on film as opposed to video. This is due to the high use of 16 mm film, which has brought the cost down. Tape is used mostly when shooting more than 60 testimonies throughout the course of a day or when the production budget has to be under $20,000.

On the low end, you can launch into DRTV for under $60,000, including both production and media. On the high end, a DRTV campaign launch can cost $150,000 or more.

Decide where to run the infomercial.

Prior to production, a media plan is submitted, outlining when and where the commercial is to be aired and at what cost. Once the schedule is approved, the time is purchased.

Generally, media are purchased at a discounted price because DRTV commercials run at the discretion of the TV stations (residual time). This way of buying is changing as more and more companies are buying a combination of fixed time and residual times.

Another way to buy airtime is on a per-inquiry (PI) basis. Basically, you negotiate with TV stations to run the commercial at no charge, and you pay only when an order is received. Many stations request an up-front fee as a guarantee. Other stations will not accept PIs at all. Strategically, PIs are a small portion of the DRTV buy or are used when seeking no more than 10,000 inquiries a year.

Track efficiency.

Based on the media buy, each commercial sent out must be assigned separate phone numbers so that the efficiency of each station can be tracked. For example, station "XYX" gets 1-800/123-4444 while station "ZYW" gets 1-800/123-7777.

There are exceptions. American Express uses 1-800/THE CARD on both its DRTV and general advertising commercials. This allows the number to be burned into the mind of the customer.

Usually, 80 percent of the calls are received within an hour after the commercial runs.

The telemarketing operator follows a script preapproved by the client. Recently client Y simplified its script, and response rates increased 20 percent.

Susan Goodrich's Coda

Does the product have mass appeal?

TV is a mass medium, reaching more households in the United States than any other medium. Furthermore, it is often difficult to target DRTV since it is sold at discounted rates, in large rotations, and with no guarantee of even airing! Since you are usually paying to reach a large and diverse audience, products with a mass appeal are more likely to work. Products that depend on a narrow target demographic incur a lot of waste when using DRTV, and are usually better off with a more targeted medium.

Is the product demonstrable?

Products that can reap big benefits from a visual demonstration will of course benefit from TV. While TV may be a more expensive medium than others (in terms of cost per thousand), it offers the unique advantage of showing the product in action. *Action* is a broad term here; some products that cannot be demonstrated may still rely on and benefit from heartfelt testimonials to close a sale.

Can the product be produced/fulfilled in large quantities?

Since TV has such a large reach, the point of using TV is to achieve volume sales. The profit per sale is usually low and therefore depends on high sales volume to make the venture worthwhile.

Can the product be produced for 25 percent or less of the selling price?

The cost to make the typical TV product is 25 percent or less of the selling price—e.g., a product that sells for $19.95 costs less than $5.00 to make.

Can you make a profit if the media cost per sale is half of your selling price?

A rule of thumb in the DRTV business is that a successful product can expect a marketing cost that is equal to half the selling price. For example, a product that sells for $19.95 would be considered successful if the TV advertising generated sales at $10.00 per order. In other words, a $100.00 air would have to generate 10 sales, or $199.50 worth of income. The target cost per order for your TV spending should therefore be half the selling price; similarly, the target return for income should be twice the TV spending, a two-to-one ratio.

Can you make a profit based on these financials?

Using a $19.95 product as an example, here's what you can expect from a successful campaign:

- TV media cost per sale: $10.00
- Answering service cost per sale: 2.50
- Cost to produce the product: 5.00
- Cost to amortize creative: 1.00
- Credit card fee: .80
- Total expenses: $19.30

- Income: $19.95
- Profit $ .65

Notes: The TV media cost includes the agency commission. The answering service cost includes taking credit card information and includes amortizing the costs associated with nonorders (inquiries, etc). The cost to produce the product includes royalties, etc. The cost to amortize creative refers to the expense incurred in making the TV spot or infomercial.

All costs associated with fulfillment are extra and would be covered by the postage and handling charge, which is always an add-on to the selling price. This should be considered when determining the appropriate postage and handling charge—which is often set high enough to allow for a little more profit.

Determining an acceptable cost per lead for lead-generating programs depends on conversion and the price of the product. Mass market lower-cost products can generate leads as low as $3 each; higher-cost products can tolerate CPLs of $20 or more. You must work with the test results, including the back end, to develop a model or formula that works for your particular product.

Are you prepared to set up a back end?

Given the small profit made on TV sales in the preceding ideal situation, many DRTV campaigns look to the back end for the real profit. In fact, some DRTV advertisers try for only a breakeven on the front end, to obtain the names needed for back-end database marketing. Back-end marketing consists of continuity programs, add-ons, upsells, and affinity products. Many companies sell the TV names to list companies.

Can you afford a heavy front-end investment?

All infomercial time and some spot time is payable to stations at least a week in advance, or the station will preempt the schedule. The creative cost is also incurred up front. Therefore the start-up expenses are quite high as you begin to roll out.

Are you willing to commit time and money to doing it right?

The media buying side of direct-response TV includes much, much more than just buying the time. Critical to a successful campaign are planning, tracking, and managing the buys so as to optimize results. This not only requires hiring a professional DRTV buyer but also means assigning the job of daily reviews and coordination to someone within your own company. The latter is often a full-time job organizing the setup and remains full-time if the project is successful and continues to a rollout.

Planning

Length.

Determine the type of ad: short form (30, 60, 90, or 120 seconds) vs. long form (half-hour infomercial). As a rule of thumb, short form is best for lead generating and products priced at $29.95 or less. Within short form, most stations sell all lengths, but the 30- and 60-second ads often get better clearance and may be necessary to air on major national cables. However, 120s have traditionally done better responsewise than the shorter length. The half-hour program length is best for complicated products, those that need longer demonstrations, and higher-priced products that require more sell. Most stations now sell infomercial time, although the available half-hour slots each week may be limited.

Strategy.

Test, test, and test again! Because direct response is so measurable, you can test different offers and price points and continually tweak the creative, the offer, the price points, and the media selection as you expand the test, until you have the best format to roll out.

Test plan.

An ideal test will take place over a one- to two-week period; will include 10 markets (one station each, various affiliations) of diverse size and location, plus a couple of national cable stations; and should utilize all day parts (daytime, late night, weekend, etc).

Budget.

The media cost for the initial two-week test should be in the $10,000-to-$15,000 range. This is enough to test the waters. If the results are terrific, roll out! If they are awful, consider cutting your losses and moving on. However, if you are anywhere in between, analyze the results data to identify which areas show promise (e.g., the best day parts, the best part of the country, etc.) and test again with your newfound knowledge as a guide. Also, continue tweaking the offer, upsells, etc., until you have a successful formula. Media costs for this stage should be an additional $10,000 to $25,000.

Rollout.

The safest way to go is to increase spending by $25,000 to 50,000 per week; a major rollout may go as high as $500,000 per week. However, if your "window of opportunity" is limited due to seasonality of the product or other limitations, it is not unusual to roll out much faster.

Buying

Target demographic.

Always reference results for products with a similar demographic if available and buy stations with a proven track record. If not, use Nielsen data to determine which stations have the best reach at the lowest cost per thousand (CPM) for your demographic—that is, stations with the most efficient delivery of the products' target demographic.

Note: It is easier to identify a target audience for spot buys, which air within programs that have a rating history. Infomercials, on the other hand, replace regular programs and therefore have no rating history. Infomercials attract their own audience from channel surfers, so it is more difficult to target the buy.

Negotiate, negotiate, negotiate.

Direct response rates are based mainly on supply and demand and can vary considerably from quarter to quarter and even week to week. DR time is usually "distress" (unsold) inventory and is priced lower than the rate a traditional advertiser (non-DR) would pay. Keep in mind that virtually any station can pay out if it is priced low enough.

DR time is preemptible.

Since DRTV time is discounted, it may be preempted by an advertiser willing to pay a higher rate. For spot, you can expect 25 to 80 percent of the time you book to be preempted, so buy more than you plan to air. The preemption level is one of the most difficult things to predict and changes constantly, but is usually lowest in first quarter, followed by third, second, and fourth. Infomercial bookings are more reliable in that only 10 percent or less of the time you book is liable to be preempted.

DR spot time is sold in rotations.

Also known as *blocks* or *day parts,* these are broad time periods such as "Monday through Friday, 9:00 A.M. to 4:00 P.M." When estimating your audience, assume you will air in the lowest-rated program within the time period, because this is most likely to be what's left as distress inventory. Sample all the time periods that appear cost-effective for your demographic. A typical spot schedule would be 10 to 15 airs per week, with 75 to 85 percent booked Monday to Friday and the rest over the weekend.

DR infomercial time is specific.

Of course, infomercial time is sold date and time specific (e.g., Monday, July 1, at 8:00 A.M.). Keep in mind that infomercial rates are based on audience viewing levels at different times of day and year.

The best time of the year for DRTV is the first quarter.

Schedules are usually bought on a quarterly basis, three months at a time. Each quarter's pricing and availability are affected by the supply and demand for airtime by traditional advertisers.

As a rule, the best part of the year for DRTV is first quarter (1Q— Jan/Feb/Mar) because audience levels are highest and rates are lowest. The next-best area is 3Q (Jul/Aug/Sep) because rates are low but audience levels are not as high as during 1Q. Next comes 2Q (Apr/May/Jun), when audience levels begin to decline due to improved weather but rates increase because traditional advertisers start to advertise more heavily than during 1Q. Unless your product makes a good Christmas gift, 4Q (Oct/Nov/Dec) may be the toughest to crack since rates are at their highest due to high demand from traditional advertisers; audience levels start increasing again at this time of year, but most consumers are focused on Christmas spending.

The seasonality of the product is important to consider as well: if your product is related only to summer activities, it doesn't make much sense to advertise it in 1Q just because the rates are lower.

Reach and frequency are not as crucial in DRTV as in traditional TV.

It is hard to target these parameters since preemptions are such a big factor in DRTV. Think of each air as a stand-alone display with the consumer walking by; it has to reach out and grab the customer right then and there. Frequency of airing will improve results some 10 to 25 percent early in a campaign; very high frequency eventually results in wearout and a diminishing return for each air. When wearout sets in on a station, it's time to con-sider reach; add new time periods, new stations, or new markets.

Tracking Response

Track response in terms that are appropriate.

Typically results are measured in terms of cost per order (CPO), cost per lead (CPL), and income-to-cost ratio (return). CPO may be based on credit card orders only or may include mail orders as well. CPL is used for lead-generating campaigns; if orders are also tracked, a conversion of leads to orders is often included in results (e.g., a 20 percent conversion means that 20 percent of the leads turned into sales). The return expresses sales income in ratio-to-media cost (e.g., a $1,000 air that generates $1,700 in income has a return ratio of 1.7 to 1, or 170 percent).

Correct sourcing is crucial to a successful campaign.

Do not use an answering service that does not have experience with sourc-ing TV leads. Use an answering service bureau that can supply hourly media counts on a daily basis, reporting all calls/orders for a given day by station, by hour. The calls/orders are "sourced" to a station by using dif-ferent 800 numbers for different stations. The answering service bureau uses equipment and computers that identify the 800 number the caller dialed, compares it to the list of stations assigned to that number, and decides which station generated the call by matching the caller's zip code to the station's coverage areas.

Measure results for each and every air, station by station.

Once you have this data, you can quickly identify which stations (and which time periods on those stations) are profitable and which ones are not. Note that not all response comes in at the time of the air; drag calls may come in for days and even weeks after an air. People will write down the number and think about ordering for a while before calling or get a busy signal at first and call back later, for example. Drag calls often make the difference between an air paying out and not and must be attributed to the air that generated them. This difficult assignment relies on experienced buyers/managers who know how to identify response patterns for different stations and time periods.

Database all results.

Once you have this information databased, you can sort it in different ways to identify the larger patterns at work. For example, sort your results by time period, market size, market geography, station affiliation, etc. You may find that mainly small markets work, or only southern markets, or mostly late-night time periods, or just weekends.

Track results on a daily basis.

Don't wait until the week or the test is over to assess results. Campaigns usu-ally improve as they gain frequency, but keep in mind that the "race is to the swift." The faster you can identify and manage winning and losing stations, the better your overall results will be.

Mail orders don't count.

Or, don't count your chickens before they hatch! Only 10 to 25 percent of people who say they will send a check actually do so. Therefore, don't count mail-order "promises" as results—wait until the check is in the bank before you count it. Don't plan a rollout based on mail-order hopes, wait until you have the real data.

Track inquiries.

These are the calls (also called *customer service calls*) that don't become a credit card order or a mail order. These should never outnumber total orders. Examining the main reasons for inquiries can help you identify a problem with your creative or the offer or the fulfillment.

Response is inconsistent.

Keep in mind that TV is not a static medium with the same circulation week after week. Audiences are in constant motion, and even the same daily program will get changing audience levels throughout the week. Therefore, you cannot expect response to remain constant for the same air or station. While you are databasing response for each air, you need to calculate the average response for a station or time period before you can act on it.

Managing results

Negotiate, negotiate, negotiate.

Once again, this is the key to successful direct-response campaigns. No matter how successful your campaign may be, there will be stations and time periods within stations that are not profitable. Negotiate lower rates based on the response you need to pay out.

For example, an air costing $100 generates five orders for a CPO of $20. You need a CPO of $15 to be profitable, so you can afford to pay $75 for the spot (5 orders times $15 each). If the station can accommodate you at a lower rate (i.e., it has enough excess inventory), it will agree. If not, you can cancel that time period. Also, since DRTV is usually sold in rotations, you may find that only certain programs within a rotation pay out; in this case you may negotiate by keeping the rate the same but trying to narrow the rotation to the successful program(s).

Manage quickly.

A station's response rarely improves more than 10 percent as a result of frequency—and bad stations usually just get worse. Waiting and hoping for improvement is often costly. Start cutting back the really poor performers within a week. Begin negotiating as soon as you see poor results. Note that spot TV time can usually be canceled or renegotiated with two business days' notice; infomercial time usually requires two calendar weeks' notice.

Identify patterns.

Database and combine your response so as to identify patterns that work. This will then dictate the best way to roll out. For example, if only weekends are working for you, plan to buy mainly weekends as you roll out.

Note the difference between response and results.

The response refers to the number of calls and orders and income you get when you air; results take those numbers and relate them to the cost of the air. For example, an air that costs $100.00 and gets 10 orders has a $10.00 CPO. If the cost for the same air increased to $125.00, but the response remained constant at 10 orders, your result would be $12.50 an order. Your response did not fall off, but your results got worse due to the rate increase. Determining why your cost is up is crucial to taking the right steps to optimize your profit.

Volume of response is driven by the target.

The higher your target CPO/CPL, the more stations you can carry and the more orders or leads you can generate. Conversely, the lower you set the target, the fewer the orders at target.

Watch for certain hallmarks of a successful campaign.

First, look for two-thirds of the stations to pay out in the first week. Once you cancel and renegotiate the losers, you can generally amortize down the first week's results to cume at target unless you start off with less than two-thirds of the stations totaling at your target. Another indicator of a successful campaign is good drag, that is, people keep calling to order. Third, expect good management to improve your overall results by a maximum of 25 percent, which means you need to be within at least 75 percent of your target at the beginning of a campaign. Finally, when credit card orders outnumber mail orders and constitute 50 percent or more of all calls, you have a successful campaign.

There are only two mistakes you can make in managing DRTV: (1) generating too few orders at a great (low) CPO and (2) getting too many orders at a bad (high) CPO.

There are only three ways to improve your results: (1) negotiate lower rates, (2) buy new stations/markets, and (3) try new creative or offers.

Be prepared for the law of diminishing returns to kick in.

Don't be fooled into thinking success will last forever. Constant vigilance is necessary to keep your initial profit from turning into a long-term loss. Stations wear out over time. Expect to renegotiate or cancel and replace them with new ones. Creatives get tired, generating less and less response. Always have new creative on hand to inject new life into a campaign. Finally, products wear out. It is important to know when to call it quits.

Use an agency that has DRTV experience.

Agencies and buyers that have experience only with traditional buying are not prepared to handle the complexities of planning, buying, tracking, and managing direct-response television. Make sure the company you use has a functional computerized tracking system in place; ask to see the kinds of reports you will be getting and find out how often and how quickly you will be receiving them. An experienced DRTV agency can maximize your profits if your product is successful and conversely will cut your losses quickly if it is not.

Envelopes

 Everything within the system that gets put into the mail, from solicitation mailings to letters to bills, gets wrapped in an envelope. The tips in this chapter apply to all kinds of envelopes holding all kinds of notices, offers, and promotions.

Herschell Gordon Lewis's Precept
The only purpose of the carrier envelope, other than keeping its contents from spilling out onto the street, is to get itself opened.

Axel Andersson's Formula
Spelling out the offer on the envelope is a dangerous ploy in mailings to cold lists.

> According to freelancer and author Herschell Gordon Lewis, you cannot make a sales case on the envelope. The only purpose of the envelope is to get the mailing opened. For example: "Save 20% on Your Automobile Insurance" is of interest only to people who have been bothered by the thought that they are paying too much for automobile insurance. A far stronger headline (and promise): "Put $200 cash in your pocket next week!"

Jay M. Jaffe's Tip
For insurance offers, envelopes that have an official look are more likely to be opened.

Gary Halbert's Reminder
Remember that people sort their mail into two piles, the A pile and the B pile, and your goal is to get your mailing into the A pile.

> The A pile is the important stuff: letters from the kid in college, notes from the IRS, social security checks, insurance premium notices, and bills. This is

the mail that must be dealt with first. Everything else goes into the B pile and can wait.

To get your messages into the A pile, never use a window envelope. Instead, the name and address should be typed personally (or handwritten) on the front of a plain, closed-face (nonwindow) envelope. Always use a stamp (as opposed to a printed indicia). And never put promotional copy on the front of the envelope, because that signals junk mail, something that can be dealt with later or not at all. The only allowable copy is a return address in the upper left-hand corner.

Bill Jayme's Dissent
Never disguise the fact that it is advertising mail.

Your outer envelope is where your prospect decides whether to stop, look, and listen. It's the come-on—the headline on the ad, the cover of the catalog, the dust jacket on the book, the display window outside the store, . . .

This holds true for the business arena as well. Any competent secretary can recognize bulk mail. The secret to overcoming the "secretary barrier" is to create an envelope that looks interesting.

Comment by Denny Hatch: Who's right: Halbert or Jayme?

In the more-than-200 long-term controls isolated and analyzed by Axel Andersson and me—mailings that proved successful over a period of three or more consecutive years—not one fit the Halbert model.

Richard Armstrong's Reconciliation
Halbert and Jayme are both right.

The apparent conflict results from Halbert's not having thought through his A-pile/B-pile theory thoroughly enough. Gary is right that people separate their mail into A piles and B piles, but he has failed to notice two important points: (1) Junk mail letters with loud teasers occasionally get into the A pile (especially when it's extremely well-targeted; for example, I'm interested in casino gambling, and all my casino gambling junk mail immediately goes into my A pile). (2) In most cases the B pile does not go directly into the wastebasket but is subjected to a second sorting. Some people do sort their mail directly over the trash can, but this is not as common as many of us in the business fear. It's the second sort that allows well-written teaser headlines for commercial and fundraising efforts to do their job.

If I had to bet my life on the success of a direct mail package, I'd do it the way Halbert suggests. But in the real world, where we're usually betting only money (not lives), the Jayme model often proves to work best at a lower financial risk.

Pat Farley's Approach

Fight with clients who want you to start selling or presenting the product on the envelope; they don't understand that the envelope's job is to get opened, not to sell.

Lea Pierce's Model

All direct mail gets opened over the trash can.

> You have three seconds to live or die. Devote as much time to your outer envelope as to the rest of the package.

Malcolm Decker's Doctrine

Your envelope stands between you and orders.

> More prospects see your envelopes than will ever see what's inside them. So make sure your envelope not only carries the message but also does everything possible to set up the sale.

Pat Friesen's Six Outer Envelope Hot Spots

Corner card/return address.

Addressing—window, label, computer, handwritten.

Postage.

Teaser copy.

Back envelope flap.

Back teaser copy.

"Rocket" Ray Jutkins: Dr. Vogele's Five Truths About Envelopes

> People first look at their name.
> If it is spelled correctly, if the initials and title are right, the envelope is for them!

> The second thing people look at is the teaser copy.
> They look especially at the teaser copy that is close to their name and then at teaser copy elsewhere on the envelope.

The third thing people do is look at who sent them this piece of mail.
"What person, company, or organization sent me this piece of ad mail?" This
shows how important the corner card of your ad mail envelope is.

Next is the type of postage and how it is applied.
Most often live stamps get the most attention and meter mail gets the least.

The fifth thing people do is turn your envelope over.
Three out of four people who touch your ad mail envelope will turn it over
before opening.

What does all this say? It says the following questions need to be answered
on your envelope:

- Is this ad mail package for me?
- What is it all about?
- Who is it from?

Jutkins's Four Possible Actions People Can Take When They Receive Mail

They open it immediately.
If it's important, interesting, and something about it gets their attention
immediately, they open it at once.

Or they put it in the stack to read at night or on weekends.
If it's interesting but not important, it can wait. And how many of us are
caught up with our nighttime and weekend reading stack?

They route it to somebody else.
When it seems not for them but for someone else, they circulate it to another.
This happens at home as well as in the office.

They round-file it.
They simply throw it away. And what's most interesting is that the decision
to take one of these four actions—read it, stack it, route it, or toss it—takes
place in just two or three seconds per piece of mail. This says your offer better be good and better be interesting!

Denny Hatch's Precept
Always have envelope tests in the mail.

With very few exceptions, direct mail packages tire over time and results begin
to flag. When people have seen the same envelope come in over and over again,

whether or not they read the package the first time, they say, "Oh, I've seen this before," and pitch it.

Clothe your package in a new envelope, and you've got a shot at those folks who dismissed the first version based on the envelope alone and who never read the contents.

When Rapp & Collins superstar writer Emily Soell wrote the launch package for *Condé Nast Traveler,* it became a five-year control. Whenever results started to flag, the color of the envelope was changed and it was once again unbeatable. I saw it in red, yellow, green, blue, white, black, and polywrap.

Fulfillment

Fulfillment is the key function in the direct marketing process. At this point in the process you are delivering on all the promises you have made. For some reason fulfillment historically has been allocated to a nebulous area called *operations*. In fact, fulfillment is a market function.

The Gospel According to Bill Christensen
The sale begins when the customer says yes.

When you get an order, you can't simply send product a week later. The customer will have forgotten. Rather, you must reexcite the customer by reselling the customer. This is the absolute key to all marketing, direct or other. In the case of a magazine where the subscriber comes in on a soft offer (e.g., "Take a free issue and then decide"), the conversion (billing) efforts must be created by a professional.

The copywriter whose work brought in a subscriber from a particular list or database should be the one who sends all follow-up correspondence from the magazine so that the subscriber is handled by the copywriter who successfully made the initial sale.

The dean of American freelancers, Bill Jayme, once told me that he wrote the launch packages for 39 magazines. "I was writing to my people," Jayme said. "I know them, and they respond to me."

When Jayme is hired to launch a magazine, the editor tells him what articles and features will be in the magazine, but frequently Jayme ignores the editor and slots in his own ideas. As a result, the magazine can end up shaped more by Jayme than by the publisher or editor. "I know what these people want to read," he says. "I know what will get them to subscribe."

Marilyn Black's Rule of Product Excellence
When the product arrives, ideally it should be better than what the customer expected.

Denny Hatch's Corollary
When the product arrives, it should be ready to use.

When the product arrives, the customer should be able to plug it in and listen to it or watch it, wear it, hang it on the wall and admire it, or open it and read it. Clothing that needs to be altered, a radio that needs batteries, a picture with no frame may sit around for a while, increasing the chances of returns and reducing your chances of getting paid.

Don Jackson's Caveat
Make sure the product is accompanied by instructions clear enough for an idiot.

Before you commit to the final fulfillment package, make up five dummies that include the product and all the accompanying literature and give them to five strangers as a test. If all five get the product up and running with as little fuss as possible, go with the package.

Denny Hatch's Law
The length of time it takes for the product to arrive is inversely proportional to the probability of retention and payment.

The longer it takes the product to arrive, the less memory the person will have of having ordered it and the greater the chance it will be returned.

Hearst magazines has a caveat on all subscription order cards: "Please allow 6 to 8 weeks for delivery of your first issue." Think of it! With the same hardware that put men on the moon, Hearst takes up to two months to deliver a magazine! So you fall in love with the copy and the offer. You send in the reply card for your free issue. Then nothing for three months. Suddenly, out of the blue, you get an issue of a magazine you don't remember ordering, followed by a series of bills.

This is *not* as it should be.

Coleman Williams Hoyt's Three Immutable Rules for Keeping Customers

If you want to get paid, date the outside of your billing envelopes.
It amazes me how many major mailers have still not caught on to this obvious secret. If you don't believe this, test it—or look at your own personal bills. Chances are the bills you open and pay last are the undated ones. Putting a date on your outgoing billing envelope is the easiest way to collect your outstanding accounts receivable a week (or a billing cycle) sooner.

If you want to prevent angry customers, post their payments like lightning.
One axiom in this business is to spend money setting up a system for shipping an order fast; a less well-known but equally powerful axiom is to spend money setting up a system to prevent unnecessary follow-up bills, by posting payments *fast*. Remember that "claims paid" is the most common customer complaint.

If you want repeat customers, acknowledge their orders immediately.
This is especially true if it will take time to get the product delivered to the customer. Sure, you say, that's obvious. But far too many companies in the direct-response business remain sloppy about letting customers know that their order has been received and is on its way, with *thanks*.

Karen Boyle's Dozen Ways to Wreck Your Fulfillment

Offer material that you don't actually have on hand yet.
Prepare fulfillment material ahead of time. Don't advertise your products until you know you can deliver. Don't offer premiums or information pieces until you have them on the shelf.

Provide reply cards or coupons which allow illegible, handwritten address information.
Preprint names and addresses on mail reply cards. Provide boxes to check if possible. Leave plenty of space and say, "Please type or print."

Fulfill when convenient or "as practical."
Stipulate fulfillment within 48 business hours. Follow up by phone. Tell inquirers, "I called to let you know that your material will be in the mail tomorrow. Is there any way I can help now?"

Fulfill with confusing material.
Example: printed folders containing information about an entire line without highlighting the specific information requested. Send a personalized letter with direct references both to the source of the inquiry and to the specific product of interest.

Spend big money to get each inquiry, then send a cheap response to inquirers.
Responders' names are far more valuable than when they were only suspects on the original list. Treat them that way.

Refer inquirers to the wrong dealers or distributors.
Use a fulfillment computer program to identify your closest outlet to each prospect.

Promise a follow-up without actually providing one.
Don't promise any personal follow-ups if you can't control them. Furnish an 800 number so the prospect can call a knowledgeable individual for information.

Fail to follow up regularly by mail, by phone, or in person.
Remember, prospects often inquire long before they buy.

Fail to build a database of responders containing everything you know about them.
Learn all you can about the characteristics of these qualified prospects. Use and profit from the database you develop.

Ignore new techniques such as fax and on-line computer services that can potentially improve fulfillment speed or costs.
Get expert help to match new technology to your needs and budget as quickly as practical.

Let unskilled people handle requests.
Make sure your fulfillment is handled by a fast, accurate, trained, and professional fulfillment service.

Do fulfillment yourself, sharing a computer with accounting or some other department.
For fulfillment, use a specialist dedicated to customer service or devote an entire department with its own equipment to fulfillment functions.

Fundraising

Fundraising has used the processes, techniques, and media of the direct marketing concept with enormous efficiency and effect. The volume of good that has been generated is difficult to measure. It was the application of the direct marketing concept that moved fundraising from the drawing rooms of the very rich into the living rooms of regular folks. From the integrated techniques of the Jerry Lewis Telethon to the on-air auctions conducted by PBS to the in-the-mail appeal for dozens of charities and organizations, post–World War II America has opened its heart and its collective pocketbooks to help where help is needed.

Roger Craver's Three Principles

You need a streak of outrage. You need a sense of injustice. Without outrage, I don't know how the hell you can do this work.

Always say thank you; it's the polite thing to do.

Donors are continuity buyers of ideas.

Max Hart's Accumulated Wisdom

The Five Only Ways to Increase Net Income

Reduce mailing cost.

Increase the average contribution.

Increase the percent response.

Increase the mailing frequency.

Increase the donor base.

Max Hart's Three Ways to Increase Average Contributions

Copy can influence the percent of response and/or average contribution.
Good emotional copy will motivate donors to give more. Disabled American Veterans tests five or six pieces of copy on each major mailing. The *average* contribution differential can vary from a few cents to as much as a dollar on certain donor categories. This translates into millions of dollars for DAV. Maximizing your net income through the use of the best possible copy is important. We cannot overemphasize testing and the use of the most productive copy money can buy.

Upgrade through personalization.
For a number of years, DAV has mailed highly personalized upgrade mailing called Commanders Club. The suggested upgrade is by table lookup with the lowest of two suggested donations being 50 percent greater than the donor's last contribution to the DAV.

Use premiums, long one of the most powerful incentives employed by nonprofits to increase results.
First, let's differentiate between a front-end and a back-end premium. Front-end premiums—also known as "freemiums"—are inserted in the mailing package, so a contribution is not required to receive them. Back-end premiums are available only to those who respond. Many nonprofit organizations do not have the pulling power to succeed in their fundraising effort through a straight appeal solicitation (letter, reply form, brochure, and reply envelope), so they must turn to promotional techniques such as sweepstakes, matching check programs, and premiums.

Max Hart's Seven Rules for Using Premiums

Use premiums that have a logical tie-in with your organization.
DAV's best successes in back-end premiums were with historical or patriotic books. Name-and-address stickers with the American flag have been one of the most powerful front-end premiums used by the DAV over the years. Heavy emphasis has been placed on red, white, and blue in our graphics, which is in keeping for a veterans' organization with a patriotic heritage.

Use premiums with the highest perceived value at the lowest cost.
This usually occurs with printed matter, such as name stickers, certificates, cards, seals, newsletters, pamphlets—in general, ink on paper. Intangible premiums also meet this qualification, such as memorial books, special masses, listing on honor rolls, and listings in special newsletters or bulletins. Do not confuse *low cost* with *poor quality*.

Feature the premium in the copy.

Use four-color printing and first-quality graphics. Copy should be developed around the premium offer, particularly if there is a logical association between your organization and the premium.

Use premiums that require periodic replacement.

Consumable items such as greeting cards and name stickers, which necessitate resupply, are usually well received, and subsequent mailings are actually welcomed by the donor or potential donor. Replacement can also be created by dating the year of membership on membership cards or certificates given to special recognition groups to encourage renewal. Personalization is highly effective on premiums. People like to see their name in print.

Provide quality premiums.

A good print job generally does not cost any more than one of poor quality. A poor-quality certificate will definitely hurt future renewals and stimulate complaint mail.

Use premiums only when cost-effective.

This goes back to the old adage of "spending money to make money." Make sure your return on investment justifies the additional expense. Do not simply insert or offer premiums because you think it is clever strategy.

Be able to fulfill on the premium offer.

It is important to fulfill your commitment in a timely manner, so give thought to fulfillment when you offer a premium.

Max Hart's 15 Membership Strategies

Offer free months.

The highly personalized copy reads: "Gerald, I've already enclosed your membership card because I'm confident you'll like the DAV once you've tried it. Yes, I'm giving you four free months of DAV membership with no obligation." We go on to offer an additional year of membership for only $10, which is discounted from regular dues of $15 to $35, depending on the state and chapter. This strategy brought in 44,000 new members on a 900,000 mailing. The budget was $320,000 and produced first-year dues of $4,000 with a lifetime dues value of $4 million.

Save!

A powerful word. "Save 40 percent on the first year dues of $8.95 and 50 percent on $14.95 for two years." The two-year option did four times better than the one-year offer.

Easy payment terms and discounts.

Three hundred thousand DAV annual members were offered a "Deal You Can't Refuse" on life memberships. The teaser copy featured a $20 discount voucher. There is that word *discount* again. The copy read: "Edward, this year I'm sending you a part-life membership card . . . not an annual membership card . . . because I've got a deal you can't refuse." Life memberships range from $150 to $75, depending on age. In Edward's case, it was $100. When the $20 savings voucher was deducted, the cost came down to $80. Edward's annual dues were $12, so for a down payment and eight easy quarterly payments of $8.50 each, Edward had us off his back forever. This mailing to 307,000 annual members brought in 48,000 new life members and renewed the annual memberships of 15,000 members. Lifetime dues volume was $5.8 million on a budget of $122,000.

Use premiums.

See "Seven Rules for Using Premiums" on page 172.

Incentive programs work.

"What do the big guys do?" is a center spread in the DAV magazine offering premiums ranging from a leather bomber jacket for recruiting 50 new members to a quill pen for only two new members.

Sweepstakes can work, too.

DAV has also successfully used sweepstakes for both membership renewal and acquisition.

Try personalization.

We have referred to the prospective member's home state, the number of disabled vets in the prospect's city, the name of the nearest DAV chapter, the exact amount of a life membership based on the prospective member's age, the war era served, issues and services relevant to the war era served, the nearest DAV office telephone number, and the DAV membership strength in the state.

Perhaps the most technically difficult use of personalization by DAV on a membership solicitation was a "Member-Get-a-Member" mailing in 1984. We matched 556,880 eligible prospects against the DAV active member file and brought together the nearest member and prospect. For this example, we asked Oliver Hanger, who lived near Thomas Rockfor in Alaska, to contact Thomas and ask Thomas to join the DAV. The application had Thomas Rockfor's name and address prelasered. All Oliver had to do was complete the balance of information and return it with Thomas's dues check.

Action devices have increased results.

We have used yes-no pressure-sensitive labels tipped on the outside of the carrier envelope, which are affixed to the reply form and the DAV seal, which was transferred to the reply envelope.

The National Audubon Society also used a pressure-sensitive label action device on the outgoing envelope, which is placed on the acceptance (reply) form to receive a free backpack. Other strategies included a tipped-on membership card and a special introductory membership for $20, which is $10 off the regular membership.

Don't overlook Post-It notes.

Although DAV has not tested them, I really like the personalized simulated Post-It notes used by the American Institute for Cancer Research on its annual fund mailing. This note reads, "Mr. Hart, I hope we can count on you this year! Marilyn." Marilyn is Marilyn Gentry, Executive Director of the institute.

The Smithsonian Institution also used a personalized note directed to Max Hart from its publisher, Ron Walker, which reads, "Since the invitation enclosed includes several months of *Smithsonian,* I want you to know that we make every issue a totally fresh experience in the wonder of discovery. For that alone is surely ample reason to accept this special offer."

Max Hart's Six Strategies That Didn't Work

Name your own deal.

"I'm so sure you'll like the DAV, I'll give you special membership through June 30th at whatever price you think it's worth!" was a bomb.

Totally free membership.

"We'll give you a free membership for a year. Just check the free option and return the reply form."

Cartoon.

The cartoon said: "Hart! You don't need all these benefits, do you?" This also had the four free months options with an additional year for $10.

Desert camouflage didn't make it.

Free copy of the magazine.

Polybagged free issue of the DAV monthly magazine also bombed.

Penny mailing with a penny taped on was a disaster.

The strategy was to equate DAV membership to pennies a day. Perhaps we should have used a dime.

Max Hart's Seven Tips for Small Nonprofit Mailers

Desktop publishing places recognition devices such as certificates within the production capability and budget of the smallest mailers.

Intangible premiums such as honor roll book listings for minimum contributions are relatively easy and inexpensive to produce.

Name sticker mailings can be produced economically in relatively small quantities.
We handle a turnkey program for your state organizations to approximately 500,000 members, which goes in the mail for $200/M including postage.

Comment: The date of this material was March 19, 1992.

Word processors and desktop laser printers allow small mailers to upgrade through personalization.

Monthly pledge programs are applicable to small mailers.

Small mailers should segment and purge low donors at an early point in time.

Upgrading can be augmented through notes or simulated Post-It notes.

Bob Stone's Formula
You will collect far more money in a fundraising effort if you ask for a specific amount from a purchaser.

Likewise, you will collect more money if the appeal is tied to a specific project.

Mal Warwick's Seven Challenges Facing Direct Mail Fundraisers

The successful fundraiser will point out that the starting point in planning a direct mail fundraising program is where the process ends—on the back end.
The catchall phrase *back end* refers to the tasks of caging, cashiering, and acknowledging donors that an organization relates to the majority of its donors. In this interface, the bulk of the list—the organization's most valuable asset, which it built and nurtured, and its lifeblood, the donors—is introduced to the organization's daily conduct.

All too few nonprofit organizations have database management systems that permit them to record and update gift histories in a timely and consistent manner. Inaccurate and outdated addresses accumulate. Duplicate records multiply unchecked. Unresponsive prospects linger, year after year, devouring precious resources as they receive (and ignore) mailing after mailing.

If the back-end functions aren't firmly in place before the first direct mail appeal wends its way to the post office, much of the value of the mailing may be lost.

Even among nonprofit organizations with detailed individual donor histories at their fingertips, far too few make effective use of the information by segmenting their mailings.

Much more commonly, nonprofits heedlessly mail the same generic appeal to everyone on the house file, every time they mail—and often ask all their donors for the same generic amount of money (assuming they ask for any specific amount at all!).

"Mailing smart" requires cutting costs by mailing less frequently to a list's least productive segments—and spending more money on the most productive segments with more frequent mailings and telephone contacts, using first-class postage and personalization techniques and providing lots of information to the best prospects.

Few nonprofit organizations of any level of sophistication have determined the long-term value of their donors.

Most nonprofit trustees and executives still look on direct mail fundraising in the most simplistic terms—as a way to raise money *this* year to meet today's budgetary needs. Donors' attrition, the long-term costs of donor cultivation, and upgrading rarely receive attention. Similarly, few nonprofits focus on the substantial long-term prospects for major gifts from direct mail–acquired donors or members. But no direct mail fundraising program can achieve its full potential without a deep understanding of both the costs and benefits involved.

Despite years of rising postal and production costs, increasing competition, and generally declining response rates, nonprofit leaders still typically expect that donor or member acquisition programs will, at the very least, break even.

The notion of *investing* seems foreign to most charities. They're limiting their prospects for growth, of course—even sometimes literally dooming themselves to extinction—by insisting rigidly that fundraising mailings make money.

Only by calculating long-term donor value—and comparing it to the short-term cost of acquiring new donors—can any organization determine how much to invest in prospecting. All too often this decision is made arbitrarily, based largely on cash flow requirements.

The prevailing attitude in the nonprofit world is that frequent fundraising appeals are likely to alienate donors—and are wasteful to boot.

"Everyone complains about getting too many fundraising mailings," the argument goes. "And every time we mail a fundraising letter, somebody on our board calls up and chews us out." It's the rare nonprofit executive who understands that a direct mail fundraising program is, first and foremost, a communications effort that requires constant reinforcement, repetition, and cultivation if it's to bear fruit.

Fundraisers are almost always surprised when I cite focus group findings that uniformly show donors underestimate the frequency of mailings they receive from their favorite charities—and that active donors want more frequent opportunities to learn about the organizations they support. (Yes, many of them want more opportunities to give money, too!)

Recent survey research makes it clear that donors want more control over their relationships with the charities they support—including, ideally, the ways in which their gifts are to be used.
Yet less than one nonprofit in a hundred now offers donors the opportunity to request that their names not be rented or exchanged with other organizations. Direct mail fundraisers that have learned this lesson and incorporated this simple donor option into their fund appeals have typically found that only a fraction of donors elect it. And gift earmarking programs are usually thought to be anathema, because they're said to create budgeting nightmares. As United Way has been learning the hard way in workplace giving campaigns, however, today's donors demand choices—and they're more generous if given opportunities to declare their preferences.

Large numbers of donors truly enjoy the fundraising calls they receive from their favorite charities.
If I've heard it once, I've heard it a thousand times: "Our board will never allow us to do telemarketing, because people *hate* to get phone calls like that." I hate to get phone calls like that, too, and I'm in the business! Nevertheless, donors prove their receptiveness to phone solicitations by returning generous gifts, by increasing their response to subsequent direct mail appeals, by renewing their memberships at a faster rate than do members who aren't called, and by remaining active longer. Nonprofit leaders need to learn that their own instincts and preferences aren't often an accurate indicator of the response they can expect from donors.

Mal Warwick's 12 Ways to Combine Direct Mail and Telephone Fundraising

Use the phone to handle new (or renewing, or upgrading) donors—and as soon as possible after you receive their gifts.
Time after time, tests demonstrate that organizations with the foresight to invest in kid-glove treatment of their donors are likely to receive bid dividends for years to come: higher renewal rates, larger gifts, and higher rates of donor retention.

Send a "lead letter"—one that *doesn't* ask for money.
The lead letter states the case and promises the phone call. Or you might promise donors you *won't* call if you receive a gift before a certain date. (In a small-donor variation, you might send a postcard instead of a letter.)

Most of the time, this and other combinations of phone and mail fundraising efforts yield greater net revenue than the sum of isolated direct mail and telephone fundraising campaigns targeting the same donors.

Call in advance of a high-dollar mailing.

The purpose of the advance call is not to ask for money but to thank donors for past support and ask them to watch for letters on the way. This is one more form of donor cultivation; it's been known to work wonders, especially when the message delivered in the advance call includes important or interesting news.

Phone follow-up to a mailing typically doubles response.

Within two weeks of a mailing, a phone call can be used to discuss the issues raised by the letter and to urge that donors send gifts without delay.

If you expect a high enough response and a large enough average donation *without* phone follow-up, this can be the route to increase net revenue greatly.

Phone members (or subscribers) to ask them to renew, either early in a renewal series, to maximize early response and speed up cash flow, or late in the series, to cut telephone costs and maximize response from marginal members.

If there is any single *best* application of telemarketing in the fundraising process, this is probably it. Using the telephone, you can reach more people who have proven highly resistant to direct mail appeals. A strong telephone fundraising program can break even or even raise net dollars from a group of direct mail–acquired members or subscribers on whom you've long since given up.

Use the telephone as recruitment for a monthly sustainer program.

With or without a direct mail lead letter, you can call new (or newly renewed) members or donors and ask that they join a monthly pledge or sustainer program. (In these efforts, an electronic funds transfer [EFT] option may also be introduced smoothly.)

Using the telephone to recruit monthly sustainers may well triple or even quadruple the conversion rate—and the economics of monthly sustainer programs are extremely favorable for organizations with the wit and the wherewithal to set them up. If you assume an average monthly donation of anywhere between $10 and $20—it's around $17 in all programs with which I'm personally familiar—a little simple multiplication will show that you can raise really big bucks with a relatively small investment in telemarketing.

With or without a direct mail lead letter, you can call high-dollar prospects—generally donors who have contributed at least $100 on at least one occasion—to offer membership in an annual giving club at the $250, $500, or $1,000 level.

While my experience at Mal Warwick & Associates and The Progressive Group, Inc., shows that prospects can, indeed, be persuaded to send such donations in response to very special high-dollar direct mail packages, the response rate is typically even higher in a well-run telephone fundraising program. (And a combination of a high-dollar lead letter and a high-dollar follow-up call can be even more productive!)

Use the telephone to announce a special fundraising campaign.

Once leadership gifts have been pledged, you can call your next-best donors or prospects to announce the launching of a capital, endowment, or other special fundraising campaign. The next step is to follow up by mailing materials tailored to donors' gift levels. If necessary, you can phone again to solidify or confirm pledges—and to thank donors for their support.

The special, personalized attention you're able to give donors through a telephone call—which is, after all, genuine person-to-person fundraising—is the next-best thing to a personal visit. And I can think of situations in which a call is even *better* than a visit. (So can many donors!)

Use a mail-phone-mail sequence in place of two or three special appeals.

To launch a short-term fundraising campaign among your membership and achieve maximum impact and the highest possible response rate, you can announce the campaign with a mailing, follow up by phone seven to 10 days later, and mail a second time one month afterward—an appeal to those who haven't responded and a thank-you to those who have. (And don't forget the people for whom you can't get phone numbers or can't reach by phone—or who refuse to pledge by telephone: mail them a special version of your follow-up letter.)

In many situations this may be the optimal combination of mail and phone fundraising techniques. It's the sort of carefully planned and coordinated effort that the very best direct marketers use to sell high-ticket consumer products or business services, but it's all too rare in the fundraising field. Why can't we learn a lesson from our peers in the commercial world?

Dedicate a telephone line for fundraising inquiries—in thank-you letters or in an insider's newsletter for a monthly sustainer program or giving club you can tell donors they may call a special "inside" line in your office to discuss their concerns or ask questions.

National organizations may wish to offer toll-free numbers to high-dollar donors.

The very best time to approach a donor for a new (and bigger) gift is just after you've received the last one!

Within 60 to 90 days of receipt of a new member's first gift—and after the welcome package and the first newsletter have been mailed—you might phone to introduce an important, broadly appealing program and to solicit immediate support. Far fewer than you imagine will resent the request.

Survey top donors by phone.

A few weeks in advance of a major appeal, you can phone your top 50 or top 500 donors. In a conversational but entirely consistent way, ask as many of them as are willing to cooperate to answer a series of predetermined questions about the work of your organization, its image, your fundraising plans and programs. Ask for suggestions about how to improve your operations; don't ask for money.

The information you receive about your donors' perceptions of you and your work may prove to be important; far more important, however, is the information you get about your individual donors' attitudes and preferences. And don't be surprised if a survey of this sort actually proves extraordinarily lucrative; many donors will either send unsolicited gifts after you've talked to them or respond more generously to your next appeal.

Roger Keeling's Standard
With fundraising letters, four pages generally pull better than two, and six generally pull better than four.

This is true despite complaints recipients often voice about long, time-consuming direct mail letters. But you *must* have interesting things to say and *must* be able to sustain momentum; if not, go with a shorter letter. In addition, while a six-pager may pull better than four, it may not always pull better enough to pay for the extra expenses involved.

Explanation: People only rarely read direct mail top to bottom, word for word. They jump around, glance it over, and move on. This, of course, is why we use underlining, headlines, indented paragraphs, bullets, and all the other tricks of our trade.

So, everything else being equal, a four-page letter is *twice* as likely to catch the recipient's eye somewhere as a two-pager.

Even in charitable fundraising the word *free* is the strongest word in the language. I wrote a package for the Sierra Club years ago that did so-so with my first teaser but slammed through control when the teaser was changed to "Your FREE decal enclosed." That package—after dominating for a year or two—bobbed around for several more years, dropping in and out of control. Always the offer of a free decal, stamps, or Sierra Club calendar proved a vital element.

In charitable giving, people are suckers for "bargains" that they can activate on behalf of the cause. Matching grants—wherein a large benefactor or major foundation offers to match dollar for dollar (or, better, two dollars for every dollar) whatever the prospect gives—routinely do well in fundraising. Folks love the idea that their modest $25 or $30 gift will become $50 or $60 or $75 or $90, just like magic.

Roger Keeling's Matching Grant Corollary
The matching grant must be legitimate.

Donors will grow wary or cynical if they learn that the matching grant was in the bag all along. In terms of maximizing response, the absolute best situation is when such a grant really *could* be partially lost if donors don't respond in a timely fashion or with sufficient dollars.

Roger Keeling's Hint
Copywriters should submit fundraising copy that's as strong as possible because all too often it will be watered down by the busy fingers of the client.

> This watering down will almost certainly occur even if the package starts off tepid as dishwater, so you need to put in something for the busy fingers to cut later if you want anything with tooth to survive.

Roger Keeling's Supposition Corollary
The extent of this watering down is directly proportional to the number of employees and volunteers at the nonprofit who are allowed to review and approve copy.

> The more reviews, the more they'll try to bowdlerize it. Illustration: Do you remember the famous "Kiss This Baby Goodbye" cold prospect package from Greenpeace? The one with a cute little harp seal pictured on it? That carrier was Greenpeace's control for years. It was created by the legendary Hank Burnett, who told me wistfully that "that teaser copy was about the *only* part of my letter they used."
>
> Back then, scads of folks at Greenpeace got a say in approving copy. When Hank's first "Kiss This Baby Goodbye" draft came back, it was *buried* in edit marks. One, signed by an 18-year-old college student who'd just joined the group, simply said, "This copy sucks." Hank noted that it was a humbling comedown for a guy considered one of the top 10 direct mail writers in the nation.
>
> And . . . a couple of rules in memory of the late and very great Peter Tagger, who was one of the masters of the direct mail craft and was also my dear friend and one of my three mentors in the business.

Peter Tagger's Rule 1
Fancy inserts in nonprofit fundraising appeals can actually *suppress* response.

> The presumed reason is that they distract the recipient from the appeal at hand. And, like many rules, this one is occasionally wrong—but not so often that you should violate it lightly.
>
> Peter told me that he first discovered this when he was handling mailings for the San Francisco Exploratorium. The museum had a stockpile of brochures—pretty, professionally done, and quite expensive—that it wanted to use up. The staff kept insisting that Peter include them in his cold prospect mailings, and he had a hard time arguing against it because they *were* attractive and *did* seem appropriate.

Still, on a lark and sans approval of the museum, he decided to mail some test panels *without* the brochures. Response rates were astoundingly higher.

So, if you've got a brochure you were thinking of using, be *sure* to test with and without it. There's a real chance it won't pay for itself and even the possibility that it'll dampen response.

Peter Tagger's Rule 2

If clients insist they can write a better letter than the professional copywriter you want to hire, invite them to do so and bet dinner on the outcome of a head-to-head test.

More than once Peter told me that he'd often made such bets with his clients . . . and he'd never bought dinner yet.

Susan K. Jones's Suggestions

Just as smart direct marketers of consumer products "strike while the iron is hot" with seasonal offers, fashion items, and fads, fundraisers can take advantage of valuable momentum by requesting money to support causes that are very much in the news.

Acknowledge and thank donors promptly.
Immediate turnaround when donations are received is essential. If practical, a personal note from the group's president or executive director makes an excellent acknowledgment. Donors to Northwestern University's John Evans Club, who often send checks of $1,000 or more at a time, usually receive three separate letters of thanks: from the president of the university, from the dean or development officer whose school will benefit from the money, and from the alumni relations officer.

Grand Rapids–based fundraiser Daryl Vogel says that organizations should "find seven ways to thank donors before asking them for more money." These might include thank-you notes, progress updates, newsletters, invitations to events, membership credentials, etc.

Frank Greco's Yardstick

In direct mail fundraising, revenue comes from two sources: (1) the 10 percent to 20 percent of your donors who respond to the mailing; (2) the 1 to 3 percent who respond to your acquisition mailings.

Greco's 12 *Musts* for Successfully Cultivating Donors or Customers

You must promptly send each donor a receipt.

Make sure the name, address, and amounts are correct and legible. This process should require no more than five working days from the date of receiving the donation to mailing the receipt.

You must say thank you.
The two words that are always underutilized are *thank you.* Send your donors personalized acknowledgment letters, notices of upcoming events, and newsletters.

New donors should receive a welcome package providing information about your organization, programs that their gifts help to fund, addresses of local offices—even a special toll-free telephone number they can call.

You must handle nondonors' concerns efficiently.
It is your ability to address the requests of nondonors that builds goodwill in the public. A nondonor who calls or writes to you may in turn be your future donor.

How efficient is your organization in responding to these questions and comments?

- Where did you get my name?
- Remove me from your mailings!
- I want only one mailing per year!
- This person is deceased—why did you write to her?
- You are wasting money on these expensive mailings!
- Are you giving my name out to others?

You must keep your promises and claims.
Very simply stated, follow up and follow through.

You must invite donors and nondonors to contact your organization.
Make it easy for them to call you by providing a toll-free number. An 800 service will also allow you to monitor calls and listen to donors' and nondonors' views and comments about your campaign and your organization.

You must follow government guidelines for tax receipts.
This will protect your organization and its contributors from any potential uncertainties. Duplicate receipts must be kept on file and posted to donor records.

You must provide donors with an opportunity to contribute more.
As a vital part of the receipt package, include a reply envelope (preferably postage-paid) and a request card for information on other programs and services your organization provides. In other words, take advantage of cross-selling opportunities.

You must solve donor problems promptly.

Use the telephone if a problem can be solved immediately. This reduces the staff time required to draft a letter, cuts postage costs, and eliminates the delay in getting back to the donor.

You must inform office staff of a campaign launch.
Make sure every staff member is ready for the launch. The most important person to be updated is the switchboard operator who handles all incoming calls. Proper training of staff will minimize headaches—yours, the switchboard operator's, and the caller's.

You must clean and update lists before and after a campaign.
Accuracy and cleanliness of the names on your database will produce better-responding campaigns through faster and more efficient processing of responses and reduce postage costs by reducing the amount of undeliverable addresses, resulting in a better net bottom line.

You must develop a procedures manual and standards for your program.
The manual will ensure that campaigns run smoothly in most cases and will protect your organization should key staff depart. It can also serve as a training tool for new staff. The manual should outline standard procedures for databasing new names, processing responses, the receipting process, accounting and reconciliation, etc.

You must maintain all names on a database.
Computers make the management of donor requests and follow-up easier.

The success of any fundraising campaign is not judged by the initial response but by your ability to retain donors and extend the value of donors to your organization over a number of years.

Max Hart's Addition
The use of first-class return postage in the form of multiple stamps is almost an institution with Disabled American Veterans.

I wish I could take credit for the concept, but it was already in place when I came to the DAV in 1969. At that time DAV was using three two-cent stamps. (Yes, first-class postage was only six cents.) My recollection was that we were stamping all $5-and-over donors on DAV's twice-a-year renewal name sticker mailings (mailed in spring and fall).

When first-class postage increased to eight cents in 1971, DAV also increased the number of stamps to four. With the 1974 rate increase, we were up to five stamps. When rates increased to 15 cents in 1978, DAV used five three-cent stamps. During those early years it was evident that the more stamps DAV splashed across the return envelope, the better the response rate and the higher the net income.

This phenomenon was demonstrated by postage tests conducted by DAV in the fall of 1981. At the time first-class postage was 20 cents. We tested five four-cent stamps (which was the control against two 10-cent stamps versus no postage). Note the control of five four-cent stamps increased the net—after the cost of the stamps and affixing—by $262/M on the $10-and-over donors and $125/M on the $5-to-$9.99 donor segment. However, the control (five four-cent stamps) beat no postage by a whopping $1,245/M on the $10-and-over donors and $465/M on the $5-to-$9.99 donors. It is rather obvious that live return first-class postage primarily increases the response by some 37 percent lift on both donor segments. Also, the greater the number of stamps, the higher the response rate.

Eight More Ideas

1. Use a minimum of five stamps on your tests to maximize your chances of success.
2. More stamps are better; the more stamps that are splashed across the reply envelope, the better the results.
3. In general, multiple stamps will probably increase your response rate 50 percent.
4. Test multiple stamps only on renewals, where you have a higher percent of response.
5. Constantly test. If first-class return postage is cost justified and you roll out, constantly retest due to the high cost.
6. Take a hard look at business reply envelopes to make sure they are cost-effective.
7. Forget metered mail; avoid it if possible.
8. Seriously consider the use of a third-class nonprofit stamp on outgoing mail.

Guarantees

 Mail-order pioneers originally used guarantees to offset their lack of brand equity. Today, as the direct marketing concept continues to expand, brand equity is not as great a concern. That does not mean, however, that guarantees are no longer necessary. Put simply, selling at a distance requires a guarantee—or, better, a bunch of guarantees—to offset prospects' natural worry about if and when you will deliver on your promise.

A good guarantee not only assures prospects they have nothing to lose by trying your product but also gives them a feel for what kind of service they can expect if they become customers of yours. Fortunately, Aaron Montgomery Ward set the guarantee stage for all of us by simply stating "If you don't like the merchandise, or if it doesn't work, you can return it or get it replaced. Period." That's the best kind of guarantee. Beware of the "conditional" guarantee, an example of the worst kind.

Jay Abraham's Postulate
You can overcome a prospect's reluctance by using risk reversal.

Even if you've done a fabulous job of selling, people may be reluctant to buy from you—because of the competitive marketplace, fear, or simple inertia. How do you overcome their reluctance to close the sale? The key is to transfer the risk from the customer to you.

After all, you already know that your product will meet your claims. The customer, on the other hand, has to go on faith. So you should be willing to back up your product with a strong guarantee.

The standard guarantee is to offer customers their money back if they return the product within 30 days. A stronger guarantee is to let them try your product for free, billing them only after the 30 days have expired. Stronger still is the "pay only if it validates" guarantee: They have to pay your invoice only after your product has made them, say, five times the price of the product.

When you offer a strong guarantee, the money you lose on customers who take advantage of you is a tiny fraction of the increased sales you'll get by offering the guarantee in the first place.

Try the Better-than-Risk-Free Guarantee, one of my favorite forms of risk reversal. In addition to the usual money-back guarantee, you offer customers free bonuses that they'll receive along with the product. (Ideally these bonuses cost you very little but have a high perceived value.) The better-than-risk-free guarantee is this: Customers get to keep the bonuses even if they return the product.

I recommend that when you make your offer you explain it this way: "These bonuses are worth more than $150, so even if you decide to ask for your money back, you'll be $150 ahead just for trying my product." Stated this way, it's almost irresistible, isn't it?

James Gribble's Three Rules for Using Guarantees

No matter what you're selling, always include a strong guarantee.

Guarantees should be simple, direct, as unrestricted as possible, personally backed by your president or owner, and, most important, must address your prospect's basic concern(s) adequately.

Before you create your guarantee, consider your potential customers. What possible concerns might these people have? Are they concerned with price, your earlier claims, a relatively unknown product, location of your company, how long you've been in business, size or appropriateness of their selection, that a salesperson may call, that they have to pay return postage, where their charitable contribution goes?

Do not encumber your guarantee with restrictions or instructions beyond "call us."

For example, do not include things such as "Return it prepaid in its original package," "Some special-order items are not returnable," "Shipping costs are not refundable," "This is a limited guarantee," "We accept only unopened merchandise," etc.

Here are a few effective guarantees (minus titles and signatures):

You must be satisfied, or we make it right—exchange, credit, or cheerful refund, whichever you prefer. We have stood behind our work for 30 years.

We sincerely want you to be 100 percent satisfied with each and every purchase. If the product you order does not meet your standard of excellence, just give us a call. We will send UPS to pick it up from you and send you a replacement or a full refund of your purchase price and all shipping costs.

We make every effort to see to it the maximum amount of your donation makes it into the hands of _____. A copy of our latest financial statement, which illustrates this fact, is available through the state of
_____ simply by calling _____. We encourage you to check
our fine record for yourself.

Jim Kobs's Edict
If you have a guarantee, put an official-looking certificate border around it.

Barbara Harrison's Vision
The guarantee: Put your money where your mouth is.

There are stronger ways to guarantee your product or service than with the generic "you must be 100 percent satisfied or your money will be refunded, no questions asked." Instead, tie the guarantee to the product's benefits, putting your money where your mouth is! For Deepak Chopra's *Ageless Body, Timeless Mind*: "If not 100% convinced that altering your perception of aging can extend your life, improve your health and even change your body, you may return *Ageless Body, Timeless Mind* within 30 days and owe nothing. The anti-aging secrets you learn during your 30-day free trial will be yours to keep and use forever."

Headlines

 Writing effective headlines is a tough job, whether for a press advertisement or for a brochure, flyer, or lift note. It looks like it should be easy, but in a very few words you have to communicate the captivating essence of your offer—and do it in an eye blink for print and under five seconds for a TV commercial. Good headlines last for generations.

Murray Raphel's Doctrine
The headline is the ad for the ad.

Seventy-five percent of the people reading your mailer or newspaper ad will read the headline; only 25 percent of those will keep on reading. Appeal to self-interest.

What benefit does the headline offer the reader? One of the bestselling headlines of all time was Dale Carnegie's "How to Win Friends and Influence People." It was the third headline he tried! It worked because everyone wants to have friends and influence people.

Other self-interest headlines that work:

"How to make a million dollars in mail order."

"How to lose 10 pounds in 10 days."

"How to retire on $75,000 a year."

"Are you spending $10 a week too much for food?"

Stop your readers with a statement that makes them ask, "How can that be?" and/or "What do they mean by that?"

Examples: Do you wonder how we can sell an all-wool Shetland sweater for less than $15?"

"How many of these 20 questions can you answer correctly?"

Important: In the copy that follows you must *answer* the question you raised. And the answer must make logical sense: because you are having a sale, because you made a special purchase, because you are offering your customers a preseason chance to buy before you advertise to the world. The prospects' curiosity must be satisfied by your explanation; otherwise they will not respond and, more important, will feel grave skepticism about any future offers from you.

The headline that begins, "This is your last chance to" is one I never finish reading. I know a similar (or better) offer will follow in the next mail.

Next, promise quick results. Americans are accustomed to speed. *USA Today* is successful because it closely parallels the nightly TV news—coverage of what happened that day without too much information. Everything is complete in one page and, preferably, in one or two paragraphs.

If you can show people how to lose weight quickly, make money quickly, or be successful in a short period of time, they will read what you have to say.

People also have a strange attraction to numbers, from the 10 Commandments to the "Seven out of ten people who . . ." to the "19 reasons why" to the "16 people who believe that . . ." Not only do people read the headline and then start reading the copy, but—more amazingly—they feel they have to read down to the last number mentioned.

The more specific you are in your headline, the more selective you are in choosing your audience. Examples: "An important message to men who are losing their hair." "How college students can earn their tuition this summer."

Harry B. Walsh's Yardstick
When writing headlines, stay under 15 words.

Before I got into mail order, my magazine ads were judged by the Starch ratings they earned. At one point, Starch did a huge review of how the length of the headline affected the read-most rating. I was used to shooting for four- or five-word headlines and was surprised to learn that headlines of up to 14 words were read as well as the short ones.

Trust is a key word in direct marketing. A recent shocking statistic: Ninety percent of Americans do *not* associate the word *trust* with the word *business*.

Drew Allen Miller's Advice
Put headlines below the illustration.

According to research conducted by Starch INRA Hooper, Inc., headlines in print ads should be placed below the illustration or photograph because the eye naturally falls on the illustrative area of an ad first. Headlines that are above the illustration force the eye to fight gravity and go "uphill," while headlines below the illustration allow the eye to fall effortlessly and begin reading.

Bill Jayme's Tip
The headline should be horizontal—not vertical, not slanting.

David Oglivy's Precept
The headline is the "ticket on the meat."

Use it to flag down readers who are prospects for the kind of product you are advertising. If you are selling a remedy for bladder weakness, display the words BLADDER WEAKNESS in your headline; they catch the eye of everyone who suffers from this inconvenience. If you want mothers to read your advertisement, display MOTHERS in your headline. And so on.

Conversely, do not say anything in your headline which is likely to exclude any readers who might be prospects for your product. Thus, if you are advertising a product which can be used equally well by men and women, don't slant your headline to women alone; it would frighten men away.

Every headline should appeal to the reader's self-interest. It should promise her a benefit, as in any headline for Helena Rubenstein's Hormone Cream:

HOW WOMEN OVER 35 CAN LOOK YOUNGER.

Always try to inject news into your headline, because the consumer is always on the lookout for new products, or new ways to use an old product, or new improvements in an old product.

The two most powerful words you can use in a headline are FREE and NEW.

Other words and phrases which work wonders are: HOW TO, SUDDENLY, NOW, ANNOUNCING, INTRODUCING, IT'S HERE, JUST ARRIVED, IMPORTANT DEVELOPMENT, IMPROVEMENT, AMAZING, SENSATIONAL, REMARKABLE, REVOLUTIONARY, STARTLING, MIRACLE, MAGIC, OFFER, QUICK, EASY, WANTED, CHALLENGE, ADVICE TO, THE TRUTH ABOUT, COMPARE, BARGAIN, HURRY, LAST CHANCE.

Don't turn your nose up at these clichés. They may be shopworn, but they work. That is why you see them turn up so often in the headlines of mail-order advertisers and others who can measure the results of their advertisements.

Headlines can be strengthened by emotional words like DARLING, LOVE, FEAR, PROUD, FRIEND and BABY.

Five times as many people read the headline as read the body copy, so it is important that these glancers should at least be told what brand is being advertised.

Include your selling promise in your headline. This requires long headlines. When the New York University School of Retailing ran headline tests with the cooperation of a big department store, they found that headlines of ten words or longer, containing news and information, consistently sold more merchandise than short headlines.

Headlines containing six to twelve words pull more coupon returns than short headlines, and there is no significant difference between the readership of three-word headlines.

The best headline I ever wrote contained eighteen words:

At Sixty Miles an Hour, the Loudest Noise in the New Rolls-Royce comes from the electric clock.*

*When the chief engineer at the Rolls-Royce factory read this, he shook his head sadly and said, "It's time we did something about that damned clock."

Avoid blind headlines—the kind which mean nothing unless you read the body copy underneath them; most people don't.

—Confessions of an Advertising Man

Ed Elliott's Thought
Headlines must be more than just big words.

Elliott's Five Major Purposes of Headlines

Grab the attention of the skimmer.

Be readable at a quick glance.
- Smaller, longer subheads are read more quickly if they are serif and not extremely bold.
- All caps are not quickly read, though for a few words can be effective as an attention getter.
- Establishing line breaks between natural phrases will help a headline communicate more quickly.

Break up the page.
Nothing is less inviting than a solid page of gray text with nothing to break it up or catch the eye.

Evoke the intended emotion.
While only a few typefaces may be appropriate for text, a greater variety of type can be used for headlines and subheads. Different moods and emotions can be communicated through the right choice of typeface, weight, color, and format treatment.

Photos, illustrations, charts, and graphs can boost your results.
- Showing a premium can increase response, particularly if it has a good design that can lift response.
- A person or even a hand holding the book or premium is stronger still.
- Pictures of people catch more attention than pictures of things.
- If you have control over the color, make it predominantly warm. Red is a great color.
- Each visual should have a caption that directs the reader back to the text.

Internet Marketing

The Internet has stormed into the marketing consciousness of uncounted companies. There is no denying that Internet marketing is sexy. But at this juncture this new medium is immature. To make it work requires media integration. Someday in the future, once a secure payment system has been embedded in the Internet, it will become the interactive medium envisioned by its current proponents. However, until it is better organized, with some controls in place, it is unlikely to blaze new trails in sales. When that time does come, as it is sure to do, concern is going to center on the "reach" of the new medium. That alone makes it the most interesting medium to come along in decades for direct marketing practitioners.

Robert C. Hacker's Seven Assumptions on the Possibility of Finding Marketing Salvation on the Internet

The receiver, not the sender, controls communication.
Prospecting strategy is based on using intrusive media with the sender controlling the content and timing of the message. Will the Internet be of benefit to companies who must use direct marketing for prospecting, particularly for products or services that must be pushed through the medium?

The Internet is global; this is touted as one of the major benefits and, indeed, it is.
But how can we count on it to support individual territories, sales representatives, or markets, particularly when the entire communications interaction is controlled by the receiver?

The Internet is anarchic; it runs itself.
All clients and agencies have been working with media that are bureaucratic, highly controlled, and very predictable. Can clients and agencies count on a communications system that nobody controls? What happens when the system hits capacity constraints and there's no central authority to fix it?

The Internet is a huge library with 2,500 branches and no Dewey decimal system.

How will people find you in the clutter? Perhaps an unpredictable medium can generate cost-efficient sales, but how do you plan around anarchy? How many sales, of which products, in which markets can you count on, and when?

The Internet is free.

Both agencies and clients have specialized in communicating through paid media. Since specialized talents are required to pay off the media investment, companies formed departments and hired agencies to maximize their return on capital. But access to the Internet is virtually free. There is no charge for the time. So production will be virtually free, too.

If the media is free, and production is free, return on investment is no longer an issue.

Since there is no economic cost for failure, there is no longer a need to invest heavily on the front end to protect the investment.

Now any department in any company can create its own home page without having to go through the marketing department for budget or technical assistance. What will that mean for marketing and communications departments? How will that affect corporate standards and brand image? Who will control interdepartmental conflicts and coordination requirements?

To maximize marketing efficiency, it might even be smarter to do it yourself than to hire professional assistance—even if you have to do it over and over again to get it right.

Remember, there is no economic penalty for failure, and even one sale guarantees high ROI.

A local interactive media company specializing in developing World Wide Web home pages for its clients confirmed my suspicions: "Everybody will be doing their own home pages within a year."

What will that mean for agencies with high overhead, particularly ones making a mad dash to expand their Internet marketing capabilities? And how will it affect freelancers and telecommuters with low overhead and all the computing power they will ever need sitting on the dining room table?

It looks like Internet marketing may be the first communications channel that will escape all corporate and agency control and become the first true guerrilla marketing medium.

Regina Brady's 10 Commandments of Marketing Electronically—Both On-Line and on the Web

Develop your marketing plans with an eye toward building your own customer and prospect file.

Think of your on-line presence as a way to stimulate a variety of ways for the customer to interact with you. For example, if you are a cataloger, you should do all of the following:

- List selected products for sale on-line.
- Allow people to order a free copy of your catalog.
- Allow customers who have your paper catalog to order from the catalog on-line.
- Run a monthly contest or promotion so that members have a reason to leave you their name and address *and* a reason to come back time after time.
- Include an option that simply says "Add me to your mailing list."

Mine your mailing list with direct and electronic mail.

When a customer orders, make sure you send an electronic thank-you . . . and then continue to send messages once a month to update what is going on in your store. Remember, you are building a relationship, and a relationship is built on open communication.

Create reasons for prospects and customers to return.

At a minimum you should be doing this monthly. The electronic world is no different from the physical world. You need to keep your inventory, your offers, and your promotions lively, interesting, and customer focused to attract and build a loyal electronic customer base.

Update, update, update.

Think about the catalog that has the same cover and the same inventory mailing after mailing. Recipients probably won't even open up the catalog if they believe they have already seen it. The same holds true for electronic real estate. You need to keep your offers fresh. Rotate your stock and you'll keep those customers coming back.

Participate! Take advantage of sponsored promotions.

Most of the on-line services do a lot to support their marketing clients. They create theme promotions on-line to attract the attention of their member bases. These promotions take time and effort for the on-line services to create—because they know they work.

A well-planned promotion will often triple or even quadruple the number of customers. Often the cost of entry for you to participate in any of these promotions is very low. They may be looking for a prize (often in the $25-to-$100 range). That can be a small price to pay for the opportunity to make a large group of members aware that your products and services are available on-line.

Communicate with the system's staff.

The staff is there to help you. It also has some experience with what has worked and what has not worked. You know your products and services better than anyone else, but the staff understands the electronic environment, so take advantage of its expertise and suggestions.

Don't be afraid to experiment; but do be prepared to analyze results.

In the on-line environment it is very easy to change inventory, offers, premiums, pricing, and more. Because the medium is so flexible, you can have a tremendous amount of marketing intelligence at your fingertips. So try some new offers and tests. You need not keep them "live" for long, but you will get some very interesting results—and quickly. The lead times are minimal compared to getting ready to launch a direct mail campaign. But do be prepared to analyze your results.

Take advantage of the medium's unique capabilities.

The medium is interactive—you can encourage direct communication with your customers and foster loyalty. It is perfect for relationship marketing.

1. Use electronic mail for questions and answers, to provide customer service, to create a dialog with your customer, to resell and cross-sell, to survey, and to run ongoing promotions.
2. Build an electronic mailing list through catalog requests and "add me to your mailing list" requests.
3. Host on-line real-time events such as "meet the celebrity or spokesperson," focus/user groups, conferences, and offering of behind-the-scenes advice.
4. Allow customers to create a profile and then deliver information that is tailored to that profile (e.g., Dreyfus asks about investment strategies, then recommends several funds): establish corporate accounts or offer new car configurations, for example.
5. Deliver customized messages based on supplied information: retail store locator upon entry of zip code, key word search, CompuCard model of lowest delivered price, or download of brochures.
6. Take advantage of the fact that the store is always open and the medium is flexible and dynamic. Be sure your messages are continually altered. Remember that lead times can be as little as days. Be aware that you have the facility to change your offer, merchandise, or premiums, create a sale, or launch a promotion.

As always, prompt and efficient customer service is a must—customer expectations are even greater with this medium.

Recognize and create a synergism between print and on-line.

Some of the on-line services offer monthly magazines free of charge to their members. At CompuServe our magazine is a powerful tool in making members aware that a particular marketer is on-line. Members can browse through the magazine at their leisure and decide what they'd like to do the next time they are on-line. Take advantage of this opportunity.

Robert Brueckner's Seven Deadly Sins of Web Marketing

Boredom.

According to David Ogilvy, "You can't bore people into buying your product." Boredom covers a multitude of transgressions, including long waits for your pages to build, big chunks of indigestible text, and not getting to the point right away!

Pride.

The notion that whatever we think is important about our company and product is worth publishing on the Web, whether or not anyone outside the corporate power structure gives a hoot, is the anticustomer or antiprospect point of view.

Sloth.

Web sites need to be updated constantly, yet many times an "update" turns out to have been made more than six months ago.

Greed.

Whenever a customer feels you are on the Web only for the money, that's greed. Making people register on your site is too greedy. Inducing them to do so is not. Inundating them with unwanted e-mail is greedy . . . and failing to offer good deals is way too greedy.

Envy.

Whatever you see on another Web site you have to shoehorn into your own site, whether it fits or not. Suit your Web content to your customers first. Forget about keeping up with the Joneses.

Confusion.

When people visit your Web site, do they feel as if they're looking through a glass darkly? Do pages trail off with nowhere to go? Do they bounce around looking for something you talk about on one page, only to find themselves back on that page through a circular reference loop? You have to spoon out information sparingly, but make it link to something else. If the "something else" is not compelling, you're being confusing.

Ignorance.

Learn about the Web: its strengths, weaknesses, idiosyncrasies, and foibles. Most Web sites today are constructed by people who have no experience in interactive marketing. Get experience. Experiment and learn. Create a new model. Explore.

A Denny Hatch Observation
If direct marketing were a human body, the head, shoulders, and most of the torso would be direct mail; you could take all the revenue generated by the Internet and on-line services and fit it into the navel with two peppercorns and still have plenty of room left over for Saddam Hussein's heart.

With a tip o' the hat to Fred Allen.

Comment: However, times are changing . . . and the Internet is going to become a major media player in the future.

Lead Generation

 Lead generation and conversion is one of the two marketing models embedded in the direct marketing concept. (The other is invitation to contract.) If you use DRTV, you are using the lead generation model, although infomercials, where payment is required before fulfillment, is invitation to contract. Most DMA member companies follow the lead generation model. It is a powerful model when you cannot specifically target your audience.

Bob Hacker's Eight Truths About Lead Generation

When the leads stop flowing, sales representatives go hungry and the company's profits and cash flow can drop dramatically.

Work backward from point of sale.
The best way to plan a lead generation campaign is to start at the point of sale and work backward toward the prospect or suspect.

To begin the process, spend quality time with the sales force.
The class war between marketing and sales is a primary reason for program failure. So knock it off. Now!

What goes on between the sales rep and the prospect? What information is needed to close the sale? How does the sales rep get the buyer to say yes? What objections come up?

Make sure "deal killers" don't creep into your copy.
Even in a defensive mode. You don't want to raise objections the prospect never thought of.

Next, define the steps in the sales process.
Who is responsible for managing and controlling each step? How can they help or hurt your program? What will they do? Keep in mind that another major cause of program failure is unrealistic assumptions regarding the behavior of people for managing the system.

In fact, according to Performark president Joseph Lethert, quoted in Richard Gibson's marketing column in the *Wall Street Journal,* in many companies "sales and marketing aren't working together. No one has responsibilities for making sure prospects are converted to customers."

Match your leads to sales capacity.

Too many leads can kill a sales force. Sales representatives work better in a drizzle than a thunderstorm. A hungry sales force will close higher. At the same time, with too few leads morale can become a problem. To maximize closing rates, deliver 70 to 80 percent of what they say they can handle.

Will the sales force be ready to handle the leads? Have they been trained properly? Are lead banking systems in place? It takes 58 days for requests for information to be fulfilled at the average company. It takes 89 days before a prospect is contacted by a sales rep. By then the potential customer may have selected a more responsive supplier.

How much prescreening and qualifying do you do?

Left to their own devices, sales reps will overqualify leads, hoping for easy sales. Why would you want to disqualify people from the sales process before they understand what the product or service is about?

You could hurt the sale by introducing information too early in the process.

For example, you probably don't want to put price in the lead package or fulfillment materials—especially if the price-value relationship is not clear to the potential buyer. Let the sales rep introduce price later.

If you've asked and answered the proper questions, your options for offer development, copy platform, list strategy, and fulfillment systems will be defined for you, by the people who convert leads to sales.

Bob Hacker's 15 Tips to Power Up Your Lead Generation Performance

Creative supports but never leads.

Start with the offer, deal, or appeal. All other creative elements such as copy platforms, layout, and design must support the sales promotion. Simplify everything so that the offer, not the package itself, grabs the reader's attention.

In lead generation, the more you tell, the less you sell.

Copy platforms should focus on generating a lead, not closing the sale. When you say too much, you often create reasons not to respond. The goal at each step of a multistep sale is to get to the next step. When you try to skip a set, you break the sales chain and scare away qualified buyers.

Tease the prospect into wanting to know more. Be strong on emotional benefits—leave the rational features and advantages to the sales rep.

Talk to the left and right sides of the brain.

Some people process information more rationally, some more emotionally. But as good as lists are, they don't segment this way . . . yet. So give two arguments to each package—even in business-to-business copy. We generally put the more emotional argument in the letter and the more rational one in the brochure. If cost is a problem, *stick with the letter and throw away the brochure.*

Your package isn't a marketing plan in drag.

Financial institutions and high-tech firms are famous for this. If the marketing plan has five major objectives for the year, then all five objectives must be covered in every piece of marketing communications. Every objective you add to a direct marketing package tends to dampen response rate. Do one thing at a time! Pare back objectives, and response rates can soar.

Strong offers, stated boldly, are the key to success.

If the offer is a 25 percent discount, tell me now! Don't bury it in the brochure or the sixth paragraph of the letter. Tell me if I can't survive without it. "Billboard" the offer with Johnson boxes, boldface, underlining, highlighting, and inserts. And tell me often in the letter, brochure, and response form.

Test ugly early.

Pretty packages soothe. Ugly disturbs, and disturbed people respond better than peaceful people. And there's more good news: ugly usually costs less, which brings down cost per response.

Assume readers don't care.

They *don't* care about you or your product. They want to know what's in it for them. First tell them what they get. Then, if that grabs them, they may sit still for your story.

Sell salvation, not products.

Sell hope, the promise of a better tomorrow, being recognized by the boss, beating peers in the race up the corporate ladder, wealth, popularity, or being there first! The product is just the way to get there.

Use the great motivators.

Greed, anger, fear, guilt, exclusivity. Fear of loss and desire for gain have sold more product than all other offers combined. Use the ephemeral if you want to win awards; use the visceral if you want to sell product.

Copy the sales reps' most successful techniques.

Are they using a drop close? Then a discount offer might be one of your best test ideas. Are they using a take-away close? Then an offer built around limited availability might work. Are they using a budget close? Then you might use a free financing offer. By matching up-front offers to back-end closes, you can often increase both response and closing rates.

Loosen it up and make more sales.

In consumer product sales, the most qualified people often will not allow themselves to be qualified! So be careful, particularly with high-cost products that have hard-to-understand features and utility. If the prospect doesn't really understand the product or the price/value relationship, it's very difficult to prequalify.

Use words that sell.

Pepper your copy with words like *understand, proven, health, easy, free, guarantee, money, safety, save, love, new, discover, right, results, truth, comfort, proud, profit, deserve, happy, trust, value, fun,* and *vital.*

Avoid response killers.

Words to avoid: *cost, pay, contract, sign, try, worry, loss, lose, hurt, death, buy, bad, sell, sold, price, decision, hard, difficult, obligation, liable,* and *fail.*

Appeal to everyone and miss them all.

When a package fails, it's tempting to change the package to "appeal to everybody." Instead your effort loses focus, and you end up appealing to nobody. So ignore the 90 to 95 percent who will never respond and concentrate your efforts on converting just one or two more for each 100 you mail.

Use colors that sell.

Throw away your pastel PMS swatch book. Use bold primary colors—red, yellow, blue. Avoid designer tones, particularly muted earth tones. Appeal to the visceral, not the cerebral. Agitate. Don't pacify.

Axel Andersson's Approach

Don't try to sell expensive products or products that need an elaborate explanation with a one-step technique.

A two-step approach for such offers is always more profitable. First get the inquiries and then pursue those inquiries with a powerful follow-up series.

Andrew J. Byrne's Principle

Use short copy to get an inquiry but never to make a sale.

Harry Kraus's Caveat
When seeking qualified leads, sell the offer, not the product.

Bob Stone's Gauge
The closure rate from qualified leads can be two to four times as effective as cold calls.

> Telephone-generated leads are likely to close four to six times better than mail-generated leads.

Letters

 Direct marketing practice uses, literally, thousands of letter types—solicitation letters, billing and collection letters, customer service letters, thank-you letters . . . and dozens more types. In direct mail the letter is *the* critical element in the mailing package. The letter is your salesperson, and to get the sale your salesperson must be outstanding.

Harry B. Walsh's Double Prescription

The tone of a good direct mail letter is as direct and personal as the writer's skill can make it.

Even though it may go to millions of people, it never orates to a crowd but rather murmurs into a single ear. It's a message from *one* letter writer to *one* letter reader.

Tell a story if possible.

Everybody loves a good story, be it about Peter Rabbit or King Lear. And the direct mail letter, with its unique person-to-person format, is the perfect vehicle for a story. *Stories get read.* The letter I wrote to launch the Cousteau Society 20-some years ago has survived hundreds of tests against it. When I last heard, it was still being mailed in some form or another. The original of this direct mail Methuselah started out with this lead: "A friend once told me a curious story I would like to share with you. . . ."

Andrew J. Byrne's Writing Rules

Use short words, short sentences, short paragraphs.

Double spacing makes it more difficult to read, not easier.

Break sentences at the bottom of every page except the last.

Eliminating the first paragraph improves most letters.

Dick Benson's Admonition
Letters should look and feel like letters.

Malcolm Decker's Primer
The letter itself is the pen-and-ink embodiment of a salesperson who is speaking personally and directly to the prospect.

The letter is the most powerful and persuasive selling force in direct marketing once the product, price, and offer are set. The writer creates the salesperson, usually from whole cloth, and you must be certain that this sales representative is truly representative of your product or service as well as of your company.

The letter is likely to be the only "person" your market will ever meet—at least on the front end of the sale—so don't make it highbrow if your market is lowbrow and vice versa.

Make sure the letter speaks your prospect's language. A Tiffany salesperson writes in one style; if a grapefruit or pecan farmer or a beef grower writes differently, I develop as clear a profile of my prospect as the available research offers and then try to match it up with someone I know and "put him in a chair" across from me. Then I write to him more or less conversationally.

The salesperson in the letter is doing the job he or she obviously loves and is good at. He or she knows the product inside and out and is totally confident in and at ease with its values and benefits—even its inconsequential shortcomings—and wants to get the prospect in on a good thing. Here is someone with a sense of rhythm, timing, dramatic effect, and possibly even humor—getting attention, piquing curiosity, holding interest, engaging rationally, anticipating and assuaging doubts, and ultimately winning the confidence (and the signature on the order) of the prospect.

The personal technique is seen most clearly in long letters.

How long should a letter be? The best-known answer to that age-old question is "As long as it has to be."

That doesn't tell you much, but perhaps it suggests two important criteria: economy and—above all—efficiency.

As a sometime angler, I get a better sense of length by remembering a fishing trip to Maine when we used dry flies with barbless hooks. Unless you kept up the tension all the way to the net, you lost the trout. Try it. You should feel the same sort of tension when you write and when you read a letter. If not, reel in the slack.

Because the direct mail letter is the most highly personal, intimate form of commercial writing . . .

. . . It is *not* a monolithic corporation addressing a computer-generated market profile; it is not impersonal in tone, form, or content.

. . . It is *not* one or more pieces of 8½- by 11-inch paper with a letterhead on top and a signature on the bottom and the most cherished sales pitch of the marketing VP sandwiched in between.

. . . It is *not* set in standard type, is not illustrated with photographs, is not printed in four-color process, does not have a bang-tail or envelope pocket or other device attached.

A long letter—four pages and especially upward—needs a bit of help, even if you're an expert angler. Therefore . . .

. . . It *can* have an eyebrow or Johnson box above the salutation to tease, tantalize, or help the reader preview what's coming in the letter—especially if it's four or more pages.

. . . It *can* have handwritten notations in the margins, a scrawled P.S., or underlining for emphasis in a second color of the same hue and hand as the signature. But be sure the handwriting in the margins matches that of the signature, or you've lost all the verisimilitude of personalization.

. . . It *can* be printed on two sides (as long as the stock is opaque). The color, weight, quality, and texture of your letter stock communicate, too. Choose them very carefully. They're your salesperson's clothes.

Be sure the right person signs the letters. Some time ago, two investors' newsletters—*Advance Planning Letter* and *Investors World Intelligent Report*—sent out long (12- and 16-page) highly technical promotional letters filled with forecasts with recommendations. The former was signed by Bobbie Bunch, Assistant to the Publisher; the latter was signed by Joan Pendergraft, Executive Assistant to Sid Pulitzer. Obviously neither wrote the letter, so believability went out the window.

Don't overlook the color, size, and vitality of your signature; they're your salesperson's handshake.

Even people who aren't graphologists pick up a lot from the way a name is signed. It's interesting to compare the signature of Carolyn Davis (*Reader's Digest*) or Carol Wright with that of Salvador Dali or Gloria Vanderbilt. Then ask yourself why the former are so lackluster and the latter are so distinctive.

The other signature that can work for you is your company name and logotype. Use it to tell your prospect what kind of company you are: traditional, avant-garde, industrial, financial, and so on.

Whatever your marketing stance, a good designer can help you express it, and that helps your reader identify you. The objective is individuation—to stand out in the increasingly competitive marketplace of the mailbox—so that when it comes time to toss the me-too mail, yours won't be part of it.

The letter *must* be quickly scannable: that is, a reader should get the gist of the proposition simply by reading the (1) eyebrow, (2) lead paragraph, (3) crossheads, (4) wrap-up, (5) P.S.

If not, send it back for surgery, because without a strongly integrated skeleton the body of the argument will slump.

The letter *must* be easy on the eyes, open, inviting, and varying in texture. It should have normal margins, individual paragraphs with line space between, at least one crosshead or subhead per page (two per page for long letters), occasional variation in paragraph width, a quotation, underlined sentence or phrase, numbers or bullets to list benefits, and/or other bits of "color" to maintain reader interest by promising visual variety.

The longer the letter, the more important these techniques.

Roger Keeling's Beacon
The top of every page deserves a new lead!

You never know where people will start reading—it may not be on page 1. And you never entirely know where their eyes will skip to. But the tops of every page are likely candidates. So don't waste this opportunity: start every page with a punchy new sales pitch . . . a golden opportunity to *grab that customer*!

Keeling's Corollary
Prospects often open their direct mail, half-pull the letter out, glance at the first page, then lift it and glance at *the third page* (or second, if printed on one side only).

With a six-pager, they'll possibly glance at the top of the fifth page. Therefore, the page 3 (and page 5, etc.) "top of the page lead" is especially important.

Don Hauptman's Techniques

Use a typewriter-style font.
Split tests of typewritten vs. typeset letters appear to yield contradictory results; sometimes typewritten beats typeset, while other tests show no difference.

Still, it seems wise to continue employing the "old-fashioned" typewriter look. When people open an envelope, they expect to see a letter, with its familiar conventions. The image of a personal, me-to-you message may indeed be an illusion, but it's one that most of us have come to expect. What's more, the typewriter format helps differentiate the letter from other components of the package. Courier, a typeface available with most of today's software and impact and laser printers, is closest to the familiar typewriter look.

Avoid circusy tricks.
A serious (and common) typographic error is the use of dizzying variety of fonts, sizes, etc. After all, people may reason, it's easy, so why not? Don't even use boldface or italic; you wouldn't (or couldn't) have done it with your old manual or electric.

Indent the first line of each paragraph.
How much of an indent? Four to six characters. The "neat" look of blocked paragraphs (i.e., the left margin flush with subsequent lines) was once fashionable. But tests (and common sense) suggest that paragraph indents make for easier reading.

To avoid a gray "wall" of type that discourages reading, paragraphs shouldn't be more than seven lines long.

A visual and dramatic break can be provided by an occasional paragraph of one sentence, one line, or even one word. But don't mail a letter that consists of all one-sentence paragraphs unless it's intended for toddlers.

Use a ragged-right margin.

Again, it's so easy for a computer and printer to execute flush-right (justified) margins that people do it without realizing that it detracts from the typewriter-letter illusion.

Don't break words at the end of a line.

The "word wrap" function of most word-processing programs can be instructed not to hyphenate.

Avoid a dangling *a* or *the* at the end of a line; keep such articles adjacent to their nouns.

Use familiar attention-getting devices.

Even if the bells and whistles offered by desktop publishing are eschewed, as I recommend, certain techniques can be used to relieve the gray look of a typed letter and to flag and emphasize key points:

- Underscore key words, sentences, and even entire (short!) paragraphs. Always underscore with a continuous rule (i.e., not "hatched" or broken between words). Unfortunately, some fonts and printers create a rule that cuts into the lower edges of letters; use a font that cuts a hairline space above the rule.
- Bullets, round or square (always solid), can be inserted via computer (depending on your software), or added later by the designer if necessary. Do *not* use asterisks, hyphens, periods, or the letter *o* to substitute for bullets. Checkmarks work nicely, especially for a list of benefits.
- Subheads help break up long copy. They should be centered, capitalized, and underscored. For greater emphasis, set them in a larger size.
- Inset paragraphs, centered (10 or so characters' worth of space both left and right) and blocked, are useful for calling attention to important points.
- Handwritten notes—brief simulated pen script messages in the margins—work well if not overdone. According to Toronto designer Ted Kikoler, the best use of this device is to pull the browser into the text (e.g., "Could this idea benefit you?" followed by an arrow pointing to the specific words referenced). Other mock handwritten devices: wavy underscores, double parentheses, asterisks, circled words. All of these must be added legibly to the printout by hand.
- If your letter will be printed in a second color, by all means use it for most of the attention-getting devices. But use black for underscoring

and for all typewritten text. A sudden paragraph in orange or purple is more disconcerting than emphatic and often hard to read.

- Use page breaks to arouse curiosity. Ideally, every right-hand page should break in the middle of a sentence that is so exciting that the reader cannot resist turning the page ("Harold then discovered that the secret of eternal life is . . ."). Realistically, it's tough to achieve this goal throughout a long letter, but it's worth making the effort on page 1. Adding, "over, please" at the bottom of the first page can't hurt, but I suspect that many readers find it offensive on every page.

For the signature, use the second color.
Blue is frequently recommended, but if your sole extra color is red, you won't have this option. Solution: Try a 50 percent screen of black, which creates the effect of a third color (gray) at no extra cost.

Secretary's subscript can't hurt, especially to a business audience.
I once had a client who used the subscript as the package key code.

Always include a P.S., say experts.
It can restate the guarantee, premium offer, or major benefit or make a provocative point that kicks the reader back into the letter. Use a hanging indent—the entire message is positioned to the right of the *P.* and *S.*

Logo, address, and phone numbers are best placed at the bottom of the last page if the letter has a display headline.
I'm always amazed to see letters—and other components—that omit this vital information.

Arrange pages appropriately.
Pages can be printed on both sides unless you are aiming for a high-class effect. For four pages (and multiples thereof), 11- by 17-inch sheets are usually best. In a long letter, cut sheets are likely to become disordered. In all cases, pages should be numbered at the top.

Why honor these ancient letter traditions in the post-pentium period? Despite all the technological changes, human nature remains very much the same. We still read newspapers even though news is obtained more efficiently via TV, radio, fax, computer screen, or wireless pager. And that helps explain why seemingly archaic conventions—such as typewritten letters—continue to work.

Start with the prospect, not with the product.
Sales letters that start by saying, in effect, "We have a product we want to sell you" are making a big mistake. A better way is to start is with a series of

sentences that begin with the prospect: "You'll profit by," "You'll save time by," "You'll be the first to know," and so on.

Avoid superlatives and brag-and-boast language.

Wherever possible, incorporate anecdotes, testimonials, success stories, and other believable elements of human interest.

Do research.
Interview customers, ask questions, and listen carefully. My favorite question is "What are your [the prospect's] greatest problems, needs, and concerns right now?" At least half the time I spend on an assignment is pure research—before attacking the blank page or computer screen.

Use specifics to add power and credibility.
Use precise, documented figures and facts in advertising. Cite data or opinions from outside, impartial sources. A lot of copy is anemic and ineffective because it's superficial, vague, and unspecific. Concrete statements and detail supply the ring of truth. But to find this kind of material you often have to dig.

Don't try to change behavior.
It's time-consuming, expensive, and often futile. It's usually wise to capitalize on existing motivations. In other words, preach to the converted. Unless you have an unlimited budget, avoid products and services that require the buyer to be educated or radically transformed.

Be a "creative plagiarist."
You can learn by studying the work of others. But don't imitate; emulate or re-create. When you see an idea you admire, try to identify the principles behind it, then apply those principles in a fresh, original way to your own work.

Bob Hacker's Key Direct Marketing Copy Drivers
Fear, Guilt, Anger, Greed, Exclusivity, and Salvation.

If your letter isn't dripping with one or more of these, tear it up and try again.

Pat Friesen's 12 Letter Hot Spots
Letterhead/masthead. Salutation. First sentence, first paragraph. Johnson box—billboard above the salutation and letter body. Last paragraph. Signature. Title with signature. P.S. and P.P.S. Copy indented from both

margins or underlined. Copy in bullet form, second color, or boldface type. Indented sub headlines. Anything added in handwriting.

Dick Hodgson's Pronouncement

Of all the formats used in direct mail, none has more power to generate action than the letter.

> Any package containing a letter will generally pull greater response than a package without a letter; extensive testing has proved this to be true in most cases.

Lift Pieces

 A lift piece is an extra element slipped into a mailing package in order to "lift" response. The first documented lift note was by Paul Michael for the old Greystone continuity series. It was a slip of paper folded in half. On the front was the line:

Frankly, I'm puzzled . . .

Inside was a letter from someone other than the person who signed the main letter saying, in effect,

Frankly, I'm puzzled. . . .

I cannot imagine you are not going to take advantage of the FREE offer, because the first volume really is FREE. . . .

Harry B. Walsh's Example
In the old days, second letters—which usually reiterated the no-risk guar-antee—*always* gave between a 10 percent and 12 percent lift, no matter what copy was used.

They've fallen out of favor in some quarters, but I still recommend testing them. People don't change that much.

Malcolm Decker's Strategy
If your prospect is sitting on the fence, a quick little shove in the form of a lift letter could get him or her on your side.

But be careful—because those already on your side will read it, too. It should be another voice—for example, not the person who signed the main letter— but a personality like Madonna or Gloria Steinem or David Letterman speaking very plainly to point up a benefit, reassure a fence-sitter, or disarm a nay-sayer. It should never introduce anything new; that's the top sales-person's job.

Barbara Harrison's "Break the Rules" Rules of Effective Direct Mail Copywriting

Forget the old, tried-and-true but tired lift note.

Don't waste paper on "Read this note only if you have decided not to respond to this offer." Instead, make the lift note work harder by introducing a disarming, startling, or unexpected selling point that may not be appropriate for the full-length letter.

This can be a letter from a woman who made dried flower arrangements for her daughter's wedding from what she grew in her garden, for Meredith's *Floral & Naturecrafts* magazine . . . a note on herb lore, like "Daniel Boone Sold Ginseng," for *Rodale's Illustrated Encyclopedia of Herbs* . . . a note from the editor-in-chief, speaking as a woman who is also a doctor and the mother of four daughters, for *Harvard Women's Health Watch*.

If one lift note is good, two are better.

For the Tufts School of Veterinary Medicine's newsletter, *Your Dog,* I wrote a letter from the dean of the Veterinary School emphasizing the credentials and expertise of its canine authorities. Then I added a second lift note—from a dog—explaining why dogs hate the newsletter. (It makes their owners too knowledgeable, and teaches owners how to break dogs' bad habits!)

Humor is usually risky, but can prove highly effective.

In the Tufts newsletter it added significantly to the strength of this control.

Don't limit the lift note to the lift note.

Lift notes can go anywhere in the package. I've built them into the P.S. of the letter (a note from the publisher added to the long letter from the editor) and into the brochure. For *Better Homes & Gardens Craft & Wear* magazine, I featured the managing editor's most recent creative crafts project—with a full-length photo and enthusiastic note—on the back of the brochure.

Lists

Richard V. Benson's Law

Lists are the most important ingredient in the success of any promotional mailing.

I know of no mailer who spends enough time on lists.

Rose Harper's 21 Inviolable Principles

A mailing list consists of the names and addresses of a group of people or companies all having one or more things in common; the list represents a meaningful grouping.

Direct marketing companies do not have a single mailing list; they have many.

How many? Only segmentation will tell. The opportunities to segment the customer file into marketing units when purchasing behavioral characteristics are vast. Thus, where the Marketing Information Network (MIN) offers more than 20,000 published lists on-line, if you take into consideration the segments, you are looking at more like 200,000 separate and distinct lists.

Always bear in mind that consumers are purposeful human beings with goals and interests—and a distinct purchasing behavior.

Too often you hear, "The list doesn't work." How about the creative message? Did it address the audience, the consumers on the list?

Direct mail can be a powerful persuader if the right message is sent to the right prospect at the right price. The relationship between product and copy is clear, as should be the synergism between copy and list. Copy language has an infinite number of possibilities. Lists have a "flavor." You're juggling important forces in the promotional effort.

To establish an effective business relationship with a list broker, consider it a partnership, a strategic alliance.

Bring the broker into the picture at an early stage to help in the approach to the market—and profits.

Give the brokers the time to do a skillful job since they must make specific recommendations and also supply such critical information as selectivity, balance counts, state counts, and usage.
The more a pro knows, the more help you will receive in achieving your own goals for a mailing.

Most companies rent their lists to make money.

Renting your list can be a form of market research.
Many companies may improve their own selection of rental lists by monitoring the successful outside usage of their house file.

In direct mail you can control your package, your offer, and your product, but the rental list so important to your success is the one factor you can't really control.
You don't own it. Nor did you produce it. You are entirely dependent on outside parties for the accuracy of the information on which to base your decision. Data cards you receive from brokers or managers are necessarily truncated. Usually there is more to a list than what's shown on the data card.
     It is essential to learn all you can about the lists you want to test. Ask for mailing pieces or samples of recent advertisements and find out where these ads appeared so that you get an idea of the "flavor" of the list. If the source of the list was a TV infomercial, find out which stations and during which time slots it ran.

Every mail should consider matching the mailing tape vs. the response tape to understand the geodynamics of response.
Population redistribution is an ongoing and flexible trend. In the ever-shifting society, some formerly high-revenue areas may be down in response. A possible reason: a big new shopping mall that is convenient and lures consumers away from catalogs. A fascinating exercise would be to match a list of major malls against the geo factors. It may be that you will want to suppress certain zip codes from your prospect mailings where major malls have been built.

Mail every month to find out when your customers and prospects are most likely to buy; you may uncover a good new season that is right for you.

All orders should be traced by lists for collectibility, renewability, and lifetime value.

We must avoid the draining effects of inconsistent analysis. It is essential to compile a list of critical variables to be included in the analytical procedures on a consistent basis. For example, we know that the response rate is the key. What about bad pay rates?

Look at list selection as an investor looks at a stock portfolio: choose mostly safe, guaranteed moneymakers, some slightly more speculative, and some with an element of risk that have a chance of a big payoff.

"Hot line" (recency) segmentation is very important and in some cases as important as the affinity factor.

Be sure that the hot line is hot—not the last 12 months. Also, be sure it's a paid transaction, not just the name of someone who just received the premium, the free issue of a magazine, the free catalog, or the introductory record or book on club offers or who was a "no" respondent to a sweepstakes offer.

Follow these standard list selection guidelines.
- Descriptions (subscribers, members, buyers, donors, expires, former buyers)
- Affinity (based on consumer profile, previous list history, or a subjective extension of interaction or experience)
- Source used to acquire names (direct mail, space, radio, TV, telephone)
- Recency of acquisition, such as hot line names
- Frequency (i.e., multibuyers)
- Unit of sale

In original studies, these last three elements or standards (recency, frequency, and monetary value) controlled 90 percent of the reasons why customers repeat at a certain sales volume. The weighing of these factors in the total value of 90 percent of all factors was broadly as follows:

Frequency: 50 of 90 percent
Recency: 35 of 90 percent
Monetary: 15 of 90 percent

The RFM theory cannot be used in list selection for outside lists.

This theory is applicable to the customer file only. In list selection, *recency* means when the customer came on; *frequency* is defined on list rental fields as multiple buyers; *monetary value* is the unit of sale.

Don't look at the success or failure of a single list; think categories such as household, leisure, recreation, fashion, gourmet, travel, sports, do-it-yourself, children's, or pet.

Some products are demographically self-defining, e.g., acne treatments, disposable diapers, designer jeans, toys, and denture cleaners.

For example, let's take a look at some discretionary purchases:

Dorothy Brown

9/1/95	Suede Suit	$600
5/8/96	Evening Dress	$300
		$900

Jane Smith

9/2/95	Nest of Tables	$200
	Gourmet Cookware	$250
	Corn Popper	$ 50
6/1/96	Decorative Screen	$250
	Hostess Dress	$100
		$850

The dollar amounts are in the same ballpark, but the purchased items are not. To the computer these are data—not information. It's what you do with these data—how you humanize them—that yields valuable information.

Obviously, Dorothy often goes out; Jane Smith is a hearth hugger who prefers home-based activities. A correlation study of this kind of purchasing behavior allows you to:

- Know your customer.
- Create specialized mailings or catalogs for groups of customers.
- Gather the necessary research to expand your market and product line.
- Segment your customer file to produce effective promotions and generate additional rental income.

The more you know about your own customer, the more directed the test list selection.

People classify themselves by what they buy and where it comes from. A customer database that has been segmented to effectively create customer portraits directs you to the appropriate lists to test.

It is important, particularly in a start-up situation, to understand that in most instances the first mailing does not yield a profit.

Actually, it should be considered a research and development (R&D) expense, which must be related to the stated goals of the business plan. Even though you will get some orders that offset some of the expense, the most important result of the direct mail test is the information. You will be able to determine the degree of acceptance of the product or service. You will also learn which piece, which promotional appeal, and which type of list works best. All in all, this research is much more directional than many other research methods.

It is logical to assume that the same group of names that pulled .19 percent in January will not pull the same response in August.

A second solicitation in a six-month period will be less productive than the first. If you can afford a 15 to 30 percent drop in response, the list could be worth repeating. However, if the list is an active one with new names being added and old names dropped, the "repeat" becomes less repetitive, and the list should hold up within a 10 to 15 percent range.

Caveat: Coordination of all the various suppliers and creative resources requires a high degree of sophistication and professionalism.
Companies should not attempt to undertake this function with people who are not completely familiar with all aspects of direct mail marketing. If no one within the company has this expertise, use a consultant or direct marketing agency. As many major corporations entering the direct marketing field have learned, assuming that general marketing principles apply to the direct marketing discipline can lead to absolute disasters.

Paul Goldberg's Strategy for Picking Lists
Of all the elements that go into a direct mail effort, the most important single purchase is the list.

It's not simply spending $70/M or $100/M for names. That's just the beginning. Once you've ordered a list, you're committed to sending something to the names on it. That means you're spending additional money for printing, folding, inserting, mailing, bagging, or traying. If a mailing in test quantities costs $600/M, then every 5,000-piece cell costs $3,000.

There are two ways to order lists: (1) use a broker or (2) do it yourself. By *broker* I don't mean an organization. Basically, all brokerage companies are the same. They have access to the same mailing lists; they charge the same prices; their data cards are more or less the same. Instead, choose a list broker for the specialist working there. Does he or she know the market and do the hard work of digging, screening, and analyzing every which way to Sunday so that when you get a series of recommendations you *know* you've got a good shot at success?

Use different brokerage houses for different products. At one house, I feel my broker is the best person in the country in the field of art and collectibles. At another, there's a person who knows catalog lists inside out. If I have a fundraising client, I turn to two individuals whom I trust completely. All work for different brokers, and if any of these professionals changes companies, *I follow the person.*

Chances are if you call the average list broker and describe your product or service and the market you are trying to reach, the broker will push some buttons and the computer will spit out 100 or more data cards; this means *you*—not the list broker—will have to do all the work.

Goldberg's Seven Rules for Dealing with Data Cards

Divide the cards into three piles: A, B, and C.

Put the likely candidates in the A pile, the marginal in the B pile, and the obvious rejects in the C pile.

Next, call the broker and *ask for samples of the direct mail control packages* **for all the cards in your A and B piles**—those mailings responsible for turning prospects into paying customers whose names are on those lists.

Most brokers have these mailings. If not, chances are they will reside in the massive *Who's Mailing What!* archives in Philadelphia and you can get copies for a fee.

For list selection, the direct mail efforts are far more valuable than the products themselves, copies of the magazines, or samples of the merchandise the person ordered.

By studying the mailings, you discover what these people actually responded to. You want to see what made these people act, not what they actually bought.

Was the mailing a buckeye sweepstakes? Does the offer include an irresistible premium? Does the package have the look, feel, and style of what you are doing, or is there a real clash?

If space or DRTV sold, get copies of the ad or commercial plus the media it ran in and the dates and times.

Once you have chosen your lists, go back to the list broker and find out who else has used the list successfully.

You want to know both who tested it and did not roll out as well as the rollouts. Some brokers will automatically add this information to the data card. With this information in hand, you should have a sense of which lists are logical candidates to test.

Beware the data card.

Remember who has written the data card—usually the list owner or manager. While I don't believe either would deliberately misrepresent a list, they are often overenthusiastic in their descriptions. One wag once pointed out that data cards represent some of the greatest fiction ever written.

After all, list rental income is free money. It might cost 75 cents to switch on a computer and run 1,000 names; those names are rented for up to $150/M or more—a 300 percent markup. This is hugely profitable business.

Try to read between the lines of a data card, and if you have any doubts, check with the broker or manager. Also, look carefully at additional charges for special selects. Many of these charges are totally unnecessary.

Beware of special pricing unless you have gotten an agreement in writing that the owner will hold to that special price through a rollout.

Ask that a sample dump of each list be sent to you in hard copy at the same time your mag tape is being shipped for merge/purge.

How do you know if you are getting the list you ordered? A tough question. Remember, after all the alchemy, enhancements, and merge/purge, the ultimate output of any computer run is a series of names and addresses in zip code order.

It seems most mailers' complaints are in the area of compiled lists in general and business-to-business lists in particular. Two examples: When one of my clients ordered a compiled list of presidents of large manufacturing companies and other organizations, he got a file filled with data processors, engineers, individual names, and P.O. boxes—and virtually no presidents. When he ordered a totally different compiled list of executives, he found individual names in totally unrelated areas throughout.

In both cases—since the client asked to look at the file before it was mailed—he saw the actual printout of part of the file, so he quickly ordered new lists and saved himself a lot of money.

In another case a seed and garden cataloger ordered a list of suburban and rural new movers—a logical marketing technique since people in new houses often have gardens.

New mover lists are acquired by researchers prowling through real estate transaction records in municipal courthouses. Among the data they record: name and address (of course); type of dwelling, amount of the sale, amount of the mortgage, and name of the mortgage holder.

On this seed catalog mailing, the addresses read as follows:

John Smith
Columbia Savings Bank
1234 Main Street
Evanston, IL 00000

Somehow the name of the institution holding the mortgage got on every label, giving the creeps to the recipients. Had the bank rented their names? What was going on?

When Denny Hatch wrote this up in his newsletter—and later used the illustration in a speech—he received a blistering letter from the catalog firm's attorney requesting he not mention his client by name in future talks. "At the least I trust you will note that the incident occurred years ago, was the compiler's fault, and led to corrective action."

Hatch wrote back:

> The fault was not with the list compiler. The list compiler gets the information—including the name of the bank and the amount of mortgage—and sells that information to mortgage insurance companies. [Your client] wanted part of that information for another purpose.
>
> [Your client] either gave the wrong specs when ordering the list or it was a glitch by the list compiler. Either way, [your client] did not have a knowledgeable person eyeball the list before the mailing went out. [Your client] was the mailer. Its name was on that catalog. The buck stops there. . . .

All of this unpleasantness could have been avoided if someone who cared had taken a look at the hard copy before it went on the catalogs.

Mary Lou Probka's List Arrival Checklist

Demand at least a portion of your list in hard copy.
Rarely is it practical to look at the contents of a full magnetic tape. You have two ways to go:

1. Ask for a file dump of X number of records from a certain spot on the tape. If you don't specify, you'll get the first 50 records or so. A marketer may prefer to get a certain number—say 200 from the middle of the tape or 200 from particular zip codes (such as your own zip area or one where you have an interest).
2. Ask for a galley of X number of records by a certain criterion. (A galley doesn't give computer info, such as record length; it will give name, address, code, etc.)

You can ask for 100 records in a certain sectional center facility or the records on a certain key code or zip code, etc.

Did you get the quantity you ordered?
You may have been sent the wrong select. Is the list one zip string or did they give you half and run it twice?

Is the key code there—on all labels—and is it correct?
This is especially important if you've asked for two codes to be merged into one order.

Is the list in zip order if so requested?

Are the titles and businesses appropriate for the select you ordered?

Check the selections you were given versus the selection you didn't make; you could have the reverse.

Are there obvious duplications (errors)?

Are the labels printed for proper cutting by the Cheshire machine?

Are there home addresses where you expected business addresses?

Are zip codes missing that you didn't exclude in your order?
See if some states don't appear at all or if you got only three states when you wanted the entire United States.

Check titles and companies in zip codes where your industry is concentrated to see if they make sense.

Check your own zip code or your local metro area to see who's there.

Did your list come with the first page showing errors (no zips)?
Sometimes it's worth looking up the rest of the information.

Do any or all of your lists have a heavy concentration of zips in one area?
You may want to send some first class or stagger the mailing. Too many pieces arriving at one time to some companies or government agencies result in your mail being trashed.

Check for foreign names.
If you ordered only U.S. names, did you somehow get 20 pages of foreign names?

If you ordered fifth-digit names ending in zero, check that all the labels are correct; see if every sixth name has that zero.

If you ordered only female names, did you get one-third male names?

If you asked for an A/B split, did you get two sets of identical names?

You, the marketer, are still responsible for results. Check your lists . . . and don't trust the new person at the front desk; do it yourself.

Andrew J. Byrne's Precept
Direct-response mailing lists outpull compiled lists, even those that mirror the demographics and psychographics of the customer list.

If hot line names don't work, skip the list.

James Gribble's Tenet
Mail hot line lists while they're still hot.

I define a hot line select as those individuals on a list rental file who responded or purchased within the last three months. This is the industry standard, although you will see list owners advertise their hot lines as updated every month or every week.

Why does a hot line select exist? Mailers have known for some time that many offers work best with hot line names. The theory is that people go through buying or responding phases, so hit them while they're hot.

Consequently, the more quickly you can get to people after they've responded to another offer, the higher your response will be. This is simply a fact of life for many opportunity seekers and low-end general merchandise mailers and for many fundraisers. Without the availability of hot line names, they would be unable to mail profitably.

I have tested and proven this phenomenon many times. Here are actual results of a well-structured timing test of one hot line selection that shows the power of recency in the RFM formula:

Activity	Calendar Days from Initial Response Purchase	Actual Response Rate	% Diff.
Prospect respond or buy	0		
Names are added to list rental file	+7		
Names are rented, delivered, and divided into 5 test panels	+12		
Panel 1 mails	+14	4.5%	
Panel 2 mails	+21	3.9%	−13%
Panel 3 mails	+28	3.2%	−29%
Panel 4 mails	+35	2.8%	−38%
Panel 5 mails	+42	2.7%	−40%

Fran Green's Rubric
Don't think lists; think people.

Most product managers think in terms of which lists work for their offer. Techies love to overlay databases and manipulate lists to shake out potential nonbuyers, thereby making the offer to people who are statistically most likely to buy.

While this is all well and good, why not consider another tack? Take a cue from the creatives.

Talk to any direct marketing writer—or read any book on the direct marketing creative process—and you'll hear the same thing: "I imagine I am writing to one person. I visualize that person sitting across from me reading my letter and studying my brochure. If it's a telemarketing script, I hear the conversation in my head. Like a method actor, I have *become* that person. I have to feel the resistance to my offer and overcome those objections. I have to be compelling, fascinating, and continually interruptive. I can't be dull or irrelevant or offensive; otherwise, my letter will be tossed aside. I am engaged in what Stan Rapp calls 'intimate advertising'."

What does this have to do with picking lists? Everything!

For example, American List Counsel was selected by Roger Craver to be list manager for all the clients of Craver, Mathews, Smith & Co., America's greatest fundraising agency specializing in liberal causes. Among Craver, Mathews, Smith accounts: Planned Parenthood, the Fund for the Feminist Majority, and the National Organization for Women. Chances are, if a list broker recommended, for example, the National Organization for Women to a commercial client, the account executive or product manager would skim over the data card and mutter to him- or herself: "Why are they suggesting this list of radical feminists?"

But stop. Think. Look at the data card: nearly 100,000 women have paid to become members.

Get hold of the current mailing piece. The letter is totally issue-oriented, with emotionally charged copy.

Now think of the individual donor.

She is literate—*a reader of her mail who has responded*. What kind of person is she *really*?

She wants equal pay for equal work; she resents being put on "the mommy track" by law firms; and she wants freedom of choice.

Is she a radical feminist *really*? Most are hardworking professional women who don't want to be pigeonholed because their plumbing is different from that of men. And they are successful.

Average gift: $28. That's the average single gift; the majority of these donors give three or four times a year. This means they are giving $100 or more annually—not chopped liver.

They join book clubs and buy magazines. Catalogs—perhaps not Victoria's Secret but certainly Bedford Fair. After all, they have to dress for work and don't have a lot of time for shopping. Certainly they are candidates for Day-Timers and Hold Everything with those wonderful organizers, and very likely Nightingale-Conant will have some self-improvement materials that they would gladly invest in.

Doesn't this knowledge create a wider universe for your product or service?

Of course it does, because donor files open up new avenues of opportunity for direct marketers. These philanthropic individuals are inundated with fundraising appeals while being virtually ignored for commercial offers. In essence, they present uncharted territory for catalogers, publishers, and business offers. Mailers who look beyond the scope of their current testing patterns to consider the potential of donor fields will prosper when other mailers don't.

Doesn't a test of 5,000 or 10,000 make sense? This isn't rocket science. It's old-fashioned logic.

Arlene Clanny's Guide
Observe mailing patterns.

Brokers and managers know Victoria's Secret mails its sale catalogs in January and February. So, unless you're looking for bargain hunters, you might want to avoid those hot line names.

Richard V. Benson's Vision
Thirty-day hot line names will overcome seasonality.

Architectural Digest conducted a seasonality test by mailing segments of the same lists every month to measure the effect or response of the season. The results showed very little deviation by month. The book division tested a new cookbook in late December, with good results. Based on its seasonality study, it rolled out in May—with disastrous results. This wasn't really surprising since May is a poor mailing month for most products.

When I looked into "Why the disaster?" I found the seasonality test had been done with 30-day hot line names.

Mailing lists do not show much better results mailed with a year's rest than with six months' rest.

Mike Manzari's Indicator
Seasonality means that a mailer will mail at the best times of the year.

Manzari's Corollary:
Seasonality is not as simple as it looks.

For example, just because early January and Labor Day are historically the best times of the year for business-to-business newsletters and magazines, this is not necessarily the best time to mail for all business publishers. For instance, if your audience includes wealthy farmers, these could be the worst times to get them to respond.

Doug Flynn's Caution
If all your list tests work, you haven't tested enough.

Denny Hatch's Dictum
If someone offers to give you a free list, think twice before accepting the offer.

Some list owners (e.g., Boardroom) will offer a free test. Before you say yes, learn everything about the list—and the original source of the names—to be sure you have a logical mesh.

If a typical mailing costs $500/M and someone offers you a list that normally sells for $100/M, but it's the wrong list, you're blowing $400/M. That's a bad deal.

Malcolm McCluskey's Checklist of Broker's and Mailer's Responsibilities

Before you get started selecting, renting, and enhancing lists, you'll need to hire a broker to help you find what you're looking for. Having worked in the mailer, brokerage, and management segments of the industry, I know the importance of research in acquiring lists that will work for direct mail campaigns.

One of the basic steps to finding good lists is to work with a list broker who is an experienced marketer. Shop around for a broker who is compatible and understands your specific market. Find out if the broker is currently working with other mailers of similar background.

I have also found the mailer's participation critical to list research; you need to give your list manager and brokers as much information as possible on your company and products.

Eight Responsibilities of a Broker

A good broker knows the mailer's competition.

A good broker knows what the mailer's competition is mailing and what's working.

A good broker maintains a well-developed network in the list management community.

A good broker secures accurate test and universe counts—including roll-out potential.

A good broker provides pricing information, along with possible discounts.

A good broker knows how the list is refined—appended data, new segments, related usage (did it work?), the source, how often the file is updated and run through National Change of Address (NCOA), who the service bureau is.

A good broker has the availability of a list database that is continually updated with fresh information and is segmented into list categories.

A good broker offers a professional support staff to assist in follow-through and provide backup.

Seven Things the Mailer Must Provide
Samples of the complete mail package.

Product pricing.

Details on all offers.

Costs to produce the packages (excluding list costs).

Demographics—recent studies available plus what demographics are working for you.

Mail schedules (so brokers can more effectively recommend lists that will provide the best universes for future rollouts).

An index of what has worked in the past . . . and what hasn't.

Mike Manzari's Reality
If a list is going to be good, it will never be more responsive than when it first comes to market.

James Johnson's Observation
Data cards rarely describe what a list "update" really means.

If the list is drawn from an active mail order catalog customer list, *update* usually means that new names have been added to the file.

If the list is an assembly from primary-source information, it is nearly impossible to determine if names have been added, changed, or deleted.

The title of the list is seldom the most important component of the list use question; usually it is a selection from the various data available on the list that makes "the list" work.

Todd Waldman's Code
When you have three lists that look the same and offer identical selects, usage can be the deciding factor in helping you choose the list with the proven track record.

Bob Stone's Test
Merge/purge names—those that appear on two or more lists—will out-pull any single list from which these names have been extracted.

> Overlays on lists (enhancements), such as lifestyle characteristics, income, education, age, marital status, and propensity to respond by mail or phone, will always improve response.

Bob Foehl's Limitation
Never mail a list outside of your merge/purge.

Foehl's First Corollary
When you can't get a list into a merge/purge, don't automatically throw it out.

> This could be an untapped gold mine. It may simply be that a list is not used often because it's difficult to work with. Individual list integrity must be maintained.

Foehl's Second Corollary
If you combine a group of your core lists into one big field, you'll save money and sometimes boost response.

> Direct Media has created some mega-lists from some of the customer files. The approach works well for seminar mailers, for instance, because the characteristics of potential attendees that are most predictive—geographic proximity to the convergence and business category and title—can be isolated across several lists and are, in fact, more important than the original list source.
> Usage, usage, usage—always try to find out who's using a list.

Foehl's Third Corollary
Don't be fooled by usage reports.

> If you see your competitors' names, ask some questions: Did the other mailer test it or continue? What offer was mailed? It could have been a totally different division or a new product test. Don't assume that because someone else mailed it at some point it'll work for you.

Craig Huey's Statute
Reserve your mail date.

The very best mailing lists require a reserved mail date. Beware any list that doesn't! It could mean other mailers have had poor results and so no one uses the list, or it may mean the list owner is not protecting your mail date. Other mailers could mail at the very same time, decreasing your response. A good list has many users, but the owner should not let anyone mail for one week on either side of your mailing.

Paul Goldberg's Caveat
If your mailing is delayed, you must reclear the mail date with each list owner.

Don't give your list broker hell when he or she can't come up with a list; do it yourself!

If no published list exists in a vertical market, you will not find it in Standard Rate and Data Service (SRDS) or on the Marketing Information Network (MIN) on-line service. No broker can get it; no manager is touting it. It doesn't exist. Quite simply, you have to create it.

Goldberg's Five Time-Honored List-Building Techniques
These techniques from the 1970s are just as valid today.

Contact advertisers.
This was not an assignment either Denny Hatch (who wrote the package) nor I relished. But we were starting out as freelancers, and you took whatever paid the rent so long as it was not a fraud.

The client wanted to take on the three "barbershop" magazines—*Playboy* and *Penthouse,* which would not rent their lists, and *Hustler*, which was strictly newsstand.

It quickly became apparent that I was going to have to be innovative to find the names for a mailing large enough to allow the publisher to raise his advertising prices and broaden his advertising base.

The word *advertising* was the key to building lists successfully. I bought every equivalent magazine in existence and called every advertiser I could reach whom I suspected might have a decent-sized customer file. I struck gold.

Yes, they had lists; no, they had never thought about renting them; yes, they loved the idea of getting money for the list rentals. In fact, on reflection, if I'd had the stomach for it, I probably should have gone into the compiling business at the time.

Find affinity organizations.
In its quest to recycle existing editorial material, the *Financial Times* of London created a magazine for U.S. corporations doing business abroad—*World Business Weekly*. Existing lists were far from being responsive enough to build the needed numbers economically.

Lou Isadora, then publisher of the magazine, hired a very bright young man, Clyde Brown, whose sole purpose was to develop lists to be used for *World Business Weekly*. Brown was amazing. When a special report on a specific country was announced for publication in an upcoming issue, Brown would hunt for organizations that had affinity with that country and talk his way into borrowing the list. These names were put on file, and a sampling program was set up; these subscribers were then converted to paid. Isadora nicknamed the operation "Scoop and Dip." The program had a dual purpose: (1) It enabled us to meet the rate base by using the controlled free names whenever we needed them. (2) The conversions to paid were the most profitable.

Clyde Brown then hit pay dirt when he convinced two large hotel chains to allow the use of the names of those clients they identified as frequent travelers. In some cases the hotel allowed us to distribute magazines in their name as a perk, which in turn gave us an excellent conversion rate.

Offer a piece of the action to an association.

The enormously successful founder of Jeno's Pizza, Jeno Palucci, wanted to create a magazine that would make his fellow Italian-Americans proud of their heritage at a time when the only Italians making news were the Mafia.

A few ethnic compilations existed at the time, but they were filled with errors. For example, one such list of Italian-Americans was designed around names from the phone book that ended in *a, e, i,* and *o*. One publisher—it may have been Meredith—had done research and offered ethnic selects on its house file. But the numbers were not large enough to build a subscriber file.

The solution: We approached every Italian-American organization and every ethnic newspaper we could put our hands on—on both a national and a regional basis (e.g., the Sons of Italy, the Columbus Club)—and offered them a percentage of every sub we sold through them. They could do the promotion or we could. It was only then that we were able to reach our circulation goals.

Another version of this technique is to offer your product as a benefit of membership in an analogous association—such as a museum. This enables you to piggyback your offer in someone else's mailing, thus saving you the cost of solo mail.

Be your own clipping service.

When the *Financial Times* purchased a group of privately held, exorbitantly priced newsletters, I thought I had returned to the Dark Ages again. *International Reports* (at the time a whopping $750 a year) and its sister publication, *International Country Risk Guide* ($2,500 a year) were aimed at international bankers, traders, investors, LIBOR experts, and the Gnomes of Zurich, whose names may have been in annual reports but emphatically were not on any lists.

The business was the brainchild of Guenther Reiman, a brilliant and incredibly energetic German economist in his 80s, whose prime source was his own prospect file that was neatly put up on, of all things, Speedomat plates. Reiman's prospecting technique: scour every financial publication in the world for the mention of important executives. Once a week, Reiman would drift into the fulfillment office with a fistful of new names, which he would drop on a desk, and then tell the circulation director to send three people a personal letter.

Another of his sources was the New York Public Library, where his people studied every directory published that related to foreign trade. He then purchased those directories most likely to work and put them up on his file. Another source: the lists of every foreign Chamber of Commerce member in New York, Chicago, San Francisco, and Los Angeles.

When I began working with *International Reports,* I tried to make existing lists (e.g., *Business Week* Hotline) work to avoid using the Speedomat monster. Was I ever wrong. What I had not taken into account was how carefully Reiman had compiled the lists on the stencils. The file was updated once a year with a "Return Postage Guaranteed" mailing. Reiman was the only economist I ever knew who was an authentic marketing genius.

Use selects in "reverse."

Another difficult list challenge was a magazine aimed at upscale black women. It was the brainchild of a minority-owned aerospace company in Maryland. For circulation director, they hired Edna Greenbaum, who had successfully converted *Black Enterprise* from controlled to paid and really knew her way around that market. Between the two of us, we came up with a plan that produced some remarkable results for *Élan.*

The first step was to select zips across the country known to house a high-percentage black population. Then we went to every large magazine that rented its lists and asked for a female select in those areas only. That was the easy part. No one turned us down on the selects.

Next, we knew of a major service bureau that had developed a program designed to eliminate known names of blacks, the original purpose of which I do not remember. However, when used in reverse, it could help us identify blacks. So we ran the rented lists against this program and mailed only the hits.

Now for the tricky part: In each case we asked for a net name charge so that we would pay for only the names we mailed. As you can imagine, we ran into a bit of a hornet's nest since that was the first time that the net name concept had been floated. However, persistence and an appeal to social conscience won out in most cases. The result: a whopping 99 percent accuracy and only a single complaint letter from a recipient who was neither black nor female. On a couple of lists we hit double-digit responses.

Alas, *Élan* was wildly underfinanced, and after three exquisite issues it ceased publication.

Jerry Gould's Five Traps to Avoid in Mailing List Rentals
Note: These five caveats first appeared in *Successful Magazine Publishing*.

Beware of the Small-List Syndrome.
A very common error of new launches is wishful thinking or inadequate research about the size of the list universe. Just because there are, say, 25,000 members of the National Association of Home Brewers (a fictitious example), and no other lists available specifically for home brewers, don't think you can start an independent, paid-circulation magazine for home brew aficionados and achieve a circulation goal of 25,000. Probably you can't. On an annual basis the most subscribers you will be able to cull from the NAHB list is probably 2,500 to 3,500 (10 to 15 percent), presuming, of course, that the association would let you use the list in the first place.

Depending on whether your publication is paid or controlled, consumer or business, the net response from any profitable list in a specific mailing effort will range from 0.5 to 10 percent, with rare exception. As my six-year-old says philosophically: "That's the way life's gotta be." Use these figures to determine how large a universe of real prospects there needs to be to support your circulation goals before spending good money on a bad launch.

When you are launching a new product that is heavily dependent on direct mail, make sure you have a universe of lists available large enough to support your circulation goals. Don't put your trust in a few lists that are obviously good for your product but represent too small a universe.

Beware the trap of believing list description or data cards.
This is the error of naïveté. List descriptions, commonly called *data cards*, are marketing tools, not objective descriptions. They are not audited by BPA or any other independent auditing agency. Need I say more?

Actually, many and perhaps most list data cards are fairly accurate. However, if you do not have experience with a specific list, you have no way of knowing whether the data card in front of you is anywhere near correct. And that's what you need to know.

You need the same skills to ferret out information about lists as you do to be a good journalist. And, in fact, good list brokers can help you, because they are rather like good journalists. They have a strong streak of skepticism about the list information that comes across their desks, and they should be passing along their honest judgments to their clients.

Protect yourself from weak, imprecise, or downright incorrect or out-of-date information on data cards by asking lots of questions of your list broker, the manager of the list, or any other resource available. Be skeptical.

Beware of operating under the idea that "My subscribers are like me."
This is the egotist's error—believing that your subscribers are identical to you in taste, personal habits, and demographics. It is an error that occurs particularly with enthusiast magazines and newsletters and can lead to some crazed

list-buying decisions. For example, if you are a farmer's wife and also a sewing enthusiast, don't assume that farmers' wives are going to respond in large numbers to your offer of a general-interest sewing magazine. Your primary market is other sewing enthusiasts and, in particular, subscribers to other sewing publications, regardless of their demographics.

There is an unrelated but similar error: assuming that a few demographic characteristics are sufficient to make a list work. Say, for example, you want to launch a newsletter for bond buyers. You have discovered that most bond buyers are over the age of 50 and make more than $50,000 a year. Therefore you mail your offer of a $195 per year *Bond Buyer's Alert* to well-heeled 50-year-olds. The mailing bombs, of course. In that case the most important characteristic of a successful list is not the demographics at all but interest in investment and particularly in bonds. And the principle usually holds. It shouldn't matter, after all, where or under what circumstances your subscribers live, so long as they are interested enough in your publication's subject matter to subscribe to it.

Rent lists of people who have spent money on a product as similar to yours as possible. Don't depend on demographics as list selection criteria. Demographic lists generally have disappointing results for circulation offers.

Beware of inadequate monitoring of suppliers.

Your suppliers in mailing list transactions are, of course, your list broker, your merge/purge house, and your letter shop or mail house. Visit them. See how they do the work on your account and watch the process from the beginning through the actual mail drop. Don't be shy about making some procedural suggestions. As a publisher of a small magazine, you are only one of many clients of these suppliers, and you are competing for their attention against clients that are probably larger and represent more business. You'll enhance your leverage with your suppliers by being visible and making helpful suggestions.

With list brokers specifically, make sure they are paying your bills on time. Many brokers make a practice of aging the money that you paid them for another 30 days or longer before they pay the list management company. The benefit to the list broker: the interest earned while "floating" your money.

There are absolutely no benefits to you in this arrangement, and in fact your credit at list management companies may be damaged or jeopardized without your knowledge. That can make it more difficult for you to obtain lists in a timely fashion, particularly if you should change list brokers. If you suspect your broker of aging payments, insist that the broker pay your bills within a week of receiving your funds. Check independently to be sure the broker is doing so.

Beware of in-house list brokerage.

Many small magazine publishers are do-it-yourselfers, and this is a do-it-yourselfer's error. It's the old idea that you can save money by ordering lists yourself and talking the list owner into giving you a commission. In fact you'll generally lose more than you'll gain with this approach.

Let me put in a good word for the real list brokers and the commission they make. List brokers normally make 20 percent commission on the base price of a list, and that is their only source of income. Believe me, they earn it. Just on the labor spent in telephone calls back and forth to list owners, monitoring shipping, and other production matters, a list broker can actually save you money.

But of course the real reason a broker is valuable is the quality of information and recommendations he or she makes and what the broker knows about list procedures and direct mail generally. Typically a list broker will be working with anywhere between five and 25 other mailers on an active basis, seeing hundreds of mailing list descriptions daily as well as having dozens of conversations about specific lists and their characteristics. That experience is very useful to you, and the only way you can have access to it is by working with a list broker.

In addition, a list broker is a creative resource—he or she should regularly be coming up with new ideas for you. The broker is, essentially, a free direct mail consultant and should be used as such—so long as you are giving the broker your list-buying business.

Finding a good list broker is not an easy task, especially if you are a small publisher who orders in relatively small quantities. Typically a list broker needs orders from you of one to two million names a year to consider you a minimally profitable client. If you order fewer than this quantity of names from a broker who is doing a good job for you, you are very fortunate. So if you are using more than one broker and spreading that quantity of names between them, think about consolidating your orders with the best of them or with someone better than either of them. You will probably get better service.

There's also real danger in *not* using a good list broker: being too narrowly focused, myopic, closed off to new ideas, out of date on new lists and developments in the direct mail industry. If you're using lists to build or maintain circulation, they are your lifeline. Use the best resource available to find and obtain them.

Let me qualify my criticism of in-house brokerages by noting that there is a very small handful of them that manages to do a good job. They are the exceptions to the rule.

In general, you should forget trying to save on broker commissions. If you are lucky enough to find a good list broker, count your blessings.

Denny Hatch's Addition
If you do your own in-house list brokerage, be sure to claim a 20 percent brokerage commission deduction on all lists you rent.

However, unless you have a very sophisticated in-house list research department and vast connections throughout the industry, you're nuts to (1) not use a good list broker and (2) not pay your broker full commission.

Exception: when you're too small to be a worthwhile client for a busy list broker. Then, I'm afraid, you're on your own.

Don Chilcutt's Practice
Use one list broker.

> A client has to test each list anyway. This way we build a relationship—we get to know what works and what doesn't. The client doesn't need another broker unless the names I supply don't work or I say there are no more lists to test.
>
> What I don't understand is how a broker can sit in a little cubicle in downtown Manhattan and make recommendations without ever having seen or touched the merchandise that the names on a particular list responded to. We go into clients' businesses and get to know their merchandise and how they fulfill orders. We meet their employees, and we let them meet the people from our company with whom they'll be working.

Arlene Clanny's Stricture
Nobody wants to sell a list as something it's not, or you won't come back; then the broker will have to face the list owner and explain what happened.

Andrew Harwin's Demand
Expect your broker to go beyond the routine.

> For instance, subscription publications always look at other subscriber lists, and many catalogers are adamant about getting only a mail order buyer. When I was a list manager for the Kleid Company, which manages a lot of magazine lists, I routinely had to wear down the resistance of brokers working with catalogers to get them to look at subscriber lists as a source of new blood. They think very narrowly, and this tends to wear out their core lists, which have a limited amount of new blood at any given time.
>
> A broker must paint a picture of the potential buyer.
>
> When we helped launch *Vibe,* a new magazine covering music and popular culture, it was so new we were not sure of the audience. We looked at every possible angle to find subscribers: all sorts of music lists, students, different age brackets, from people on the cutting edge who are living this culture to those who want to be *au courant*—over 30 but still interested in being hip. Based on that *au courant* theme, we tested magazines with a median age much higher than you'd expect our subscribers to be.
>
> The challenge is getting mailers to be courageous. But then that's tricky since the economics don't always work for mailers. They need to get a certain response, and although you might be able to generate a response, it might not be enough to make a difference for them. It depends on their budget and their goals.

Denny Hatch's Dictum
Negotiate list rental fees, but always pay full brokerage commissions.

As a percentage of the $400M–$600+/M cost of solo mail, the brokerage commission is peanuts. A broker can steer you to lists that work and, more important, can steer you away from poor lists. As Martin Edelston and Brian Kurtz of Boardroom state unequivocally, paying full commissions means brokers will go the extra mile for you. As Kurtz says, "It's so tempting to negotiate. But if the broker can get better base prices, waiver of selection prices, and exchange deals, the commission is well worth it."

Annette Brodsky's Indicator
If you are unfamiliar with the source of the list, ask to see the promotional material that got the name.

Brian Kurtz's Maxim

All data cards are guilty until proven innocent.
Today's test may not be tomorrow's continuation, and today's continuation might not be a continuation a year from now.

Competition in the list business is really coexistence; the best lists can work for you and me both.

Data cards offering exact counts can be misleading, because by the time a list manager puts a count on a data card and mails the list promotion, the numbers on that list have almost certainly changed.

There are three elements to picking lists to test and three elements only: (1) research, (2) research, and (3) research.

To paraphrase the late Dick Benson, no one spends enough time on lists. To ensure a list makes sense for a test or roll out, Boardroom has come up with the criteria that follow. Not only do Boardroom's product managers have to fill out as many sections as possible, but our brokers have to fill out some of the sections as well (e.g., Outside Usage: Who else has not only mailed this list, but rolled out with it? What selects do you recommend?). Because Boardroom mails in the 10s of millions every year—and, as company policy, pays full brokerage commissions—brokers fill out these sheets for us. This discipline makes them ask questions they normally might not. In fact, thinking about the criteria helps them and, I feel, makes them better brokers.

The sheet has 14 elements to be filled in. You create your own by using the following headings—with lines or space to be filled in under the headings—by either the product manager or the list broker.

As you review the headings, keep in mind that the overall sheet is greater than the sum of its parts. No single question will tell you to test or not to test.

List manager and owner.

Usually a mailer won't care who the manager is, but Boardroom always asks for that information from the broker. The reason: If you are not familiar with the list, the manager's reputation could weigh in as a favorable or unfavorable factor.

Knowing the owner can tell you the promotional techniques used to generate the names. For example, a list for Hachette Filipacchi or Time, Inc., may well be sweepstakes sold. Also, when you know who the owner is, you can ascertain whether or not you have a corporate list exchange policy that impacts the budget.

Selects.

Let's get specific. What selects should be made? Does more than one select make sense? This question forces brokers to think the challenge through and rank their reasons.

Estimated total annual universe.

This tells you the rollout potential of a list.

Pricing.

If you are testing a list outside your core market, ask for a discount on the list price and see if you can avoid paying for selects—at least in the test. A list owner who wants the business—and all the possible juicy rollout orders—should play along.

Conversely, when you are renting your own list to another mailer and choose to give test quantity discounts, be sure to get in writing that the arrangement is for testing purposes only; for additional names, regular prices will be charged.

Source.

Here's where data cards can be guiltiest. What's really behind such ambiguous wording as "direct mail sold" or "direct response generated"? Was it through space ads, statement stuffers, informercials, agents, surveys? Are the names inquiries? Sweeps NO entries? Expires?

Recency or frequency of update.

Consumer lists go out of date at the rate of 2 percent a month; business lists age 1 percent a week (roughly 50 percent a year). If the update system is not spelled out, you could find yourself mailing an old list. What does that mean? If you are paying $400/M for a mailing to a list that is 20 percent out of date, your real cost is $400/800 or $500/M. Of course, if the list brings in orders at an acceptable cost per order (or cost per paid order), you go back to it. However if it's breakeven or a loser, age could be part of the problem.

Further, if the list is updated annually and your test goes out to it right after the update, those results will not hold up in the rollout.

Seasonality of the list.
What is the advertising or promotion schedule of the list owner? For example, if the owner blitzes customers with big mailings twice a year, it makes sense not to mail into the teeth of those efforts.

Sample attached.
Always insist brokers attach to the worksheet a sample of the mailing piece that generated the names. This is key in the case of a new list.

For example, if you are renting a list of magazine subscribers, the magazine itself is not nearly as important as the mailing package, TV infomercial, or phone call to which the subscriber initially responded.

Two examples:

1. Boardroom uses wildly colorful "magalogs" and "bookalogs"—filled with illustrations and jarring design—to sell its books and newsletters. Yet the actual products are staid, editorially driven publications with little color.
2. Are they sweeps sold? You can know that only by seeing the actual mailing package. Sweeps buyers are a breed apart. If sweeps sold, your mailing had better be a sweeps effort—or look like a sweeps—or chances are it will bomb. If your mailing is not a sweeps, you can still test the list, but order "non-sweeps-sold buyers only."

If the broker can't get a sample, often you can tap into a direct mail archive such as the one maintained by the newsletter *Who's Mailing What!* in Philadelphia, with information about more than 100,000 mailings in 200 categories of consumer, business, and nonprofit catalogs.

Also, find out the product mix. ABC Company electronics items buyers could be anything: portable radio, automatic sift-and-flush cat litter box, pocket Rolodex/phone dialer. Which fits the profile of your prospect and which does not?

Category.
If you get a "reco" (recommendation) of 100 lists, it is imperative that you put them into such general categories as consumer catalog, health, high-tech magazine, animal activist charity, etc.

Take computer magazines. You can't test everything. So ask your broker to rank the top six in priority order. Then "test the tip of the category"—maybe the top two lists. If results are good, delve deeper later.

It is also imperative that the list recommendations be prioritized by the broker. A hundred data cards are helpful, but you should get your broker to make a habit of always prioritizing them.

House usage.
Boardroom can have up to 15 products being offered at one time. Knowing how a list performed for other house products is crucial for cross-selling and upselling others.

Usage on boardroom lists.

If the list owner has rented your list—and rolled out to it—it indicates affinity. Here too is the possibility of a money-saving list exchange program.

Outside usage.

Quite simply: Who has rolled out to this list? A lot of people may have tested it, but who rolled out? Who made it work? What were the offers and packages that were used in these rollouts?

Here is where the rubber meets the road. Who's mailing what list is the most prized and secret information in direct marketing. Well-networked brokers know and will share that information with one another—and with you on a highly confidential basis. Still, often you can't know specifics—which selects, what seasons, etc. But any and all information is invaluable.

The credibility of a list is determined by who has rolled out with it.

Comments.

Boardroom insists brokers fill this in. I push brokers to make comments—to make meaningful connections.

I don't mean ordinary, easy connections (e.g., "You used a health list last time; here's another health list").

I want connections that take some creative thinking (e.g., "You used such-and-such a list; *University of California Wellness Letter* is using that list; you should try it").

It's our chance to find out what their thinking is in recommending a list. Example: "This list looks like another list that worked well for the company."

Final recommendation.

Boardroom product managers and list brokers working together come up with the decision to test or not to test. My personal system for how to rank lists:

5. You'd be crazy not to test it.
4. You have multiple reasons to test it.
3. Better than even money it will work.
2. One little (or big) reason to test it.
1. Gut feel.

Lists do get tested because of gut feel—often because of what turned up on the worksheet.

Reason not approved.

Disapproved lists go into a ticker file that contains extra lists in a category. Product managers often share the information with their brokers and even give them a chance to "fight back" one more time.

Filling out the sheet is time consuming. Don't feel guilty about asking brokers to do so. It's not "busy work." Remember, you're spending $2,500 to $5,000 on a list test. The worksheet helps list brokers, and it helps us clarify our thinking on which lists to test—and continue with.

Paul Goldberg's Five Techniques for Creating Your Own Lists

Sometimes no list exists for a new product launch; in that case you'll have to create your own. Many years ago Barbara Kumble and I wrote a musical dramatization for Direct Marketing List Day. The skit featured a hypothetical company about to get into the direct marketing business. The hit song (to the tune of "Matchmaker, Matchmaker" from *Fiddler on the Roof*): "List broker, list broker, find me a list. Find me a list that doesn't exist. . . ."

What do you do if you have a clearly defined product or service, but no list exists in that vertical market and no published list in active commerce parallels the profile of your prospective buyer?

If no published list exists in a vertical market, you will not find it in SRDS or on the Marketing Information Network (MIN) on-line service. No broker can get it; no manager is touting it. It doesn't exist.

Quite simply, you have to create it!

Here are some case histories of mailers who had to create their own lists. Although I'm talking about what existed in the 1970s, the techniques are just as valid today.

Use advertisers to create a list.

The client: publisher of a no-holds-barred adult magazine.

This was not an assignment either Denny Hatch (who wrote and designed the package) or I relished. But we were starting out as freelancers, and we took whatever paid the rent so long as it was not a fraud.

In the mid-1970s, *Playboy* and *Penthouse* existed but would not rent their lists. *Hustler* is strictly newsstand. Your client has a publication and a known audience; how do you find it?

The client, by the way, was something out of Damon Runyan, with offices on the third floor of a seedy walk-up in the east seventies in New York City. When I first met him, he was sitting at his desk counting piles of $10 bills; back then, nobody wrote checks or charged credit card accounts for a subscription to such a publication; it was a cash business.

In these pre-SRDS (*Standard Rate & Data Services*) days, a precious few lists were available through "selected" list brokers. But it became quickly apparent that I was going to have to be innovative to find a sufficient quantity of names to mail a large enough volume to give the publisher the numbers he was looking for in order to raise his advertising prices and broaden his advertising base.

The word *advertising* was the key to successfully building lists. I bought every equivalent magazine in existence and called every advertiser I could reach whom I suspected might have a decent-sized customer file. I struck gold.

Yes, they had lists; no, they had never thought about renting them; yes, they loved the idea of getting money for list rentals. In fact, on reflection, if I'd had the stomach for it, I probably should have gone into the compiling business at the time

Find affinity organizations—Scoop and Dip.

The client: *World Business Weekly*. In its quest to recycle existing editorial material, *The Financial Times of London* created a magazine for U.S. corporations doing business abroad. Existing lists were far from being responsive enough to build the needed numbers economically.

Lou Isadora, then-publisher of the magazine, hired a very bright young man, Clyde Brown, whose sole purpose was to develop lists to be used for *World Business Weekly*. Brown was amazing. When a special report on a specific country was announced for publication in an upcoming issue, Brown would hunt for organizations that had affinity with that country and talk his way into borrowing the list. These names were put on file, and a sampling program was set up; these subscribers were then converted to paid. Isadora nicknamed the operation "Scoop and Dip." The program had a dual purpose:

- It enabled us to meet the rate base by using the controlled free names whenever we needed them.
- The conversions to paid were the most profitable.

Clyde Brown then hit pay dirt when he convinced two large hotel chains to allow the use of the names of those clients that they identified as frequent travelers. In some cases, the hotel allowed us to distribute magazines in their name as a perk, which, in turn, gave us an excellent conversion rate.

Offer a piece of the action.

The client: Jeno Paulucci and *Attenzione*. The enormously successful founder of Jeno's Pizza wanted to create a magazine that would make his fellow Italian-Americans proud of their heritage at a time when the only Italians making news were in the Mafia.

A few ethnic compilations existed at the time, but they were filled with errors. For example, one such list of Italian-Americans was designed around names from the phone book that ended in *a, e, i,* and *o*. One publisher had done research and offered ethnic selects on its house file. But the numbers were not large enough to build a subscriber file.

The solution: We approached every Italian-American organization and every ethnic newspaper we could put our hands on—both on a national and regional basis (e.g., the Sons of Italy, the Columbus Club) and offered them a percentage of every sub we sold through them. They could do the promotion or we could. It was only then that we were able to reach our circulation goals.

Another version of this technique is to offer your product or service as a benefit of membership in an analogous association, such as a museum. This enables you to piggyback your offer in someone else's mailing, thus saving you the cost of solo mail.

Create it name-by-name.

The client: *International Reports*.

When *The Financial Times* purchased a group of privately held, exorbitantly priced newsletters, I thought I had returned to the dark ages. *International Reports* (at the time, $750 a year) and its sister publication, *International Country Risk Guide* ($2,500 a year), were aimed at international bankers, traders, investors, and the gnomes of Zurich whose names may have been in annual reports but emphatically not on any lists.

The business was the brainchild of Guenther Reiman, a brilliant and incredibly energetic German economist in his 80s, whose prime source was his own prospect file that was neatly put up on—of all things—Speedomat plates. Reiman's prospecting technique: Scour every financial publication in the world for the mention of important executives. Once a week Reiman would drift in to the fulfillment office with a fistful of new names which he would drop on a desk and tell the circulation director to send these people a personal letter.

Another of his sources was the New York Public Library, where his people studied every directory published that related to foreign trade. He then purchased those directories most likely to work and put them up on his file. Another source was the lists of every foreign Chamber of Commerce member in New York, Chicago, San Francisco, and Los Angeles.

When I began working with *International Reports,* I tried to make existing lists work (e.g., *Business Week* Hotline Names) in order to avoid using the Speedomat monster. Was I ever wrong! What I had not taken into account was how carefully he had compiled the lists on the stencils. The file was updated once a year with a "Return Postage Guaranteed" mailing. Reiman was the only economist I ever knew who was an authentic marketing genius.

Zip select.

The Client: *Élan*—another difficult list challenge, as this was a magazine for upscale black women. It was the brainchild of a minority-owned aerospace company in Maryland; it already owned a successful recording company and wanted to diversify more. For circulation director, they hired Edna Greenbaum, who had successfully converted Black Enterprise from controlled to paid and really knew her way around that market. Between the two of us, we came up with a plan that produced some remarkable results.

The first step was to select zips across the country known to house a high-percentage black population. Then we went to every large magazine that rented its lists and asked for a female select in those areas only. That was the easy part. No one turned us down on the selects.

Next, we knew of a major service bureau that had developed a program designed to eliminate known names of blacks, the original purpose of which I do not remember. However, when used in reverse, it could help us identify blacks. So we ran the rented lists against this program and mailed only the hits.

Now for the tricky part: In each case we asked for a net-name charge so that we would only pay for the names we mailed. As you can imagine, we ran into a bit of a hornet's nest, as that was the first time that the net-name concept was ever floated. However, persistence and an appeal to social conscience won out in most cases. The result: A whopping 99-percent accuracy rate and only a single complaint letter from a recipient who was neither black nor female. On a couple of lists, we hit double-digit responses.

Alas, *Élan* was wildly underfinanced, and after three exquisite issues it ceased publication.

The whole point of all these stories: Don't give your list broker hell because he or she can't come up with a tailor-made list for your small universe; nor should you be aggravated when you can't find anything in SRDS or on MIN.

Do it yourself, and you will find those lists that don't exist.

John Klingel's Recipe
Whenever renting lists for a nonsweeps offer, stipulate that all sweeps-sold names be eliminated.

Michael Sass's 12 Reasons to Decoy Your Mailing List
You want to know:

Who is mailing your list.

When your list is mailed.

What mail piece is being sent to your list.

If you are receiving compensation for all your list rentals.

If any unauthorized mailings are being sent to your list.

If your own mail is being delivered.

How long it takes to be delivered.

If all inserts were in proper order.

If there were any printing errors.

The best months to mail.

If you are receiving all your business reply mail.

How long it takes to process an order.

Paul Goldberg's Misuses and Abuses of Lists

There are three essential ingredients to any direct mail campaign—product, offer, and lists—if any one of the three is wrong, you have a loser, no matter how impeccable the logic of your assumptions.

In any transaction where lists are rented, there can be up to four key players: list owner, manager, broker, and renter.

Each of them is in a position to knowingly—or unknowingly—give the other a royal rooking. And this happens far too often for my liking.

Nine Misuses by Owner or Manager

Frequency: Beware of overmailed lists.

If you own a list and you can rent it, that's free money. A 100,000-name list rented at $80/M is $8,000 in your pocket (less commissions). Rent it 24 times a year, and you've picked up $192,000. Turn it over 80 times a year and, in my opinion, you're a thief.

Why? Because when someone orders a list for rental, *theoretically* he should have an exclusive window on that list for a week or two; during that time, no one else (including the list owner) should mail those names. Otherwise the mailing could hit the same day as a competitor's, and the chances of getting an order are halved. This rule is broken frequently by the greedy list owner or manager who would say, like the legendary Tammany Hall politician of the 19th century George Washington Plunkett: "I seen my opportunities and I took 'em."

The old nth Name Scam: Beware of owners who frequently load tests with hot line buyers or multibuyers.

A list becomes very profitable when a mailer tests it, the test is a success, and the mailer comes back for a rollout. It's also axiomatic that the most recent names—or hot line buyers—will respond best, as will multibuyers. If a mailer asks for an nth name selection for a test, it is assumed the nth name *across the entire list* will be delivered.

Don't count on it. List owners frequently load tests with hot line or multibuyers. The result is a dishonestly high response on the test, which brings you running back for more names—only to suffer death and destruction on the rollout.

What can *you* do about this? Nothing—except be damned careful to forecast lower results on your rollout than your test. Some direct marketers say never step up more than five times (e.g., if you test 5,000 names, don't go back for more than 25,000). I disagree. Know your lists, know your broker, know your list owner, and be guided by your experience.

Beware of dirty lists.

Particularly annoying are list owners who rent their lists out to make money but don't bother cleaning them.

What can you do about this problem? Analyze your nixies, demand credit for them, and raise hell with the list owner.

Beware an incorrect run of names.

You ask for one select and get something else.

Beware the inability to give a special select.

Frequently list owners will claim they can't give you a select, to force you to take the whole list rather than just the juicy parts that should work for you. Recently I wanted to rent a publisher's list of subscribers. When I talked to the manager, I was told the list consisted of 16,000 subscribers and inquiries and that he could not select out just the subscribers from the file. I turned him down flat.

It's also a rip-off when you are charged a lot extra for a special select, which is a simple programming function. But many list owners do.

Beware the inability to merge/purge.

Duplication of mailings can be horrendously expensive. For instance, take a 50,000 rollout that goes to 35,000 net names and includes 15,000 duplicates. If the in-the-mail cost is $500/M, then the mailing to that list before it has been merged/purged equates to $7,500 in wasted direct mail!

Put another way, for that wasted $7,500 you could have mailed an additional 15,000 pieces.

Beware of no record of previous usage.

When you take an nth name selection for a test, the computer should eliminate those names on the rollout. Frequently it doesn't happen, and you find yourself mailing to the same name twice.

Beware confusion in terminology.

Despite the number of glossaries in the list business, there is still a fierce lack of communication. For example, if you want to test several packages to the same demographics of a list, be sure to order *comparable* cross sections. If you ask for an identical cross section, you might find yourself with several sets of the very same names, which happened to me once, and the whole test was blown. The lesson here: Spell out exactly what you want and make sure all the other people in the transaction are on the same semantic wavelength.

Beware the forbidden rollout.

One of the nastiest tricks a list owner can play is to rent you the list for a test, realize your product may be competitive, and then refuse to let you have the balance for a rollout. What can you do about it? Nothing—unless you have an agreement *in writing* up front.

Four Misuses by Broker or Renter

Beware the mailing of a different package.

Before agreeing to rent names, a list owner has every right to see precisely what is going out to the list—a sample of the mailing package itself or, if it's in production, copies of the copy and design. If the product is too competitive or pornographic, the owner can turn down the list rental order.

Sometimes a mailer will submit one package for approval and then mail another—a strictly dishonest and illegal stunt.

What can you do about it? Seed your list carefully and then spend the time to track everything.

Beware net-name arrangements.

Duplication can be expensive. And there are many duplications on affinity lists. For example, subscribers to *Time* are frequently subscribers to *Newsweek* and *U.S. News*. So it is possible to make arrangements to mail on a net-name basis. This means you merge/purge; the duplicate names are knocked out and mailed only once; and you pay only for the net names you mailed.

However, there is a pool of names left over—not just ordinary names but multibuyers who appeared on more than one list. These are the hottest prospects in your entire mailing, and they are not yours to mail unless you've paid full price for all three lists. Many marketers go ahead and mail them anyway and don't tell the list owners.

Beware illegal double usage.

Frequently a mailer will rent names with the idea of following up the mailing with telemarketing. This is multiple usage, and the list owner should be paid an additional sum—and frequently isn't.

Beware of uncleared mailing dates.

If a list is rented for a mailing scheduled to go out on a specific date and the mailing is delayed for any of a hundred reasons, it is imperative that the mailer—or the broker—call each list owner and reclear the mail date. Otherwise there could be two or three competing mailings going out to the same list and hitting the mail stream on the same day. Through laziness, ignorance, stupidity, or time crunches, few list brokers or mailers adhere to this practice—to the detriment of everyone concerned.

In short, if you're dealing with mailing lists that are not your own, expect the worst and don't be surprised by *anything*.

Don Nicholas's Gospel
Always order an odd number of test names.

Most data cards require a 5,000 or 10,000 minimum. A lot of people will just order 5,000 names as their test quantity. I recommend that you order 5,200 or 5,500 and change the number each time you do it. I do this because there are some list managers and owners who do not run a 5,000 test panel for every order of that type that comes in. They take their subscriber file of 200,000, and once a quarter they knock out 5,000 names that are going to be used to fulfill tests. So, everyone who orders tests in that three-month period gets sent the same 5,000-name tape! I don't want to be part of that because it's being mailed much more than everything else is. I want to get my own tape.

An even worse potential problem with even orders of 5,000 can occur when you order something other than standard active subscribers. Let's say you've decided that you want only people who have renewed or people with a particular job title. If you order an even number, they may still give you the plain old select! If they don't do that, they might confuse your order and give you someone else's 5,000-name selection. If you give them an odd number, you're much more likely to get what you asked for.

Business Lists

If not enough attention is paid to consumer lists, the same holds true for business lists. Business-to-business lead generation is a critical application in business expansion. There are some unique characteristics of this technique:

Mike Faulkner's SOP
Lists addressed to a name and title look more personal and targeted and therefore have a greater chance of being delivered by the mail room or "gatekeeper."

Dick Benson's Dissent
Contrary to popular opinion, we found no difference in results in addressing by title as compared to addressing by name.

Tracy Butzko's Six Ways to Clean and Standardize a Business List in Addition to Merge/Purge
Do an ACR (address correction requested).

Mail the list first class to receive address changes.

Send a postcard to every name on the list with a free offer or sweepstakes, requesting verification of the name and address.

Pay an enhancement or lookup service to verify names and addresses.

Send a free gift to companies' mail room supervisors along with your current roster and a business reply envelope and ask for any changes in personnel.

Obtain name and address verification during a telemarketing call—and make the changes in your database.

Etta Davis's Beacon
An excellent source of business lists is trade publications that reach unique and targeted audiences.

Anver Suleiman's Method
Stagger mail for greater impact.

> Split lists to business addresses for delivery over time (without losing postal advantage) so that a company with 10 names on a mailing list does not get 10 pieces in one day. Five pieces on each of two days is better than 10 in one. And one per day for 10 days is even better!

Media

A "medium" in advertising is an "agency, means, or instrument." Media is defined as the means of communication. So, logically media carries your message. Television, radio, direct mail, press advertising, *sales people*, telemarketing, and even matchbooks all are "mediums". . . collectively known as media. The medium may or may not be the message; but where and how you communicate with your audience can be as important as what you communicate.

Denny Hatch's Seven Questions to Ask Before Choosing Media

Is it to be a one-step or a two-step offer?
The overriding factor: price. In the words of Margaret Rose Roberts, whose specialty is taking direct mail packages and turning them into moneymaking space ads: "You have to use a two-step to sell anything over $200; even at $100 you're pushing it."

The exception, according to guru Axel Andersson: high-ticket items where the payments are broken up. An example: a continuity series where the total sale price of 20 volumes could be over $400 but you are shipping one every three or four weeks at $19.95 plus postage and handling.

What's the prior marketing history (successes and failures)?
Is this an established product or service? Is it a household word? Or is it brand-new to the marketplace?

Are the benefits of the product or service easily understandable, or is the proposition complex, requiring an elaborate explanation?

Is this acquisition or retention marketing?

Is the offer being made to consumers at home or consumers in the workplace—or both?

What kind of order flow do you want, and how much can you handle?

Do you want secrecy, or doesn't it matter if the whole world (including your competitors) knows what you're up to?

The obvious media for talking to your customers are mail and phone; you know who they are, how to reach them, and what they have responded to in the past.

What's more, since it costs five times as much to acquire a new customer or donor as it does to service an existing one, you can afford to use the mail and the phone—the most expensive, precisely targeted personal medium—to reach your extended family (commonly called the *house file* or *database*).

It is in acquisition marketing where direct marketers really need to weigh the advantages and disadvantages of the various media.

Denny Hatch's Six Advantages to Direct Mail

You can take plenty of space to tell your complete story. It's the ideal medium if you have a complex product or an elaborate offer.

Mail enables you to target your audience with exquisite precision.
Remember, you are able to cash in on the high technology of the list business with its myriad selects, enhancements, and credit screens, which can refine your prospecting efforts down to a gnat's eyebrow.

It's a wonderful medium to use for testing.

Direct mail is secret.
Whereas a space ad or a TV commercial becomes record once it hits, you can drop small tests around the country, and no one will be the wiser.

Mail is the most personal for printed media, allowing you to fire your message at point-blank range.
Everybody in the country is sure to stop off at one place during the course of the day: the mailbox (or the in box at the office). By getting it into the mailbox, you are virtually guaranteed of your prospect's at least seeing your effort.

Direct mail is the only participatory medium.
The recipient makes it happen, opening it, examining each piece at his or her leisure. It can be infused with all kinds of toots and hollers—plastic cards, sweepstakes, personalization, freemiums (goodies such as pens or balloons or slide charts), scratch-offs, etc. In short, it's fun! Everybody loves mail. In the words of the dean of American freelancers, Bill Jayme: "Nobody likes to come home to an empty mailbox."

Denny Hatch's Six Disadvantages to Direct Mail

Direct mail is expensive—averaging $400/M with $800/M to $1,000/M or more for tests.

You are wholly dependent on the U.S. Postal Service, whose record—while generally good—has forced a number of direct mailers to eat hamburger where they once dined on lobster and truffles.

Remember, the USPS is directly under the thumb of the U.S. Congress, those wonderful folks who brought you the $6 trillion national debt and who are currently using the Postal Service as a debt reduction scheme.

Direct mail requires long lead times.

It can take several months to get a new mailing out; two to six weeks to repeat an existing mailing. Add to that the time it takes to get delivered and the additional time needed to wait for receipt of the reply mail.

Much mail is undeliverable as addressed because many list owners are sloppy in their maintenance.

According to Charles Messina of the USPS, some lists are so badly maintained that they can be up to 40 percent undeliverable.

Example of the arithmetic: If your mailing costs $400/M and your list is 20 percent undeliverable, your real cost is $400/800, or $500/M. Can your budget stand that? (Yes, if the list brings in responses at an allowable cost per paid order.)

Ballpark stats: Consumer lists go out of date at the rate of 2 percent a month; lists of people in the workplace go stale at the rate of 1 percent a week.

Direct mail is a print medium in an environment where illiteracy is on the rise.

You have to pay postage—the most expensive element in the mailing—in advance.

The USPS doesn't have a bill-me option.

Denny Hatch's Seven Advantages to Space Ads

Use a space ad, and your offer can be in your prospect's hands quickly—in a couple of days if you run in a daily newspaper, in a couple of weeks if you place it in a weekly.

Your offer is in everyone's hands at the same time.

This may also be a disadvantage unless you're set up to handle a rush of orders.

With space you can reach the same audiences for less money than mail.
For example, if spending $400/M to reach subscribers of a certain magazine does not pay in terms of the allowable cost per order, you can reach those folks via a space ad in that magazine for $20/M to $30/M—or less if you negotiate. Since they all read the magazine, this may be worth a test.

With space you can reach wider audiences.
Example: If you have a general-interest business or a consumer product or service, you can reach likely prospects in out-of-the-way places, such as in-flight magazines.

Print ads are far easier to create than full-dress direct mail packages.

Unlike mail, you can negotiate for even lower CPMs.
In the immortal words of freelance media consultant Iris Shokoff, "I've never bought an ad at full rate in my life."

If you have credit, you can run the ad and be billed later, paying for the ad out of revenues.
Remember, the USPS demands full postage in advance or you don't mail.

Denny Hatch's Two Disadvantages to Space Ads

Your offer is public knowledge on the day of publication, opening you up to copycat offers from your competition.

You are severely limited in terms of space; it cannot be a highly complex or difficult-to-explain offer.

Denny Hatch's Four Advantages to Telemarketing

A ringing telephone is the most powerful sound in the world.

The telephone is a truly interactive medium.
When objections are raised, they can be dealt with at that moment, rather than on page 3 of a letter, which may be too late to save the situation.

The telephone is a marvelous test vehicle; you can change the script and analyze the response within minutes.

Telemarketing is the ultimate stealth medium; it leaves no paper trail, so your competitors have a very tough time tracking what you are doing.

Denny Hatch's Four Disadvantages to Telemarketing

Outbound calls can be intrusive, especially to the consumer at home. It is also rife with scams, many of them highly publicized, thus making the prospects' teeth itch.

In the consumer arena, telemarketing is really effective only when a prior relationship exists.

With dozens of phone reps talking to your customers, you can lose control over what they say.

The growth of any telemarketing operation is limited by the ability to find and train presentable reps.

Denny Hatch's Six Advantages to Direct-Response Television

No other medium can show a product in action like television.

No other medium can create action where no action exists.
Example: clips of exciting sporting events when selling a static magazine like *Sports Illustrated*.

If you need orders in a hurry, run your offer on TV; you'll get 75 percent of your orders within 15 minutes.

DRTV spots go for huge discounts—as much as 30 percent to 80 percent under what general advertisers pay.

DRTV works beautifully in conjunction with retail sales.
According to Steve Doorman of the *Infomercial Marketing Report,* for every item you sell via DRTV you will sell six to eight at retail as a result of the TV exposure.

DRTV is a great test medium.
As Steve Doorman points out, if you can sell a product for $595 on DRTV, retailers cannot cry that the MSRP (manufacturer's suggested retail price) is too high.

Denny Hatch's Four Disadvantages to Direct-Response Television

Direct-response television ain't cheap.

It can cost $150,000 to $400,000 to create a 30-minute infomercial. (Amazingly, that's about the same as general agencies charge to create a 30-second spot.)

DRTV is volatile.
Consultant Iris Shokoff points out that while you pay 30 to 80 percent of the regular cost of airtime, DRTV spots can be preempted by anyone paying full rate. You have no guarantees about when you will be running. So you have to book twice as many spots and hope half of them run.

Unlike regular television advertising—where you contract for a specific time on a specific channel, as a DRTV advertiser you have to catch the channel surfers who find you by accident at weird times.
As Steve Doorman points out, at this point you have to be so totally enthralling that they will stay with you to the end and actually pick up the phone and order.

You must use an inbound telemarketing service that can handle the peaks and valleys of DRTV.
A spot can run unexpectedly, whereupon the 800 lines are ringing off the hook. Use the wrong telemarketer, and you can lose thousands of orders in minutes.

Denny Hatch's Eight Possibilities for Alternative Media

Package inserts.
Get your product or service into the shipment of a mail order package. Presumably the mail order buyer is so happy with the merchandise that he or she will be in the mood to buy something else by mail at that moment.

Movers programs.
People who have just moved spend money. You can reach movers via a local telephone company co-op within a day or two of the move. However, you do not reach them by name; only at the new address.

Other movers media exist, but (1) there is a delay in getting the names onto a file and (2) you're back to using mail or the phone.

One tremendous advantage of mover programs is that people move every month of the year, so you can get a steady flow of orders.

Card decks.
Very cheap and worth testing. Virtually no room for sell copy, so you must have an immediately recognizable product or service and a great offer.

Supermarket take-ones.

Ecologically sound. Instead of mailing out 100 pieces only to have 98 go into the landfill, you can put 100 cards in the supermarket take-one rack and all will be taken by people interested in the offer. According to Rodale Press, pay-up and CPO are nearly as good as for direct mail.

Supermarket take-ones are also a good medium for testing copy and design for later adaptation to other media.

On-line marketing.

Prodigy, CompuServe, AOL, a home page—some marketers include them in the mix. It costs virtually nothing, and you can get up and running quickly. Generally you'll have to use other media to drive browsers to your Web site.

Freestanding inserts (FSIS).

A few marketers use them—for collectibles, greeting cards, designer checks, etc. Include your promotion in the Sunday newspaper and you're there with 30,000 other ads, not to mention news and the sports pages—many of which are probably more compelling than your offer.

ADVO/saturation mail.

Reach every consumer at home in a specific zip code for a fraction of what you would pay for a solo mailing. These offers go by address, not by individual consumers' mail.

Member-get-member (MGMS).

If you have a good product or service and happy customers or donors who believe in what you do, put them to work for you!

Andrew Cohen's Eight Reasons to Use DRTV

DRTV, more than any other medium, brings the customer directly to you.

You simply encourage the prospects to make themselves known by picking up the phone. It also brings the product directly to the prospect and shows it in action.

As with other direct-response media, DRTV is testable.

It can be designed to unfold slowly and carefully so that results can be analyzed on a small scale before expanding. A common practice is to test two different offers using the same creative execution in two matched markets (similar to using the same direct mail package but altering the price of the product being sold).

DRTV can be affordable.

The efficiency of DRTV is measured in cost per order (CPO), cost per acquisition (CPA), or cost per lead (CPL). Basically, the CPO is determined by dividing the number of orders obtained by the cost of the media and telemarketing. The cost of production is often amortized into the overall advertising budget. CPOs and CPLs start as low as $4.

DRTV is aggressive; if properly executed, it can preempt the marketing efforts of the competition and leave them scrambling.
Monsanto used DRTV as a strategic defense against a competitor whose advertising budget was three times as large. Monsanto's DRTV campaign offering a free sample cleverly demonstrated the benefits of its stain-free carpet while 200,000 responses were generated (as was awareness)—all within a limited budget.

DRTV can tap into qualified leads not reachable by major mailing lists.
In addition, once customers call, you can ask as many questions as you desire to build qualified lists.

DRTV can provide clarity and cohesiveness to the company's overall marketing effort and set the tone for direct mail and other promotions.

DRTV can reach your target audience while simultaneously uncovering an underlying market waiting to be tapped.
For example, company X needs to attract a younger target audience (ages 30 to 40) without alienating its older, more mainstream audience (55-plus). DRTV can effectively reach both.

DRTV can also be used to increase lift in direct mail or support a free-standing insert.

Marilyn Gottlieb's Four Rules of Radio

Radio is a good test medium.
What works on radio can often translate into other media with comparable results.

With radio, you know your markets.
You can pick stations by age, by sex, by interest.

Radio is quickly measurable.
You can test a radio script and see the results within minutes.

You can get into radio and get out.
You can test a radio spot, see if it fogs the mirror, and then either get out or roll out.

Iris Shokoff's Four Tips for Buying Radio Spots

Get target ratings and programming by station.

You can get this information from ratings services such as Arbitron. Amassing this mountain of information will take time and a lot of digging, but you absolutely cannot negotiate the best rate without it.

Compare station rates.

This sounds rather obvious, but you can't simply compare prices to prices. You must first determine the reach and the frequency; one station may have cheaper rates but have a smaller reach than a slightly more expensive station.

Negotiate for "no charges."

Radio is a frequency medium. The more often your spot is aired, the better your chances of making more sales. However, paying for each spot is expensive. Try to negotiate for free spots—time the station needs to fill—when drawing up your initial contract, explains Francie Barson, senior vice president and media director, A. Eicoff & Co., Chicago.

Leverage your buying power.

If you are a small marketer, the best approach is to consolidate your budget in a limited number of stations in a market. You can achieve greater impact with 20 spots on one station than scattered among multiple stations.

Offers

According to Gary Kauffman, people accept offers in larger numbers than they buy products. As we've seen, prospects are interested in what's in it for them. In short, what's the deal? In direct marketing the offer is complex, made up of many parts, and nothing can influence the success of a program more.

Claude Hopkins's Dictum
The right offer should be so attractive that only a lunatic would say "no."

Axel Andersson's Corollary
If you want to dramatically increase your results, dramatically improve your offer.

Bob Hacker's Gospel
It's the offer, stupid!

If performance isn't what it should be, check the offer first.

Jim Kobs's Checklist of 99 Proven Direct Response Offers (Plus Three More!)

Basic Offers

Right price.
This is the starting point for any product or service being sold by mail. Consider your market and what's being charged for competitive products. And make sure you have sufficient margin for your offer to be profitable. Most products sold by mail require at least a three-time markup.

Free trial.

If mail order advertisers suddenly had to standardize all their efforts into one offer, this would no doubt be the choice. It's widely used for book and merchandise promotions. Viewed from the standpoint of a consumer, the free trial relieves the fear that you might get stuck buying by mail, because the advertiser is willing to let you try the product before getting your money. Most free trial periods are from 10 to 15 days, but the length of the trial period should fit the type of product or service being offered.

Money-back guarantee.

If for some good reason you can't use a free trial offer, this is the next best thing. The main difference is that you ask the customer to pay part or all of the purchase price before letting him or her try your product. This puts inertia on your side. The customer is unlikely to take the time and effort to send a product back unless he or she is really unhappy about it.

Cash with order.

This is the basic payment option used with a money-back guarantee. It's also offered with a choice of other payment options. Incentives (such as paying the postage and handling charge) are often used to encourage the customer to send his or her check or money order when the order is placed.

Bill me later.

This is the basic payment option used with free trial offers. The bill is usually enclosed with the merchandise or follows a few days later. And it calls for a single payment. Because no front-end payment is required by the customer, the response can be as much as double that of a cash offer.

Installment terms.

This payment option works like the preceding one, except that it usually involves a bigger sale price with installment terms set up to keep the payments around $10 to $20 per month. Usually this is a necessity in selling big-ticket items by mail to the consumer.

Charge card privileges.

This offers the same advantages of "bill me later" and installment plans, but the seller doesn't have to carry the paper. It can be used with bank charge cards, travel and entertainment cards, and specialized cards (like those issued by the oil companies or large retailers).

Cod

This is the U.S. Postal Service acronym for cash on-delivery. The postal worker collects when he or she delivers the package. Not widely used today because of the added cost and effort required to handle COD orders.

Free Gift Offers

Free gift for an inquiry.
This offer provides an incentive to request more information about a product or service. It usually increases inquiries, though they become somewhat less qualified.

Free gift for a trial order.
Sometimes called a "keeper" give because the customer gets to keep the gift just for agreeing to try the product.

Free gift for buying.
Similar to the preceding offer, except the customer gets to keep the gift only if he or she buys the product or service. The gift can be given free with any order, tied to a minimum purchase, or used as a self-liquidator.

Multiple free gifts with a single order.
If one gift pays out for you, consider offering two or more. You may even be able to offer two inexpensive gifts and spend the same amount as one more expensive item. The biggest user of multiple gifts is Fingerhut Corporation, which currently offers three or more free gifts for a single order!

Your choice of free gifts.
This can be a quick way to test the relative appeal of different gift items, but it will seldom work as well as the best gift offered on its own. The choice probably leads to indecision on the consumer's part.

Free gifts based on size of order.
Often used with catalogs or merchandise suitable for a quantity purchase. You can offer an inexpensive gift for orders under $25, a better gift for orders running between $25 and $50, and a deluxe gift for orders over $50.

Two-step gift offer.
This offers an inexpensive gift if the customer takes the first step and a better gift for taking the second step. Example: a free cassette for trying a new stereo set; a deluxe headset if you elect to buy it.

Continuing incentive gifts.
This offer is used to get customers to keep coming back. Book clubs often give bonus points to save up for additional books. Airline frequent flyer programs also fall in this category.

Mystery gift offer.
Sometimes this works better than offering a specific gift. It helps if you can give some indication of the item's retail value.

Other Free Offers

Free information.

Certainly this is an inexpensive offer and a very flexible one. The type of information you provide can range from a simple product catalog sheet to a full-blown series of mailings. If the information is not going to be delivered by a salesperson, this should be played up.

Free catalog.

This can be an attractive offer for both the consumer and the business market. In the business field catalogs are often used as buying guides and saved for future reference. In the consumer field you can often attach a nominal charge for postage and handling or offer a full year's catalog subscription.

Free booklet or video.

This offer helps establish your company's expertise and know-how about the specific problems of your industry, especially if the booklet contains helpful editorial material, not just a commercial for your product or service. A video brochure can be an effective way to show your product in action. The booklet or video should have an appealing title, like *How to Save Money on Heating Costs* or *29 Ways to Improve Your Quality Control System*.

Free fact kit.

Sometimes called an *idea kit,* it's usually put together in an attractive file folder or presentation cover. You can include a variety of enclosures from booklets to trade paper articles to ad reprints. Be sure to secure permission to reprint from the author or the publication.

Send me a salesperson.

This one is included here because the offer is actually a free sales call with wording like "have your representative phone me for an appointment." It normally produces more qualified inquiries than a free booklet or fact kit. Those who respond are probably ready to order or are seriously considering it.

Free demonstration.

This is important for things like business equipment that has to be demonstrated to be appreciated fully. If the equipment is small enough, it can be brought into the prospect's plant or office. If not, the prospect might be invited to a private showing or group demonstration at the manufacturer's facilities.

Free "survey of your needs."

Ideal for some business products or services like chemicals sold for various water treatment problems. Offering a free survey by a sales representative or technical expert is appealing and gives you the opportunity to qualify a prospect and see if your product or service really fits his or her needs.

Free cost estimate.

Many large business or industrial sales are made only after considerable study and cost analysis. The offer of a free estimate can be the first step in triggering such a sale.

Free film offer.

Many mail order film processing companies have been built with some variation of this offer. Either the customer gets a new roll of film for sending one in for processing or the first roll is offered free in the hope that it will be sent back to the same company later for processing.

Free house organ subscription.

Many business firms put out elaborate house organs for customers and prospects that contain a good deal of helpful editorial material. You can offer a free sample issue or, better yet, a year's subscription.

Free talent test.

Popular with home-study schools, especially those that offer a skilled course, such as writing or painting. Legal restrictions require that any such test be used to measure real talent or ability, not just as a door opener for the salesperson.

Gift shipment service.

This is one of the basic offers used by virtually all mail order cheese and gift-food firms. You send them your gift list, and they ship direct to the recipients at little or no additional cost. Also used at holiday time by magazines.

Discount Offers

Cash discount.

This is the basic type of discount. It's often dramatized by including a discount certificate in the ad or mailing. However, it should be tested carefully. In most cases a discount offer will not do as well as an attractive free gift of some value.

Short-term introductory offer.

A popular type of discount used to let somebody try the product for a short period at a reduced price. Examples include "Try 13 weeks of the *Wall Street Journal* for only $34" and "30 days of accident insurance for only $1." It's important to be able to convert respondents to long-term subscribers or policyholders.

Refunds and rebates.

Technically this is a delayed discount. You might ask somebody to send $5 for your catalog and include a $5 refund certificate good on the first order.

The certificate is like an uncashed check—it's difficult to resist the urge to cash it.

Introductory order discount.
This special discount used to bring in new customers can sometimes cause complaints from old customers if they're not offered the same discount.

Trade discount.
This is a discount usually extended to certain clubs, institutions, or types of businesses. Magazines sometimes offer a professional courtesy discount to doctors and dentists.

Early-bird discount.
This offer is designed to get customers to stock up before the normal buying season. Many Christmas cards and gifts have been sold by mail with this offer.

Quantity discount.
This discount is tied to a certain quantity or order volume. The long-term subscriptions offered by magazines are really a quantity discount. The cost per copy is usually lower on a two-year subscription because it represents a quantity purchase—say 24 issues instead of 12.

Sliding-scale discount.
In this case the amount of the discount depends on the date or size of the order. For example: a 2 percent discount for orders up to $50, a 5 percent discount for orders over $50, and a 10 percent discount for orders over $100.

Mystery discount.
This offer is used most commonly by retailers. Customers bring in a special ad or mailing, and a mystery spot is rubbed off to reveal their discount amount.

Sale Offers

Seasonal sales.
When successful, pre-Christmas, summer vacation, and other seasonal sales are often repeated every year at the same time.

Reason-why sales.
This category includes inventory reduction, clearance sales, and similar titles. These explanatory terms help give the sale a reason for being and make it more believable to the prospect.

Price increase notice.
A special type of offer that's like the limited-time sale, this gives customers a last chance to order at the old price before an increase becomes effective.

Sample Offers

Free sample.
If your product lends itself to sampling, this is a strong offer. Sometimes you can offer a sample made with or by your product. A steel company, for example, uses take-apart puzzles made from its steel wire, or a printer offers samples of helpful printed material it has produced for its customers.

Nominal-charge samples.
In many cases making a nominal charge for a sample—like $.50, $1, or $5—will pull better than a free sample offer. The charge helps establish the value of the item and screens out some of the curiosity seekers.

Sample offer with tentative commitment.
This is also known as the *complimentary copy*—or *comp copy* for short—offer used by many magazines. In requesting the sample, the prospect is also making a tentative commitment for a subscription. But if the prospect doesn't like the first issue, he or she just writes *cancel* on the bill and sends it back.

Quantity sample offer.
This specialized offer has worked for business services and newsletters. One example might be a sales training bulletin where the sales manager is told to "just tell us how many salespeople you have, and we'll send a free sample bulletin for each one."

Time Limit Offers

Limited-time offers.
Any limited-time offer tends to force a quick decision and prevent procrastination. It's usually best to mention a specific date, such as "This special offer expires April 5th," rather than "This offer expires in 10 days."

Enrollment periods.
Mail order insurance companies often include a specific cutoff date for their enrollment period, implying that there are savings involved in processing an entire group of enrollments at one time.

Prepublication offer.
Long a favorite with publishers who offer a special discount or savings before the official publication date of a new book. The rationale is that it helps them plan their printing quantity more accurately.

Charter membership (or subscription) offer.
This offer is ideal for introducing new clubs, publications, or other subscription services. It usually includes a special price, gift, or other incentive for

charter members or subscribers, and it appeals to those who like to be among the first to try new things.

Limited-edition offer.
This is a proven way to go for selling plates, coins, art prints, or other collectibles. The edition may be limited by date (e.g., a "firing period for plates") or quantity.

Guarantee Offers

Extended guarantee or warranty.
Examples include letting the customer return a book up to a year later, offering to refund the unexpired portion of a magazine subscription anytime before it runs out, and extending the manufacturer's warranty if a product purchase is made with a certain credit card.

Double-your-money-back guarantee.
This offer really dramatizes your confidence in the product. But the product better live up to advertising claims!

Guaranteed buy-back agreement.
While it's similar to the extended guarantee, this specialized version is often used with limited-edition offers or coins and art objects. To convince the prospect of their value, the advertiser offers to buy them back at the original price during a specified period that may last as long as five years.

Guaranteed acceptance offer.
This specialized offer is used by insurance firms with certain types of policies that require no health questions or underwriting. It's especially appealing to those with health problems who might not otherwise qualify.

Build-Up-the-Sale Offers

Multiproduct offers.
Two or more products or services are featured in the same ad or mailing. Maybe you've never thought about it this way, but the best-known type of multiproduct offer is a catalog, which can feature 100 or more items at a time.

Piggyback offers.
Similar to a multiproduct offer, except that one product is featured strongly. The other items just kind of ride along or "piggyback" in the hope of picking up additional sales.

The deluxe offer.
A publisher might offer a book in standard binding at $19.95. The order form gives the customer the option of ordering a deluxe edition for only $5 more.

It's not unusual for 10 percent or more of those ordering to select the deluxe alternative.

Good-better-best offer.
This one goes a step further by offering three choices. It's often used as part of a catalog's merchandising strategy.

Add-on offer.
A low-cost item related to the featured product can be great for impulse orders. Such as offering a wallet for $19.95 with a matching key case offered for only $5 extra.

Write-your-own-ticket offer.
Some magazines have used this with good success to build up the sale. Instead of offering 17 weeks for $14.45, which is $.85 per issue, they give subscribers the $.85-an-issue price and let them fill in the number of weeks they want the subscription to run.

Bounce-back offer.
This approach tries to build on the original sale by enclosing an additional offer with the product shipment or invoice.

Increase and extension offers.
These are also follow-ups to the original sale. Mail order insurance firms often give policyholders a chance to get increased coverage with a higher-priced version of the same policy. Magazines often use an advance renewal offer to get subscribers to extend their present subscription; when that extension offer is made on the bill for the current subscription, it is known as a *renewal at birth*.

Sweepstakes Offers

Drawing-type sweepstakes.
Many sweepstakes contests are set up this way. The prospect gets one or more chances to win. But all winners are selected by a random drawing.

Lucky number sweepstakes.
With this type of contest, winning numbers are selected before the mailing is made or an ad is run. Copy strategy emphasizes, "You may have already won." And for those winning numbers that are not actually entered or returned, a drawing is held for the unclaimed prizes.

"Everybody wins" sweepstakes.
No longer widely used, this offer was a real bonanza when first introduced. The prize structure is set up so the bottom or low-end prize is a very inexpensive or nominal one. And it's awarded to everyone who enters and doesn't win one of the bigger prizes.

Involvement sweepstakes.

This type requires the prospect to open a mystery envelope, play a game, or match his or her number against an eligible number list. In doing so, the prospect determines the value of the grand prize he or she wins *if* that entry is drawn as the winner. Some of these involvement devices have been highly effective in boosting results.

Talent contests.

Not really a sweepstakes, this offer is effective for some types of direct marketing situations, such as the mail order puzzle clubs, which offer a simple puzzle to start so contestants will pay to play.

Clubs and Continuity Offers

Positive option.

You join a club and are notified monthly of new selections. To order, you must take some positive action, such as sending back an order.

Negative option.

You are notified in advance of new selections. But under the terms you agreed to when joining, the new selection is shipped *unless* you return a rejection card by a specific date.

Automatic shipments.

This variation eliminates the advance notice of new selections. When you sign up, you give the publisher permission to ship each selection until you tell the firm to stop. It's commonly called a *till forbid* ("until you forbid any more shipments") offer.

Continuity load-up offer.

This offer is usually used for a continuity book series, such as a 20-volume encyclopedia. The first book is offered free, but after you receive and pay for the next couple of monthly volumes (which establishes your creditworthiness) the balance of the series is sent in one "load-up" shipment. However, you can continue to pay at the rate of one volume per month.

Front-end load-ups.

This is where a music or book club gives you, say, four books or CDs for $1 if you agree to sign up and accept at least four more selections during the next year. The attractive front-end offer persuades you to make a minimum purchase commitment. And the commitment usually has a fixed time period for buying your remaining selections.

Open-ended commitment.

This offer is like the front-end load-up, except that there is no time limit for purchasing your four additional selections.

"No strings attached" commitment.

Like the preceding two offers but more generous, because you are not committed to any future purchases. The publisher gambles that you will find future selections interesting enough to make a certain number of purchases.

Lifetime membership fee.

You pay a onetime fee to join—usually $10 or $20—and get a monthly announcement of new selections, which are normally offered at a discount. But there's no minimum commitment, and all ordering is done on a positive-option basis.

Annual membership fee.

Here you pay an annual fee for club membership. It's often used for travel clubs where you get a whole range of benefits, including travel insurance. Also used for fundraising, where a choice of membership levels is often effective.

Specialized Offers

The philanthropic privilege.

This is the basis of most fundraising offers. The donor's contribution usually brings nothing tangible in return but helps make the world a better place in which to live. Sometimes the offer is enhanced by giving gummed stamps, a membership card, or other tokens of appreciation.

Blank check offer.

This offer was first used in the McGovern presidential fundraising campaign. Supporters could fill out blank, postdated checks that were cashed one a month to provide installment contributions. Later adapted for extending credit to charge card customers.

Matching check.

In this popular fundraising offer a gift from a large donor is used to encourage and match contributions from individuals.

Executive preview charge.

This is a successful offer for such things as sales training films and videos. The executive agrees to pay $25 to screen or preview the film, but if he or she decides to buy or rent it, the preview charge is credited against the full price.

Yes/no/maybe offers.

This offer asks the prospect to let you know his or her decision. In most cases the negative responses have little or no value. But by forcing a decision you end up with more yes responses. A maybe option is sometimes used to indicate a tentative commitment.

Self-qualification offer.

Uses a choice of options to get the prospect to indicate a degree of interest in your product or service. Such as offering a free booklet or a free demonstration. Those who request the latter qualify themselves as serious prospects and should get more immediate attention.

Exclusive rights for your trading area.

Ideal for selling some business services to firms who are in a competitive business. Such as a syndicated newsletter that a bank buys and sends to its customers. You give the first bank that responds an exclusive for its trading area. The percentages that order are such that you seldom have to turn anybody down.

The superdramatic offer.

Offers like "Smoke my new kind of pipe for 30 days—if you don't like it, smash it up with a hammer and send back the pieces" are sometimes very effective.

Trade-in offer.

An offer like "We'll give you $100 for your old typewriter when you buy a new electronic model" can be very appealing.

Third-party referral offer.

Instead of renting somebody's list, you get the list owner to make a mailing for you—using their firm's name—and recommend your product or service. Usually works better than your own promotion because of the rapport a company has with its own customers.

Member-get-a-member offer.

Known in the business as an MGM, this offer is often used to get customers to send in the names of friends who might be interested. Widely used by book and music clubs, which give their members a free gift if they get a new member to sign up.

Name-getter offers.

A firm can offer a low-cost premium at an attractive price through this offer, usually designed for building a prospect list.

Self-liquidating premium.

A premium is offered at the advertiser's cost if you send proof of purchase from regular products.

Purchase with purchase.

Widely used by cosmetic firms and department stores, this is an offer of an attractive gift set at a special price with a regular purchase.

Delayed billing offer.

The appeal is "Order now and we won't bill you until next month" (or "after the first of the year"). Especially effective before holidays when people have heavy expenses.

Postdated checks.

Similar to the preceding offer, in this one advertisers promise not to cash your check or process a credit card charge until after a trial period. Air France has used it in offering travel videos. You can watch and return the video at no cost, but if you don't return it by a deadline date, Air France automatically charges it to your credit card.

Reduced down payment.

This offer is frequently used as a follow-up in an extended mailing series. If the customer does not respond to the regular offer, you reduce the down payment in later mailings to make it easier for the customer to get started.

Stripped-down products.

This one is also used in an extended mailing series. If the prospect doesn't order the deluxe model featured in the first mailing or two, you switch emphasis to the standard model at a lower price.

Sweeten-the-pot offers.

First used in TV support by CBS records. The commercial offered an extra bonus record for those who wrote the album number in the "secret gold box" on the order form.

Rush shipping service.

This is an appealing offer for things like seasonal gifts and film processing. Customers are often asked to pay an extra charge for this service.

The competitive offer.

This can be a strong way to dramatize your selling story, an example being Diner's Club's offer of money to prospects who turned in their American Express card.

The nominal reimbursement offer.

This offer is used for research mailings. Here a token payment is offered to get somebody to fill out and return a questionnaire. In some surveys, a $1 bill is included in the mailing.

Establish-the-value offer.

With an attractive free gift, you can build its value and establish creditability by offering it in your catalog at the regular price.

Comment: In 1995, *Target Marketing* ran a list of my 99 proven direct-response offers, and we challenged readers to come up with some worthy additions.

The response was at the same time pleasing and disappointing. I was pleasantly surprised by receiving 113 suggestions, that came from coast-to-coast. (I even got one from a staff member at Kobs, Gregory Passavant!) But I was disappointed because quite a few of the submissions showed confusion about what constitutes an offer. Readers submitted a lot of good ideas, but many were creative, positioning, or format ideas—not offers.

So, just to set the record straight, here's how I define the offer in my book, *Profitable Direct Marketing:*

> The offer is simply your proposition to the prospect or customer, what you will give the customer in return for taking the action your mailing or ad asks him or her to take.

What does the offer include? Your product or service, the price and payment terms under which the customer can get it, any incentives you're willing to throw in (like a free gift), and any specific conditions attached to the offer. Sometimes the offer includes free literature or booklets as a first step to selling the actual product or service.

I should also point out that it's not easy to add to a list of 99 offers that have been around for over 20 years, but I went over all 113 suggestions and found three additions worthy of note:

Terry Reilly and Sue Stone's (Walker Direct) Offer
Free shipping.

> This one's so obvious that I'm embarrassed it wasn't on my original list. And I must admit, it's been a pretty popular offer lately. Some catalogers have been featuring free shipping, particularly on larger orders. —*Jim Kobs*

Tom Meyer's (Creative Directors Group) Two Additional Offers

Private retail sale.
This has long been a staple offer for large and small retailers alike. Tom Meyer suggested you use it with personalized VIP admission passes.

First 50 gift.
Some people call it a "fast 50" or "nifty 50" offer. The idea is to give an extra gift, such as a small TV, to the first 50 people who order from a given mailing. I've seen results that show how effective this offer can be. But I must admit, it's not one of my favorites. I think you run the risk of displeasing too many customers who rush to get their order in, only to find they aren't among the first 50.

Claude Hopkins's Duet

Cheapness is not a strong appeal.
Americans are extravagant. They want bargains but not cheapness. They want to feel that they can afford to eat and have and wear the best. Treat them as though they could not and they resent your attitude.

People judge largely by price.
They are not experts. In the British National Gallery hangs a painting that the catalog states cost $750,000. Most people at first pass by the painting with just a glance. Then, when they get into the catalog and learn what the painting cost, they return, surrounding it.

One Easter a department store advertised a $1,000 hat, and the floor could not hold the women who came to see it.

Bob Stone's Quintet

Credit card privileges will outperform cash with order at least two to one.

Free-gift offers, particularly where the gift appeals to self-interest, outpull discount offers consistently.

A yes/no offer will consistently produce more orders than offers that don't request a no response.

It is easier to increase the average dollar amount of an order than it is to increase the percentage of response.

The "take rate" for negative option offers will always outpull positive option offers by at least two to one.

Frank Vos's Canons

First of all, list selection and the structure of the offer are far more important than copy and artwork.
But even when lists, offer, and presentation are well done, at least 95 of every 100 pieces that one mails generally become landfill, usually unread.

A substantial portion of unheeded mailing pieces are thrown away simply because the offer is understood too easily and quickly by those not seeking the product at the moment.
Therefore, I often tried to include in the forefront of each mailing a physical device of seeming value (or usefulness) that was not immediately rejectable [e.g., a stamp sheet for the RCA Record Club, membership cards for hospital insurance efforts]. With this technique I was able to compel prospects to read

my sales story to discover the purpose of the dissonant element in the mailing. I reasoned that if my product had merit, a broader readership would produce greater sales.

Axel Andersson's Consideration
Don't try to sell the main offer and the premium at the same time.

Sell your main offer and give your premium away free. Charging for a premium is a no-no. To charge for a premium means that the prospect has to make two decisions, and as a rule two decisions hurt response.

Murray Raphel's Maxim
Offer purchase with purchase.

The cosmetics people have this down to an exact science. If you buy one of their products, you receive a gift for free or for a fraction of its true value.

John J. Fleider's Recipe
An add-on offer to your current customer for a specific product can generate a response 10 to 20 times that of the initial offer.

When people have already gone through the decision process to buy from you via direct response—and if you've met *all their requirements*—offer them more of the same. They are preconditioned to buy it! They know and have your product. They've found your company trustworthy and your offer of value. So they are ready to buy more. "Because you are already our customer, you can get twice as much of the stuff for only $XXXXXX!"

Drayton Bird's Doctrine
Offers work because they enlist one vice—greed—to overcome two others: sloth and fear.

People are too idle to read or reply, and they fear if they do they will end up with something they either don't need or can't pay for. Greed, carefully harnessed, invariably triumphs.

Walter Weintz's Two Principles

First, get action (that is, orders) by offering prospective customers a special introductory bargain.
The offer must really be special—that is, not generally available elsewhere every day of the year.

Use an action device or hot potato.
This technique was developed and refined by Frank Herbert of *Reader's Digest*. Frank didn't just offer you a half-price subscription; he mailed you a $1 discount certificate, which you could use to secure a subscription for half-price. If you used it, it was worth a dollar to you. If you threw it away, in effect you had lost a dollar. It was a "hot potato" you had to do something with, one way or the other. The difference between a physical, tangible, valuable object and a vaguely worded offer was all-important.

Dick Benson's 11 Epigrams

The offer is the second most important ingredient of direct mail (after lists).

You can never sell two things at once.

A credit or bill-me offer will improve results by 50 percent or more.

The increase of orders generated by the use of installment payment is 15 percent.

The more believable a special offer is, the more likely its success.
Our experience proves another rule of thumb: Whenever you can present a believable reason for a special offer, response will be increased above and beyond that to be expected by the deal itself.

The addition of installment payments for an item over $15 will increase results by 15 percent.

In all my experience, I've found it profitable either to decrease the total price, bringing payments down to end in .95, or to take in extra money without adversely affecting response by increasing payments so they end in .50 to .99.

You can expect the same result when you sell "open end" by mail on a credit card.
The customer never faces a direct renewal decision. The longevity of the customer is increased dramatically.

An exclusive reduced price to a house list will more than pay its way.

An incentive to pay cash when you offer both cash and credit options reduces net response.

The same product sold at different prices will result in the same net income per thousand mailed.

In merchandising plates, when the initial plate was sold at $17.50, we received twice as many orders as when it sold at $35. Prices between the two pulled proportionally.

Ted Nicholas's Precepts

When marketers make offers, they really are making requests.
A direct-response offer asks the prospect to do something. If the prospect doesn't do what you ask, your effort has been wasted. Direct response is a success only when it brings in orders. Because of that, your "offer" has to be a planned sales piece. In it you will anticipate what salespeople refer to as objections, or common reasons that prospects give for not buying.

Each product has its own set of customer objections.
A salesperson needs to have an answer ready for all the objections and a countering argument for why the prospect needs to buy right now. When selling through the mail or in ads no salespeople are involved. Objections must be anticipated and answered in the copy. A knowledge of selling must be applied to the offer.

Nicholas's Four Ways to Turn Up Sales Volume
Run bigger ads in publications that are now working for you.

Run ads or do mailings more often in the same publications and to the same lists.

Try other publications or lists that are similar to the ones you're using now.

Try different ads for the same product.

Andrew J. Byrne's Test
Choice between offering a "free gift" and a discount? Offer the gift if it's pertinent to the prospect.

Richard Jordan's Strategy
Harness the pulling power of promotional-integral premiums.

Promotional-integral premiums are editorial premiums that take first place in a direct mail promotion. You sell the free premium, with the only condition being that the product comes along with it for trial. (This contrasts with the usual positioning of a premium whereby you sell the product and the premium is offered as an add-on, an extra inducement for action.)

Examples:

- "9 Proven Ways to Make a Million in Canadian Business Today"—yours with a no-risk trial subscription to *Canadian Business*.
- "14 Little-Known Ways to Get (and Stay) Very Rich." "Venture's 15 Top Entrepreneurial Opportunities for 1997."
- "How to Double—and Triple!—the Yield of Your Garden!"

Promotional-integral premiums are not easy to do; they are not especially cheap; but they can be incredibly effective.

Corollary on Offers
Never ever forget to dramatize the offer.

You may have the greatest offer in the world, but it will do you little good if it's buried where your prospect can't find it.

Make a bargain offer tangible with certificates, coupons, vouchers, checks, etc. Always get your offer out in front of the prospect early and often. Mention it in your letter superscripture or Johnson box or use a corner slash to do the job. Drive your designer nuts by insisting that the offer be displayed somewhere on every reading surface, with an overliner, a burst, a panel, or whatever. Recap the offer on all elements of the mailing: in the letter, the folder, the outer envelope, the lift note, and, of course, the order form.

If you possibly can, weave some kind of copy story around your offer—e.g., "My boss says I'm nuts to make you an offer this big, but I think you'll prove the boss wrong."

Andrew J. Byrne's Policy
Sell *one* product in a mailing—not more.

Paul Goldberg's Absolute
Confuse 'em, ye lose 'em.

Exception to Byrne and Goldberg
Catalogs, obviously.

Andrew J. Byrne's Estimate
Limited-time offers continue to outpull conventional offers.

Bob Stone's Confirmation
Time limit offers, particularly those that give a specific date, outpull those with no time limit practically every time.

Maxwell Sackheim's Advice
If you are making a time limit offer, give a reason for it—a good reason.

Denny Hatch's Addendum
If you have a firm date on your limited-time offer, be prepared for your offer to die very dead on that date and expect no more orders or inquiries thereafter.

> If you have a firm date on your limited-time offer, be very careful about how and when you send it.
>
> Many credit card issuers that have cutoff dates on their offers mail them first class, thus guaranteeing speedy handling and the return of nixies. If you go third class with a deadline, you take a terrible chance. If you put the deadline date too far into the future, it will invite procrastination and have little power; if you set it too soon after the drop—and the U.S. Postal Service diddles with your mail—the offer may arrive on or after the deadline, which means you've wasted the entire effort.
>
> This is a case where you *must* have a world-class letter shop that works closely with the USPS in your behalf.

Pat Friesen's Summary
Every offer must contain certain elements.

> • Free sample • Pricing/discounts (quantity, wholesale, early bird)
> • Referral request • Response options (phone, mail, fax, e-mail, walk-in) • Payment methods (cash, check, money order, time payment, house credit, purchase order, credit card, bill-me, send no money now) • Offer statement (e.g., buy-one-get-one-free vs. two-for-one) • Guarantee • Deadlines • Free case histories • Free summaries of research • Entry into drawings, sweepstakes, contests • Invitation to participate, attend, etc. • Comparison checklist (your product vs. the competition) • Price comparison checklist • Free gift • Article reprint • Gift certificate • Free guide • "Fast 50"—incentive for one of the first 50 to respond

Order Forms

 Order forms for catalogs, applications for insurance or credit cards, inquiry forms . . . in a sense they all fit under this broad heading. Keeping it simple is key. Make it easy for your prospect or customer to respond and you're well on your way to the sale.

Anver Suleiman's Obvious Admonition
No response device—no response.

> Include a response device in all your mailings, whether going for an order or not. Make it easy to find and use. And test it before you print.

Donna Stein's Next Obvious Admonition
Never underestimate the importance of your response form copy.

> This piece ought to be able to stand on its own and make your sale. State the terms of your offer clearly and simply and make it easy for your reader to respond.

Pat Friesen's Five Order Form/Response Device Hot Spots
• Call to action • Restatement of benefits • Payment options
• Shipping and handling charges • Anything highlighted as free

Elsworth Howell's Absolute
Make it as easy as possible for the customer to order.

Frank Watts's Two Rules
Always ask for the order.

Once you have the order in hand, stop selling. Like an Arab, fold up your tent and leave.

Malcolm Decker's Six Propositions

Give the order card more time and effort per square inch than any other piece in the package.
It's time well spent. It's the net that secures the trout, so it can't have any holes in it.

Create the order form in conjunction with the people who do your order processing, telephone sales, white mail response, and customer service.
Give them the final vote. It must be simple, clear, direct, and—if you can possibly imagine it—foolproof. Use the combined talents of your most clever people to write it, but make sure even a fool can understand it.

The order card should also sell.
But basically it has a particular job to do: it should reprise the essence of the letter in the reader's voice. That is, the writer (salesperson) has had his or her say, and now the prospect (customer) responds.

The order card should contain absolutely nothing new; it should stand on its own feet and crystallize everything that's gone before it.
Its purpose is to speed the action.

If you're looking for maximum response, it's better to check off or call toll-free than fill in; better to tear off (no pencil required) than check off.
However, you must decide (by testing) whether the fastest order card in the West gives you the quality of customer you require.

If you are offering payment by credit card, never use a business reply card.
No one wants this highly personal and valuable information to go naked through the mail for strangers to see (and steal). Instead, enclose a reply envelope. An envelope also encourages cash.

Bill Christensen's Advice
Try to create a "visual fascination" with the order card.

It's the one piece of the package you want to get into the hands of the recipient. If you can entice readers to want to see the order card, you stand a better chance of getting them involved enough to place an order.

Axel Andersson's Triumvirate

Don't put a different offer on the back of the order card.
For example, if the front of the order card offers information about language courses, don't promote writing courses on the back of the card.

The back of the order card should be left blank (unless, of course, it's a business reply card (BRC).
The late Ed Mayer believed that nothing should interrupt the ordering process, and copy on the back of the order form might do that. The majority of the Axel Andersson Award winners leave the back of the order form blank—particularly in the magazine subscription field.

Of the 71 Axel winners, only BMG used the back of the card to solicit the names and addresses of others who might be interested in receiving a BMG mailing. Nightingale Conant routinely puts referral requests on the back of its BREs; this does not interrupt the ordering process, because the order is already in the BRE and the customer is licking the flap when this request is noticed.

If you use a sticker or token on the order card, make the prospect move it from left to right, vice versa, or up or down; do not ask that it be pasted on the back.

Wisdom from USA Direct, Inc.

If any single component of the direct mail package can kill an order, it is a poorly constructed reply document.

Once a prospect is motivated to respond by the sales letter and all the other components of the package, the reply should make it as easy as possible to act. The reply can do little to change a mind in favor of positive response, but it can stop an order cold.

USA Direct's Order Form Checklist

Is the form easy to read?
Does it have adequate type size for readers whose eyesight will vary? Is it easy to understand—simple to complete with plenty of room to include credit card, size, color, item number, or other information important to the completion of the order?

Are the customer assurances such as return/refund policies and guarantees featured clearly?
Where appropriate, are the discounts for upselling displayed prominently?

Have you preaddressed the form so the customer isn't bothered with completing repetitive information?

Have you included code and account information to be able to track the results of the mailing?

If you are using scannable bar codes or OCR lines, have you confirmed with the back end that they are legible to the equipment you use?

Does the reply form easily fit into the postage-paid return envelope you've provided without need for additional folding?

Did you prominently feature a toll-free number for quicker response? How about fax orders?

Dick Benson's Certainty
Tokens or stickers always improve results.

In all my years of testing I recall very few pure tests of order card designs or sizes, but I recall lots of tests of tokens and stickers. I use tokens or stickers frequently, and on head-to-head tests I can't remember when their addition didn't pay off.

Denny Hatch's Adage
A yes/no offer can raise the net number of yeses, even though you are paying postage for nos.

You can also rent the curmudgeonly no responders to burglar-alarm companies, guard-dog kennels, and liberal cause organizations.

Bob Matheo's Checklist: The Eight Things an Order Card Must Do
It must recap the essence of the proposition.

It must speak in the voice of the reader, not the seller.

It must evoke good feelings that spring from using the product.

It must emphasize the guarantee or risk-free nature of the offer.

It must feature your telephone ordering option if you have one.

It must look—and be—easy to use.

It must provide a mailing address in case the BRE is mislaid.

Ultimately, it must put the reader in control of the transaction.

Premiums

 Premiums (free gifts or self-liquidators) work in wondrous ways. An appropriate premium can boost response, conversion, payments, next orders, and so on. Insurance direct marketers call these tokens of gratitude *gifts,* because *premiums* are what they collect from customers.

Dick Benson's Five Observations
A premium is a bribe to say yes now.

Promptness is often the best reason for giving the premium.

Dollar for dollar, premiums are better incentives than cash discounts.

Desirability is the key element of a premium; the relationship of the premium to the product isn't important.

Two premiums are frequently better than one.

Dan Capell's 10 Premium Tips

Test more than one premium.
You don't test one list or just one new business package idea at a time. Premium testing is no exception. Premium testing usually requires more tries to find a winner than package testing.

Try focus panel research.
Properly conducted, focus group research can help you assemble a group of 10 or more *probably solid* premium ideas to test. Use your current subscribers to probe their interests. Don't be surprised if their main premium interests are not related to the editorial content of your magazine.

Use premium specialty firms very carefully.
Don't give them carte blanche. Guide them and ask for premium suggestions that are as specific as possible. Attend premium shows as well for new ideas.

Use your own insert cards to test premium ideas.
Try a multipremium insert card test (test five to 10 premiums). Use the test to determine the relative strength of various premiums. Caution: Multipremium tests will depress overall insert card response.

Try a multipremium test in direct mail.
Design a multipremium brochure as an additional insert into one of your new business direct mail test cells. (Make sure the order card reflects the offer.)

Try a creative think tank session.
Devote a half day away from the office with your staff to think about new premium ideas, direct mail test packages, and creative new business offers.

Look for a premium with a high perceived value.
Time Warner is expert at this. All of its premiums look as if they are worth $50 or more; obviously they are not and cost far less in volume.

Avoid editorially related premiums.
Few companies (Rodale is a notable exception) have made editorial premiums work. Test noneditorial premiums first; your editor may love editorial reprints, but they will probably bore your subscribers to death!

Stay out of the warehouse.
Just because you have 5,000 umbrellas or 10,000 posters left over from some flawed ad sales promotion scheme, do not assume these will work as subscription premiums.

Build your direct mail package around the premium.
Don't just add a premium to your existing control package. At least add a brochure that sells the premium as hard as the rest of your package sells your magazine or your offer.

Axel Andersson's Law
Don't try to sell the main offer and the premium at the same time.

Sell your main offer and give your premium away free. Charging for a premium is a no-no. To charge for a premium means that the prospect has to make two decisions, and, as a rule, two decisions hurt response.

Don Jackson's Practice
Logical premiums pull better than illogical premiums.

Information premiums (like books and booklets) pull well in insurance and financial services, membership offers, and high-priced offers when there is a logical association with the product. The same was true for magazine subscription promotion before publishers got trapped by sweepstakes.

Hard goods premiums—watches, jewelry, knickknacks—appear to work well with hard offers such as exercise equipment and automobiles . . . although watches also work well when you are trying to get people to pay their bills. Generally, however, the more logical and connected the premium is to your offer or your product or service, the more effective it is.

Reply Envelopes and Cards

 Pay the postage or let the customer pay the postage? There have been dozens of tests—perhaps hundreds—over the years. Let this pool of practitioners stimulate your thoughts about this thorny issue and others.

Susan K. Jones's Approach

Repeated tests show that the cost of providing a business reply envelope is justified in that it encourages a greater level of response.

The customer finds it much easier to return an order in a postage-paid, self-addressed envelope than to search around for a plain envelope and a stamp.

Business reply envelopes also serve an excellent purpose for the recipient: they may be coded by color, size, or other means to allow for a quick and dirty way to visually read daily response even before the orders are input.

To use a business reply envelope, you need a permit from the local postal office.
To get one, you have to fill out a form and pay a yearly fee. Then you'll receive a reply number to use on your envelopes and pay the current first-class rate plus a small surcharge for all orders returned to you. If you provide the post office with money in advance to draw against as mail arrives, you'll avoid some delays in receiving your mail.

Business reply envelopes must be designed and sized in accordance with USPS rules.
The specifications for BREs and BRCs are available at your post office and in the USPS publication *The Domestic Mail Manual.* Art directors and production specialists must be very familiar with these rules, because violations waste time and money.

Make sure that the business reply envelope you select is machine insertable into your outer mailing envelope and that the reply form fits easily into your reply envelope, preferably without folding.

Since the reply form will be hand-inserted into the BRE, the size can be slightly larger than if it was to be machine insertable.

When your prospect is returning only an inquiry or reservation, and no payment is required, you may opt for a postage-paid business reply card (BRC), which the prospect can simply drop in the mail. But when you are asking for a check or money order in payment, you'll need a BRE.

A BRE is also appropriate when you are asking for any confidential information—a credit card number or the prospect's age, for example—or when the prospect might want to keep his or her response to the offer confidential.

Denny Hatch's Corollaries
You may want to test an order card with a business reply face plus a business reply envelope.

Make sure your business reply card is on stock heavy enough to meet USPS requirements.

Dick Benson's Hint
Whether to pay return postage is testable.

> The only product category I know that consistently pays return postage is new magazine subscriptions.
> Fundraisers, particularly for political campaigns, often put stamps (multiple) on reply envelopes. Several times I've tried this device on products—unsuccessfully.

Max Hart's Experience
Without going into a lot of numbers, for Disabled American Veterans a third-class stamp is most productive, followed by a permit, with the meter imprint bringing up the rear.

Denny Hatch's Observations
If you put live stamps on your reply envelopes, you are adding upward of $300/M to the cost of your mailing; with business reply mail, you pay only for the envelopes that are returned to you.

Never use a business reply envelope in a sweepstakes offer.

Space Ads

 Space advertising is a mainstay for direct response. It has always been a primary choice of book clubs, video clubs, and CD clubs as well as continuity programs. It is a rich milieu for some of the most creative ads ever produced by direct-response copywriters. Take a visual stroll someday through the supermarket tabloids. The art of creating effective space advertising is exemplified in this medium.

Claude Hopkins's Standard
Mail-order advertising is the court of last resort.

You may get the same instruction, if you will, by keying other ads. But mail-order ads are models. They are selling goods profitably in a difficult way. It is far harder to get mail orders than to send buyers to the store. It is hard to sell goods that can't be seen. Ads that do that are excellent examples of what advertising should be.

Ted Nicholas's 13 Steps for Using the Hidden-Benefit Technique to Create Million-Dollar Ads

Before you test the hidden-benefit technique against your control, which is most likely an obvious-benefit ad, review the basics of writing an ad or sales letter.

Begin the process by studying your product. Write down all the obvious benefits from the prospect's point of view on 3- by 5-inch cards. Often you'll get the best headline you could ever find from this step. In that case, prepare your ad using the obvious-benefit headline.

If the obvious-benefit headline doesn't bowl you over or you just want a comparison, test a hidden-benefit ad against your obvious-benefit ad.

To create the hidden benefit, answer this question: If I had unlimited god-like power, what is the single most compelling benefit my prospects would like to gain from my product?

Often the hidden benefit has nothing directly to do with the product itself. The answer to this question can become your most powerful benefit—and thus your headline.

"How to Get Enthusiastic Applause
—Even a Standing Ovation—
Every Time You Speak!"
Leadership in all fields today <u>requires</u> you to be
an outstanding public speaker.

This headline in a successful ad prepared for *American Speaker* consists of a hidden benefit.

Don't you agree that the headline captures exactly what every speaker wants deep down? When you speak, isn't enthusiastic applause and possibly a standing ovation what you want? Of course! Everyone who speaks wants these results.

Here are some more specific points that helped this headline and this ad succeed.

Add power to your headlines.
Notice the headline is in quotes. Why? Studies show that an ad headline draws 28 percent more attention if quotation marks are around it! It appears much more important because someone is being quoted. Therefore, it should be read. And this is your first task. If the ad is not read, you have no chance of a sale.

Make sure your first sentence has power.
The first letter in the body copy of the *American Speaker* ad is oversized and bold. This is called a *drop cap,* and it increases readership. How? The reader's eye is drawn up and toward the left, so the likelihood that the first sentence will be read is much higher.

Now, read the first sentence:

"Picture yourself enjoying the smiles and the pleased look of excitement on the faces of your audience."

The sentence is powerful. It's strong enough to be a headline or a subhead.

When you write copy, make sure your first sentence has power. There are three reasons why you should spend time crafting that sentence:

1. The sentence helps set the tone for the rest of the ad.
2. The headline is reinforced by the first sentence.
3. The reader is induced to read the second sentence.

The rest of the copy amplifies the headline theme. Note the benefits and features. A great exercise is to pick out the benefits and features in a successful ad.

Here is a helpful tool in learning to write copy that sells: Sit down and copy by hand a successful ad you particularly like. Handwrite it on a yellow pad. You'll start getting a feel for sentence construction and flow: long sentences, short sentences, bullets, subheads. You'll actually get into the mindset of the author when it was written! Then have it set in type so you actually experience the whole process.

Typefaces are important.

The featured ad employs the old classic Times Roman typeface in the headline. Either serif or sans serif typefaces can be used for the headline.

In the body copy, the typeface is also Times Roman. Reason? It's easy to read. *Never* use a sans-serif typeface in body copy.

Strive for an editorial look. The ad should appear similar to an article in the magazine or newspaper in which your ad will run. I call it an "advertorial" style. Five times as many people read editorial material than messages that scream out "I'm an ad!" If an advertorial is prepared in accordance with the following techniques, it can do up to 500 percent more in sales.

Test photography.

The sample ad is being tested both with and without a photograph. Early results up till now are mixed. In some publications, the photo adds response. In others, the ad works better without a photo. Photos often lift response, but remember to use a caption; many marketers overlook this.

Column width is important.

The size of the columns in your ad is also important. Your prospects' reading habits are formed largely by reading magazines and newspapers. Therefore, your column width should be approximately the same size as the editorial columns in the publication where you run the ad.

Set your 7- by 10-inch ads in a three-column format. The right side can be justified or ragged right; I have found no difference from either style.

Use a free bonus.

Results from any offer can be improved with an attractive free bonus. Add bonuses to successful offers and watch sales increase dramatically.

There is one exception, however. The bonus must be desirable. When I first began direct marketing, I tried using slow-moving or even failed products as bonuses. It doesn't work. If you can't sell it, you can't give it away!

Ask for the order.

Unsuccessful marketers are reluctant to ask for the order. For any offer to be successful, you must be clear and explicit in how you ask for the order. Include every detail. Make it easy for the prospect to buy.

When you ask for the order is also important. The prospect must be primed for the close. The sequence is crucially important. In your sales letters, wait until the end of the message to reveal the price and ordering instructions. If your offer includes a brochure and an order form, separate them from the letter. This strategy will increase response. Put the brochure and order form in a sealed envelope. On the outside of the envelope, say, "Please don't open until you have read my letter."

Always have a guarantee.
Offer a money-back guarantee. A guarantee increases your credibility, and your response will be higher, whether you're marketing a product or a service.

I notice the Hampton Inns, a hotel chain, is using this guarantee:

> Money-Back Guarantee
> If you are not completely
> satisfied with your
> accommodations, just let us
> know, and you will be issued
> a full refund or credit.

A money-back guarantee increases orders on any offer, especially for any service business that depends completely on customer satisfaction, feedback, and referrals to build the business.

I've found 10-day, 21-day, 30-day, 60-day, and one-year guarantees are all effective. Once again, you should test to be sure.

A coupon is usually a good idea.
Results from my coupon versus no-coupon tests have been inconclusive. Sometimes one outpulls the other and vice versa. A lot depends on how "tight" I am for copy since a coupon usually takes more space.

When you do use a coupon, keep the dotted line surrounding it thin. You don't want the reader's eye to be drawn to the coupon too early. Remember, you must stage your offer in a sequence. Most graphics people tend to use a heavy coupon unless otherwise instructed.

Pay attention to your graphics.
Graphics, even in all-copy ads, are very important, but be sure to choose graphic designers who understand the marriage needed between graphics and copy. Only one in a hundred graphics people has grasped the principle that the role of graphics is to support, embellish, and strengthen the copy. The most important ad element is the copy. The graphics can help set the stage. The mood is the offer.

The big ad agencies sometimes waste a fortune on graphics that do not support the copy. Instead the graphics fight with or conflict with the copy, thus reducing the power and the effectiveness of the ad.

Copyright your ad.

When you create winning ads and sales letters, others will copy you. The best no-cost easy form of protection is to use the proper copyright notice: Copyright © 1997 by [your company name]. This is what is known as *common law copyright protection*. Use it on all your ads, brochures, and sales letters—all your printed material.

You can also register everything you create with the U.S. Copyright Office for even more protection if you so choose. And when someone steals your ad copy, sending a "cease and desist" letter usually stops them.

Margaret Rose Roberts's 35 Steps to Successful Space Ads

Space advertising may provide you with a large universe of untapped buyers.

Test a full-page ad.

To get paying customers, don't skimp on space. Most mail-order products need as much selling copy as possible. Avoid the temptation to test a small ad first. It will rarely give meaningful results. Full-page ads command attention.

To save on cost, use a large ad in a small-circulation magazine rather than a small ad in a large-circulation book.

Full-page ads are more cost-effective and command better attention in print.

Consider a recent test for a women's diet offer. With a budget of $10,000 we developed a media plan for full-page ads in five publications: a women's magazine, a weekly tabloid, a fitness magazine, a health magazine, and a regional newspaper. More than 1.4 million potential buyers were reached at an average of $7/M, spreading the risk and improving the odds for a winner.

However, if your product is very inexpensive or self-explanatory, you may be able to test with a small display ad or even a classified ad.

High-ticket items (over $200) are sometimes tested in a two-step approach, with a small display ad to generate inquiries.

Stick with the best elements of your proven mail offer.

Don't change prices or add elements unless there is a strong reason to do so.

Make every word count!

This is the real challenge of space ad copy. Use the guts of what makes your mail package successful. Make careful, though painful, cuts to your mail copy.

Most advertisers find that long, strong copy pulls best.

Use long copy rather than big graphics.
Use illustrations that draw readers to the ad or don't use them at all. Photos of people tend to work better than photos of products alone.

Test one ad that you consider your best shot.

Be sure you make it easy for customers to respond. Check the basics—does the coupon have enough space for customers to fill it out?

Toll-free numbers offer a good opportunity to upsell.

Fax numbers work well for business offers, particularly overseas.

Look for editorial fit—magazines that directly tie in with the nature of your product.
If your offer ties in with a specific newspaper classification, such as business services or real estate, you will reach your target audience in well-read sections of the paper.

Look for a small, least-expensive publication in a category of magazines that have competition. (If the ad is successful, you want to have a few ready places to try next.)

Go with the medium whose demographics most clearly match your target audience.
Advertising media kits supply the basics on audience, but don't hesitate to ask specific questions. Many magazines have independent readership surveys. Some also have a research analyst to help explain various data available.

Look for audited paid-circulation figures.
People who pay for a magazine are more likely to read it carefully than those who receive it free. Use only the paid-circulation figures to compute the cost per thousand (CPM). Often media will promote readership figures, but these data are often unreliable and exaggerated.

The price you pay often determines your long-term success or failure in space, so be prepared to bargain!
With most media it is critical that you be prepared to bargain or have an agency that will do so for you. Your margin of profitability is determined largely by what you pay for what you get.
  See if the publication offers:

- A mail-order discount (up to 25 percent is common)
- A special test rate for new advertisers
- Standby ad space (Tests at the media's convenience can save 50 percent.)
- Last-minute remnant space

If a publication seems very eager to get your business, suggest that it run on a per-inquiry (PI) basis—or per order. You have no risk and pay the media an agreed percentage of your sales or X dollars per inquiry.

None of this information will be volunteered by the publication! Ask for everything, and you will often get some type of rate break. Recognized advertising agencies get a 15 percent commission. A good agency can save you 20 to 80 percent.

As with price, you must bargain for position.

In magazines, a right-hand page in the front will usually be better read than a left-hand page or a page in the back. Some publications charge a position premium to honor special requests. Often you can bargain these premiums away if they really want your business. Having your ad run opposite or surrounded by editorial helps it stand out.

In newspapers, the best position is on a right-hand page, above the fold on the outside corner.

Be aware of timing; for example, monthly magazines close their books for orders 30 to 60 days ahead of issue.

You may have an additional week or two to supply them with artwork. If you're in a hurry, newspapers, which have two- to three-day closing deadlines, are a natural.

Don't buy the frequency line; it is a myth that you need to run at least three times before the ad will start to pay out.

The best results almost always come from the first exposure of the ad in a new publication. Thereafter, let the extent to which the audience of the publication changes and how strongly the publication pulled on the first test be the guide to determining how often you run. Experiment and test (and ask for a frequency discount while you're at it).

Unless an offer depends heavily on color visuals, it is best to start out with black and white.

Color can add 20 to 40 percent to your cost.

Split test.

Many advertisers get tired of their own ads or make what they believe to be improvements to the ad, only to have poor results convince them they made a mistake. To avoid risking heavy loss, test any change—whether large or small—by way of a split test.

On the other hand, any ad will eventually get tired. It pays to test new creative, changes to the offer, bonuses, pricing, illustrations, color, or even different products.

An A/B split is the only way to eliminate outside influences and get a true reading on the performance of one ad against another.

With a perfect A/B split, you provide the media with artwork (coded separately) for your control ad and for the test ad. Every other copy of the publication comes off the press with the same ad. There is no geographic bias. Both ads appear in the same issue, in the same position, surrounded by the same editorial, so that any significant differences in response can reasonably be attributed to the ad itself.

Newspapers that offer an A/B split will usually charge less for the split fee than magazines.
However, it is best to conduct the test in your best media, regardless of cost. If you run in different media, try to schedule the same test in at least two or three places to see if results are consistent.

Beware of 50/50 splits.
Publications sometimes offer an "imperfect" A/B split or a "cluster" split. Instead of having the ideal mix of every other copy, the issue is batched in groups of 50 to 500. Publications that offer a 50/50 split guarantee only that each ad will be distributed to 50 percent of the circulation. Be sure there is no geographic bias to the distribution.

If you want to test one region against another, some publications will accommodate geographic splits at no charge, so long as the territorial splits tie in with their normal distribution boundaries.

Many media are not set up to do splits.
Others will do splits only on full pages. Split charges can vary from zero to $3,000, so it pays to bargain. Try to conduct A/B splits in your most profitable media. *TV Guide* offers a split run nationally or within each of eight regions. *Delta Sky* in-flight magazine will do a four-way (A/B/C/D) split, which provides an easy way to test travel and business offers.

Measure your results!

Be sure every ad is coded separately so you can track results.

In measuring the results of a split run, look for a clear winner.
If results are separated by only a small margin, you gain nothing. Unless the test outpulls a control by 20 percent or more, it is not a clear winner over a control ad that has had prior exposure in the publication.

Track ad results as long as possible but for no less than three months.
Some ads pull orders years after the issue date. This is particularly true of magazines that tend to hang around barbershops or doctor's offices.

Don't be discouraged if your initial results are not blockbusters.

I work with an advertiser whose test ad ran in three magazines. Two of the three failed and the third was only marginal. With what we learned, we were still able to build a long-term successful ad campaign that helped double the client's subscriber base.

Marketers continue to stretch the boundaries of what can be sold profitably in print advertising.
Recently full-page ads and inserts with ticket prices of up to $2,000 have succeeded.

Iris Shokoff's Three Techniques

Never buy retail.
Only if you absolutely must have page 3 or page 5 of a major magazine should you pay full price. The reason: Virtually all magazine publishers and reps negotiate and will sell space at up to 60 percent off.

One technique: Hang back until closing and then call at the last minute.
Most magazines will take a space reservation up to 10 days after closing. Have the ad ready and money set aside in your budget so you can move quickly and take advantage of a deal.

For budgeting purposes, start with a projected response of one order per thousand circulation and work down or up from there based on experience.

Denny Hatch's Two Ideas

If you bypass an agency and place your own insertion orders, insist on receiving the agency's 15 percent commission as a discount for yourself.
But you're probably better off using an agency unless you know precisely what you're doing.

Never contract out a direct-response space ad to a writer and/or designer who have no experience in asking for an order/lead/contribution.
Before hiring any creative help, get samples of their work and references.

Bud Pironti's Beacon
In space advertising, there has been a fallacy that holiday issues and/or the summer months are not appropriate times for testing.

While strong items perform best in January, February, October, and November, a dog is a dog and can be found out on December 15 or June 15.

Bob Stone's Prediction
A print ad with a bind-in card will outpull the same ad without a bind-in up to 600 percent.

Denny Hatch's Caveat
Test a bind-in before you roll out with it. (In fact, test everything before you roll out.)

Andrew J. Byrne's Four Precepts
The smaller your ad, the more cost-effective it will be in getting inquiries.

The headline is the most important part of the ad.

A successful ad is one that convinces the prospect that the product's benefits far exceed in value the price paid for them.

Tests prove photographs sell better than drawings in ads.

Maxwell Sackheim's Dogma
If a picture doesn't tell a story—a complete story—it isn't the right picture.

David Ogilvy's 17 Truths

A display subhead of two or three lines between your headline and your body copy will heighten the readers' appetite for the feast to come.

If you start your body copy with a large initial letter, you will increase readership by an average of 13 percent.

Keep your opening paragraph down to a maximum of 11 words. A long first paragraph frightens readers away. All your paragraphs should be as short as possible; long paragraphs are fatiguing.

After two or three inches of copy, insert your first crosshead and thereafter pepper crossheads throughout.
They keep the reader marching forward. Make some of them interrogative, to excite curiosity in the next run of copy. An ingenious sequence of boldly displayed crossheads can deliver the substance of your entire pitch to glancers who are too lazy to wade through the text.

Set your copy in columns not more than 40 characters wide.

Most people acquire their reading habits from newspapers, which use columns of about 26 characters. The wider the measure, the fewer the readers.

Type smaller than nine-point is difficult for most people to read.

Serif type is easier to read than sans serif type.

Widows increase readership except at the bottom of a column, where they make it too easy for the reader to quit.

Break up the monotony of long copy by setting key paragraphs in bold-face or italic.

Insert illustrations from time to time.

Help the reader into your paragraphs with arrowheads, bullets, asterisks, and marginal marks.

If you have a lot of unrelated facts to recite, don't try to relate them with cumbersome connectives; simply number them, as I am doing here.

Never set your copy in reverse (white type on a black background) and never set it over a gray or colored tint.
The old school of art directors believed that these devices forced people to read the copy; we now know that they make reading physically challenging.

Leading between paragraphs increases readership by an average of 12 percent.

The more typographical changes you make in your headline, the fewer people will read it.

Set your headline, and indeed your whole advertisement, in lowercase. CAPITAL LETTERS LIKE THESE are much harder to read, probably because we learn to read in lowercase. People read all their books, newspapers, and magazines in lowercase.

Never deface your illustration by printing your headline over it.
Old-fashioned art directors love doing this, but it reduces the attention value of the advertisement by an average of 19 percent. Newspaper editors never do it. In general, imitate the editors; they form the reading habits of your customers.

Axel Andersson's Five Tips

If you contract for the back cover of a publication, never split a full-page ad into two half pages with different offers on each half page.
To my knowledge, nobody has made this as profitable as just making one offer on the page.

The split of the fourth (back) cover into two half-page ads is the ideal technique if you want to test two different products against each other. That split will answer your test question. But it will not give you any indication of what response to expect if you had advertised only one of these products on the page.

Sideways ads inside a magazine are a no-no.
Sideways ads with a strong layout for book clubs and home study courses have been successful on the fourth cover of magazines over many years in the United Kingdom and in Germany, lifting response 10 percent to 15 percent. In other words, with a strong layout the fourth cover sideways is a yes, but inside, it's a no-no.

Do not open an ad with this sequence: headline at the top of the page, main illustration, text beneath with no subhead or display line over the text.
If you insist on placing the headline above the main illustration, make sure there is a secondary display line (subhead) above the text to pull the eyes into it. The line or lines that appear above the illustration should provide a complete reading thought, as should any lines that appear below it.

When a headline is long, it should not be broken up so that part of it appears above the illustration and the rest of it below.

David Ogilvy's Two Proverbs

The wickedest of all sins is to run an advertisement without a headline.

Don't get cute with coupons.
Some advertisers try to be creative in their coupons. I have seen coupons looking like a slice of bread, a piggy bank, an egg, etc.

Tony Antin's Dictum

A coupon (order form) should be—must be—an artistic cliché.

Rectangular. Surrounded by dash lines. Not even dotted lines because one connects dots. One cuts along dashes. Moreover, the coupon should be where it belongs, at the lower outside. The coupon should stand out from the rest of the ad.

Craig Huey's 40-Point Primer
Headlines

Position your headline.
Your ad must position your product and its benefits for your target audience—not the total readership of the publication but only those readers who are likely to respond to your offer.

Don't be afraid of long headlines.
Long headlines are often more effective than short headlines. In a long headline you can better target your audience with specific features and benefits.

Put *you* in the headline.
For example: "How You Can Look Younger and Feel Healthier in 30 Days."

Clearly state a benefit in your headline.
For example: "Slash Your 1997 Taxes by $1/3$."

Use hot words: "At last . . . ," "Announcing . . . ," "Now . . . ," "the secret of . . . ," "New!"

Use geography or occupation to build credibility: "How One Businessman from New York Saved $10,000 on His Travel Expenses."

Use numbers.
They give a feeling of reality. They are specific (that's why an odd number is better than an even one, especially one rounded off). Here's an example: "Turn $9,575 into $214,311 in two years!"

Consider telling readers what they might lose by not responding.

Use quotes in a headline to draw attention and create interest.

Use simple words.
Remember, even the *Wall Street Journal* uses language that's understandable to a 17-year-old student. The front page can be understood by a 15-year-old. Even the best-educated people prefer to read without strain or heavy concentration.

Copy

Long copy works.
The more you tell, the more you sell. In fact, the reason ads don't do as well as direct mail is you don't have the space to tell your story as strongly. In just one study, McGraw-Hill reviewed 3,597 ads in 26 business magazines. It found that ads with 300 or more words were more effective than shorter ads in creating awareness of the product, prompting action, and reinforcing a buying decision.

A few years back, Merrill Lynch ran a very long ad in the *New York Times*. Its 6,450 words received a lot of criticism for being "ugly," for having "too much copy and not enough graphics." The headline was long, too: "What Everybody Ought to Know About This Stock and Bond Business."

Despite all the negative reviews, it received 10,000 responses without even a coupon.

Practice preventive advertising.
Anticipate questions and objections. Then answer them in your copy. Ignore them and doubt, indecision, confusion, or objections can kill your response.

Back up your claims.
Don't make a big claim or promise without backing it up. People will always be skeptical. You must verify your claims with facts, testimonials, and/or case histories. Puffery alone doesn't sell.

Don't use humor.

Make your copy reader-oriented.
Don't just write about your product or service. Instead, your copy should be about the readers and how your product or service will benefit them.

For example, "Our computer is unique."

Write instead, "You'll discover it's easy to use and no software is required. . . . You'll save time and money."

Avoid bragging about yourself.
Your prospects want to know why a response is in their self-interest, not your history or achievements.

Simplify, focusing on one offer, simplified as much as possible.

Use powerful subheads.

Use a strong close.
Be forceful and specific. Your prospect will more fully respond to firm directions. Never ask a question or fail to ask for a response now.

Give your prospect response options: phone, mail, fax, credit card.

The more generous your offer, the higher your return.

Use emotion and reason.
Ads must create the desire to respond and a reason to respond. Desire is emotional, but it must be built on a good, logical rationale that provides the motivation to act.

Create tension.
Test phrases such as *limited quantities, first come, first served,* or *offer subject to change without notice.*

Design

One-color ads often generate greater response than two-color ads, because readers associate black-and-white photos with news.

Your visual should use people in action.

Photos are more convincing than line drawings.

Always use a caption with your visual; it will be the most-read part of the ad.

Highlight your toll-free number.

Use bullets, checkmarks, and numbers to break up the copy.

Avoid reverse type for any copy block of three words or more.

Use color to help draw the eye to key sales points and your call to action.

Use serif type in body copy, not sans serif type; it's more readable and will bring a better response.

Type should be 10 to 12 points.

Order Coupon

Always use a broken-line border.

Always put it on the right-hand side, for right-hand placement.

Always include your address and telephone number above—and in—the coupon.

A post office box alone can be a credibility killer; always use a street address.

Always use a positive acceptance statement: "Yes, I want to make $1,000,000 using your widget."

Always leave enough room to fill out the name and address; otherwise you'll lose orders.

Always say, "Please print."

David Ogilvy's Touchstone

A good advertisement is one that sells the product without drawing attention to itself.

Strategy

Strategy is a plan, method, or series of stratagems for obtaining a specific goal or result. It is, in fact, a broad statement of an organization's goals, encompassing its vision for the future and the processes it intends to employ to achieve those goals. Today, in a major paradigm shift, the new business model is described as the *purpose-process-people* model. It emphasizes the interactive, connected systems of business all leading to the notion of customer delight.

Maxwell Sackheim's Five Rules
First you must have a good product.

Is it light in weight in proportion to its price? Except for other disadvantages, the ideal product for mail-order selling would be a diamond. It is ideally light and ideally expensive. Conversely, the worst product is probably an anvil. Your mail-order product must not be handicapped by excessive transportation charges in proportion to its total cost.

Second, you must be adequately capitalized so you can afford to buy customers instead of expecting to make a profit on every initial sale.

Third, you can't afford to dilly-dally in building up a list of customers, for if your pace is too slow, your overhead will devour you.
This may be no different from other methods of doing business, but in selling by mail you can do a lot to control the speed of gaining new customers.

Fourth, you must continually go after repeat orders and multiple sales, for they make it possible to invest money in obtaining new customers.

Fifth, you must be on the alert to expand operations and lengthen the selling and buying season.

Elsworth Howell's Supposition
Every direct marketing effort must stand on its own. You cannot operate on the possibility that the cumulative effect of your advertising will
elicit trackable orders.

> *Comment by Denny Hatch:* General agencies make money when they cre-
> ate a space ad or TV commercial and run it and run it and run it, taking the
> commission for placing the space or buying the airtime. The object of gen-
> eral advertising is to create awareness through repetition.
>
> In direct marketing—according to Elsworth Howell, former president of
> Grolier Enterprises and proprietor of Howell Book House—an offer must
> stand on its own. If you go out with a series of messages or offers, it is impos-
> sible to track which one worked unless each has a specific key.
>
> Yet in a customer-oriented culture, the business of a company is to cre-
> ate customers in the long term, not the short term. Read in a strategic light,
> Howell's comment indicates that a business must measure itself constantly to
> prove it is successful.

Denny Hatch's Commentary
Direct-response TV and radio are exceptions.

> Remember, with a mailing or a catalog, the prospect can go back and reread
> it. A broadcast ad is gone in a wink. A person may need one or more repeats
> before ordering.

Cecil Hoge, Sr.
More money is lost in mail order from poor product selection than in
any other way.

MacRae Ross's 12 Ways to Kill Your Business
Selling what your customers need rather than what they want or desire.

Having no margin to spend on advertising or marketing.

Thinking that your product superiority, technology, innovation, or company size will sell itself.

Depending on word of mouth.

Neglecting or ignoring your current customers while chasing glamorous
new ones.

Trying to be like Coca-Cola and using institutional advertising for prestige.

Turning advertising over to a junior executive.

Turning sales over completely to your sales force or distributor.

Making things easy for you rather than your customers.

Spending the whole budget in one place.

Caring more about what you want to make or do than what your customers want to use or buy.

Being too early or too late to use new techniques or technology.

Martin Gross's Five Strategies
Anyone who overlooks the influence of current events in planning a mailing will be ambushed by them.

She who knows herself will soon know her customers.

Losing an illusion about your prospects makes you wiser than finding a truth.

When reading results, get your mind accustomed to doubting the numbers and your heart to accepting the inevitable.

Bad results are bitter pills that you're better off swallowing than chewing.

Drayton Bird's Six Rules
A complete sale takes more persuasion than an inquiry.

An inquiry about something important takes more than one about something trivial.

It's easier to take small money than it is to take big money.

It's easier to sell a new product with no competition than an old product with lots of competition.

It takes less to sell something made by a well-known company than by an unknown one.

A well-known product requires little explanation; a little-known one requires a lot.

Wendell Forbes's Paraphrase of John Ruskin . . . and Other Ideas

There is hardly anything in this world that some man cannot make a little worse and sell a little cheaper, and people who consider price only are this man's lawful prey.

There is usually more than one good way to solve a problem or accomplish a task, and good managers will understand that *their* way may not be the *only* way.

Let initiative bubble up from within the organization.

No business can survive that weds itself forever and intractably to its original premise.

Businesses are like biological organisms and must grow and change and divide and contribute as do blood and flesh and plants. Otherwise they die.

Marilyn Black's Coda
Underpromise and overdeliver.

George Mosher's Motto
You can run a smooth, profitable business by evening out mailings.

Bill Josephs's Edict
Always offer a real and perceived value.

Dick Benson's Principle
A follow-up mailing dropped two weeks after the first mailing will pull
50 percent of the original response.

When we initiated follow-up mailings [for American Heritage], they pulled 50 percent of the original mailing. The 50 percent figure continues to hold up today almost without fail when we mail a carbon-copy follow-up two weeks after the first mailing with overprinted copy to the effect that "If you missed the first one, here is a second opportunity."

Denny Hatch's Techniques
If your allowable cost per order is reached when you hit 1 percent and you pull 4 percent, jump back into the mail to that list and you should pull 2 percent; if the 2 percent holds, jump right back in and seize your additional 1 percent.

Be sure to negotiate a special rate with the list owner for multiple usage.

Anver Suleiman's Wisdom

Create models for success and then perfect them. Don't try to make every opportunity a new model. Use proven models and tweak them until you get them operating at optimum profitability.

Develop a model for "placing your bets"—i.e., mailing and remailing—and stick to it in, for example, frequency, depth, package, product, geo, list, etc.

Buy/rent/barter credibility.
Form strategic alliances for instantaneous credibility. And then be sure you deliver the quality implied.

Andrew J. Byrne's Prescription

Never underestimate the amount of business brought in by a follow-up mailing.
A surprising number of people respond to the follow-up mailing with the "original" response piece. Original mailing gets too much credit, follow-up too little.

Forget about your advertising campaign. Keep running your most effective ad until another ad can beat it in an A/B split-run test.

Regardless of techniques used, no research is more valid than an A/B split-run test to determine the most cost-effective advertising approach.

Don Nicholas's Tenet
Mail dates should be carved in stone.

Missing a mail date by any significant number of days is really serious—even grounds for firing. There are a couple of reasons for this.
  If you are a magazine with advertising and you are rate base driven, missing a mail date by, say, a month or two could mean that you miss rate base because you don't get orders in on time to replace other subscribers that are falling off. This could force you to "grace" copies—keeping people on the file past expiration, serving them with more than their 12 issues to make rate base. In severe situations, gracing might not cover your shortfall, and you could actually miss rate base, an economic disaster for any advertising-driven magazine.

Even if rate base is not an issue and you are just trying to market subscriptions for their own profitability, missing drop dates can still be a firing offense. One campaign, if dropped on January 1, would yield, say, a 3 percent response. But if the same campaign is dropped two months later, it might draw only a 2.4 percent response. In terms of dollars on the bottom line, you just knocked 20 percent off the profitability of that mailing.

Jack Maxson's Policy
Remember, your client knows more about his or her business than you do.

Don't make any assumptions about your client's business. Listen and learn! If you don't understand, ask! Even if yours is a long-term relationship, keep your ears open. The message may change over time.

Ray Schultz's Rubric
The only dumb question is the one you didn't ask.

The Hauptman/LeBarron client quiz.

When taking on a new project or client, you have to learn everything you can about the business quickly before you can put your direct marketing know-how to work.

In the course of writing subscription promotion packages for dozens of newsletters, freelancer Don Hauptman found himself asking similar questions of new clients. As a result he put together a questionnaire for the client to fill out in advance of their first meeting. The purpose: to save time . . . to get the client's input in writing . . . to be absolutely sure all bases are touched . . . and to have at hand answers to questions that might come up later when the client can't be reached.

This exercise is invaluable in two situations. The first is when a new product or service is being launched and, for the most part, exists only inside the heads of one or two people. It gets the clients thinking through "their baby" and putting those ideas into writing. The second is when the publishers or editors of a magazine give you a very precise idea of what they think they are publishing but when you read the last 12 issues, you find it to be something quite different. If the copy reflects what you believe the magazine to be about—as opposed to what they perceive it to be—chances are the copy will be rejected. By getting their thoughts in writing in advance, you can thrash all this out before fingers touch a keyboard.

Whereas Hauptman's pioneering questionnaire is slanted toward newsletters and publications, freelancer Denny LeBarron has adapted it to come up with an all-purpose questionnaire; it works for products, publications, and services, consumer or business. It should be extremely useful not only for writers but also for account executives, consultants, and list brokers. In addition, if you are a mailer who uses outside creative help, take some time to fill out this form. Then give it to each new copywriter or agency you hire.

Client Questionnaire

1. Client   Address

    Phone Number: Contacts

    Fax Number:

2. DESCRIPTION of product/service. (In 50 words or less, what is being offered? Complete this sentence: This is the only magazine/newsletter/widget/etc. for _____ that offers _____.)

3. PURPOSE of the product. (What does it do? How does it work? How does the prospect use it in his/her daily work or life?)

4. PRICE. (How much does it cost?)

5. What is the OFFER? (Special introductory savings? Premium? Limited-time offer? Two-for-one sale? Free information? Etc. Do you want the copywriter to recommend a new "breakthrough" offer?)

6. What are the FEATURES of the product? (All facts and specs.)

7. What are the BENEFITS? (What will it do for me? What specific problem does it solve, and how does it solve it? How will it make or save me money? Save me time or work? Make my life easier or better? For publications, what specific "information gap" does it fill? What information will it give me that I can't get anywhere else?)

8. OTHER COPY POINTS? (How and why is it new, better than, different from what's already available? Is it unique or exclusive?)

9. **What is our ASSIGNMENT?** (Ad, direct mail package, brochure, insert, DRTV offer, complete campaign?)

10. **What is the OBJECTIVE of the project?** (Inquiries or leads, direct sale, announcement, image building, contribution?)

11. **What's the BUDGET?**

12. **What's the SCHEDULE?** (Be sure to allow enough time for concepts, copy, and revisions.)

13. **Who is the main PROSPECT?** (In business, what is his or her title/responsibility? What are the biggest concerns, fears, attitudes, possible objections? How will the product be used to get ahead or keep from falling behind or save money or make money? For consumers, what main interest/desire/fear does it appeal to?)

14. **Who are your SECONDARY PROSPECTS?** (Are there enough of them to versionalize the copy so the offer appeals more directly to them?)

15. **What LISTS/MEDIA will you use?** (What have you used in the past? What worked and what did not? What is the performance by source?)

16. **Do we have a SAMPLE of the product/service?** (If a publication, send six to 12 months of back issues; media kit—to see what the magazine says about itself; the four bestselling newsstand covers; editorial plan for the next six months.)

17. **Do you have SAMPLES OF PREVIOUS PROMOTIONS?** (Winners and losers? And the results?)

18. **Do you have any TESTIMONIALS, celebrity endorsements, media coverage?** (If not, provide names and phone numbers of 12 current users of your product I can interview for testimonials and information.)

19. **Do you have any COMPLAINTS?** (Letters from unhappy customers?)

20. Will you be conducting any TESTS? (Price, offer, copy?)

21. What copy points MUST be included?

22. What TABOOS do you have? (Anything that must never be said or promised?)

23. What about COMPETITION? (Why are you better? Product? Price? Service? Can your prospect make price comparisons with others, or do you have an exclusive?)

24. Any IN-HOUSE COMPETITION that might affect positioning, copy approaches, etc.?

25. Any operational RESTRICTIONS? (e.g., no 9- by 12-inch outer envelopes, four-color, etc.)

26. What is the METHOD OF PAYMENT? (Cash with order; bill me; PO required? Visa, Mastercard, American Express?)

27. Will you accept TELEPHONE ORDERS? (What percent of your business comes in by phone? Do you have a toll-free 800 number? Fax? An e-mail address? Are your telephone sales representatives trained? What hours are the phone lines open? Do you accept collect calls?)

28. What's the GUARANTEE? (100 percent money-back anytime? 15-day trial? Other?)

29. What about your COMPANY? (Special history of the company, personality of the owner, authority of the seller, achievements, or anything else of sales importance?)

30. ANYTHING ELSE? (As much research and background material as you can supply.)

31. Recommended BACKGROUND READING and OTHER PEOPLE I SHOULD TALK TO.

Sweepstakes

 In the magazine subscription promotion area during the 1960s sweepstakes were wonderful. A whole coda developed regarding sweeps applications—and magazines large and small got into the frenzy. The sweepstakes concept was even tried by the insurance direct marketing folks—with little success, sad to report. Sweepstakes have earned a vaunted place in the history of direct marketing. Hence—some observations.

Bob Stone's Canon

Sweepstakes, particularly in conjunction with impulse purchases, will increase order volume 35 percent or more.

Dan Capell's 15 Sweeps Tips

Everyone hates sweeps.

Publishers and editors generally despise sweepstakes. Even the magazines that are effectively using sweeps wish they could find another marketing approach. The bottom line is that sweeps can double the front-end response for some magazines without any damage to the quality of the subscribers generated.

Expect to spend $50,000 to $60,000 to run a sweepstakes test.

Expenses include about $10,000 to administer the test, $20,000 for art and copy, and another $20,000 to $30,000 for prizes.

Design a sweeps package rather than trying to turn your existing control into a sweeps effort.

Find a sweeps direct mail copywriter and begin from scratch. The prizes should be the star of your package, not the product being sold.

Relate the prizes to the product if possible.

Unless you can afford to give away $1 million or more, try to keep the "dream value" high and the prizes related in some way to the interests of your readers.

The more chances to win, the better.
Have a choice of a grand prize and at least five or six lower tiers of less valuable prizes.

Hire a sweepstakes consulting firm to worry about the nuts and bolts of running a sweepstakes.
The rules and regulations are mind-boggling, and the cost is nominal for the services provided.

Get a year's mileage out of the sweeps.
Run the sweeps long enough to get at least two or three direct mail campaigns under the umbrellas of the same sweeps; it helps to defray the costs.

The more mailings you make under the sweeps umbrella, the less the sweeps costs. (For example, mail a million pieces for a $1 million sweeps and your cost is $1 each or $1,000/M; mail 10 million and your cost drops to 10¢ each or $100/M; mail 100 million pieces and your sweeps cost drops to $10/M.)

Sweeps have unique response patterns.
Returns will come in earlier and faster than nonsweeps direct mail.

Use an early-bird device.
Use a smaller, additional contest (with a quicker deadline than the grand prize) to improve response.

Avoid your inventory of leftovers.
Your premiums left around the office are probably not good sweeps prizes—except for the lowest tier of prizes.

Don't try TV support.
Only a handful of very large mailers have enough mail volume to justify the use of TV support advertising (namely Publishers Clearing House and American Family Publishers).

Use the sweeps umbrella for all other sources.
Make certain that the sweeps is a corporate promotion; then all your other sources and company activities can take advantage of the same giveaway and reduce your costs.

Use all the standard gimmicks.
Sweeps packages are enhanced by all the favorite junk mail devices—tokens, stamps, ink-jet, scratch-off, etc.

The ratio of nos to yeses will vary tremendously by list and by whether you pay return postage or not.
Remember that some companies have had success with renting or even remailing the nos at a later date.

Winning numbers can be preselected or chosen by random drawing. Review the costs of both approaches.

Wendell Forbes's Tips

If you sell by a sweepstakes, you must renew with a sweepstakes and you must sell at exactly the same rate as when the person first came in. Sweeps-sold magazine subscribers who bought from Publishers Clearing House or American Family Publishers will renew at about 18 percent as opposed to 25 percent from a publisher's own sweeps. I believe they should be converted by a sweeps at the same price. (Once having made the huge investment in a new sub, we want to retain as many as possible.) I believe that the PCH 18 percent can be lifted to 28 percent with a sweeps conversion offer and the publisher's own from 25 percent to 32 percent.

People who respond to sweepstakes give a magazine a more dynamic readership—a fresh audience that has responded to strong graphics and copy—and so are better prospects for the advertiser than those who mutely renew year after year.

Gordon Grossman's Insight

While a sweepstakes renewal of sweeps-sold subs will bring in 35 to 40 percent renewals, you can jack this up another 4 to 5 percent with really hard work on the copy, presentation, and prize structure.

A sweeps renewal effort to a non-sweeps-sold sub is confusing and will actually depress response.

Henry Cowen's Addendum

A nonsweeps renewal effort to a sweeps-sold sub will pull half as well as a sweeps renewal effort.

The beauty of sweepstakes is that you can use the same sweeps umbrella for both new and renewal subscribers.

As you use the sweeps across more and more offers, the cost per thousand continues to decline.

Halbert Speer's Wisdom

Part of the confusion over sweepstakes subs is that there are two kinds of sweeps—your own and the direct mail agencies' (Publishers Clearing House, American Family Publishers) sweeps—and the economics are different.

You've got to remember that PCH and AFP pay the publisher a "remit" up front. That is, the publisher gets some net cash for every copy the agencies sell—both new and renewal—and he hasn't invested a cent in direct mail to sell those *new* subs. But the mail agencies do more than just sell the subs. They *collect* from the subscribes. In other words, the publisher doesn't have to *sell* the subs and doesn't have to *collect* for them. And the publisher gets a net payment without having to lift a finger. Guaranteed. Not a bad proposition.

Why else do publishers sell through mail agencies? Most publishers sell *some* new subscriptions to lists that net them some kind of "profit," others sell new subs to lists on which they break even, and others to marginal lists. Viewed in this light, PCH/AFP business is mighty attractive, especially if you can use it instead of that awful direct mail to marginal lists.

If 15 percent or more of these subscribers who bought in the first place "because of the sweepstakes" renew their subscriptions *without* a sweepstakes, that's a pretty good indication that they want your magazine. Maybe they wanted it in the first place, and the sweepstakes was mostly a way of getting their attention.

Of course the real payoff comes when you improve your own renewal promotion to hold more of these people and even persuade some of the ones who might have renewed via the PCH/AFP stamp sheet to respond to *your* offer this time around. But even if they persist in "riding the stamp sheet," you still net *more* from these people than you would from direct mail to marginal lists. Of course my bias in favor of stamp sheet marketers is conditioned by the three years I spent as a consultant to Publishers Clearing House.

Hal Speer's Three Rules for Renewals

Publishers should pay more attention to tracking the renewal behavior of all their subscribers, including their mail agency subscribers.

Publishers should pay more attention to costs and income from all renewals.
A proper analysis may disclose that they are frantically selling renewals (on those 10th and 11th efforts or through their own sweepstakes) that net them even less than they net from marginal direct mail.

This blind quest for renewal percentages at all costs may be the result of trying to maintain impossibly high rate bases.

Denny Hatch's Observations

Sweepstakes buyers are a breed apart; they care more about the winning prizes than your product or service.

Use sweepstakes only to hype one-shot products or services, such as a single book or a magazine subscription.

Sweeps entrants buy because they believe they have a better chance of winning. If you use a sweeps to hype a book club or a continuity series, you'll attract a house file of nonbuyers. The exception: *Reader's Digest* Condensed Book Club.

Never use a business reply envelope in a sweeps mailing.

You'll take a postage bath on people letting you pay for the nos.

Dick Benson's Duo

A sweepstakes is a bribe, a chance to win a big prize for making a yes or no decision.

Sweepstakes will improve results by 50 percent or more.

Overall, I must have been involved in some 200 sweepstakes. No more than five of them were successful.

For many years I found no difference in the quality of orders received from sweepstakes. The pay-up on sweepstakes-generated orders was as good as for nonsweeps; they also renewed as well as nonsweeps. Today quality of orders can't be taken for granted. There are many cases in which pay-up is poorer and renewals can also be poorer.

Axel Andersson's Yardstick

Stay away from skill tests; they don't work as well as sweepstakes.

Never give away as a sweepstakes prize the thing that you are trying to sell.

Why should a prospect buy if there's a chance of winning it free? Anything that gives the prospect a reason to put off the buying decision is a no-no. The exception: automobiles. Auto dealers offer free car prizes because it draws people into the showroom. Once in the showroom, the pigeons are surrounded by gleaming cars and the smell of new leather. The most successful test-drive traffic builder is a sweepstakes offering the car you want the person to test drive.

Never use a sweepstakes where the grand prize is something other than cash.

Second in popularity is a car, and the third prize can be travel. But always offer the cash option. Prizes such as a scholarship—once offered by Encyclopedia Britannica—expensive paintings, collector's items, etc., don't seem to work.

DMA/USPS List of 14 Points That Must Be Set Forth Clearly in Sweepstakes Rules

Disclosure of the fact that no purchase of the advertised product or service is required to win a prize.

Procedures for entry.

If applicable, disclosure that a facsimile of the entry blank or promotional device may be used to enter the sweepstakes.

The termination date for eligibility in the sweepstakes. The termination date should specify whether it is a date-of-mailing or receipt-of-entry deadline.

The number, retail value (of noncash prizes), and complete description of all prizes offered and whether cash may be awarded instead of merchandise.

The approximate odds of winning a prize or a statement that such odds depend on the number of entrants.

Disclosure of the fact that a cash prize is to be awarded by installment payments when that is the case, along with the nature and timing of the payments.

The method by which the winners will be selected.

The geographic area covered by the sweepstakes and those areas in which the offer is void.

All eligibility requirements, if any.

Approximate dates when winners will be selected and notified.

Publicity rights regarding the use of the winners' names.

A statement that taxes are the responsibility of the winner.

Provision of a mailing address to allow consumers to request a list of winners of prizes over $25 in value.

Telemarketing

Telemarketing is big business. In fact, inbound and outbound telemarketing accounts for the largest annual expenditure—over $58 billion—for media within the direct marketing concept. It is the fastest-growing medium, too. But, telemarketing does not stand alone. It is usually part of an integrated media plan, supporting direct mail as well as television, radio, and most of the other direct marketing media.

Lord Lew Grade's Theorem
You can't wait for the phone to ring; you have to ring them.

Mary Ann Falzone's Primer of Telemarketing Practices

To succeed, the telephone element must be a budgeted, integrated, well-planned component of the overall direct marketing campaign.
If telephone-based contacts are added to a direct response campaign as a last-minute afterthought when somebody realizes "Hey, don't we need somebody to take those 800 calls?" the effort usually falls apart.

When follow-up calls to non-responders are carelessly thrown into the mix after a campaign does not produce projected results—with no pre-planning and no real investment in telemarketing program development, measurement, training, or follow-through—the time spent is often wasted.

Whenever the telephone portion of a major direct marketing push is conceived and executed in a vacuum, completely independent of the various other media, departments, and vendors involved, it will be fraught with both problems and lost opportunities and will be counterproductive to the entire program.
The prospect expects the representative to be able to answer any possible question about the product or service—how to use it, the offer, the terms, pay-

ment or financing options, related products, the company, competing companies and products/services, the needs of similar customers . . . you name it!

Prospects expect all of the reps to be intimately familiar with the commercial, print ad, mail piece, flyer, or catalog at hand and to be skilled at helping them make a buying decision that may go far beyond the parameters of that particular product, offer, or campaign.

Prospects expect all of the contacts they've received from a company, regardless of the medium, to be tied together in a coherent and related effort to solve their problems as potential or current customers.

Prospects hate to be told that the answer to their question or the recommendation they seek is not in the script or the help screens at the rep's disposal and will simply take their business elsewhere.

Prospects expect the telephone rep to immediately access information about every other transaction, contact, or correspondence with the company and be able to respond accordingly.

None of these prospect expectations can be met without a significant investment in time, planning, resources, expertise, and coordination. Without it, all previous funds spent on creative, copywriting, design, printing, production, database, and fulfillment will be wasted at the point of contact—the most critical factor in turning an inquiry into a closed sale, confirming that the buying decision will be backed with service and support, and establishing a long-term customer relationship.

The days when customers were willing to fill out order forms, write out a check or money order, mail it all in, and wait four to six weeks for delivery are gone forever. Buying decisions often require consultation with well-trained and informed inside sales specialists who can answer questions and offer recommendations within a short conversation.

Contrary to popular opinion, telephone programs do not magically spring forth from prewritten, restrictive scripts; scripting approaches evolve gradually from well-designed telephone programs.

A corollary to this rule also holds true: Beware the program objective that ignores (1) the needs of the prospect and (2) the conversation that naturally flows from those needs.

One of the most common mistakes in getting a telephone effort off the ground is writing a script in a vacuum and then presenting that unproven script cold to representatives as their main (and often only) instruction on how to conduct the calling program.

Like any effective direct mail piece, the telephone presentation must be researched thoroughly and based on facts and evidence—not assumptions— to be successful. The effort should include input from a sampling of individuals who have hands-on contact with potential or current customers. Creating a process flowchart will show how the telephone contact is integrated with other media, departments, and processes and how follow-through and follow-up efforts will affect everyone involved.

Understand everything you possibly can about your prospects or current customers before you begin to outline a dialogue with them.

Who are they? Why do they need what you have? How would they use it? What else do they buy from you or your competitors? What problems would your product or service solve for them? How important are these problems/solutions to them? What obstacles, real or perceived, need to be overcome before they're likely to make a purchase? Who else might influence this decision? What impression, if any, do they have of your company or companies like yours?

What other communications have you had with them, now and in the past (including correspondence, direct mail, advertisements, contacts with field sales, or within the retail environment, etc.)? If they're current customers, how long has it been since they last purchased from you? What kinds of things do they usually buy? Have there been any problems (with product quality, delivery, bad publicity, etc.) that might come up in the discussion?

Whittle all of this data down to a core benefit or set of benefits that will get and keep their attention. Basically, focus on how what you're selling can help them get something they want—cost savings, recognition, peace of mind, convenience, etc.—or avoid something they don't want: pain, problems, delays, embarrassment, etc.

Keep in mind that this core "punch line" has to be presented from the prospect's point of view, briefly and in a way that's easy to understand.

On an outbound script in today's highly competitive telemarketing environment, representatives will have about 10 seconds to identify themselves and your company and entice a consumer to listen further by using a compelling punchline.

When calling businesses or professionals, you may have a few more seconds to play with, but not much more.

These days, most folks are overworked and underpaid and have little patience for solicitations that interrupt their workday. (This, of course, leaves no time for the overused and ineffective "How are you today?" that is a totally inappropriate greeting from a stranger on a business call.)

The punch line should be backed up by intriguing facts about how this benefit has actually been achieved by others like the prospect or prospect's company.

If overstated, this hook will sound too good to be true and lose its punch.

If you're successful in winning a few more moments of attention from prospects, you can ask some questions to hone in on particular needs and understand how your product or service might best serve them.

Falzone's Five Classic Faulty Scripts

The "one size fits all" script that is inappropriate for the market segment and annoys prospects who quickly realize you don't understand them.

The "announcement" script that focuses on the product, special promotions, the company—anything but the prospects and their needs.

The "assumptions" script that doesn't give prospects the opportunity to talk about their problems and work up an interest in what you have to offer.

The "no, good-bye!" script full of questions that invite a brush-off: "Did you get our mailing?" "Do you need anything today?" etc.

The tendency to literally write scripts that must be spoken and should sound conversational. Tape and retape your initial call guide, then transcribe your most natural sounding version.

More of Falzone's Primer of Telemarketing Practices

Once you have a prototype script, thoroughly crash-test it.
First do a verbal run-through with a select group of knowledgeable colleagues within your company who have hands-on contact with prospects/customers, no ax to grind, and won't hold your clumsy first drafts against you. (Yes, that's a lot to ask, but if you haven't built those kinds of relationships across departmental lines, you won't get the kind of cooperation needed to make the telephone effort a smash hit either.)

These folks will tell you where you're off base and on target and will give you valuable alternate perspectives to work into your next revision. They'll pick up on issues involving your original process flowchart and how what you're planning must be coordinated through other individuals. And they'll also be flattered that you asked for their counsel and will be more likely to cooperate on the program instead of opposing it.

Next take the script outside the company to friends and acquaintances with no insider knowledge or company culture bias. Try to find people who are fairly representative of the region, class, educational level, and interests of your target market. Simply call them up by phone and role-play the dialogue with them. You'll find they'll be more willing to share honest feedback if you explain that you are researching one of the company's customer contact programs rather than testing out a script that you, personally, created.

Listen carefully for verbal and nonverbal reactions and try to keep a lid on your pride of ownership. Document their questions, objections, and misunderstandings about what you're presenting. Afterward, try to find out what they were *thinking* during the call: Were they expecting something else, based on your opener? Did they feel reluctant during the needs analysis questioning? Were parts of the conversation more interesting or boring to them than others? Don't accept a jovial "Sounds good to me!" without probing for the why and how.

If possible, try to get a cooperative friend or relative *who matches the profile of the kind of representative who will be using the script* to take on the role of the caller as you play the prospect.
This will give you a much better feel for how someone at a different level who was not involved in creating the call guide will interpret and present it. And, as you hear and participate in the dialogue from the prospect's side of the fence, you will gain yet another perspective to work into your next round of revisions.

Once revisions are complete, you're ready to make some live test calls into an nth record sampling of the calling list.
Yes, you! Without hearing, firsthand, the actual reactions and results your presentation is getting, you'll be handicapped in making the needed changes: what's not working, what is, what other information you'll need, answers to questions and objections you hadn't anticipated, access to additional data, different follow-up mail materials or literature that must be faxed, a different decision maker or influencer than the one you targeted, and so on.

Most representative-level staffers are not as well prepared as you are to handle live crash-test issues or implement solutions.
First impressions about a calling program carry a lot of weight with reps. If you can load the deck in your favor from the start and the calls pretty much go as you train the reps that they will, the campaign will run a lot smoother from that point on. When reps are the first to shake down a completely new telephone effort, and they aren't as well equipped to deal with the inevitable problems, the people they called will get the short end. The reps will then sour on the program just when they need to build confidence during the learning stage, and you'll be facing an uphill battle.

Once you have the bugs out of the call guide, have pulled all the accompanying processes into place, and it's time to train your reps on the campaign, first *put away the script!*
The first thing your reps will need to learn is how to think, talk, and listen intelligently during the dialogue with the customer. They can't do that right

out of the box by reading a script. Remember, the prospect doesn't have a script and won't necessarily follow the one you designed.

The most successful reps are those who are "light on their feet"—who listen carefully and respond quickly and accordingly when the conversation veers off the script (which is most of the time).

Once the prospect's questions are answered, issues are covered, and misunderstandings are dealt with appropriately, the well-trained rep can gracefully guide the conversation back into the flow of the call guide and the desired outcome.

Reps must develop a working, "talking" understanding of many of the issues researched in creating the initial script: a profile of the targeted prospects, their needs and problems, and a thorough knowledge of the product, your company, the offer, pricing and terms, product uses and benefits, the competition, and so on.

The ultimate goal is for reps to feel so comfortable with the material that they can respond easily and naturally to any off-the-cuff question or concern from the prospect.

At this stage in their training, conduct a group discussion about the main call objectives, benefits, questions, and answers reps feel will be key to the calling program.

You'll find that they will come to many of the same conclusions you did, especially if they've had previous contact with the target audience. (You'll probably pick up one or two great ideas to work into your final script.)

Let them know that you will incorporate their insights and suggestions into the final version of a guide designed to help lead them through the telephone sales conversation. Immediately following this session, introduce the call guide as a structure to mesh their "talking learning" with the "presentation/persuasion" learning involved in following a scripted approach.

Be prepared for the fact that the introduction of a formalized call guide will make reps temporarily forget some of the stuff they had down pat before they ever laid eyes on the script.

Be patient. You may have to take away the call guide for a while if they get bogged down and go back to the thinking/talking training until reps can meld the two.

Even though you go to all that trouble to train reps to ad-lib successfully, you still need a script.

Successful telephone campaigns, like any other direct marketing effort, must be *measurable*. The different personalities and delivery styles among your representatives already represent a significant wildcard variable without encouraging each rep to shoot completely from the hip on the presentation approach as well. If every rep said something different to prospects on the phone, it would be very difficult to troubleshoot the program and duplicate successes.

And most reps feel much more comfortable with a preplanned, structured approach they don't have to make up from scratch on every call.

Once reps are confident enough with the call guide and the rest of their training to "go live," monitor calls intensively during this initial phase of the program.

You'll continue to make revisions and learn valuable lessons as you fine-tune the program. Emphasize to your reps that you'll be working together during this time to enhance the campaign, that there will be some changes coming, and that change is a good thing when it serves the needs of customers.

Recognize and reward flexible behavior as a qualitative goal in addition to your quantitative objectives on productivity and results.

The process outlined is very similar for structuring call scripts/screens and training for inbound calling programs.

Telephone training must be continuous to be effective.

Corollary: Training alone, however, can never counterbalance other negative factors that may be toppling your telephone campaign.

Managers tend to forget that every action they take will produce an equal and opposite reaction from their people and customers—and it usually *isn't* the outcome they had intended.

Pushing for higher productivity via simply dials, calls, and connect time may have a chilling effect on sales and profitability as reps rip through lists and speed-talk through incoming calls, trying to reach the goals you set. You may, in fact, decrease the average time on hold (or some other management objective) only to find that it now takes callers less time to reach a rep—who doesn't seem to want to talk to them, uncover their needs, or provide solutions that will make the sale.

Don't confuse process training, which is relatively easily learned and retained, from progress training, which involves radical behavior change.

Identify the specific results you want the training to achieve. Identify the most probable equal and opposite reactions that your training actions may produce.

Use alternative resources—where appropriate—to handle incoming calls. With the great preponderance of 800 numbers and inbound campaigns, many companies are augmenting live representative call coverage with automated call-handling systems. Pressures to cut costs and provide 24-hour, seven day-a-week accessibility and service have led the way for many inbound calls to be automated—either partly or entirely—through voice response equipment.

George Mosher's Adages

Telephones must be answered and handled professionally by *everyone*.

You want as many sales calls as possible handled by a select group of higher-trained individuals, presumably in the sales department.

The person taking the call is to get the order if at all possible; he or she always has to ask, "Can I get your order started?"

Taking orders is a quality process that guides the customer through the order; it is *not* a conversation.

Always ask, "Do you want this on MasterCard or Visa?"

Customer calls must be answered competently without delay or hassle; do not put your telephone on "make busy" (on hold) when you are at your desk.

FTC Telemarketing Prompt Oral Disclosure Rule

A telemarketer making an outbound call must promptly disclose, in a clear and conspicuous manner, four items of information:

The identity of the seller.

The seller is the entity that provides goods and services to the consumer in exchange for payment. The identity of the telemarketer, or person making the call, need not be disclosed if it is different from the identity of the seller. If the seller commonly uses a fictitious name that is registered with appropriate state authorities, that name may be disclosed instead of the seller's legal name.

That the purpose of the call is to sell goods or services.

The rule does not require any "magic" words or phrases to explain the purpose of the call. The rule requires only that the purpose of the call be disclosed promptly to consumers. How the purpose of the call is described or explained is up to the seller or telemarketer, so long as it is not likely to mislead consumers.

The nature of the offered goods or services.

This is a brief description of the items offered for sale.

In the case of a prize promotion, that no purchase or payment is necessary to participate or win.

If the consumer asks, the telemarketer also must, without delay, disclose instructions on how to enter the prize promotion without paying any money or purchasing any goods or services.

The termination date should specify whether it is a date-of-mailing or receipt-of-entry deadline.

John Hamilton's Precept
The success of any telemarketing effort is directly proportional to the investment in training the reps.

Testimonials

 Getting people to "tell it like it is" is as powerful in direct-response advertising as it is in general advertising. The difference is the direct marketer uses testimonials as the "prove it" part of the pitch. Simply put, there is nothing more powerful than credible testimonials to give you a competitive edge.

Denny Hatch's Formulary

If you make outrageous, self-serving claims about your own product or service, you can get into trouble with the regulators—not to mention opening up a credibility gap with your readers. If you can get a satisfied customer to make the same claims, you're golden.

If you promise people they can eat all they want of everything they love and lose 30 pounds in 30 days, you could get into trouble with the FTC. If you can get a customer to say she used your diet system, ate like a pig, drank like a fish, and lost 30 pounds in 30 days, it's legal. That's because the First Amendment guarantees the right of free speech.

Testimonials are powerful selling tools; use them.

The generally recognized sequence of events in marketing is (1) finding a suspect, (2) making the person a prospect, (3) turning that person into a customer (or donor), and (4) converting the customer into a renewer or multibuyer or a regular customer or donor. Nirvana is (5) when that person becomes an advocate—likes you so much that you will get a testimonial and referrals.

If a customer writes, or tells you on the phone that your product is really appreciated and gives the reasons why, immediately ask if you can use those comments as a testimonial.

Ask if you can use the customer's name or just the testimonial. The testimonial might be signed—Mrs. J.L., Jackson, Mississippi, for example.

David Ogilvy's Ideal
If one testimonial tests well, try two.

> But don't use testimonials by celebrities unless they are recognized authorities, like Arnold Palmer on golf clubs.

Bob Martel's Warning
There are too many cases of testimonials being used in direct marketing campaigns without prior knowledge of the client/customer.

Donn Richardson's Guide
Always be clear about what you intend to use the testimonial for, get the customer's permission, and ask the customer not to date it; that way you can use it for quite a while without arousing curiosity about the time lapse.

Bob Wells's Process
For testimonials, have the customer type the text onto his or her letterhead.

Richard Armstrong's Tip
Real testimonials have a genuine sound to them that's very hard to reproduce—maybe the grammar is ever so slightly off, there's a peculiar choice of words, or a point is made that no professional copywriter ever would have considered—try to use these real raindrops wherever possible before you start seeding the clouds.

> Back in the days when silver dollars were common currency, bartenders and store clerks used to drop the dollar on the counter and listen to the ring because it was distinctly different from the dull sound made by lead counterfeits. I've found the same to be true of testimonials. People can spot the real ones from the made-up ones a mile away. So while I don't disagree with the preceding rules, I'd be very careful about doing too much rewriting, suggesting, and editing.

Testing

Remember, testing is what really separates the direct marketing concept from any other form of business model. Investment is governed by *result*. While vertical industry segments may have to put up millions of dollars to retool for product, a direct marketer, using market testing methods, can tell for a fraction of the costs if the major investment is worthwhile. Someday, the other people are going to "get it." Until then here is some accumulated wisdom.

Don Nicholas's Hypotheses

The Holy Grail of direct marketing is the single-variable test.
You want only one thing to change in each test. If you're going to test price, then you test two packages that are the same in all respects except for price. If you want to test outer envelopes, you change only the outer envelope.

The goal is to make sure that when something wins or loses on a package or a panel, you know the cause of the difference so you can repeat it if it wins. The exception, of course, is breakthrough testing—as with an entirely new package or approach.

On multimailings, fire your best shot first and use the follow-up to reinforce.
Theory: If they say no to a first offer, nothing will convert them. (Doesn't apply to inquiry generation.)

Anver Suleiman's Observations

Let your competitors test for you.
Don't test stuff your competition has already tested, especially the big competitors. If they tried a certain approach and dropped it, assume it didn't work. And if they are using something over and over, assume it does work. No need to retest and reinvent until your model proves itself.

Provide an incentive to buy today, but don't make it a penalty to order tomorrow.

Rose Harper's Yardstick

Greater productivity in direct mail is a function of gathering, understanding, and using information.

It's axiomatic that if we don't understand where we've been, it's very hard to figure out where we're going.

Where do we start? With recordkeeping. Not piles of computer printouts, but disciplined, comprehensive, and systematic recordkeeping.

Once the integrity of your system has been established, the data collection function (manual or computerized) should not be difficult to follow. Without complete and information-packed records, decisions can be haphazard to the health of your mail plan—and costly.

Consider the mail plan analogous to strategic planning—a process of gathering facts about your business, asking questions, and developing decision criteria.

In reviewing the previous plan (whether results were good or bad), what did you learn? What matters in a cause-and-effect analysis is not a subjective defense of the plan but an objective and thoughtful evaluation.

Six Key Questions to Ask

What influences can be specifically measured that will assist in positioning the assumptions for the next campaign?

Were there too many tests affecting overall results?

What would have been the outcome if some of these tests had been excluded?

Were the tests significant (as in breakthrough)?

Tests cost money. In the words of one consultant, "Don't test whispers."

What influences can be measured specifically?

For example, were the assumptions used in developing the plan realistic?

Were the house files used to the fullest extent possible?

Can additional segmentation techniques be applied?

Were financial resources allocated on the basis of how much you are willing to invest in new-customer acquisition versus how much you are willing to invest in retaining present customers?

It is essential to develop methods of comparing actual performance to planned objectives, identifying trends, and taking corrective actions when needed.

Reports should highlight key variances and trends to be investigated. This is the information that will prepare you for developing future campaigns.

The unprecedented availability of information has made data selection just as critical as the data themselves.

Sometimes decisions are difficult to make either because data do not exist or they exist in such volume that critical facts are lost in the mess.

To estimate the results of a mail plan, certain variables must be identified and assumptions relative to the effect of the variables must be used in the projections.

This is analogous to economic advisers who look at leading indicators and sometimes reach different conclusions. It's a question of interpretation and the weight given to certain factors. For example, if the total quantity mailed was and will be governed by the need to meet a rate base rather than the quantity that could be mailed at a break-even level, a high weight must be given to this objective and the financial implications of it.

Five Variables That Have a High Impact on Results

Seasonality: Each company should determine, through controlled testing, which months or seasons are best for its product or service.

Years of study and evaluation seem to show that certain categories of products sold by direct mail have certain time periods of the year in which the climate is better than others. Some are obvious, such as fall fashion catalogs in July or August or Christmas catalogs in the fall. In certain parts of the country, late winter to early spring is better for gardening products. In other parts of the country gardening products can be sold practically throughout the year.

Seasonality tests can be done on a monthly basis by mailing the same offer at the same time every month to comparable but different names from the same list. Then the company can carefully tabulate the results.

Price test: Testing price is easier to quantify than seasonality.

If the new price was tested, you should have a good idea of its impact on results. For example, you sold your book at $14.95 in January but tested $17.95 on the lists being used to test seasonality—hot line and changes of address. Response dropped by 10 percent on the $17.95 price, but increased revenue per thousand indicated that, nevertheless, the price should be used in the fall mailing.

The back end: Don't base future decisions totally on front-end response.

In one recent situation where a price test was conducted, the new price depressed initial response and increased the cost per order. However, when the response was tracked, conversions were up by 11 percent, resulting in a substantial increase in net revenues per converted order.

The mailing package: If the new package produced a 50 percent lift on a test panel, it would be unwise to apply this substantial increase over an entire continuation volume.

Very frequently a new package is tested in a relatively small quantity. From experience it would be unwise to apply a 50 percent lift on a test panel over an entire continuation volume. A more conservative approach is indicated. A 10 percent or 25 percent increase might be more reasonable, and the cost of the package should be adjusted to reflect the economies of scale.

Test to continuation: In actual practice, it is rare that the larger-quantity continuation runs parallel to test results.

In my experience it is not so unusual, in some instances, to experience a significant drop-off.

Reasons Why a Continuation Might Be Disappointing

The test was not a true representative sampling of the list.

There was a long time lag between the test and the follow-up.

The test was mailed in a good season, and the run in a poor season.

The test was small (5,000) and the continuation quantity was 100,000.

There were external influences such as weather, dramatic news events, or poor economic news.

Competition may have been a factor.

Repeat usage of names: A second solicitation to the same names in a six-month period will be less productive than the first.

If the response on a particular list produced well above the overall response in a particular mailing, you know something about these prospects. Repeat usage could be considered. But it is logical to assume that the same names that pulled 2.9 percent in January will not pull the same response in August.

The standard procedure on list results is to request omission of names previously used. This is based on experience that in general repeat usage affects response negatively.

If you can afford a 25 to 30 percent drop in response, the list could be worth repeating. However, if the list is an active one with new names being added and old names dropped, the repeat becomes less repetitive and the list should hold up within a 10 to 15 percent range.

In general, if you deal with a vertical market such as professionals (doctors, lawyers, teachers), these targeted files can be used more frequently.

Mail-date allocation: If you have several products that appeal to similar markets and mail two times a year, the allocation of mail dates needs to be measured and assigned on a formula basis.
This assessment is important because it provides a basis for allocating today's resources against tomorrow's business. A successful product with a high return on investment may continue to generate a reasonable profit even if assigned a low-priority mail date. Conversely, a new product that does not yet contribute to profits might need to be assigned a high-priority mailing period to accelerate the return on investment.

In a financial sense, you're considering the risk-reward trade-off and return-on-investment balancing act.

Lew Smith's Precept
The success of any direct marketing effort depends on three things: product, offer, and lists.

Everything else—creative, paper stock, format—is secondary and tertiary.

Ed Mayer's 40-40-20 Rule
Success in direct [mailing] is dependent on the following ratios: 40 percent lists, 40 percent offer, 20 percent everything else.

Bob Hacker's Corollary
The success of a direct marketing project is 30 percent offer, 30 percent lists, 20 percent package cost, and 20 percent creative. If you pay too much, you can never recover.

Denny Hatch on the Art and Science of the Dry Test

For introducing a new product, a dry test is cheaper than a wet test and more reliable than a focus group.
You have a fire in your belly to publish a magazine or book; you've invented an electronic gizmo; you've dreamed up the ultimate weight-loss program. You have three choices: focus group, dry test, wet test.

With a focus group, you are dealing in the subjunctive.
("If you were offered this product and if it cost this price, would you buy?")
In the quiet comfort of a conference room stocked with sandwiches and soft

drinks, you might say yes. In the real world of a crazed household with screaming kids or under the pressure of the workplace, you might say no.

Wet tests are expensive.
You have to spend money creating and producing the product. If it bombs, you will lose a fortune.

The sensible and economical compromise is a dry test—making an offer for a product that does not yet exist and asking people to buy (or subscribe or donate). You have moved from the subjunctive to the active.
Further, if the dry test is a success and you go ahead with the product or service, you have in place a direct mail package ready to roll, so you're ahead of the game. If the test bombs, you've saved yourself a ton of money by not producing the product.

Even if the dry test is successful, you are not home free.
If the product is no good, people will return it (their absolute right under FTC regulations). If it's a magazine that fails to live up to its billing, subscribers will not renew. You can't know that until you've served up the product. But the dry test can give you a good indication as to whether or not you have a business.

Do not use space or TV for a dry test.
Use either of these media and what you are doing is public knowledge the moment the ad breaks.

Do not use a double postcard unless you have a narrowly defined product going to a precisely defined audience.
Cigar Aficionado magazine debuted via a double postcard because it was what it was and it went to cigar aficionados.

The cheapest dry test is to create an ad—one-page or a two-page spread—and send it to likely buyers with a letter.
The letter says, in effect:

> Here's a preview of an ad we will be running shortly in national media. Because of who you are, I wanted you to see it in advance of the general public and to take a special 25 percent discount. . . .

If you get nothing back, you'll know you have a problem; if you get a few orders back, it fogs the mirror. The proposition has some life. If you get a ton of orders, go to the next step—a dry test.

The point of a dry test is to create a mailing package that makes this proposed product or gleam in a publisher's eye so real and so appealing that the prospect simply has to have it!

In the late 1970s, a client of mine did some elaborate market research to his database of customers and came up with about eight products that he knew would make money. One of the products to be dry-tested was a card continuity series—much like the cooking cards and gardening cards offered by International Masters or Margrace. The subject was the Civil War. I personally thought the idea was nuts, but my client said it was sure money and to do it.

In his department was one of the greatest professionals I have ever worked with, a young product manager named Cindy Cooper whose true passion in life was hurling herself out of airplanes; back when I knew her, she had made more than 2,000 jumps. Where many entrepreneurs are fuzzy-headed dips who give a writer vague direction, this woman researched the project to death and sent a giant carton of information, illustrations, background material, and a detailed analysis of the universe to whom I would be writing. She was organized and prompt and pleasant. Quite simply, she was the best in the world at what she did.

As proprietor of the world's greatest archive of direct mail, I was able to quickly find a number of mailings dealing with collector's cards. I immediately settled on a 6- by 9-inch format. All the other card offers showed the free storage box full of cards, so it was imperative that the client have dummies of at least a few cards. Freelancer Herschell Gordon Lewis calls this technique verisimilitude—creating an image so indistinguishable from reality that to the recipient it becomes reality.

I did the following to create the necessary verisimilitude:
Running down the left-hand column of each page of the four-page letter in tiny type: titles of all the cards (which did not yet exist). Verisimilitude.

The cover of the brochure depicted a box of the cards (which didn't yet exist) with one of the dummy cards shown full size. Again, verisimilitude.

Inside the brochure, another shot of the card box full size with a pair of full-size human fingers holding one of the cards. (Actually, the fingers were slightly smaller than actual size and the cards slightly larger so as to make the cards look bigger.) Verisimilitude.

Back cover of the brochure: a hand holding a set of cards (that didn't yet exist) with a cascade of prototype cards ringing the copy and juxtaposed against an old etching. More verisimilitude.

In the prospect's mind, the cards existed when they did not.

Technically, true dry tests are illegal.
In the good old days of mail order—before bureaucrats and lawyers got involved—you simply did a dry test and then wrote a "delay letter" to those who ordered, returning any money sent in. According to the FTC, if a product does not yet exist, you must say so. You cannot offer something for sale that you knowingly cannot deliver within 30 days without saying so.

If you say in the piece that the product does not exist, the whole concept of verisimilitude goes out the window. What's more, you certainly don't want to use a piece that says the product doesn't exist when the product does, in fact, exist; the validity of the dry test is blown to hell. (The product *exists;* it just isn't available.)

Technically, you have to be upfront about the product not existing. Lawyers will urge you to qualify it with such weaseling phrases as "Preproduction Preview," "When ready," etc.

In fact, the whole business of dry testing is a mine field; if you get convicted of mail fraud, you're liable to a $10,000 fine per count (with each piece of mail representing one count).

But, if you don't ask for payment, you can say, "What are the damages? Who's been cheated?" The point is, non-existent magazines do dry tests all the time. And, in the words of my longtime mentor and former employer, guru Walter Weintz: "If lawyers had their way, nobody would mail anything, which means nobody will get into trouble."

What did my client do? The company's lawyers were very uncomfortable with the dry test program. Legal and creative did a long, complex Waltz-Me-Around-Again-Willie and settled on a line of copy both could live with. On the brochure coupon and on the accompanying order card, in tiny (maybe nine-point) type under the name and address, a single line of copy was tested:

This offer is contingent upon receiving a sufficient number of orders.

What happened?

It raised response 15 percent!

It was tested again, and it raised response 15 percent.

As a result, the company put that line of copy on every order form—even on controls that had been working for years.

Guess what?

It bumped response 15 percent on everything!

It's a crazy, crazy business.

Pat Farley's Five Rules for Beating Controls

Make sure your tests are clean and the offer is exactly the same for all creative efforts so you have a true reading on which creative won.

Separate format from creative approach.
I've won tests big by combining the format from an old winner and the creative approach of the latest winner.

Justify expenses.
Don't just add a costly element because you always wanted to do it. You must feel strongly that the additional expense is going to produce revenues far in excess of the cost.

Examine the winners of the past to identify elements they have in common and make sure your new effort contains all those elements.

Examine losers of the past to identify elements they have in common; double-check to see if these elements are missing in the winners; avoid anything you find.

Ed Capano's Ethic

There are certain hard-and-fast rules in direct marketing that should never be violated.

Always test.

Wendell Forbes's Idea

If you make a mistake, call it testing; if you make a big mistake, call it research.

Bill Josephs's Control

Never test in a market that cannot be rolled out in larger volumes.

Richard Jordan's Regulation

Spend the most money on testing where the results matter most and the least where results are least important.

> I've seen this rule violated time after time. In renewal testing, for instance, most marketers test an entire renewal series, which means they're spending as much creatively on the final effort as they are on the first effort—even though the first effort might produce 50 percent of the eventual cumulative renewals, while the final effort might account for only 2 or 3 percent.
>
> While the late great Red Dembner was riding herd as circulation director of *Newsweek* in a period of explosive growth, he preferred to spend his renewal testing money on the early efforts, where the results were most strongly leveraged. During the two years I was at *Newsweek,* we tested constantly—but never got further into the series than the D renewal effort. The other 12 or so efforts—it was a monstrously long series—never got tested at all.
>
> Another example: Many marketers spend big bucks on the cold, up-front effort but little behind it. This can be disastrous with an offer such as a magazine comp copy offer, where 75 or 80 percent of the takers never pay up. Wouldn't it be smarter for the magazine to spend a little less up front and put some heavy dollars into the conversion series in an attempt to plug this profit drain?

Martin Gross's Three Concepts

Mistakes are all right when you're designing a test, but you don't have to drag them along into a control.

Guessing at results is as pernicious as misreading them.

What a test market does should not be considered an action but a symptom.

Jack Maxson's Maxim
Test everything (except your boss's patience).

> Even seemingly unimportant variables can surprise you. Test them even if they don't make sense at first. And keep testing them; tastes and preferences change. Yesterday's dumb ideas may become tomorrow's runaway successes.

Dick Benson's Rule of Thumb
Test-mailing packages are best when they come from independent creative sources.

Malcolm Decker's Two Inviolable Basic Rules
There are two rules in direct marketing and two rules only:

> Rule 1: Test everything.
> Rule 2: See Rule #1.

Maxwell Sackheim's Stricture
Confine your tests to important changes, not trivial ones. You will never get the exact same answers over again.

Ed Mayer's Corollary
Don't test whispers.

> Test $9.95 vs. $9.98 or blue paper vs. pink paper or Garamond vs. Times Roman only after you have exhausted every other possible test.

Axel Andersson's Formula
For a test to be a clear winner the number of responses must be more than double the square root of total orders.

> Example: You have two tests that bring in 100 orders. The square root of 100 is 10. Thus if test A brings in 60 orders and test B brings in 40 orders, test A is the winner by 20 orders—or double the square root. But be cautious: keep in mind that the larger the numbers, the more reliable the result.

Bibliography

The greatest library of direct marketing publications is maintained in Palm Coast, Florida, by consultant/guru Axel Andersson. His collection includes books and periodicals from all over the world, collected and subscribed to over his 50 years in the business. With Andersson's help, we have assembled this bibliography, which we expect to add to with each successive edition of this book. Our thanks to Axel Andersson for his invaluable help.

Books

Andrews, Francis S. *Billions by Mail.* Tabor Oaks, 1984.

Bacon, Mark S. *Do It Yourself Direct Marketing.* New York: John Wiley & Sons, Inc., 1992.

Baier, Martin. *Elements of Direct Marketing.* New York: McGraw-Hill, 1983.

_____. *How to Find and Cultivate Customers Through Direct Marketing.* Lincolnwood, IL: NTC Business Books, 1996.

Baines, Adam. *The Handbook of International Direct Marketing,* 2nd ed. The European Direct Marketing Association, 1996.

Baker, R. A. *Help Yourself to Better Mail Order.* Printer's Inc., 1953.

Baker, Sunny, and Baker, Kim. *Desktop Direct Marketing.* New York: McGraw-Hill, 1995.

Bayan, Richard. *Words That Sell.* Chicago, IL: Contemporary Books, Inc., 1984.

Benson, Richard V. *Secrets of Successful Direct Mail.* Lincolnwood, IL: NTC Business Books, 1982.

Bird, Drayton. *Commonsense Direct Marketing.* Lincolnwood, IL: NTC Business Books, 1994.

Bly, Robert W. *Ads That Sell.* Asher-Gallant Press, 1988.

_____. *Business to Business Direct Marketing.* Lincolnwood, IL: NTC Business Books, 1993.

_____. *The Copywriter's Handbook*. New York: Henry Holt & Co., 1990.

_____. *Direct Marketing Profits*. Asher-Gallant Press, 1987.

Bodian, Nat. *Direct Marketing Rules of Thumb*. New York: McGraw-Hill, 1995.

_____. *Encyclopedia of Mailing List Terminology*. Bret Scot Press, 1986.

_____. *NTC's Dictionary of Direct Mail and Mailing List Terminology*. Lincolnwood, IL: NTC Business Books, 1990.

_____. *Publisher's Direct Mail Handbook*. Phoenix, AZ: ISI (dist. by Oryx), 1987.

Brady, Frank R., and Vasquez, J. Angel. *Direct Response Television*. Lincolnwood, IL: NTC Business Books, 1995.

Brady, Regina, with Forrest, Edward, Mizerski, Richard, and American Marketing Association Staff. *Cybermarketing: Your Interactive Marketing Consultant*. Lincolnwood, IL: NTC Business Books, 1997.

Brann, Christian. *Cost Effective Direct Marketing*. Paramus, NJ: Prentice-Hall, 1988.

Burnett, Ed. *The Complete Direct Mail List Handbook*. Paramus, NJ: Prentice-Hall, 1988.

Burstiner, Irving. *Mail Order Selling*. Paramus, NJ: Prentice-Hall, 1982.

Burton, Philip Ward. *Advertising Copywriting*, 6th ed. Lincolnwood, IL: NTC Business Books, 1990.

Cannella, Frank. *Infomercial Insights*. Burlington, WI: Cannella Response Television, 1995.

Caples, John. *How to Make Your Advertising Make Money*. Paramus, NJ: Prentice-Hall, 1983.

_____. *Making Ads Pay*. Paramus, NJ: Prentice-Hall, 1957.

_____. *Tested Advertising Methods*. Paramus, NJ: Prentice-Hall, 1974.

Cohen, William A. *Building a Mail Order Business*. New York: John Wiley & Sons, 1991.

Cross, Richard, and Smith, Janet. *Customer Bonding/Pathway to Lasting Customer Loyalty*. Lincolnwood, IL: NTC Business Books, 1994.

Deloitte & Touche. *Profitable Retailing Using Relationship and Database Marketing*. Direct Marketing Association.

Direct Marketing Association. *Direct Marketing: Directly Improving the World You Live In* (video). New York: DMA.

_____. *DMA Environmental Resource for Direct Marketers*, 2nd ed. New York: DMA.

_____. *Economic Impact: U.S. Direct Marketing Today: A Landmark Comprehensive Study Conducted by the WEFA Group*. New York: DMA, 1996.

Eicoff, Al. *Direct Marketing Through Broadcast Media,* new ed. Lincolnwood, IL: NTC Business Books, 1995.

Emerick, Tracy, and Goldberg, Bernard. *Business-to-Business Direct Marketing*. Yardley, PA: Direct Marketing Publishing, 1991.

Evans, Craig R. *Direct Response Television*. Paramus, NJ: Prentice-Hall.

Fenvessy, Stanley. *Fenvessy on Fulfillment*. Stamford, CT: Cowles Business Media, 1988.

Forrest, Edward, and Mizerski, Richard. *Interactive Marketing: The Future Present*. Lincolnwood, IL: NTC Business Books, 1996.

Gnam, Rene. *Rene Gnam Direct Mail Workshop*. Paramus, NJ: Prentice-Hall, 1990.

Gross, Martin. *The Direct Marketer's Idea Book*. ANACOM/American Management Association.

Grossman, Gordon W. *Grossman on Circulation–1995*. Philadelphia, PA: North American Publishing Company, 1995.

_____. *Grossman on Circulation–1996*. Circulation Management, 1996.

Hallberg, Gary. *All Consumers Are Not Created Equal*. New York: John Wiley & Sons, 1995.

Hatch, Denison. *Million Dollar Mailings*. Chicago, IL: Bonus Books, 1993.

_____. *Target Marketing's Guide to Direct Marketing Creative Services*, 3rd ed. Philadelphia, PA: North American Publishing Company, 1995.

_____, ed. *Target Marketing's Guide to Direct Marketing Suppliers*. Philadelphia, PA: North American Publishing Company, 1995.

Hawthorne, Timothy. *Infomercial Marketing: The Complete Guide*. Lincolnwood, IL: NTC Business Books, 1996.

Hiebing, Roman G., Jr., and Cooper, Scott W. *The Successful Marketing Plan*. Lincolnwood, IL: NTC Business Books, 1995.

Hill, L. T. *How to Build a Multimillion Dollar Catalog Mail Order Business by Someone Who Did*. Paramus, NJ: Prentice-Hall, 1984.

Hodgson, Dick. *Dick Hodgson's Complete Guide to Catalog Marketing*. Chicago: Dartnell Corp., 1996.

_____. *Direct Mail and Mail Order Handbook,* 3rd ed. Chicago: Dartnell Corp., 1980.

_____. *The Greatest Direct Mail Sales Letters of All Time*. Chicago: Dartnell Corp., 1995.

Hoge, Cecil C., Sr. *The Electronic Marketing Manual*. New York: McGraw-Hill, 1993.

_____. *Sears & Wards: The First Hundred Years Are the Toughest*. Berkeley, CA: Ten Speed Press, 1988.

_____. *Mail Order Moonlighting,* rev. ed. Berkeley, CA: Ten Speed Press, 1988.

Holtman, Arthur F., and Mann, Donald C. *The New Age of Financial Services Marketing*. Naperville, IL: Sourcebooks, Inc., 1992.

Hopkins, Claude C. *My Life in Advertising & Scientific Advertising.* Lincolnwood, IL: NTC Business Books, 1986.

Hughes, Arthur M. *The Complete Database Marketer,* 2nd ed. Burr Ridge, IL: Irwin Professional Publishing, 1995.

Hunter, Victor, with Tietyin, David. *Business-to-Business Marketing: Creating a Community of Customers.* Lincolnwood, IL: NTC Business Books, 1996.

Imber, Jane, and Toffler, Betsy-Ann. *Dictionary of Advertising and Direct Mail Terms.* Hauppauge, NY: Barron's, 1987.

Jackson, Donald R. *151 Secrets of Insurance Direct Marketing Practices Revealed.* Wilmington, DE: Nopoly Press, 1989.

_____. *Insurance Direct Marketing 1996: Special Report on the Companies, the Practices, the Standards and the Benchmarks.* The Jackson Consulting Group, Ltd., 1996.

_____. *Insurance Direct Marketing 1997, Special Report on the Companies, the Practices and the Benchmarks.* The Jackson Consulting Group, Ltd., 1997.

Jackson, Donald R., and Lowen, Irwin. *Winning, Direct Marketing for Insurance Agents & Brokers.* Naperville, IL: Financial Sourcebooks, a Division of Sourcebooks, Inc., 1992.

Jackson, Robert R., Wang, Paul, and Petrison, Lisa. *Strategic Database Marketing.* Lincolnwood, IL: NTC Business Books, 1995.

Jones, Susan K. *Creative Strategy in Direct Marketing,* 2nd ed. Lincolnwood, IL: NTC Business Books, 1993.

Jutkins, "Rocket" Ray. *Power Direct Marketing* (video). Tudor Direct.

Kobs, Jim. *Profitable Direct Marketing,* 2nd ed. Lincolnwood, IL: NTC Business Books, 1991.

Kremer, John. *The Complete Direct Marketing Source Book.* New York: John Wiley & Sons, Inc., 1992.

_____. *Mail Order Selling Made Easy.* Ad-Lib, 1990.

Lambert, M. P., and Welch, S. R., eds. *Home Study Advertising Handbook.* National Home Study Council, 1993.

Lautman, Kay Partney, and Goldstein. *Dear Friend: Mastering the Art of Direct Mail Fund Raising,* 2nd ed. Detroit, MI: Fund Raising Institute, A Division of the Taft Group, 1991.

Lepper, Ron. *Secrets of a Successful Mail Order Guru: Chase Revel.* New York: John Wiley & Sons, Inc., 1988.

Lewis, Herschell Gordon. *Copy That Sells.* Paramus, NJ: Prentice-Hall, 1984.

_____. *Copywriting Secrets and Tactics.* Chicago: Dartnell Corp., 1991.

_____. *Herschell Gordon Lewis on the Art of Writing Copy.* Paramus, NJ: Prentice-Hall, 1987.

_____. *How to Make Your Advertising Twice as Effective at Half the Cost.* Paramus, NJ: Prentice-Hall, 1986.

_____. *How to Write Powerful Catalog Copy.* Chicago: Dartnell Corp., 1990.

_____. *Power Copywriting*. Chicago: Dartnell Corp., 1992.

_____. *Sales Letters That Sizzle*. Lincolnwood, IL: NTC Business Books, 1994.

_____. *Selling on the Net*. Lincolnwood, IL: NTC Business Books, 1997.

_____. and Nelson, Carol. *The World's Greatest Direct Mail Sales Letters*. Lincolnwood, IL: NTC Business Books, 1996.

_____. *Your Most Brilliant Mailing Will Fail If the Envelope Doesn't Say OPEN ME NOW!* Chicago: Precept Press, 1996.

Ljungren, Roy G. *The Business to Business Direct Marketing Handbook*. American Management Assn., 1989.

McKenna, Regis. *Relationship Marketing: Successful Strategies for the Age of the Customer*. Reading, MA: Addison-Wesley, 1993.

Meyer, E. N., Jr. *How to Make More Money with Your Direct Mail*. Printer's Ink, 1960.

Miller, Richard N. *Multinational Direct Marketing: The Methods & The Markets*. New York: McGraw-Hill, 1995.

Muldoon, Katie. *Catalog Marketing,* 3rd ed. Lincolnwood, IL: NTC Business Books, 1996.

Nash, Edward, editor-in-chief. *Database Marketing: The Ultimate Marketing Tool*. New York: McGraw-Hill, 1993.

_____. *The Direct Marketing Handbook,* 2nd ed. New York: McGraw-Hill, 1992.

_____. *Direct Marketing: Strategy/Planning/Execution,* 3rd ed. New York: McGraw-Hill, 1995.

Nicholas, Ted. *The Golden Mailbox*. Chicago: Enterprise-Dearborn, 1992.

_____. *Magic Words That Bring You Riches*. Nicholas Direct, Inc., 1995.

Nichols, Judith E. *Growing from Good to Great*. Chicago: Bonus Books, 1995.

Norrins, Norrins. *The Complete Copywriter*. New York: McGraw-Hill, 1996.

Ogilvy, David. *Confessions of an Advertising Man*. New York: Macmillan, 1963.

_____. *Ogilvy on Advertising*. New York: Random House, 1987.

Peppers, Don, and Rogers, Martha, Ph.D. *The One-to-One Future*. New York: Currency Doubleday, 1997.

Powers, Melvin. *How to Get Rich in Mail Order*. North Hollywood, CA: Wilshire Book Company, 1992.

Raphel, Murray, and Raphel, Neil. *Up the Loyalty Ladder: Turning Sometime Customers into Full-Time Advocates of Your Business*. New York: Harper Business Books, 1996.

Rapp, Stan, and Collins, Tom. *Beyond MaxiMarketing*. New York: McGraw-Hill, 1994.

_____. *The Great Marketing Turnaround: The Age of the Individual—and How to Profit From It*. Paramus, NJ: Prentice-Hall, 1990.

_____. *MaxiMarketing,* 2nd ed. New York: McGraw-Hill, 1987.

Reitman, Jerry. *Beyond 2000: The Future of Direct Marketing*. Lincolnwood, IL: NTC Business Books, 1996.

Roberts, M. L., and Berger, P. D. *Direct Marketing Management*. Paramus, NJ: Prentice-Hall, 1989.

Roman, Ernan. *Integrated Direct Marketing*. Lincolnwood, IL: NTC Business Books, 1995.

Rosenfield, James R. *Financial Services Direct Marketing*. Naperville, IL: Financial Sourcebooks, 1991.

Sackheim, Maxwell. *Billion Dollar Marketing*. Vancouver, WA: Towers Club USA, Inc., 1995.

_____. *Maxwell Sackheim's Complete Guide to Successful Direct Response Advertising*. Vancouver, WA: Towers Club USA, Inc., 1995.

_____. *My First Sixty Years in Advertising*. Paramus, NJ: Prentice-Hall, 1970.

Schmid, Jack, and Weber, Alan. *Desktop Database Marketing*. Lincolnwood, IL: NTC Business Books, 1998.

Schultz, Don E. *From Advertising to Integrated Direct Marketing* (video). Lincolnwood, IL: NTC Business Videos.

Schwab, Victor O. *How to Write a Good Advertisement*. Harper Bros., 1962.

Schwartz, Eugene M. *Breakthrough Advertising*. Paramus, NJ: Prentice-Hall, 1996.

_____. *Mail Order: How to Get Your Share of the Hidden Profits That Exist in Your Business*. Greenwich, CT: Boardroom Books, 1982.

Shepard, David, Associates. *The New Direct Marketing*, 2nd ed. Burr Ridge, IL: Irwin Professional Publishing, 1994.

Simon, Julian. *How to Start and Operate a Mail-Order Business*, 5th ed. New York: McGraw-Hill, 1987.

Sroge, Maxwell. *How to Create Successful Catalogs*, new ed. Lincolnwood, IL: NTC Business Books, 1993.

_____. *101 Tips for More Profitable Catalogs*. Lincolnwood, IL: NTC Business Books, 1960.

Stein, Donna Baier. *Write on Target*. Lincolnwood, IL: NTC Business Books, 1997.

Stone, Bob. *Direct Marketing Success Stories*. Lincolnwood, IL: NTC Business Books, 1995.

_____. *Successful Direct Marketing Methods*, 6th ed. Lincolnwood, IL: NTC Business Books, 1994.

_____. *30 Timeless Direct Marketing Principles* (video). Lincolnwood, IL: NTC Business Videos.

Stone, Bob, and Wyman, John. *Successful Telemarketing*. Lincolnwood, IL: NTC Business Books, 1995.

Throckmorton, Joan. *Winning Direct Response Advertising,* 2nd ed. Lincolnwood, IL: NTC Business Books, 1997.

Vavra, Terry G. *Aftermarketing: How to Keep Customers for Life Through Relationship Marketing.* Burr Ridge, IL: Irwin Professional Publishing, 1995.

Vos, Gruppo & Cappel, Inc. *Interactive Direct Marketing: A Planning Guide to New Media Opportunities.* New York: Direct Marketing Association.

Warsaw, Steve. *Successful Catalogs: Award Winners That Sell.* New York: Retail Reporting Bureau, 1989.

Warwick, Mal. *999 Tips, Trends and Guidelines for Successful Direct Mail and Telephone Fundraising.* Berkeley, CA: Strathmoor Press, 1993.

Weintz, Walter H. *The Solid Gold Mailbox.* New York: John Wiley & Sons, 1987.

Winston, Arthur. *Direct Marketing and the Law—What Managers Need to Know.* New York: John Wiley & Sons, Inc., 1993.

Annuals

Adcock, Edgar. *Direct Marketing Market Place: The Networking Source of the Direct Marketing Industry.* New Providence, NJ: National Register Publishing.

Direct Marketing Association. *Statistical Fact Book.* New York: DMA.

Gottlieb, Richard. *The Directory of Mail Order Catalogs.* Lakeville, CT: Grey House Publishing.

McKenzie,Leslie. *The Directory of Business-to-Business Catalogs.* Lakeville, CT: Grey House Publishing.

Oxbridge Communications. *The National Directory of Catalogs.* New York: Oxbridge Communications, Inc.

Target Marketing. *Directory of Major Mailers & What They Mail.* Philadelphia, PA: North American Publishing Company.

List Information Sources

MIN (Marketing Information Network). *21,000 Mailing Lists Online* (on-line service). Oklahoma City: Marketing Information Network.

Standard Rate & Data Service. *Direct Marketing List Source* (6 times a year plus 6 updates). Lincolnwood, IL.

Magazines

Advertising Age. New York: Crain Communications, Inc., 50 times a year.

Adweek. New York: BPI Communications, Inc., 48 times a year.

Catalog Age. Stamford, CT: Cowles Business Media, 12 times a year.

Circulation Management. New York: Ganesa Corp., 12 times a year.

Direct. Stamford, CT: Cowles Business Media, 18 times a year.

Direct Marketing. Garden City, NY: Hoke Communications, Inc., 12 times a year.

DM News. New York: Mill Hollow Corp., 48 times a year.

Folio: The Magazine of Magazine Management. Stamford, CT: Cowles Business Media, 12 times a year.

Fund Raising Management. Garden City, NY: Hoke Communications, Inc., 12 times a year.

Non-Profit Times. Cedar Knolls, NJ: Non-Profit Times, 12 times a year.

PROMO Magazine. Wilton, CT: Smith Communications, Inc., 12 times a year.

Target Marketing. Philadelphia: North American Communications, 12 times a year.

Newsletters

Business Mailer's Review. Arlington, VA: Pasha Publications, 24 times a year.

DeLay Letter. Westport, CT: Bob DeLay, 24 times a year.

Direct Response. Torrance, CA: Creative Direct Marketing Group, 12 times a year.

The Direct Response Specialist. Tarpon Springs, FL: Galen & Jean Stilson, 12 times a year.

Friday Report. Garden City, NY: Hoke Communications, 51 times a year.

Newsletter on Newsletters. Rhinebeck, NY: Newsletter Clearinghouse, 12 times a year.

Publisher's Multinational Direct. New York: Alfred M. Goodloe, 12 times a year.

Subscription Marketing. Sudbury, MA: Blue Dolphin Communications, 12 times a year.

Who's Mailing What! Philadelphia: North American Publishing, 12 times a year.

Archive Services

LTS Advertising Services, Smithtown, NY.

Who's Mailing What! (direct mail), Philadelphia.

Index

A. Eicoff & Co., 258
A/B splits, 121, 223, 294–95, 308
  imperfect, 295
ABC Company, 239
A/B/C/D splits, 295
Abraham, Jay, 102–3, 187–88
Ace, Goodman, 74
Acquisition allowance. *See* Allowable
  acquisition (marketing) cost
Acquisition marketing, 331
  affordable, 37
  as an investment, 37–40
  media for, 250
  retention vs., 30–31
Action devices, 174–75, 275
Action photos, 51
Add-on offers, 267, 274
Advance Planning Letter, 207
Advance renewals, 61
Advertisers, contacting, 230, 241
Advertising agencies, 294, 296
Advertorial style, 290
Advo/saturation mail, 256
Affinity organizations, 230–31,
  241–42
Ageless Body, Timeless Mind (Chopra),
  189
Albert Constantine, 17
Allowable acquisition (marketing)
  cost, 28, 56, 58
Allowable cost per order,
  31–32, 307
Allowable cost per package, 33
Allyn, Jim, 79
Alternative media, 17–23
  eight possibilities for, 255–56
  glossary of, 17–19
American Association of Retired
  Persons (AARP), 58
American Family Publishers, 145,
  314, 315–16
American Institute for Cancer
  Research, 175
American List Counsel, 225

American Speaker, 289
Analysis, 24–29. *See also*
  Measurement
Andersson, Axel, 74, 101, 133, 146,
  162, 203, 250, 259, 274, 281,
  284, 299, 317, 339
Annual membership fee, 269
Annual reports, 112, 113
Answering services, 158
Anticipation, 7
Antin, Tony, 299–300
Architectural Digest, 226
Arithmetic, 30–43. *See also*
  Measurement
  acquiring vs. retaining customers,
    30–31
  allowable cost per order, 31–32
  allowable cost per package, 33
  cost per sale, 33
  lifetime value, 35–43
  loaded cost per response, 33
  package cost at any quantity,
    33–34
  raw cost per response, 32
  response rate required to hit
    breakeven, 33
Arizona Mail Order, 17
Armstrong, Richard, 76, 77, 163,
  329
Arrowheads, 298
Asterisks, 98, 298
Asymmetrical layout, 71
Atlas Pen & Pencil, 17
Attention span, 144–45
Attenzione, 242
Audited paid-circulation figures, 293
Automatic shipments, 268
Automobile sweepstakes, 317

Back-end marketing, 44–50
  direct-response television and,
    155
  in fundraising, 176
  testing and, 332–33

Back-end premiums, 172
Ballooning number rule, 96
Bar charts, 52
Barson, Francie, 258
Basic offers, 259–60
Behavior, attempts to change,
  74, 211
Benson, Richard V., 10, 12, 22, 44,
  60–61, 74, 136, 137, 206,
  215, 226, 237, 248, 275–76,
  282, 283, 287, 307, 317, 339
Benton and Bowles, 104
Best-in-class examples, 6
Better Homes & Gardens Craft & Wear
  magazine, 214
Better-than-Risk-Free
  Guarantee, 188
Billing series. *See* Collection series
Billing systems, 48–49, 57
Bill-me option, 32, 61, 260, 275
Bind-in cards, 19, 297
Bird, Drayton, 13, 24, 79, 274, 306
Black, Marilyn, 167, 307
Black Enterprise, 232, 243
Blank check offers, 269
Block-group models, 120
Blocks, 157
Blow-ins, 19
BMG, 18
Boardroom, 237, 238, 239, 240
Boldface, 298
Bonus drive sales, 151
Booklets, free, 262
Boredom, 104, 198
Bounce-back offers, 267
Boyle, Karen, 169–70
Brady, Regina, 195–97
Bragging, 211, 301
Brainstorming, 149–50
Brand equity, 11
Brochures, 51–54
  captions for, 52–53
  complete information in, 136
  copy for, 52

headlines for, 51–52
hot spots in, 53
letters vs., 136, 202
percentage of orders gained
    from, 134
versionalizing, 135
visual elements in, 52
Brodsky, Annette, 237
Brokerage commissions, 235, 237
Brokers
    list. *See* List brokers
    for package inserts/co-ops, 19
Brown, Clyde, 242
Brown, Lou, 231
Brueckner, Robert, 198
Build-up-the-sale offers, 266–67
Bullets, 130, 209, 298, 302
Burnett, Hank, 182
Business reply cards (BRCs), 169,
    280, 281, 286–87
Business reply envelopes, 61,
    286–87, 317
Business segments, 55–61
Business-to-business marketing, 55
    database for, 112–13
    lists for, 55, 248–49
Butler, Bill, 43
Butzko, Tracy, 248
Buyer's Choice, 19
By-products, 10
Byrne, Andrew J., 77, 105–6, 131,
    203, 205, 223, 276, 277,
    297, 308

Callahan, Linda, 17–19
Capano, Ed, 338
Capell, Dan, 313–15
Capital letters, 97, 298
Captions, 52–53, 130, 302
Card decks, 18–19, 255
Carnegie, Dale, 190
Case histories, 105, 112
Cash discounts, 263, 283
Cash payments, 275, 280
Cash with order, 260
Catalogs, 62–71, 144
    bind-ins and blow-ins for, 19
    design of, 70–71
    four tips for, 69
    free, 262
    long-range plan for, 66
    nine rules of inventory, 65–66
    pricing strategy for, 70
    short-range plan for, 66–67
    sixteen musts for success, 66–69
    thirty-two-point checklist for
        starting, 62–65
Celebrity testimonials, 329
CHAID program, 119–20
Charge card privileges, 260
Charter membership offers, 265–66
Charts, 52, 193

Cheapness, 273
Check recovery plans, 48–49
Checkmarks, 209, 302
Chilcutt, Don, 236
Chopra, Deepak, 189
Christensen, Bill, 75, 77, 108–9,
    167, 280
Cigar Aficionado, 335
Clanny, Arlene, 226, 236
Client questionnaire, 309–12
Close, in copy, 301
Closure rate, 204
Club offers, 55, 268–69
Cluster splits, 295
COD, 260
Cohen, Andrew, 152–53, 256–57
Cold lists, 136, 162
Collection agencies, 48, 49
Collection programs, 46
Collection series, 30, 47–48
Collins, Tom, 87
Colonial Penn, 58
Color
    black-and-white copies of, 131
    four vs. two, 128
    in letters, 209–10
    purple, 129
    selling with, 203
    in space ads, 294, 302
    warm vs. cold, 128
Columbia, 18
Column width, 129, 130, 290,
    297–98
Commissions, 235, 237, 296
Commitment, 7
    open-ended, 268
Common law copyright
    protection, 292
Competitive offers, 271
Competitors
    copying, 133
    meeting or exceeding service
        of, 6–7
    testing by, 330
Complimentary copies, 265
CompuServe, 197
Condé Nast Traveler, 124, 166
Conroy, Martin, 103
Constructors, 114–15
Contests, 111, 113
Continuity, 333–34
Continuity load-up offers, 268
Continuity offers, 55, 268–69
Contrast, 131
Conversions, 24, 25
Co-op mailings, 18, 19–22
Cooper, Cindy, 336
Copy, 72–101. *See also* Words
    avoiding formulas in, 87
    ballooning number rule, 96
    for brochures, 52
    for catalogs, 70–71

claiming proprietorship in, 98
for collection series, 47
creating tension with, 302
design and, 82, 129
for direct mail, 137
directed at one person, 83–84
drama in, 87
for the ear, 86
eight laws for, 82
eight phrases for getting
    action, 95
eighteen steps to commonsense,
    85–86
five canons, 77
five techniques for writing direct,
    73–74
fundraising and, 172
humor in, 89, 214, 301
interaction with reader in, 78–79
length of, 79, 203, 301
ninety-nine magic phrases, 90–95
one hundred motivations for
    people to buy in, 80–82
percentages vs. money in, 101
persona in, 99
premiums in, 173
repeating in same package, 128
selling results vs. circumstances
    with, 99
seven absolute truths about, 72–73
simplicity in, 301
for space ads, 292–93, 301–2
specifics in, 73
surprise in, 86
ten dos and don'ts for, 88
that makes sense, 72–73
thirteen proven tips for getting
    response from, 84
thirty questions to ask before
    submitting, 89–90
three elements of, 82–83
three-day rule for, 87–88
twenty-eight emotional
    appeals, 74
Copyright, 57, 292
Copywriters
    four most important
        characteristics of, 78
    full package creation by, 83
    of fundraising material, 182, 183
    real job of, 83
    respecting, 129
    tampering with work of, 82–83,
        182, 183
Cost. *See also* Price
    allowable acquisition (marketing),
        28, 56, 58
    allowable per order, 31–32, 307
    allowable per package, 33
    of conversions, 25
    of direct-response television,
        254–55, 256–57

of lead generation, 25
media and production, 25
of order processing and
fulfillment, 64–65
of sweepstakes, 313, 314
Cost estimates, free, 263
Cost per acquisition (CPA), 256
Cost per lead (CPL), 158, 160,
256–57
Cost per order (CPO), 158, 159,
160, 256–57
Cost per sale, 33
Cost per thousand (CPM), 25, 293
Coupons, 129, 291, 299–300,
302–3
Courier type, 124, 208
Cousteau Society, 205
Cowen, Henry, 315
Cox Direct/Donnelly Marketing, 14
Craver, Mathews, Smith & Co.,
225
Craver, Roger, 171, 225
Creative Directors Group, 272
Creativity, 102–9
client changes and, 107–8
getting to the point, 106
psychology in, 102
ten rules of, 105–6
Creators, 114–15
Credibility, 308
Credit card payments, 69, 273, 275,
280, 287
Credit-granting programs, 46
Credit-screening programs, 46–47
Customer base, mining, 40
Customer profiles, 28, 116
Customer segmentation, 36, 47,
48, 177
Customer service. *See* Service
Customer-driven marketing,
117, 143
Customerizing, 9
Customers
acquisition of. *See* Acquisition
marketing
building repeat with catalogs,
63–64
capturing, 142–44
collection series for, 47
delighting, 15
lifetime value of. *See* Lifetime
value
objections to product, 276
projected sales value of after one
year, 27
reaching and attracting with
catalogs, 67–68
retention of. *See* Retention
sales value from first sale, 26–27
share of, 9
special discounts to, 44
taking point of view of, 6

transaction vs. relationship
buyers, 114
types of, 26
worth of average, 34
Customization, 56, 119
Customized communications, 37, 45
Cuteness, 104, 106, 125–26, 299

Dangling articles, 209
Data cards, 228
inaccuracy in, 233
seven rules for dealing, 219–22
testing, 237–40
Database marketing, 110–22
catalogs and, 68
constructors and creators in,
114–15
data integrity in, 115
defined, 110
direct-response television
and, 158
eleven ways to use, 111–12
forty nevers for, 116–22
fourteen tenets for, 113–15
in fundraising, 185
incremental nature of, 113
jargon in, 118
length of time needed to establish
system, 114
limiting data in, 114, 118–19
outsourcing construction in, 113
processing power in, 118
relevant, clean data in, 115–16
as a state of mind, 110–11
thirteen business-to-business
ideas, 112–13
visual displays in, 115
Davidson, Martin, 128
Davis, Carolyn, 14, 207
Davis, Etta, 249
Day parts, 157
Decker, Malcolm, 5, 45, 53–54, 83,
136–37, 164, 206–7, 213,
280, 339
Definite articles, 99
Delayed billing offers, 271
Delta Sky, 295
Deluxe offers, 266–67
Dembner, Red, 338
Demographics, 156, 217–18, 293
Demonstrations, free, 262
Design, 123–32
busy, 131
catalog, 70–71
copy and, 82, 129
cuteness in, 125–26
directing reader's eye with,
126–27
getting product into reader's hand
with, 126
human involvement in, 124
jolting the reader with, 125

neatness in, 131–32
physically leading readers to
letter, 125
repeating in same package, 128
shouting via, 124
six features to avoid, 131
of space ads, 302
twenty-seven tips to lift response,
123–28
Desktop publishing, 123–24
Direct mail, 133–37
direct-response television
and, 257
eleven production and quality
control procedures for, 139–40
feel for, 146
fundraising and, 176–78
fundraising and, with
telemarketing, 178–81
machine insertion and, 138
multipremium tests in, 284
postal service and, 138–39, 252
premiums in, 284
production of, 138–41
six advantages to, 251
six disadvantages to, 252
sweepstakes in, 315
versionalizing, 135
Direct mail control packages, 220
Direct Media, 229
Direct-response media buyers,
21–22
Direct-response rates (DR), 156
Direct-response television (DRTV),
149–61, 305
agencies for, 161
aggressiveness of, 257
best time of year for, 157
budget for, 156
capitalizing on exposure, 150
cost of, 254–55, 256–57
eight reasons to use, 256–57
flawed premises in, 151
four disadvantages to, 254–55
length of presentation in,
152, 155
markup in, 149, 152
negotiation in, 156, 159
perceived value of offer in, 151
preemption and, 157
product and, 149, 153, 154
profits and, 154–55
purchasing airtime, 153
response vs. results in, 160
retail sales and, 151
six advantages to, 254
time periods for, 157
timing of response to, 153
Disabled American Veterans (DAV),
172, 174, 175, 185–86, 287
Discount offers, 174, 263–64,
273, 276

Discretionary effort, 13
DMA, 318
Domestic Mail Manual, 286
Do-not-promote file, 46
Doorman, Steve, 254, 255
Doscher, Bob, 22
Double postcards, 335
Double-your-money-back
    warranty, 266
Drag calls, 158
Drake, Ed, 59–60
Drawings, 297, 302
Drawing-type sweepstakes, 267
Drop cap, 289
Drucker, Peter, 110
Dry tests, 334–37
Dummy variables, 120
Duncan, George, 111–12, 134, 146
Dworman, Steve, 149–51

Early-bird devices, 314
Early-bird discounts, 264
Edelston, Martin, 237
800 numbers. *See* Toll-free numbers
80/20 rule, 36–37
Élan, 232, 243–44
Elliott, Ed, 129–31, 193
Emotion, 74, 108
Employees
    as decision makers, 14–15
    discretionary effort from, 13
Enrollment periods, 265
Entertainment, 108, 150
Envelope-enclosed mailers, 136
Envelopes, 162–66
    A and B piles of, 162–63
    business reply, 61, 286–87, 317
    cash payments discouraged
        by, 280
    dating of, 168
    disguising advertising nature of,
        162–63
    hot spots on, 164
    new look for, 124, 165–66
    role of, 136
    spelling out offer on, 162
    window, 138, 163
Establish-the-value offers, 271
Even-number prices, 70
Everybody wins sweepstakes, 267
Exclamation points, 97
Exclusive rights for your trading
    area, 270
Exclusivity, 8
Executive preview charge, 269
Extended guarantee or warranty, 266

Fact kits, 262
Facts, 104
Falzone, Mary Ann, 319–25
Farley, Pat, 107, 164, 337–38
Faulkner, Mike, 248

Fax marketing, 22, 23, 293
Federal Trade Commission (FTC)
    dry tests and, 336–37
    four rules of, 147–48
    telemarketing prompt oral
        disclosure rule, 326–27
Fictitious people, 14
50/50 splits, 295
Film offers, free, 263
Financial analysis, 121–22
Financial services, 56–60
Financial Times of London, 230, 231,
    241–42
Fingerhut Corporation, 17, 19, 261
First 50 gift, 272
First purchase
    sales value of customer from,
        26–27
    time between second purchase
        and, 35
Flat claims, 86
Fleider, John J., 1, 5–6, 13, 274
Floral & Naturecraft magazine, 214
Flynn, Doug, 226
Focal subheads, 51
Focus groups, 116, 283, 334–35
Foehl, Bob, 229
Follow-up mailings, 308
Forbes, Wendell, 5, 14, 101, 105,
    307, 315, 338
40-40-20 Rule, 334
Four-way splits, 295
Frank Cawood, 14
Franklin, Benjamin, viii, 87
"Free," 74, 181
Free bonuses, 290
Free months, 173
Free offers, 56, 262–63
Free samples, 265
Free shipping, 272
Free trials, 260
Free-form layout, 71
Free-gift offers, 261, 273, 276
Freemiums, 172
Freestanding inserts (FSIS). *See*
    Package inserts
Frequent buyer programs, 111
Friesen, Pat, 53, 83–84, 164,
    211–12, 278, 279
Front-end investments, 155
Front-end load-ups, 268
Front-end premiums, 172
Fulfillment, 167–70
    acknowledgment of orders in, 169
    advance preparation of, 45
    billing system and, 48
    of catalog orders, 64–65, 66, 68
    cost of, 64–65
    of direct-response television
        orders, 154
    dozen ways to wreck, 169–70
    four ways to keep below $15, 66

    instructions and, 168
    of premium offers, 173
    product excellence rule in, 167
    promptness of, 168
    ready-to-use product in, 168
    reselling in, 167
Fulfillment companies, 150
Full-dress packages, 136–37
Full-page ads, 292, 299
Fundraising, 171–86
    direct mail, 176–78
    direct mail and telemarketing,
        178–81
    donor desire for control and, 178
    fifteen membership strategies,
        173–75
    five ways to increase net
        income, 171
    frequency of appeals, 177–78
    matching grants in, 181
    postage paid in, 185–86, 287
    procedures manual and standards
        for, 185
    receipts in, 183–84
    request for specific amount, 176
    six strategies that don't work, 175
    for small nonprofit mailers,
        175–76
    thanking donors, 183, 184
    three ways to increase average
        contributions, 172
    twelve musts for cultivating
        donors, 183–85

Gabriel, Gil, 75–76
General management, 12–16
General vs. direct advertising,
    142–48
Geographic splits, 295
Gerson, Frank, 15
Gibson, Richard, 201
Gift shipment service, 263
Global Computer Suppliers, 19
Gohring, Bill, 55
Gold Card status, 114
Goldberg, Paul, 140, 219–22,
    230–32, 241–47, 277
Good manners, 104
Good-better-best offers, 267
Goodrich, Susan, 153–55
Goodwill, 5
Gottlieb, Marilyn, 257
Gould, Jerry, 233–35
Gracing, 308
Grade, Lord Lew, 319
Graphics, 47, 87, 126, 291. *See also*
    Illustrations; Photographs;
    Pictures
Graphs, 193
Greco, Frank, 183–85
Green, Fran, 224–25
Greenbaum, Edna, 232, 243

Greenpeace, 182
Gribble, James, 188–89, 223–24
Grid layout, 71
Grolier Enterprises, 305
Gross, Martin, viii, 306, 338–39
Gross margin, 63
Grossman, Gordon, 315
Grouping by product page layout, 71
Guaranteed acceptance offer, 266
Guaranteed buy-back
    agreement, 266
Guarantees, 187–89, 266
    money-back, 89, 260, 291

Hacker, Robert C., 2, 32–34,
    41–43, 77, 122, 128, 137,
    142, 144, 145, 194–95,
    200–3, 211, 259, 334
Halbert, Gary, 110, 162–63
Hamilton, John, 327
Hampton Inns, 291
Handwritten messages, 127, 131,
    207, 209
Hanover House, 17, 19
Hard copy of lists, 220–22
Hard offers, 60, 151
Hard transitions, 98
Harper, Rose, 215–19, 331–34
Harrison, Barbara, 78–79, 189, 214
Hart, Max, 171–76, 185–86, 287
Harvard Women's Health Watch, 214
Harwin, Andrew, 236
Hatch, Denny, 8, 14, 23, 30–32,
    44–45, 55, 61, 110–11, 128,
    131, 135, 136, 137, 138, 141,
    163, 165–66, 168, 199, 221,
    226–27, 230, 235, 237,
    250–56, 278, 282, 287, 296,
    297, 305, 307–8, 316–17,
    328, 334–37
Hauptman, Don, 73–74, 208–11,
    309–12
Headlines, 190–93
    for brochures, 51–52
    five major purposes of, 193
    hiding part of, 126
    horizontal positioning of, 191
    length of, 191
    for space ads, 288–89, 297, 298,
        299, 300
Hearst magazines, 168
Helvetica type, 124
Hemingway, Ernest, 86, 88
Hennerberg, Gary, 24–29, 34–36
Henry, Leon, 19–21
Herbert, Frank, 275
High-ticket sales, 41–43, 292
Hodgson, Dick, 136, 212
Hoge, Cecil, Sr., viii, 146, 305
Hopkins, Claude, 10, 102, 103,
    123, 134, 145, 152, 259,
    273, 288

Hot line selects, 217, 223–24, 226
Hot potatoes, 106–7, 275
Hot spots
    brochure, 53
    envelope, 164
    letter, 211–12
    order form/response device, 279
House lists, 64, 136, 251, 275
House organ subscriptions, free, 263
Household-level models, 120
How to Write a Good Advertisement
    (Schwab), 152
Howell Book House, 305
Howell, Elsworth, 4–5, 279, 305
Hoyt, Coleman Williams, 138–39,
    168–69
Hubbard, Elbert, 10
Huey, Craig, 229–30, 300–303
"Huh? What?" copy, 78
Humor, 89, 214, 301
Hustler, 241

"I," 76
Idea kits, 262
Ideas, 6–7, 13, 14
Illiteracy, 252
Illustrations, 131, 191, 193, 298,
    299. *See also* Graphics;
    Photographs; Pictures
Image advertising, 135
Imperfect A/B splits, 295
Impulse sales, 144–45
Incentive programs, 174
Income-to-cost ratio, 158
Increase and extension offers, 267
Indefinite articles, 99
Indicated actions, 28–29
Infomercial Marketing Report, 254
Infomercials, 150, 152–53, 157
Information, free, 262
In-house list brokerages, 234–35
Initial response, 44–45
Inquiries
    converted to sales, 26
    direct-response television and,
        159
    free gift for, 261
    by media source, 24
    receiving fulfillment packages and
        sales histories, 26
    sales force disposition of, 25
Inserts
    newspaper, 152
    package. *See* Package inserts
Installment terms, 260, 275
Insurance, 56–59, 162
Intangible premiums, 176
Integrated database marketing
    system (IDBMS), 121
Intellectual property law, 57
International Country Risk Guide,
    231, 242–43

International Reports, 231–32,
    242–43
Internet marketing, 194–99
    promotions in, 196
    Seven Deadly Sins of, 198
    syngergism between print
        and, 197
    system staff in, 196–97
    updating in, 196
Interrupting, 135, 144–45
Intimate advertising, 225
Introductory order discounts, 264
Inventory, 65–66
Investors World Intelligent Report, 207
Involvement sweepstakes, 268
Isadora, Lou, 231, 242
"It," 75, 137
Italics, 298

Jackson, Don, 3–4, 5, 8, 11, 14–15,
    37, 43, 45, 50, 59, 109,
    115–16, 168, 285
Jaffe, Jay M., 56–59, 162
Jayme, Bill, 2, 77, 134, 163, 167,
    191, 251
Jeno's Pizza, 231
John Evans Club, 183
Johnson, James, 228
Jones, Susan K., 183, 286–87
Jordan, Richard, 106–7,
    276–77, 338
Joseph, Bill, 84–85, 128, 307, 338
Jutkins, "Rocket" Ray, 95, 164–65

Kanter, Don, 83
Kauffman, Gary, 10, 259
Keeling, Roger, 82–83, 181, 208
Keepers, 261
Kennedy, Dan, 151–52
Kerr, Dorothy, 133
Key learning, 28–29
Key titles, 26
Keyhole view, 126
Keying, of inserts, 20
Kikoler, Ted, 123–28, 209
"Kiss This Baby Goodbye"
    package, 182
Kleid Company, 236
Kligge, Joseph C., 5
Klingel, John, 61, 244
Knight, Frank, 8
Kobs, Jim, 189, 259–72
Kraus, Harry, 204
Kumble, Barbara, 241
Kurtz, Brian, 237–40

Layout, 70–71
Lead generation, 200–204
    checklist for developing, 59–60
    closure rate and, 204
    cost of, 25
    deal killers in, 200

direct marketing effect on, 42–43
premature introduction of
    information, 201
prescreening and qualifying
    in, 201
response killers in, 203
sales capacity and, 201
telephone- vs. mail-generated, 204
Lead letters, 178
LeBarron, Denny, 309–12
Left-brain people, 137, 202
Lefton, John, 123
Legal issues
    in changing material, 107–8
    in fax marketing, 23
Lethert, Joseph, 201
Letters, 205–12
    attention-getting devices in,
        209–10
    brochures vs., 136, 202
    complete information in, 136
    fictitious signatures on, 14
    fundraising, 181
    hot spots in, 211–12
    key copy drivers in, 211
    lead, 178
    length of, 181, 206, 207
    lift. See Lift pieces
    logo, address, and phone numbers
        in, 210
    percentage of orders gained
        from, 134
    physically leading readers to, 125
    primer on, 206–7
    role of, 136
    specifics in, 211
    telling a story in, 205
    top of the page lead of, 208
    versionalizing, 135
    writing rules for, 205
Lewis, Herschell Gordon, 96–101,
    162, 336
Lexus, 3–4
Lifetime membership fee, 269
Lifetime value (LTV), 35–43,
    216–17
    database marketing and, 113, 114
    defined, 36
    in fundraising, 177
    in insurance, 58
    risk hedge needed for, 43
    with several product lines, 35–36
    six applications of, 37
Lift pieces, 75, 107, 135, 136–37,
    213–14
Limited-edition offers, 266
Limited-time offers, 265, 277
List brokers, 216, 219, 220,
    227–28, 236, 246–47
Lists, 215–49
    arrival checklist for, 222–23
    business, 55, 248–49
    categories of, 239

cold, 136, 162
combining, 229
critical variables in, 216–17
demographically self-defining
    products and, 217–18
disapproved, 240
double usage of, 247
estimated total annual universe
    of, 238
first mailing and, 218
five techniques for building,
    230–32, 241–44
flavor of, 215
free, 226–27
for fundraising, 185
hard copy of, 220–22
house, 64, 136, 251, 275
inadequate monitoring of
    suppliers, 234
in-house brokerage of, 234–35
Internet marketing and, 196, 197
mailing date reservations and,
    229–30
mailing delays and, 230
mailing patterns and, 226
misinterpretation of subscribers'
    interests and, 233–34
misuses and abuses of, 244–47
need for multiple, 215
odd number of test names for,
    247–48
outside usage of, 240
owners and managers of, 238,
    245–46
poorly maintained, 252
promotional material behind, 237
rental. See Rental lists
sample attached, 239
sample dumps of, 220–22
second mailing and, 218–19
selection of, 217, 219, 228
six ways to clean and
    standardize, 248
small-list syndrome and, 233
source of, 238
twelve reasons to decoy, 244
updating, 55, 228, 238
usage history of, 220, 239
usage on boardroom, 240
usage record missing, 246
usage reports on, 229
Live stamps, 107, 165, 287
Loaded cost per response, 33
Long-term value. See Lifetime value
Lounsburty, Thomas Raynesford,
    105
Lowercase letters, 298
Loyalty, 36, 45, 114, 116
Lucky number sweepstakes, 267

Machine insertion, 138, 287
Magazine advertising, 294, 295
Magnetic tapes, 220–22

Mail dates, 308–9
    allocating, 334
    reserving, 229–30
    uncleared, 247
Mail delays, 230
Mail Order Digest, 134
Mail plan, 331, 332
Mailers, 228
Mailing lists. See Lists
Mail-order discounts, 293
Mal Warwick & Associates, 179
Management principles, 15–16
Management technique, 14–15
Manzari, Mike, 135, 226, 228
Margin alignment, 130, 209
Margin notes, 131, 209, 298
Market ownership, 58
Market rental, 58
Market share, 9
Marketing Information Network
    (MIN), 215, 230
Markup, 149, 152
Martel, Bob, 329
Martin, Angel, 11
Matching checks, 269
Matching grants, 181
Matheo, Bob, 86–87, 282
Maxson, Jack, 86, 87–88, 108, 309,
    339
Mayer, Ed, 334, 339
MBA magazine, 72
McCabe, Ed, 104
McClusky, Malcolm, 227–28
McGraw-Hill, 301
McIntyre, Susan, 62–65
McLean, Ed, 1, 83
"Me," 75–76
Measurement, 7, 34, 257. See also
    Analysis; Arithmetic
Media, 250–58. See also Alternative
    media
Member-get-a-member (MGM)
    offers, 256, 270
Membership offers, 61
Merchandise-on-approval rule, 148
Merge/purge, 220–22, 229, 248
    inability to, 246
Merrill Lynch, 301
Messina, Charles, 252
Meyer, Tom, 272
Michael, Paul, 107, 213
Mill, Rebecca Klem, 31, 56
Miller, Drew Allen, 51–53, 191
Mistakes, 15
Modeling, 116, 119–20, 308
Money Mailer, 18
Money management, 15
Money-back guarantees, 89,
    260, 291
Monsanto, 257
Montgomery Ward, viii
Monthly pledge programs, 176
Monthly sustainer programs, 179

Mosher, George, 12–13, 49–50, 307, 326
Motivators, 202
Movers programs, 255
Multiple-unit pricing, 70
Multipremium tests, 284
Multiproduct offers, 116, 266
Mystery discounts, 264
Mystery gift offer, 261

Name, 164
Name-getter offers, 270
Name sticker mailings, 176
National Audubon Society, 175
Natural History magazine, 107
Neatness, 131–32
Needs
    means of satisfying, 5–6
    wants vs., 11, 305
Negative copy, 82, 87, 100
Negative option offers, 268, 273
Negative-option rule, 147–48
Net-name arrangements, 232, 243, 247
Neural-net models, 120
Newfield, 19
Newsletters, 112, 113
Newspaper advertising, 294, 295
Newspaper inserts, 152
Newsweek, 338
Nicholas, Don, 247–48, 308–9, 330
Nicholas, Ted, 276, 288–92
Nightingale Conant, 281
"No," 9–10
Nominal reimbursement offers, 271
Nominal-charge samples, 265
Northwestern University, 183
No-strings attached commitment, 269
nth Name Scam, 245
Numbers
    in copy, 96, 98, 99
    in headlines, 300
    relying on other people's, 6
    in space ads, 302

O'Brien, Don, 123
Odd-number prices, 70
Offers, 259–78
    basic, 259–60
    build-up-the-sale, 266–67
    in catalogs, 67
    checklist of ninety-nine proven (plus three), 259–72
    club and continuity, 55, 268–69
    credit screening via, 46
    direct-response television and, 149, 151
    discount, 174, 263–64, 273, 276
    dramatizing, 277
    free, 56, 262–63
    free-gift, 261, 273, 276
    generosity of, 302

guarantee. *See* Guarantees
hard, 60, 151
power of, 10
sale, 264
sample, 265
soft, 60, 151
specialized, 269–72
spelling out on envelope, 162
strong, 202
sweepstakes. *See* Sweepstakes
thrown away, 273–74
time limit, 265–66, 278
Ogilvy, David, 104, 192–93, 198, 297–98, 299, 303, 329
One-step offers, 203, 250
On-line marketing, 256. *See also* Internet marketing
Open-end mail, 275
Open-ended commitment, 268
Order forms, 279–82
    for catalogs, 71
    checklist for, 281–82
    order killers on, 281
    percentage of orders gained from, 134
    personalization of, 125
    as sales devices, 280
    standouts, 128
    versionalizing, 135
    visual fascination with, 280
Order processing, 64–65, 66
Order-screening systems, 46
Overhead, 31

P.S., 210, 214
Package cost at any quantity, 33–34
Package inserts, 255, 256
    description of, 17
    direct-response television and, 257
    four tips for buying, 21–22
    in fundraising, 182–83
    proof of receipt and delivery, 20
    ten guidelines for getting started with, 19–21
    using one, 20
Page breaks, 210
Palucci, Jeno, 231, 242
Paper, 129
Paragraphs
    indenting, 208
    size of, 209
Parentheses, 97
Patents, 57
Payment, 168, 169
    cash, 275, 280
    credit card, 69, 273, 275, 280, 287
Pay-up by effort reporting system, 48
Penthouse, 230, 241
Peppers, Don, 9
Perceived quantity, 125

Performance Diver, 17
Performark, 201
Per-inquiry (PI) rates, 153, 294
Permits, mail, 140–41, 286
Personal relevance, 8–9
Personalization
    fundraising and, 172, 174, 176
    from house vs. cold lists, 136
    overdoing, 125
    on premiums, 173
Peterman, J., 15–16
Peters, Tom, 9
Philanthropic privilege, 269
Photographs, 51, 193, 290, 297, 302. *See also* Graphics; Illustrations; Pictures
Pictures, 123. *See also* Graphics; Illustrations; Photographs
Pie charts, 52
Pierce, Lea, 75, 78, 106, 164
Pierce, Milt, 89–95
Piggyback offers, 266
Pironti, Bud, 296
Plagiarism, 74, 211
Plastic cards, 58
Playboy, 230, 241
Positive copy, 82
Positive option offers, 268, 273
Post office box address, 303
Postage, 61, 141, 252
    fundraising and, 185–86, 287
    live stamps, 107, 165, 287
    sweepstakes and, 314
Postage-paid business reply cards, 287
Postage-paid business reply envelopes, 61, 286
Postal reclassification, 141
Postal Service, U.S., 252
    reply envelope specifications of, 286
    sweepstakes rules of, 318
    three rules for working with, 138–39
Postdated checks, 271
Post-It notes, 175, 176
Postprint mailings, 134
Pre-alerts, 145
Preemptive advantage axiom, 102–3
Premium specialty firms, 284
Premiums, 283–85
    attempt to sell offers with, 274, 284
    back-end, 172
    direct-response television and, 151
    editorially related, 284
    front-end, 172
    fundraising and, 172–73, 174, 176
    intangible, 176
    logical vs. illogical, 285
    promotional-integral, 276–77

self-liquidating, 270
ten tips on, 283–84
Preprint mailings, 134
Prepublication offers, 265
Press releases, 112
Pressure-sensitive labels, 174–75
Prestige type, 124
Preventive advertising, 301
Price. *See also* Cost
    catalog strategy, 70
    database marketing focus on, 115
    for exclusive circulation, 21
    judging by, 273
    of lists, 238
    odd vs. even, 70
    in offers, 259
    of package inserts/co-ops, 20–21
    as reason to buy, 8
    same product at different, 275–76
    of space ads, 293–94, 296
    testing, 332
Price increase notice, 264
Private retail sale, 272
Probka, Mary Lou, 222–23
Process training, 325
Product excellence rule, 167
Product videos, 113
Product-driven processes, 117
Production costs, 25
Products
    direct-response television and,
        149, 153, 154
    importance of, 304
    objections to, 276
    poor selection of, 305
    unethical, 15
Profit and return on
        investment, 28
Profitable Direct Marketing
    (Kobs), 272
Progress training, 325
Progressive Group, Inc., 179
Promotional-integral premiums,
    276–77
Promotions, Internet, 196
Prospect segmentation, 47, 48
Prospects, 37–40, 47
Publisher's Clearing House, 14, 145,
    314, 315–16
Publishing, 60–61
Punkre, Jim, 82
Puns, 88
Purchase with purchase, 270, 274
Purple, 129
Purpose-process-people model, 304

Quality, 8
Quantity discounts, 264
Quantity sample offers, 265
Quintile analysis, 27–28
Quota-driven marketing, 143
Quotation marks, 96–97, 289
Quotes, 300

Radio, 257–58, 305
Rank order, 3
Raphel, Murray, 70, 129, 134,
    190–91, 274
Rapp & Collins, 166
Rapp, Stan, 225
Ratner, Bruce, 115
Raw cost per response, 32
Reader's Digest, 14, 145, 207, 275
Reader's Digest Condensed Book
    Club, 317
Reason-why sales, 264
Rebates, 263–64
Recognition devices, 175
Recommendations, 28–29
Recordkeeping, 331
Reduced down payment, 271
Refunds, 263–64
Regression models, 120
Reilly, Terry, 272
Reiman, Guenther, 232, 243
Reitman, Jerry, 8–9
Relationship buyers, 114
Remnant space, 21, 293
Renewal at birth, 267
Renewals, 73
    advance, 61
    in fundraising, 179
    in publishing, 60–61
    with sweepstakes, 315, 316
Rental lists, 216
    catalogs and, 64
    five traps to avoid in, 233–35
    inability to control, 216
    negotiation of fee for, 237
    origination of idea, 230, 241
Reply envelopes/cards. *See* Business
    reply cards; Business reply
    envelopes
Reprints, 112
Research, 73, 82, 211
Residual time, 153
Response advertising, 142
Response devices, 279
Response rates (RR), 30, 33, 35, 57
Retail sales, 134, 151, 254
Retention, 331
    acquisition vs., 30–31
    database for tracking, 114
    media for, 250
    promptness of fulfillment and,
        168
Retention percentage rate, 35
Return on equity, 31
Return on marketing (ROM), 30
Returns of merchandise, 65
Reverse type, 127–28, 131,
    298, 302
RFM (recency—frequency—
    monetary) analysis, 113, 120,
    217, 224
Richardson, Donn, 329
Ride-alongs, 17–18

Right-brain people, 137, 202
Risk reversal, 187–88
Roberts, Margaret Rose, 250,
    292–96
Rodale, 284
*Rodale's Illustrated Encyclopedia of
    Herbs*, 214
Rogers, Martha, 9
Rollouts
    direct-response television and,
        156
    forbidden, 246
    insurance and, 58
Ross, MacRae, 305–6
Ross, Max, 95
Rossi, Hank, 46–49
Rotations, 157
Rounded-off figures, 99
Rubicam, Raymond, 10
Rule of Thirds, 62
Rules, 1–2
Rush shipping service, 271
Ruskin, John, 307
Rutz, Jim, 15, 74

Sackheim, Maxwell, 44, 72, 77,
    278, 297, 304, 339
Safeco Lead Management
    System, 59
Sale offers, 264
Sales
    inquiries converted to, 26
    overdoing, 73
    quintile analysis of, 27–28
    seasonal, 264
Sales call, free, 262
Sales force, 200
Sales value, 26–27
Sample offers, 265
Sampling, 18
San Francisco Exploratorium,
    182–83
Sans serif type, 129, 131, 290,
    298, 302
Sass, Michael, 244
Save the Children, 146
Savings, 173
Scams, 245, 254
Schalit, Judith, 45–46
Schlitz beer, 103
Schmid, Jack, 66–69, 70–71
Schultz, Ray, 309
Schwab, Victor, 152
Schwartz, Gene, 78
Scientific Advertising (Hopkins),
    152
Scoop and Dip, 231, 241–42
Scripts for telemarketing, 320–21
    crash-testing of, 322–23
    five classic faulty, 322
    live test calls for, 323
    need for, 324–25
    putting away, 323–24

*Sears and Montgomery Ward: The First
    Hundred Years Are the Toughest,*
    viii
Seasonal sales, 264
Seasonality, 226, 239, 332
Second purchase
    importance of, 44
    time between first purchase
        and, 35
Secrecy, 251
Secretary's subscript, 210
Secrets of Successful Direct Mail
    (Benson), 10
Segal, Elliott, 22
Selects, 238
    hot line, 217, 223–24, 226
    inability to give, 246
    in reverse, 232
    zip, 232, 243–44
Self-liquidating premiums, 270
Self-mailers, 136
Self-qualification offers, 270
Seminars, 111, 113
Serif type, 127, 129, 290, 298, 302
Service, 8
    database marketing and, 115
    efficiency of, 7
    five ways to bolster, 45–46
    in Internet marketing, 197
    measurement of, 7
Service calls, 159
Seven Deadly Sins, 103
    of Internet marketing, 198
Shareholder value, 31
Shepard, David, 116–22
Shokoff, Iris, 21–22, 253, 255, 258,
    296
Short-term introductory offers,
    263
Sierra Club, 181
Signature, 207, 210
Single product per page layout, 71
Single-variable tests, 330
Skill tests, 317
Sliding-scale discounts, 264
Small-list syndrome, 233
Smith, Lew, 131–32, 144–45, 334
Smithsonian Institution, 175
Soell, Emily, 78, 124, 146, 166
Soft offers, 60, 151
Soft transitions, 98
Software, 48, 118
Sourcing, 158
Space ads, 288–303
    on back page, 299
    bargaining for position, 294
    bargaining for price, 293–94
    copy for, 292–93, 301–2
    dry tests in, 335
    editorial fit in, 293
    first sentence of, 289
    frequency of, 294
    full-page, 292, 299

hidden-benefit technique for,
    288–92
last-minute reservations for, 296
opening paragraph of, 297
retail price for, 296
seven advantages to, 252–53
sideways positioning of, 299
timing in, 294
two disadvantages to, 253
Specialized offers, 269–72
Speer, Halbert, 315–16
Split tests, 294
    A/B, 121, 223, 294–95, 308
    A/B/C/D, 295
Spot time, 157
Spreadsheet programs, 36
Sroge, Maxwell, 134
Stamp Collectors Society of
    America, 45
Stamp sheets, 316
Standard Rate and Data Service
    (SRDS), 230
Standby ad space, 293
Statement stuffers, 18
Stein, Donna, 87, 279
Stein, Herbert, 8
Stevenson, Robert Louis, 86
Stickers, 136, 281, 282
Stock-keeping units (SKUs), 65
Stone, Bob, 36–37, 79, 134, 136,
    152, 176, 204, 229, 273, 277,
    297, 313
Stone, Sue, 272
Storyboard, 152
Strategy, 304–12
Stripped-down products, 271
Subheads, 51, 79, 209, 297,
    299, 301
Subscription offers, 61, 265–66
Subscriptions, 73, 287
Substance, creating, 108–9
Successful Magazine Publishing, 233
Suleiman, Anver, 1, 3, 5, 30, 135,
    249, 279, 308, 330–31
Super-Coups, 18
Superdramatic offers, 270
Supermarket take-ones, 256
Survey of needs, free, 262
Surveys, 111, 112, 180–81
Sweepstakes, 61, 313–15
    business reply envelopes and, 287
    chances to win, 314
    consultants for, 314
    cost control, 314
    cost of testing, 313
    database for, 111
    designing, 313
    early-bird devices in, 314
    fundraising and, 174
    lists of entrants, 239, 244
    prizes for, 317
    relating prizes to products, 313
    response patterns in, 314

results improved with, 317
rules for, 318
television support for, 314
types of, 267–68, 315–16
Sweeten-the-pot offers, 271
Symmetrical layout, 71

Tagger, Peter, 182–83
Talent contests, 268
Talent tests, free, 263
Target audience
    for catalogs, 67
    for collection series, 47
    for direct mail, 251
    for direct-response television, 156
    for fax marketing, 22
    for space ads, 293
Teaser copy, 164
Telemarketing, 319–27
    automated systems for incoming
        calls, 325
    direct-response television and,
        150, 255
    disposition data for, 119
    follow-up calls in, 319
    four advantages to, 253
    four disadvantages to, 254
    FTC oral disclosure rule for,
        326–27
    fundraising and, with direct mail,
        178–81
    of insurance, 57
    need for informed representatives
        in, 319–20
    scripts for. *See* Scripts for
        telemarketing
    training representatives for,
        323–24, 325, 327
    understanding customers in, 321
Television. *See also* Direct-response
    television
    dry tests in, 335
    sweepstakes and, 314
Test rates, 293
Testimonials, 75, 105, 328–29
Testing, 330–39
    by competitors, 330
    of copy, 83
    of data cards, 237–40
    in database marketing, 112,
        116, 117
    direct mail and, 251
    direct-response television and,
        152, 156, 254, 256–57
    dry, 334–37
    five rules for beating controls in,
        337–38
    five variables with a high impact
        on, 332–33
    formula for winners, 339
    holiday season, 296
    of package inserts/co-ops, 19
    price, 332

radio and, 257
recordkeeping in, 331
sensible spending on, 338
single-variable, 330
six key questions in, 331
of space ads, 292, 293, 296
sweepstakes and, 313
of telemarketing scripts, 322–23
Two Inviolable Basic Rules of, 83, 339
wet, 334, 335
of whispers, 339
Third-party referral offers, 270
Thirty-day rule, 147
3602s, 140
Thompson, David, 140–41
Throckmorton, Joan, vii, 72–73, 142–44
Tighe, John Francis, 9–10, 102, 142
Till forbid, 268
Time limit offers, 265–66, 278
Time value of money discount factor (TVMDF), 38, 39
Time Warner, 284
Times Roman type, 124, 290
Tokens, 136, 281, 282
Toll-free numbers, 45, 282
on direct-response television, 150
for fax marketing, 22
in fundraising, 180
sourcing and, 158
in space ads, 293, 302
Top-of-the-page lead, 208
Tracking results
of catalogs, 68
of direct-response television, 153, 158–59
of space ads, 295
Trade discounts, 264

Trade-in offers, 270
Transaction buyers, 114
Traub, Marvin, 151
Treller, Robert H., 14
Trial orders, free gift for, 261
Trust, 191
TV Guide, 295
Two-step offers, 203, 250, 261, 292
Type size, 90, 130, 298, 302
Typeface, 123–24, 124, 208, 290

Ugliness, 128, 152, 202
Underscores, 209
Unethical products, 15
Unique selling proposition, 106
United Way, 178
USA Direct, Inc., 139–40, 281–82

Val Pak, 18
Verisimilitude, 96, 336
Versionalizing, 135
Videos, free, 262
Viking Office Products, 19
Vocabulary, 86, 88, 300
Vogel, Daryl, 183
Vogele, Dr., 164–65
Vos, Frank, 273–74

Waldman, Todd, 228
Walker Direct, 272
Wall Street Journal, 201
Walsh, Harry B., 191, 205, 213
Wants
creating better, 8
needs vs., 11, 305
Warranties and guarantees rule, 147
Warwick, Mal, 176–81
Watts, Franklin, 8, 11, 14, 279

"We," 99–100
Weber, Alan, 37–40
Weil, Bill, 115
Weintz, Walter, 75, 274–75
Wells, Bob, 329
Wet tests, 334, 335
Who's Mailing What!, 220, 239
Williams, Bill, 6–7
Williams-Sonoma, 4–5
Willing suspension of disbelief, 77
Window envelopes, 138, 163
Windows 95, 13
Wood, Frank K., 14
Word breaks, 209
Words
with automatic power, 100
to establish reader possession, 99
to establish superiority, 99
with implicit weakness, 100
to motivate, 99
to reduce power, 98
to sell, 203
twelve most powerful, 74
Work sharing, 139
World Business Weekly, 230–31, 241–42
Wright, Carol, 14, 18, 19, 207
Write-your-own-ticket offers, 267

Yeck, John, 45, 105
Yes/no offers, 269, 273, 282
"You," 75–76, 77, 99–100, 137, 300
Your Dog, 214

Zip code models, 120
Zip codes, 222, 223
Zip selects, 232, 243–44